Stephanie Bender
Ethics for the Future

Culture & Theory | Volume 288

Stephanie Bender is engaged in sowing seeds for better futures on several fields: Using the knowledge she has gained throughout her doctorate in English literary and cultural studies she teaches courses at Albert-Ludwigs-Universität Freiburg. She turns theory into practice on the fields of Community Supported Agriculture as the degrowth future of sustainable food production. And finally, she takes care of two small members of a future generation of humankind that will hopefully tread more lightly on earth than their predecessors.

Stephanie Bender

Ethics for the Future

Perspectives from 21st Century Fiction

[transcript]

This work was accepted as a PhD Thesis at the University of Freiburg, Germany.

The dissertation was generously funded by the Rosa Luxemburg Foundation.

Bibliographic information published by the Deutsche Nationalbibliothek
The Deutsche Nationalbibliothek lists this publication in the Deutsche Nation-albibliografie; detailed bibliographic data are available in the Internet at http://dnb.d-nb.de

Cover layout: Maria Arndt, Bielefeld
Proofread: Johanna Ellsworth
Printed by: Majuskel Medienproduktion GmbH, Wetzlar
https://doi.org/10.14361/9783839468203
Print-ISBN 978-3-8376-6820-9
PDF-ISBN 978-3-8394-6820-3
ISSN of series: 2702-8968
eISSN of series: 2702-8976

Printed on permanent acid-free text paper.

For those who came before me,
those who are with me now,
and those who will come after me.

Contents

Acknowledgements 11

1 Introduction 13
Challenging Times.. 17
Ethics for the Future: From Humanism to Posthumanism 23
Ethical Criticism in the 21st Century 25
Aesthetics for the Future: Popular Future Fictions.............................. 26
The Chapters 31

2 Ethics for the Future through Fiction 35
A Difficult Heritage: Humanism and Beyond 36
New Ethics for a New Age: Hans Jonas.. 39
Deconstruction, Ethics, and the Anthropocene: Joanna Zylinska 42
Towards Posthumanist Ethics 44
Actual Worlds and Possible Futures in Fiction 49
Existing Ethical Approaches to Literature 50
Ethical Criticism in Film 52
Limitations of Existing Approaches 54
Future Ethical Criticism: Worlds in the Making.................................. 56

3 Future World Ecologies: Kim Stanley Robinson's *New York 2140* (2017)
and James Cameron's *Avatar* (2009).. 65
A Political World-Ecology Approach: Kim Stanley Robinson's *New York 2140* 71
Back to "Nature" in James Cameron's *Avatar* 85
Conclusion 98

4 Transhumanist Futures: Christopher Nolan's
   Interstellar (2014) and Wally Pfister's *Transcendence* (2014).................. 101
   Transhumanist Ethics in Christopher Nolan's *Interstellar* 104
   Philosophical Essentialism: Futuristic Technologies and The Human
   in Wally Pfister's *Transcendence* 117
   Conclusion 130

5 Futuristic Digital Neoliberalism: Spike Jonze's *Her* (2013) and Dave
   Eggers's *The Circle* (2013) 133
   The Self and the Other in Digital Neoliberalism: Relationships
   and Identities in Spike Jonze's *Her* 136
   The Economy of Attention in Dave Eggers's *The Circle* 149
   Conclusion 166

6 Biopolitics of the Future: Kazuo Ishiguro's *Never Let Me Go* (2006) and Don
   DeLillo's *Zero K* (2016) 169
   The Biopolitics of Health in an Alternative Past:
   Knowing and Not Knowing in Kazuo Ishiguro's *Never Let Me Go* 172
   A Futuristic Present: The Power over Life and Death in Don DeLillo's *Zero K* 188
   Conclusion 204

7 More than Human?: Threats of AI in Dennis Villeneuve's *Blade Runner 2049*
   (2017) and Alex Garland's *Ex_Machina* (2014).................................. 209
   "To Be Born Is to Have a Soul, I Guess." Reproduction and Human(e)ness
   in Dennis Villeneuve's *Blade Runner 2049* 212
   Reflecting the Speculative Spectacle: Alex Garland's *Ex_Machina* 226
   Conclusion 239

8 Posthumanist Futures: Margaret Atwood's *MaddAddam Trilogy* (2003, 2006,
   2013) and Paolo Bacigalupi's *The Windup Girl* (2009)..........................241
   Ethics through Metafiction: Storytelling in Margaret Atwood's *MaddAddam Trilogy* 243
   Non-human Agents and Posthumanist Ethics in Paolo Bacigalupi's
   The Windup Girl 262
   Conclusion 278

9 Contemporary Imaginaries of the Future 281
   Ethical Openness versus Closure... 283
   Unmaking Capitalist Futures... 286

Otherworlds of the Future 288
Speculative Realism 291

Works Cited 295

Acknowledgements

Even though I am the author of this book, it is—like all books or works of art—a co-creation that has been made possible by myriad supporters, companions and companion species. I am very grateful for the opportunity to write this doctoral thesis and to pursue my research interests without constraints or limitations. First and foremost, this was made possible by my father, Oskar, who has always believed in me, supported me morally and financially and enabled me to go to university as the first member of our family to do so. Last year he passed away, but I know he would have been proud to hold this book in his hands.

Secondly, I want to thank Prof. Barbara Korte as my first supervisor for her reliable support and especially the freedom she gave me in choosing my own topics and approaches, as well as for letting me find my own pace of researching and writing without exerting pressure. I am also grateful for the supportive atmosphere she created in our department, which allowed us doctoral students to network and help each other. This doctoral dissertation was generously funded by the *Rosa Luxemburg Foundation*, and I am deeply thankful for its support that consisted of much more than just funding: the opportunities to network and make friends, inspiring events and meetings, helpful workshops, and—above all—the feeling of being part of a larger group of idealists who want to make this world a better place.

I could not have finished the dissertation without the help and support of my husband, David, who "covered my back", as he always said, by taking on the lion's share of care work and house work after our two lovely daughters Lotta and Maja were born. Also, he was the one who proofread my thesis at least thrice. Furthermore, I want to give a big thanks to all my friends, and especially to Mareike and Sophia, for the innumerable inspiring intellectual and political conversations, their emotional support and most importantly, for just being there—I don't think I would have embarked on this ship without them and pursued something as daring as this "doctorate thingy". Finally, I want to thank all the students who came to my classes, who inspired me and made my research "come alive".

1 Introduction

After years of corona emergency, in a world tormented by wars and the social and ecological consequences of climate change, the declaration that "the world has become a science fiction novel" (Canavan and Robinson 17) feels truer than ever. It is as if what has already been imagined in contemporary popular fiction is increasingly becoming reality. The idea of a deadly virus and a global pandemic has been played out in fiction conspicuously often, for example in Emily St John Mandel's *Station Eleven* (2014), Margaret Atwood's *MaddAddam Trilogy* (2003; 2009, 2013), and Rupert Wyatt's *Rise of the Planet of the Apes* (2011), among many others. Admittedly, the coronavirus has so far been much less lethal than its fictitious counterparts. Nonetheless, it has significantly affected and damaged lives everywhere around the globe in many ways—and we have certainly not yet seen the end of the after effects. The discourse surrounding its origins also bring its fictional predecessors to mind: is the virus an accidental side effect of biotechnological experimentation, as in *Rise of the Planet of the Apes* or Paolo Bacigalupi's *The Windup Girl*? Or was it purposefully made, as conspiracy theorists claim, as is the case in *The MaddAddam Trilogy*? Is it possibly caused by humanity's destructive relations with its non-human others, as contemporary environmental fictions like Barbara Kingsolver's *Flight Behavior* (2012) and Mireille Juchau's *The World Without Us* (2015) show? Apart from the ecological and biotechnological dimensions involved in the process of understanding the virus and tackling it, the pandemic also accelerates the ongoing digitalisation of life. In a similar vein, novels like *Ready Player One* (2011) by Ernest Cline or the *Otherland* tetralogy (1998–2001) by Tad Williams have already projected the building of entire virtual worlds existing in parallel to a wrecked physical one.

Both the current state of the world and contemporary fictional works dealing with the future show that we are living in a time which represents a radical rupture with the alleged certainties of the past. Most of all, the modern "success story" of human progress and evolution from the Enlightenment up to the present has been severely disrupted. This profoundly affects cultural conceptualisations of the future. As Reinhart Koselleck demonstrates in his seminal *Futures Past*, each historical epoch has its own relationship to the future. According to Aleida Assmann, "in modernity time had acquired the shape of an arrow that runs irreversibly from the past into the future" (42). John Urry adds that "within European societies, God's gift [of the future] was transformed into a future made, intervened in and traded" (8). For a long time, the future was thus conceptualised as a better time that could be created through human ingenuity. In contrast, the present, described as the Anthropocene, the Capitalocene, or the Chthulucene, represents a break with this teleological human history, allowing non-human actors, from viruses and digital code to CO_2 molecules, to play the leading roles in the story. Instead of being promising, "[t]he future, in short, has become an object of concern, prompting ever-new measures of precaution" (Assmann 41).

This strained relationship to the future is also expressed through the idea of risk as a pivotal concept of contemporary society, which Ulrich Beck has termed "risk society". He explains its dynamics as follows:

> The gain in power from techno-economic 'progress' is being increasingly overshadowed by the production of risks. In an early stage, these can be legitimated as 'latent side effects'. As they become globalized, and subject to public criticism and scientific investigation, they come, so to speak, out of the closet and achieve a central importance in social and political debates. (13)

Against the backdrop of a present that seems to be characterised by more and more crises, from humanitarian to ecological ones, risk has become a central paradigm for dealing with the future. The only adequate way to deal with risk is to minimise it and to keep it under control, for example through means of governmentality (Burgess et al. 12). The ideal of control that derives from the Enlightenment now finds itself in opposition to the unknown dimensions and consequences of humanity's collective actions like the ecological effects described by the term Anthropocene. Contemporary futurology or futures studies is to a large extent associated with the study of risk or probabilities and is therefore situated mainly in the natural and applied sciences rather than in the arts and humanities. Consequently, instead of thinking about alternative futures to the destructive worlds of the present, this calculating futurology is in danger of "extrapolating the future from what is present" (Urry 8) without trying to analyse, evaluate or even change it.

This "presentism" also shows in the discourse of sustainability, for example in the famous "Brundtland" report by the World Commission on Environment and Development titled *Our Common Future* and the contemporary United Nations Development Goals. Despite recognising the need for change to ameliorate the conditions in the spheres of the ecology and social equality, "[s]ustainability has been angled to 'sustain' the level of comfort and acquisition that the economy of 'growth' demands", as Tom Cohen puts it (19). It seems almost impossible to imagine a good and sustainable future that is radically different to the present with its dominance of global capitalism and consumerism. Similarly, futurological reports, like a market analysis of financial instruments or an insurance company's study of climate risks, "all fit within the distinctly modern, statistical project of 'taming change'" (Bruyn and Lütticken 7). Urry likewise asserts the idea that present power interests fundamentally shape conceptions and politics of the future by pointing out that a large proportion of futurist thinking after 1945 "was tied to powerful military and corporate agendas" (6). Is there really no alternative?

Rather than ignoring the future and focusing only on the past or present, I argue that the temporality of the future must be reclaimed from the project of control, presuming that "futurity cannot and should not be equated with linear and teleological futures" (Bruyn and Lütticken 9). Today, it even seems imperative to think about different possible futures derived from the innumerable, collaborative efforts of worldmaking in the present. We especially need to ask the question: which of these *possible* futures could be a *good* future—a future in which human *and* non-human life can flourish? In the context of this study, I will treat this question as an ethical one. Technological innovation might be able to *shape* different life worlds in the future, and statistical reports can *predict* certain outcomes based on calculation and extrapolation—but what matters now more than ever is the *evaluation* of these possible futures, the *judgement* of which future is desirable and which is not. As the philosopher Byung-Chul Han has remarked, thinking and ethics are always narrative, while data collection and pure information remains cumulative and cannot give advice about how to act right in order to live well (*In the Swarm* 52). As emphasized by Hans Jonas already forty years ago, ethics for the future require a "casuistry of the imagination" as a different mode of envisioning the future. He adds that "[t]he serious side of science fiction lies precisely in its performing such well-informed thought experiments whose vivid imaginary results may assume the heuristic function here proposed" (30).

In this book, I propose that 21st century popular fiction is a fruitful site for this kind of ethics for the future, as films and novels enable readers and viewers to *experience* possible futures aesthetically. Derived from the Ancient Greek αἰσθητικός, aesthetics originally refers to sense perception. This offers a number of theoretical and methodological angles to look at film and literature in their function of simulating possible futures through aesthetics. On the one hand, in the spirit of formalism and New Criticism, the study of aesthetics entails a study of form, including narrative form, genre, openness or closure, and other formal literary devices. To this, new formalism adds that forms are not confined to literature. As Caroline Levine points out in her outstanding study *Forms: Whole, Rhythm, Hierarchy, Network*, they include "all shapes and configurations, all ordering principles, all patterns of repetition and difference" (3). This definition of form allows for a fusion of close reading and an analysis of historical context, which is precisely what an ethical reading of fiction for the future requires.

On the other hand, aesthetics also foregrounds the role of the perceiver, in this case the reader or the viewer. As newer developments of reader response theory argue, "viewing literature as an experimental system to write the future must [...] include the reader since a text in itself is nothing but a generative matrix, frozen in a mode of virtuality" (Schwab 14). Approaching the future through fiction therefore involves considering the effects of reading novels on the reader or viewer, which have a strong emotional or affective component and rely on embodied cognition. Affective ecocriticism for example points out that "[b]oth reading and watching are highly embodied activities, not only in that we need our senses in order to be able to perceive things, but also in that our bodies act as sounding boards for our mental simulations of story worlds and of characters' perceptions, emotions and actions within those virtual worlds" (Weik von Mossner, *Affective Ecologies* 3). In this sense, the aesthetic experience of future fiction can trigger ethical reflections on the nature and consequences of contemporary world formations, dominant worlds as well as alternative or other ones.

To address and reflect on future ethical topics through popular fiction and their aesthetics, this book contains twelve exemplary close readings of what I will call "future fictions", meaning films and novels set in the future or relating to it otherwise, for example through futuristic technologies. Based on what I identify as the main ethical challenges of our times, the ethical analyses of future fictions are grouped into six chapters containing the discussion of two primary works each. The selection of the works is based on ethical topics, as well as on the visibility and cultural impact of the films and novels.

Challenging Times

As possible futures derive from the present and its seeds—although neither teleologically nor linearly—it is the present and its *plural* realities which must be scrutinised for an ethical investigation of potential futures. Therefore, I briefly want to shed some light on the main challenges of our times, which are taken up by most fictional works with a future orientation, and which provide the basic structure for my reading of future fictions in this book. The first and possibly biggest challenge of the 21st century is the ecological catastrophe, which has been conceptualised as the Anthropocene by geologists. This has by now become a mainstream term used in the sciences, the media, and the arts. Alternatively, the current period of Earth history has been called the Capitalocene by environmental historian Jason Moore and left-leaning circles, or the Chthulucene by Donna Haraway. In the following paragraphs, I will point out the differences between these terms and their epistemological function in more detail before moving on to the second future ethical junction that is relevant in the context of this book. I propose that the digital revolution and its current and potential consequences for human and non-human lives represent another momentous influence on the future and therefore require ethical reflection. Finally, I suggest that ongoing research and innovation in the realm of biotechnology is also of crucial ethical relevance for the future. To end this section on the ethical challenges of the present and for the future, I will point out that these three sites need to be seen and analysed against the backdrop of the dominant socio-economic power structures they are situated in, which are more than challenging themselves.

The term Anthropocene, which was coined by atmospheric chemist Paul Crutzen at the annual meeting of the International Geosphere-Biosphere Programme in 2000 (Horn and Bergthaller 1), marks a turning point in the history of the Earth. As the era of "the human",

[i]t encompasses a vast number of different factors and locations, ranging from global climate change to disruptions in oceanic and atmospheric currents, the disturbance of the water cycle and of other important chemical cycles [...], soil degradation, the rapid loss of biological diversity, pollution

with toxic and non-degradable substances, all accompanying a continuous growth in the number of humans and their domesticates. (2)

In other words, the Anthropocene designates an ecological catastrophe that has already been underway for some time, either from the beginning of industrialisation or starting with the "Great Acceleration" after WWII—depending on the point of view. In addition to its destructive and lethal material effects, the Anthropocene brings with it a rift in the concepts of "the human", "nature" and "technology" and their relation to each other: neither can they be seen as separate from each other, nor are they tenable any longer—instead the Anthropocene reveals webs of relationships, including historically situated groups of humans, their power structures, and their different types of socially and economically situated technologies—all in interaction with multitudes of non-human lives and geophysical agents.

As different dating systems of the Anthropocene show,[1] the causes of this phenomenon are not of recent origin, only the scale of their effects is. The effect that first and foremost comes to mind is climate change, which in turn triggers several other consequences. In its 2014 report, the Intergovernmental Panel on Climate Change (IPCC) confirmed the evidence of climate warming as a result of anthropogenic emissions and demonstrated that every decade has been hotter than the previous one (40). Despite recent efforts of national leaders in annual IPCC conferences to counter this trend, we are currently facing the highest emission rate in history (44), and there is no sign that this upward trend is going to reverse any time soon. The report also highlights the consequences of the increase in average temperature on the planet that are already perceivable: the sea level is rising, snow and ice are diminishing, and regionally, there are more regular extreme weather events (50). In addition to the effects on physical planetary systems, biological systems are also affected: in marine and terrestrial ecosystems, species shift their geographic ranges and seasonal activities, and climate-related extinctions have also been noted. Climate change furthermore has negative impacts on human and managed systems, for example on crop yields and on health-related issues due to extreme weather conditions. Apart from climate change and its effects, numerous other human activities influencing eco- and other non-human systems also contribute to anthropogenic altering of the planet: we are in the 6th Great Wave of Species Extinction, the

---

1   Some scientists argue that it began with the "Great Acceleration" after WW II, while others see its starting point in the era of industrialisation or even earlier.

destruction of natural ecosystems for agricultural production leads to massive soil degradation and desertification, and microplastics and other human waste products already show in the strata records—just to name a few examples.

While the notion of the Anthropocene serves the important function of raising public awareness for the gravity of the ecological catastrophe caused by humanity, it has also been criticised for its essentialist notion of "the human" or even "man", who seems to be at the heart of the problem. In this respect, Donna Haraway writes,

> No matter how much he might be caught in the generic masculine universal and how much he only looks up, the Anthropos did not do this fracking thing and he should not name this double-death-loving epoch. [...] But because the word is already entrenched and seems less controversial to many important players compared to the Capitalocene, I know that we will continue to need the term *Anthropocene*. (*Staying with the Trouble* 47)

As an attempt to refine the notion of the Anthropocene, Jason W. Moore proposes to call this contemporary ecological juncture "Capitalocene", the "age of capital" (77), while Haraway herself suggests to name it "Chthulucene", designating a thick present and co-presence with "the biotic and abiotic powers of this *earth*" as the main story (55). Despite their differences, what all three terms have in common is that they tackle the idea of "nature" in opposition to human "culture" and its technologies. They foreground the fundamental entanglement between human and non-human worldmaking in the *oikos*, the ancient Greek term combining the human eco-nomy (as the household) with the eco-logy (as its environment) in a dialectical process. In literary and cultural studies, these phenomena that can be subsumed into "the ecological catastrophe" are currently approached in fields like ecocriticism and critical animal studies, as well as plant studies.

The second most striking characteristic of the present age is the defining role of modern technologies of various kinds, without which the ecological catastrophe would never have occurred, but which also offer unprecedented opportunities and other unprecedented threats. Humankind has always used technology, and it is possibly precisely this ability which characterises humans, as Cary Wolfe argues: the human being is "a prosthetic creature that has coevolved with various forms of technicity and materiality, forms that are radically 'not-human' and have nevertheless made the human what it is" (xxv). While the realm of *techne* as human artisanship has long been ethically neutral in the history of ethics, today' technologies with their powers to transform ecological and distinctly human spheres, and the enormously extended reach into time and space, can no longer be seen as neutral (Jonas, 'Technology and Responsibility: Reflections on the New Task of Ethics' 38). However, just as the term "nature" proves to be problematic, as I will argue, following Timothy Morton's deconstructivist analysis, "there is, after all, no such thing as technology. There is no such thing as technology in general or technology as such: There are always instead constellations of artifacts and techniques, actually-existing and also imagined" (Carrico 48). Going back to the original idea of *techne*, technology as the employment of tools to change the world, can refer to abstract skills such as language, as well as so-called "high technologies" like the internet of things. These different kinds of technologies need to be analysed and evaluated in the context of their socio-economic contexts and with regard to their function and unintended consequences.

The most prominent or visible new techno-cultural development today is digitalisation, also referred to as the 4th industrial revolution. With world computing power doubling every two years according to Moore's Law (Urry 3), the contemporary digital landscape is proliferating quickly—and radical new forms of human worlds and humans' being-in-the-world are emerging. Everything seems to become smart, from the phone to the home to the city, and the so-called internet of things requires the building of a 5G network. The prospect of futures without work, the creation of strong artificial intelligence, automated driving and similar developments either appear as prophecies of hope or doom. Smart technology already serves medical functions, while the self becomes more and more quantifiable. Another key word in this respect is "big data", referring to the collection of digitised information by private companies or government agencies about individuals, collectives, transactions, and communications. "Screen time", as the time people spend in front of a screen, has increased severely throughout the last years. At the moment, "people generally spend an average of three hours and 15 minutes on their phones every day, with the top 20% of smartphone users spending upwards of four and a half hours" (Matei). While this may seem like a harmless waste of time at first sight, it can have severe consequences on a personal and political level, which qualifies it as an ethical problem.

Apart from the issues surrounding corporate or state surveillance, the digital poses threats that are far less visible and yet substantial, as they undermine what democratic societies are built upon—at least in theory: the free will. Statistics such as the above-mentioned show that smart phone usage and especially social media turn out to be addictive, which is the intended result of the tech companies' employment of algorithms and mechanisms to increase screen time and generate income through advertising. The former Google strategist James Williams, who is now a philosopher at Oxford, describes the contemporary digital industry as the "largest, most standardised and most centralised form of attentional control in human history". This phenomenon is currently discussed as the economy of attention, which not only structurally undermines the individual will but also erodes the foundations for democracy, as Williams further argues (P. Lewis). The digital economy of attention highlights a central characteristic of our time, which is the global centralisation of worldmaking power in the hands of very few extremely influential corporate actors alongside ever weaker democratic representation through national governments and public institutions.

In addition to these already existing ethical challenges, the digital is accompanied by discourses of potential future progressions, like the uploading of a human brain on the internet or the creation of strong artificial intelligence. These future-related hopes and dreams are brought forth mainly by a group of philosophers and practitioners who call themselves "transhumanists", referring to their aim of transcending human limitations through science and technology. Even though the ideals of transhumanists like Ray Kurzweil, Nick Bostrom, and Max More may seem extreme, I treat them as strong versions of the still dominant cultural framing of science and technology as the drivers of progress, and thus, of better futures. The frequent appearance of transhumanist aspirations in fiction also confirms this interpretation. Transhumanism further provides the link to the other contemporarily most influential new technology with future relevance, which is biotechnology. Like digital technology, it can be used to alter and potentially "enhance" the human, for example through an extension of life expectancy or augmentation of intelligence.

The *Oxford English Dictionary* defines "biotechnology" as "[t]he application of science and technology to the utilization and improvement of living organisms for industrial and agricultural production", which already hints at the fusion between organic life and its utilisation as a product on the market. In this sense, Melinda Cooper offers that "[t]he biotech era poses challenging questions about the interrelationship between economic and biological growth, resurrecting in often unexpected ways the questions that accompanied the birth of modern political economy" (3). As with digital technologies, biotechnology alone cannot be considered from an ethical standpoint, but must be seen in conjunction with the (primarily economic) power structures enabling it. As Joanna Zylinska argues, bioethics in the more common or traditional sense only interrogates "ethical issues arising from the biological and medical sciences" (*Bioethics in the Age of New Media* xii). In contrast, the bioethical inquiry I want to pursue seeks to overcome the "humanist, normative, and universally applicable" principles (xi) that make traditional bioethics appear "less as an ethics per se than a branch of policy studies within the historical development of what Foucault calls biopower and governmentality." (Wolfe xxvii).

Questions that arise in the context of these "ethics of life" (Zylinska, *Bioethics in the Age of New Media* xii) would therefore not only address contemporary and futuristic biotechnological developments like cloning or life extension but also question the idea and position of "the human" alongside other forms of life. These others may be composed of technologically made others or of animal or plant others. By including them in ethical reflections, the normative idea of "the human" as an essentially superior form of life resulting from its rational capabilities will have to vanish. Furthermore, the question of value in the double sense of ethical value versus economic value must be tackled. With regard to the evaluation of life through biotechnology, Kaushik Sunder Rajan writes: "The sort of knowledge genomics provides allows us to *grammatically* conceive of life in certain ways, [...] as that whose futures we can calculate in terms of probabilities of certain diseases happening—and this shifting grammar of life, toward a future tense, is consequential not just to our understanding of what 'life' now means, but contains within it a deep ethical valence" (14). Again, the idea of futurity through calculation and control becomes apparent as a guiding principle of the life sciences.

While these developments in the spheres of the ecological, digital and biotechnological as rather new phenomena characterise and distinguish the present and its futures, other and older developments are ongoing at the moment and will likely shape potential futures in combination with newer developments. First and foremost, there is the proliferating inequality between the world's richest and poorest countries and people: the world's richest one percent own 43.4% of global wealth, while 56.6% of the world's population own just 1.4% (Institute for Policy Studies). Instead of creating more equality between nations and their inhabitants, global capitalism has perpetuated colonial power imbalances and increased poverty in many regions of the world. The aforementioned challenges therefore affect people and regions in entirely different ways. While much of the already experienceable consequences of the ecological catastrophe hit the world's poor much more severely—and, alongside armed conflict and war, create huge waves of migration—dreams of high-technological futures are mainly dreamt of by the world's wealthiest nations and individuals. So despite the unifying tendencies of globalisation and the new media, the present is characterised simultaneously by a pluralisation of worlds, temporalities and realities, including profoundly different future prospects.

Regarding the social and cultural pluralism of the present, Leonidas Donskis concludes: "Everything is permeated by ambivalence; there is no longer an unambiguous social situation, just as there are no more uncompromised actors on the stage of world history. To attempt to interpret such a world in terms of the categories of good and evil; the social and political optics of black and white [...] is today both impossible and grotesque" (Bauman and Donskis 5). As a result, at least for modern societies shaped by moral pluralism and individualism, the decision of what is ethically good seems to be left for the autonomous individual (Rosa 38). The problem of moral agency becomes even more difficult when considering the effects of highly specified work in a global setting, which Bauman describes as enabling "sin without sinners, crime without criminals, guilt without culprits" (19). This analysis echoes Hannah Arendt's concept of the banality of evil, where evil is carried out by "normal" functionaries who neither have the power nor understanding to foresee the effects of their actions and take moral stances accordingly. This constraint on moral agency brought forward through the global division of work is accentuated when the future effects of all kinds of contemporary technologies are added to the equation. Therefore, the question is whether it still makes sense to focus on individual moral agency or whether the locus of ethics in relation to the future is not to be found elsewhere?

Ethics for the Future: From Humanism to Posthumanism

Against the backdrop of the challenges and characteristics of the present, I will argue in Chapter Two that ethics for the future require a radical reconceptualisation of ethics. In parallel with human history, the history of ethics is an anthropocentric narrative building on the alleged superiority of the human over all other beings. The contemporary view of ethics is still predominantly influenced by humanist philosophy with its anthropocentrism, focus on the individual, and emphasis on rationality and rules. Non-human beings and technologies are mostly omitted in this conception of ethics, as are the long-term or spatially removed consequences of the *collective* and *cumulative* actions of humankind. Humanist ethics furthermore tend to be rule-based, thus requiring a universalisation of situations and agents that might not do justice to the concrete actors and problems at hand. Therefore, I propose to turn towards the relatively recent theory of critical posthumanism as a foundation for future-related ethics to meet the challenges of the 21st century.

In the late 1990s and early 2000s, critical posthumanism emerged as a theoretical paradigm in philosophy and related disciplines. In distancing themselves from humanism, critical posthumanists like Rosi Braidotti, Francesca Ferrando and Cary Wolfe diverge significantly from popular posthumanism that can be equated with transhumanism (e.g. Federer 227). As Kaherine N. Halyes already pointed out in *How We Became Posthuman*, the popular idea of the posthuman privileges information patterns and cognition over embodiment and sees the human body merely as an original prosthesis of the mind (Hayles, *How We Became Posthuman* 2). In contrast, critical posthumanism is characterised by a rejection of anthropocentrism and other humanist inheritances like dualist thinking, for instance ingrained in the nature-culture or matter-spirit binary. Ferrando defines posthumanism as "a philosophy which provides a suitable way of departure to think in relational and multi-layered ways, expanding the focus to the non-human realm in post-dualistic, post-hierarchical modes, thus allowing one to envision post-human futures which will radically stretch the boundaries of human imagination" (30). While being grounded in deconstruction and post-structuralism, posthumanism also seeks to go beyond them, pursuing an "affirmative" notion towards alternative futures and ethics (Braidotti 132). Its post-structuralist legacy provides critical posthumanism with an awareness for the importance of language and narratives for human worldmaking and especially ethics. At the same time, critical posthumanism tries to take a systemic perspective on human worlds as always being co-made and co-habited by non-human actors and technologies. Most importantly, regarding ethics for the future, critical posthumanism changes the locus of ethics. It is not about the individual human actor and "his" rational reflection on potential moral laws, as for instance in Immanuel Kant's humanist philosophy. In contrast, the locus of ethics for the future is in the effects of human and non-human worldmaking on a large, planetary scale, encompassing temporalities that stretch from the past across the present wide into the future, including what Adeline Johns-Putra calls "radical posterity" as non-identitarian and ecocentric perspectives (23).

Based on critical posthumanist theory, I want to redefine ethics as an emotional and rational meta-reflection on the consequences of human worldmaking to determine whether these worlds can generate good and desirable futures or whether these futures are rather bleak and unwanted. Worlds made by humans in conjunction with non-humans consist of signification through language and aesthetics as well as hard materialities, like forms of material production and organic cycles. Drawing on the philosopher Nelson Goodman, I depart from the assumption of numerous actual worlds instead of only one actual world because I treat "world" as a metaphor for the imaginary construct which humans make to grasp the totality of everything that exists. In theory, the metaphor of worldmaking implies that there could be an endless number of worlds made by different groups of humans, each containing fundamentally different "truths" or narratives. In practise, however, there are relatively few but extremely dominant world formations alongside a plurality of minor ones. The most powerful world today, beyond any doubt, is composed of global capitalism and its sub-worlds. A future-ethical reflection of worlds also looks at the composition of these worlds in terms of narratives and power structures, but especially of their moral compasses or maps of morality which tell inhabitants what is to be valued. In addition to making visible what is naturalised, simulations of future versions of worlds need to be considered for ethics of the future, which is where fiction comes in.

Ethical Criticism in the 21st Century

Building on this new understanding of ethics, Chapter Two will also develop a methodology to approach the fictional works through future-ethical readings. A short review of different strands of ethical criticism and the work done in what has been referred to as "the ethical turn" in literary and film studies from the 1980s up to date reveals that no existing approach proves suitable for this purpose. The main reason is that previous ethical criticisms mainly built on humanist or deconstructivist conceptions of ethics, which both fail to address aforementioned challenges of the 21st century as their spatial and temporal scope is too limited. They tend to look at individual characters, authors, and maybe even readers, but not at the representation of collectively made worlds and their future effects encompassing the non-human realm. Therefore, I propose that an ethical criticism in the 21st century, which wants to pursue the quest for a desirable future, needs to take a different approach. Rather than approaching a text or a film with a predetermined idea of morality, I argue that what might turn out to be good or bad is what these fictions try to assess aesthetically—and it might be different for each viewer and reader.

The ethical question about which future might be a good future presupposes the question of which futures are possible at all from where we are. I propose that contemporary films and novels that relate to the future creatively extrapolate possible futures from existing worlds of the present. As argued before, future fictions enable a different ethical reflection than non-fictional and purely rational arguments as a result of their formal, sense-based, and emotional mode of simulating possible futures, and thus reveal the connection of ethics to cognitive and affective processes. Readers and viewers are invited to *experience* the possible worlds of the future *as if* they were in them, for example by identifying and feeling with the characters or by contemplating different futuristic landscapes and settings. This aesthetic experience triggers conscious reflection on the future worlds offered, as well as on their contemporary counterparts. Thus, in my close readings of popular future fictions of the 21st century, I will trace the aesthetic choices and formations which create the works' moral universes that form the basis for an ethical reading. To ascertain whether and how the reading or viewing of future fictions generates ethical reflections in actual audiences and readers, I will illustrate the discussion of each work with some examples of reader or viewer responses taken from online blog posts.[2] As a second step of my ethical reading of future fictions, I will turn to the depiction of possible future worlds in the films and novels. Future fictions tend to make contemporarily dominant world formations and their future consequences visible and deconstruct their seemingly "natural" foundations. At the same time, they also juxtapose them with smaller and less dominant "otherworlds", which emphasise that futures could also be radically different from the dominating forces of the present. Through a critical posthumanist lens, these worlds will be deconstructed and scrutinised for their future viabilities.

Aesthetics for the Future: Popular Future Fictions

To group films and novels that ethically relate to the future—either because they are set in the future or otherwise deal with topics that are relevant for the

---

2   While reader response theory, as represented for example by Wolfgang Iser, focuses on an implied reader, looking at actual reader or viewer responses is a relatively recent phenomenon in literary studies, for example in cognitive approaches to literature.

ethics of the future—I use the term "future fictions". Although this term sometimes appears in reference to stories or works of art engaging with the future,[3]
I have not yet encountered it in academic discussions. In turn, as a short review
of the literature will show, there are several arguments surrounding genres and
classifications of this type of fiction, which is usually categorised as science
fiction, utopian, dystopian or (post-)apocalyptic fiction. To circumvent these
wide-ranging debates and decentralise the issue of classification, I will introduce future fictions to refer to all fictional stories which are set in the future
or provide simulations of possible future consequences of human worldmaking. A similar term has been employed by Christoph Bode and Rainer Dietrich,
whose research has centred on "future narratives". It is important to note, however, that they refer to something completely different with this term, namely
narratives involving readers' or players' choices via a large degree of openness
to the narrative enabled through different possible continuations or, as they
call them, nodes (21). A prime example is the film *Run Lola Run* (Tykwer 1998),
which provides three alternative endings for the same base story. For Bode
and Dietrich, future fictions in my sense would be past narratives, as they are
mostly narrations of a future that has already happened (11).

It is true that the majority of works which I call future fictions in the context of this book are written in the narrative past and thus assume a future
perfect simple perspective: this is what will have happened. Bode and his research team take issue with this kind of narrativisation of the past projected
into the future as what they call "presentism", arguing that it does not allow for
an imagination of the future that is different from the present (100). While I
have also criticised the "presentism" ingrained in futurological discourse that
merely seeks to preserve the status quo, I nonetheless want to highlight the ethical link between present and future: we need to look towards possible futures
in order to act right in the present. It is crucial to understand how the actual
worlds of the present are made in order to deduce possible future worlds and
their consequences, especially when such worlds are collectively made systems
and not individual choices, as seems to be *Future Narratives'* take on possible
futures. The ethical decisions that matter will be collective and thus political,

---

3   A spontaneous internet search for "future fictions" for instance, came up with an art
     exhibition in London titled "Future Fictions" ('Future Fictions – Exhibition at Assembly
     Point in London'), several ratings of novels referred to as future fictions (e.g. 'Future
     Fiction Books'), and a magazine article about how stories will be told in the future in
     the context of new technologies ('Future Fictions').

and they will create non-teleological futures in conjunction with many different groups of actors—most of them non-human.

To contextualise my own approach and ground my choice of primary works, I will shortly provide an overview of the developments in fictional accounts of the future and their generic clustering throughout the last decades. As Eckhart Voigts rightly points out with respect to this group of fictional works, "[g]eneric debates are legion" (4). While there are many discussions surrounding the established genres of science fiction, utopia, dystopia, post-apocalypse, and their numerous in-betweens and crossovers, this book asks how generic traditions and conventions influence a future ethical reading of these texts. My future ethical reading investigates the ways in which aesthetic decisions on formal aspects might guide and influence readers' or viewers' feelings towards different worlds of the present and their possible future versions. The focus set on particularly popular films and novels allows for the comprehension of the dominant cultural imaginary of our times. The aim is to look at cultural products consumed by a large percentage of people to discover the contemporary cultural imaginary of the future and to illustrate how the experimental setting of possible futures affects people and invites ethical reflections. As popularity can be a slippery concept with many different and conflicting meanings (e.g. Storey 4), I define popular as having a visible cultural impact, showing through awards, reviews in newspapers and magazines with high circulation, online blog discussions, popularity ratings and rankings, as well as through influencing social realities outside of fiction.

As explained before, I approach ethics *through* aesthetics with the temporality of the *future* as the main criterion, which has for a long time been confined to the marginalised genres of utopia, dystopia, and science fiction. Many scholars around the turn of the century have remarked that there has been a fundamental shift in the long-established literary genre of utopias throughout the 20th century as a response to socio-historical developments, most prominently the two World Wars, growing industrialisation, and the collapse of the Soviet Union. These developments led to proclamations of the end of ideology (Bell 1960), the end of history (Fukuyama 1992), and the end of utopia (Jacoby 1999). However, many scholars and literary critics have rejected these diagnoses as premature and simplistic, arguing instead for the transformation of utopian thought and form and its dialectical relationship with ideology, both of which continue to exist as historical forces. Leonidas Donskis (2000), Frederic Jameson (2005) and Tom Moylan (2021) all argue for the continuation of the utopian, albeit in a different form from earlier utopian ideas and texts which tended to provide visions and concepts of the perfect utopian society, for example the Renaissance travel reports modelled upon More's *Utopia* [1516], or visions of a harmonious future society like Morris's *News from Nowhere* [1890]. Similar to Ruth Levitas, they argue that the idea of "betterment" has replaced the concept of "blueprint", and that this is increasingly situated on the microlevel, rather than on the macrolevel, in the daily constructions of society (22). While fictional utopias had been the predominant form of raising social critique or of future writing up until the 20th century, the 20th century itself saw a rise in fictional dystopias as imaginations of a bleak future or as a means to criticise the present. With canonical texts such as Orwell's *Nineteen Eighty-Four* [1949] and Huxley's *Brave New World* [1932], dystopian fiction has dominated much of the 20th century (Fitting 139), apart from the rise of feminist, anarchist, and ecological utopias during the 1960s and 1970s, which were inspired by political and social transformations of the time.

With the last traditional utopias (Jameson 216), it seems that genre classifications became much more difficult, which led to the detection of new hybrid genres. For example, Ralph Pordzik emphasises the productivity of Foucault's concept of "heterotopia", especially for postcolonial narratives (3–4), Moylan coined the term "critical utopias" to describe the interwovenness of utopian and dystopian narrative strands. Dunja Mohr invented the concept of "transgressive utopian dystopias" to symbolise the overcoming of hierarchical binary thinking, and Margaret Atwood speaks of "ustopias" in her essay collection *In Other Worlds* to point out how one is always incorporated into the other. In the context of this generic hybridity and numerous debates in the field, I find it most convenient for my aim to simply use "future fictions" to describe fictional stories set in the future or with direct relation to the future. As my focus is on ethics, which are also connected to the reception of a work, it is important to avoid a preceding evaluation of future fictions as illustrations of either a good future state of affairs (utopia) or a bad one (dystopia).

Another way of framing my future fictions would be to position them within the genre of science fiction. This classification could make sense for my purpose, considering Darko Suvin's definition of science fiction as the literature of cognitive estrangement, and taking into account that almost all novels and films deal with the effects of modern technology and science on human societies and non-human actors. Yet, I want to allow for the possibility that the future may not only and not primarily be shaped by science and technology. Also, it is important to point out that non-human life has a great deal of agency when shaping futures, and that social transformation can result from new stories and social practices not engrained in the paradigm of science and technology. Accordingly, I do not see science fiction as an overall generic term for future fictions and would argue that science fiction is a subgenre of future fictions, even though it is clearly the most dominant one.

Far from rejecting all former attempts at generic clustering, my aim is to trace how these traditions of future writing are productive for contemporary future fictions, which all draw on them in a creative manner. To bridge the gap between the familiar worlds of the present and the possible unknown worlds of the future, most of the future fictions in my case studies fuse different modes of writing and generic traditions. These include multiple degrees of realism, both in form and content, and speculative to fantastic elements as well as post-modernist modes of representation, like metafictionality and pastiche. In the context of the contemporary American novel, Winfried Fluck notes that "experimental and realistic modes of writing mix and merge in new and unforeseen ways" (82). Similarly, Caroline Edwards establishes that "[o]ne of the most striking developments of post-millennial fiction in Britain as elsewhere has been the increasing number of novels that blur the boundaries between 'genre' fiction (science fiction, fantasy literature, speculative literature, detective fiction and so on) and 'literary' fiction (traditionally conceived in terms of a particular mode of literary realism)" (5). This book will confirm these claims, also with regard to film, and propose that contemporary future fictions achieve the effect of creating proximity and critical distance to the worlds of the present through the creative play with aesthetic form.

For my ethical reading of contemporary future fictions, I have limited the scope to works published in the 21st century in English which received a fair amount of public attention and resonated with large global audiences. The downside of this criterion of selection is that it echoes Western-centric perspectives on the future and is not able to look at the potentially more rich and diverse works of postcolonial writers and film makers or incorporate perspectives from the Global South or East. For example, in the expanding field of Afrofuturism or African Futurism, publications like Nnedi Okorafor's *Binti* (2015) and *Lagoon* (2014) challenge dominant assumptions about progress and otherness. They reverse global power structures and depart from an African-centric perspective on possible futures. The Indian science fiction author Vandana Singh manages to overcome the Western divide between the sciences, the arts and traditional spirituality and foregrounds ecological, technological and social interconnectedness in her novellas *Distances* (2008) and *Entanglement* (2014). Also, the viewpoint from countries with a socialist history like China fundamentally shifts the outlook on possible futures, as Cixin Liu's *Three-body Problem* (2014) demonstrates. Instead of focusing on the destructive potential of capitalism, the novel takes a critical perspective on human nature in general in the context of ecological destruction and social exertion of power. These visions of possible futures from the Global South and East as well as postcolonial perspectives on the future have been fruitfully addressed, for example in *Ethical Futures and Global Science Fiction* (Milner et al. 2020) and Jessica Langer's *Postcolonialism and Science Fiction* (2011).

On the other hand, shifting the focus to "Western" visions of possible futures also means scrutinising precisely that cultural imaginary which is in relation with the presently and historically most powerful worldmaking agents. As a result, the selection of works mirrors the ethical challenges that arise from this unjust allocation of power and "Western" attempts to control, exploit, and dominate "nature" as well as "non-Western" "others". As displayed by my research and extensive reading of contemporary future fictions with a high cultural impact, the ethical challenges described earlier also mirror the landscape of future fictions. Therefore, the close readings of very visible future fictions in the chapters are meant to serve as examples of larger trends. While the focus is set on ecology, digital technologies and biotechnologies, other ethical issues, such as global inequality and discriminative or exploitative power structures, will also be featured in the analyses and their theoretical underpinnings.

The Chapters

After establishing the theoretical and methodological foundations of this book in Chapter Two, Chapter Three is dedicated to the ethical exploration of ecological future scenarios. Based on Moore's coinage of "world ecologies" as the dialectical entanglement of human societies and their economic structures with what has traditionally been referred to as nature, I look at fictional representations of ecological futures in Kim Stanley Robinson's novel *New York 2140* (2017) and James Cameron's blockbuster *Avatar* (2009). An analysis of the aesthetic strategies used by the fictional works to project the ecological catastrophe into the future will lead to an ethical inquiry about cultural framing and potential solutions. Comparing the works with other eco- future fictions, I treat the them as paradigmatic of larger discourses. I argue that *New York 2140* leaves little aesthetic and ethical ambiguity by blaming capitalist worldmaking as the source of the problem and hence proposes its revolutionary and political overthrow. In contrast, *Avatar* deepens precisely the problematic and destructive double-bind between capitalism and nature that it criticises on the surface. Following Timothy Morton's deconstructivist ecocritical approach, I will show how *Avatar*'s aesthetically sublime representation of nature is a capitalist product, both on an intradiegetic level and on an extradiegetic or cultural level.

Diverging from the explanations and solutions to the ecological catastrophe proposed by *New York 2140* and *Avatar*, which are either driven by a romantic conception of nature or political revolution, Chapter Four explores transhumanist answers to contemporary ethical challenges. From a critical posthumanist perspective, transhumanism represents the belief in human evolution through technology, including the transgression of physical or biological boundaries of "the human". I will argue that Christopher Nolan's *Interstellar* is a prototypical example of such transhumanist dreaming. Like the works in Chapter Three, *Interstellar* departs from the assumption of a future ecological catastrophe on a global scale, but then envisions a techno-scientific solution encompassing space travel and inhabiting five-dimensional reality. In a similar vein, *Transcendence* represents the transhumanist dream of the perfectibility of the human and human worldmaking through technologies like brain uploading and nanotechnology. I argue that its aesthetic focus on patterns rather than binaries allows for ethical ambiguity with regards to potential transhumanist futures. In contrast, *Interstellar* unambiguously celebrates the transhumanist paradigm, which I determine to be an influential undercurrent in contemporary culture and its dominant worlds.

Chapter Five is dedicated to the ethical investigation of potential digital futures and exposes their ties with neoliberal capitalism. In my analysis of Spike Jonze's *Her* and Dave Eggers's *The Circle*, I focus on neoliberal subjectivities and modes of governmentality in the context of a digital economy of attention. I argue that *The Circle* projects the already existing digital economy of attention into the future and demonstrates in an ethically and aesthetically unambiguous fashion how it undermines the free will of individuals as well as democracy as a whole. The proliferation of neoliberal conceptions of the subject through digitalisation is an important topic in Eggers's novel as well as in Spike Jonze's *Her*. While in *The Circle*, the self as digitised *homo oeconomicus* is mainly displayed in the context of work performance, *Her* focuses on the private realm and especially romantic relationships. The distorting mirror of a digital AI shows how an individualised society preoccupied with the self, its growth, realisation, and performance prevents actual bonds and relationships with others, in spite or even because of its obsession with romance. With Laurie Essig, I point out the connection between neoliberal capitalism and romance and show how digitalisation might deepen this link even further in the future.

With the examples of Kazuo Ishiguro's *Never Let Me Go* and Don Delillo's *Zero K*, Chapter Six discusses the ethics of potential futuristic biopolitical dispositions and their relations to actual worlds of the present. Taking Foucault's notion of biopolitics as the mechanism of controlling life into the 21st century, my analysis focuses on the idea of "making live" in the context of biotechnological innovation. This takes the form of producing life through cloning in *Never Let Me Go* and overcoming death through cryotechnology in *Zero K*. I will argue that both works explore the workings of power in the context of biotechnological innovation. While *Never Let Me Go* uses an alternative past setting to investigate complicity in exploitation through narrative self-creation, *Zero K*'s futuristic present defamiliarises contemporary bio-capitalism and reveals its lethal biopolitical agenda. My reading therefore also focuses on how the aesthetic choice of temporality affects potential ethical responses.

Departing from the observation that many contemporary films and novels display aspects of fear of artificial superintelligence (AI), Chapter Seven takes a closer look at this perceived threat by reading Dennis Villeneuve's *Blade Runner 2049* and Alex Garland's *Ex_Machina*. The two films approach the ethical topic of AI from different angles; while *Blade Runner 2049* envisions the biotechnological creation of human-like creatures called replicants, *Ex_Machina* departs from digitalisation as the foundation for super-intelligent robots. I argue that both films question the power hierarchies derived from an anthropocentric and normative humanist ethics. My posthumanist reader will thus deconstruct the notion of the biological human in opposition to its technologically made other and focus on issues of power and domination, including a nod to Haraway's figure of the cyborg.

While most of the works and chapters so far have been based on problematic developments and rather negative visions of the future, the last chapter aims to look towards more utopian aspects joined under the heading of "posthumanist futures". Even though Margaret Atwood's *MaddAddam Trilogy* and Paolo Bacigalupi's *The Windup Girl* in general also paint rather bleak outlooks on the future, they also offer inspiration for hope. For example, they depict otherworlds that are alternative to neoliberal capitalism, which, as the novels show, will have ruined societies and ecologies in the future. Both works end with an emphasis on the interconnection between species and technologies that can be described as an illustration of posthumanist theory: *The MaddAddam Trilogy* envisions a peaceful cohabitation of technologically made creatures, be they human or animal, and organically grown ones. The boundaries between those categories disappear, foregrounding systemic interdependence rather than separateness. Likewise, *The Windup Girl* challenges naturalised concepts like "human" and "nature" and argues in favour of complex material-semiotic entanglements of worlds within worlds. Furthermore, the novels emphasise the importance of story-telling as a pivotal human worldmaking practice and reveal its fundamental relation to ethics, illustrating Donna Haraway's claim that "it matters what stories make worlds, what worlds make stories" (*Staying with the Trouble* 12).

2 Ethics for the Future through Fiction

I want to begin this chapter dedicated to the idea of ethics for the future through fiction with a paradoxical, maybe even daring claim: the contemporary proliferation of ethics in all spheres of life is a fig leaf covering up its fundamental absence. On the one hand, there is an explosion of ethics outside of philosophy: "[T]erms such as 'business ethics', 'professional ethics', 'medical ethics' or 'bioethics' have now become part of everyday parlance" (Zylinska, *The Ethics of Cultural Studies* ix). The rise of ethics committees across the spectrum of practice areas is remarkable (Pieper 113). There is also a growing discourse surrounding "ethical consumption" with regard to social and ecological sustainability. At the same time, people who wish to behave morally by helping migrants or opting for sustainable lifestyle patterns are discredited by others with terms like "do-gooder".[1] I propose that the reason for the resentment of "do-gooders" by those who might feel that they cannot afford this kind of "ethical" behaviour can be found in the discrepancy between individual action and systemic cause—the individual is made responsible for what has been caused by global systems. This points towards the deficiencies of the contemporary understanding of ethics: if ethics remain confined to the individual and its actions, or some specialised and marginalised area of expertise, they will fail to live up to the actual challenges of our times, from climate change to digital surveillance and biotechnological enhancement. These problems are situated on the level of *collective human worldmaking* and encompass politics and economics, as well as culture and semiotics. The scale becomes even bigger when the future plays a central role in ethical considerations. Therefore, I argue that ethics for the future require a radical reconceptualisation of ethics: instead of the traditional individualistic point of view of the rational human agent,

---

1   Especially in Germany the term "Gutmensch" is often used as an enemy stereotype by
    followers of the New Right.

ethics need to be raised to a systemic and political position that incorporates humanity's relations with its non-human others and technologies—in short: ethics must become posthumanist instead of humanist.

In the context of this chapter, I will arrive at a method for a future-ethical reading of fiction as a process of reflection on human worldmaking and its future consequences, encompassing the semiotic and narrative sides of worldmaking as well as the material—predominantly economic—side. As the underlying definition of ethics may appear far from other contemporary and historical conceptualisations of ethics and previous strands of ethical criticism, this chapter wants to retrace the steps from more familiar humanist definitions of ethics and their application to literature and film to a new one which is derived from posthumanist theory. The journey begins with the attempt to shed some light on the humanist legacy of ethics, which still informs and shapes many present-day notions of ethics as well as future-related branch lines. In this respect, I will present transhumanism and Hans Jonas's ethics of responsibility as two opposing heirs of humanism. My quest for ethics for the future will follow Hans Jonas's path, which for the first time incorporates nature and technology into the realm of ethics. Diverging from this path, I will show that Jonas's ethics are limited by their roots in humanism, and therefore take a turn towards deconstructivism with Joanna Zylinska's *Minimal Ethics for the Anthropocene*. I will base my own definition of ethics for the future on posthumanist theory, which will change the locus of ethics as well as their object. This posthumanist conception of ethics will then lead me towards a new ethical approach to literature, with a methodology based on possible worlds theory.

A Difficult Heritage: Humanism and Beyond

Contemporary conceptions of ethics are mostly indebted to earlier traditions of philosophy, especially humanism. The distinguishing features of humanist ethics, as I see them, are primarily in the focus on rationality, universalism and individualism. For example, one of the most influential representatives of humanist philosophy, Immanuel Kant, privileges the faculty of theoretical reason and thus of pure rational inquiry over empirical sense-based impression and emotions. The moral law, from this point of view, is thus only detectable through theoretical reason; it is both metaphysical and an objective reality (cf. *Kritik der praktischen Vernunft* AA V 71–81 qtd. in Hiltscher 228–231). This highlights another important feature of humanist ethics, which is their being rule-based or deontological. The most famous example of this focus on rules as the foundation of ethics is Kant's categorical imperative, which reads: "Act only in accordance with that maxim through which you can at the same time will that it become a universal law" (Kant and Gregor 31). Consequently, humanist ethics imply rational subjects who are essentially free in their actions and decision-making processes. Historically, this excluded most people who lacked this freedom resulting from higher education, power, and material wealth. This concept of subjectivity also needs to be seen in the context of European history: "Humanism historically developed into a civilizational model, which shaped a certain idea of Europe as coinciding with the universalizing powers of self-reflexive reason" (Braidotti 13). In this sense, Eurocentric humanism also provided the precondition for colonialism.

Despite its difficult legacy, humanist conceptions of ethics are still foundational for most contemporary institutions. such as national states, constitutions and laws. They are expressed with ideas such as universal human rights, which again work to cover up systemically caused global injustices. This reveals the shortcomings of humanist ethics for the contemporary age and the future: they are geared towards a normative ideal of the human and are individualistic as well as anthropocentric. As Alexis Shotwell argues: "Ethics, as it is historically developed, aims to help individuals in their personal ethical decision-making, and we continue to assess moral rights and wrongs at the scale of the individual human" (109). However, with regard to collectively created catastrophes like climate change and massive species extinction, this conception of ethics is not helpful at all because it only takes *human* beings into account and is too limited in terms of temporal and spatial scales. Accordingly, "the terms of ethical thinking must change in relation to the scale of the ethical problem" (110).

Humanism's normative subjectivity as "a specific concept of the human" furthermore grounds discrimination against non-human animals and the disabled in the first place" (Wolfe xxvii). It has created hierarchies of humans and other life forms that have formed the basis for patriarchy, colonialism, ableism and cruelty against animals. At the same time, it privileges spirit over matter, therefore discrediting the physical, including the body. Cary Wolfe describes "*the* fundamental anthropological dogma associated with humanism [...] that 'the human' is achieved by escaping or repressing not just its animal origins in nature, the biological and the evolutionary, but more generally by transcending the bonds of materiality and embodiment altogether" (xiv). He thus argues that the philosophical strand of transhumanism as an inherently future-oriented kind of philosophy "should be seen as an *intensification* of humanism" (xv).

Transhumanism represents a strand of philosophy that incorporates or even necessitates the future as it aims for a transgression of current biological and physical human boundaries through science and technology. One of the most influential transhumanist philosophers, Nick Bostrom, defines transhumanism as

> an outgrowth of secular humanism and the Enlightenment. It holds that current human nature is improvable through the use of applied science and other rational methods, which may make it possible to increase human health-span, extend our intellectual and physical capacities, and give us increased control over our own mental states and moods. Technologies of concern include not only current ones, like genetic engineering and information technology, but also anticipated future developments such as fully immersive virtual reality, machine-phase nanotechnology, and artificial intelligence. (Bostrom, 'In Defence of Posthuman Dignity' 202)

The transhumanist conception of the future can be described as teleological: it builds on a notion of progress, and science and technology function as tools towards this goal. As a result, it continues the modernist conception of the future as self-made forward movement, while ignoring all contrary evidence. Transhumanism "derives directly from ideals of human perfectibility, rationality, and agency inherited from Renaissance humanism and the Enlightenment" (Wolfe xiii).

Different from humanist philosophy, transhumanism makes technology a core element of its ethics, which is geared towards the physical and psychological "enhancement" of the human. Accordingly, transhumanism treats "the human" not as a fixed and historically stable entity or concept but as a mutable condition (Ferrando 26). The idea of transcending the human condition by becoming post-human, for example through mind uploading or a radical augmentation of intelligence, is thus desirable for transhumanist thinkers. Even more than humanism, transhumanism is deeply anthropocentric, by not taking non-human creatures and environments into account, much less humanity's indebtedness to them. Therefore, the theme of the ecology is not featured prominently in transhumanist ethics, and if it is, it is only in the idea of a technological fix. In contrast, in the second half of the 20th century, Hans Jonas was one of the first philosophers to include nature, technology, and the future in his ethical theory, which I will outline next as alternative future-oriented ethics.

New Ethics for a New Age: Hans Jonas

One of the first philosophers to explicitly address the challenges posed by the effects of technological human worldmaking on nature and future generations was Hans Jonas. His most influential work, *Imperative of Responsibility: In Search of an Ethics for the Technological Age* was published in 1984 in English. Here, Jonas diagnoses that all previous ethics up until then had been anthropocentric, while both nature and technology remained ethically neutral. As a result, these ethics focused on the spatially and temporally closely related "dealing of man with man", and they were built on an alleged essence of human nature (*The Imperative of Responsibility* 4). With regard to a dawning awareness of the ecological catastrophe, Jonas points out that

> [t]he altered, always enlarged nature of human action, with the magnitude and novelty of its works and their impact on man's global future, raises moral issues for which past ethics, geared to the direct dealings of man with his fellowmen within narrow horizons of space and time, has left us unprepared. (ix)

It is what Jonas calls "modern technology" (9) that brings about these changes, which perhaps most crucially involve an unprecedented "vulnerability of nature" (6). Accordingly, nature becomes an object of human responsibility and thus of ethics, as does technology. What has been referred to as *techne* and used to be subject to clever manipulation, must now be incorporated into human ethical concern and responsibility. Especially, technology and nature should be considered together rather than separately. Nature, in this case, not only relates to external nature or that which has classically been referred to as the environment, "[b]ut man himself has been added to the objects of technology" (18). With this, Jonas mainly refers to developments in biotechnology and medicine altering human nature, as for example in the promise of immortality, the biomedical governmentality of societies, and genetic manipulation (18–21). He sees the nature of human beings transforming in the process of the application of modern technology on "man himself", which to him poses a threat with unforeseeable consequences.

A distinct feature of Jonas's ethics is the inclusion of the future and the fate of future generations of humans, which must not be put at stake for the sake of present luxuries, according to his concept of "the heuristics of fear" (27). As a result, for ethics of the future, "*[k]nowledge* [about the possible consequences of our actions] becomes a prime duty beyond anything claimed for it heretofore, and the knowledge must be commensurate with the causal scale of our action" (7–8). Knowledge about possible consequences of actions has obviously played an important role in ethics—according to Kant, basically everybody was in theory able to achieve necessary knowledge for their individual deeds, primarily through their faculty of reason, but also through experience. Jonas states that today, however, with far-reaching consequences of collective human action, which result from the usage of modern technology, this is no longer possible. Even in the domain of experts, the knowledge of possible consequences of all current actions in remote times and places can never fully be attained and "[t]he gap between the ability to foretell and the power to act creates a novel moral problem" (8). On the one hand, it calls for a "humility owed to the excessive magnitude of our power to act which exceeds our power to evaluate and judge" (8), and on the other, "[w]e [...] need a science of hypothetical prediction, a 'comparative futurology', which indeed has lately begun to appear on the scene" (26). According to Jonas, this futurology may well be based on the analysis of literary future fictions, as their imaginative power of prediction can enable a future-related knowledge fundamentally different than the natural sciences. Following the logic of Albert Einstein's famous quote that problems cannot be solved with the same thinking that created them, Jonas calls for a different mode of future-related epistemology, "a truth independent of facts" (30), which, as he argues, can be found in science fiction.

Apart from Jonas's innovative inclusion of a future perspective on ethics, another progressive feature of his philosophy is his overthrowing of the Cartesian divide between matter and spirit in his previous work on philosophical biology, titled *The Phenomenon of Life: Toward a Philosophical Biology*, first published in 1966. This turn towards a new ontology suggesting a new monism of spirit and nature (Viana 13) functions as a precondition for his theory of responsibility. While moving beyond certain features of Enlightenment philosophy, such as the mind-body dualism and the Baconian ideal of human control over nature, Jonas still perpetuates others, like the indebtedness to metaphysics, universals, and deontology. For example, Jonas formulates a new categorical imperative: "Act so that the effects of your action are compatible with the permanence of genuine human life" (*Imperative* 11). This rule-based trait, together with the metaphysical grounding of Jonas' ethics, speaks of a continued rootedness in the humanist tradition. Aligning with the complete obliviousness to social analysis and the effects of power hierarchies, his proposed practical solution for the problems at hand is to apply "a maximum of politically imposed social discipline [to] ensure the subordination of present advantages to the long-term exigencies of the future" (142). Politically and practically this would mean "[...] adhering to a temporary Marxist tyranny of a well-informed and benevolent elite" (Gordon and Burckhart 199), which should rule the world in a type of world-government, minus the techno-scientific utopianism that Jonas criticises vehemently in Marxism (Jonas, *Imperative* 186).

Despite the humanist remnants and rather dystopian, totalitarian political solution Jonas proposes, it is possible to see tentative first steps towards transgressing humanist conceptions of ethics in Jonas's ethics for the future. They seem to move towards a mode of thinking known today as posthumanism. This is shown especially in his monist ontology of life, in which spirit and matter form a unity and continuum of different degrees of freedom rather than a difference in kind, as he argues in *The Phenomenon of Life*. In his rejection of the scientific view of nature, and in the attribution of an intrinsic value to nature, he furthermore overthrows the instrumental rationality engrained in humanist thought yet replaces it with value-rationality (Klier 123–25). Like more recent posthumanist thinkers, Jonas furthermore aims the focus towards the subjective body [German *Leib* as opposed to *Körper*], which is made up of matter *and* spirit and therefore connects all living beings. In order to describe the functioning of an organism, Jonas, similar to the contemporary posthuman theorists Cary Wolfe and Neil Badmington, draws on biological concepts of cybernetics. Another point of convergence with posthumanist philosophy, but also deconstruction, is Jonas's questioning of the word "progress" that he sees to loom "largely in Western speech". Although it originated in the idea of individual spiritual development, it is mainly tied to the realm of the public and to specific kinds of technology now (*Imperative* 162). However, despite efforts to challenge the fixed human-animal divide, Jonas holds on to an essentialist notion of the human, for instance when he muses about "bypassing the human way of dealing with human problems [...] by an impersonal mechanism" ('Technology and Responsibility' 49). It therefore seems that the distinction between human and machine remains stable in Jonas, whereas posthumanists and deconstructivists also go further to challenge this boundary.[2]

Consequently, it seems that ethics, in order to meet the challenges of the 21st century that are situated in the relationship human-nature-technology and the problematic implications of each term, must go further still in departing from humanism. Deconstruction has shifted the focus towards signifying

---

2   Most prominently, for example, in Donna Haraway's "A Manifesto for Cyborgs: Science, Technology and Socialist Feminism in the 1980s"

practices and language as a means of world construction, which deeply impacts ethics as well. Therefore, I will now move on to a more recent theory of ethics that has emerged from the realm of cultural studies and builds on the legacy of deconstruction: Joanna Zylinska's *A Minimal Ethics of the Anthropocene*.

Deconstruction, Ethics, and the Anthropocene: Joanna Zylinska

Most deconstructivist theories of ethics caution against a certainty of knowledge about the other and about the world, and therefore take a stance comparable to philosophical scepticism. This is also true for Joanna Zylinska and her understanding of the Anthropocene including the problems it presents. Different from the definition mentioned in the introduction, Zylinska's "own use of the term 'Anthropocene' [...] is first and foremost as an ethical pointer rather than as a scientific descriptor. In other words, the Anthropocene serves here as a designation of the human obligation towards the geo- and biosphere, but also towards thinking about the geo- and biosphere as concepts" (*Minimal Ethics for the Anthropocene* 19). Quite revolutionary in its take, this definition draws a link between the phenomenon of the Anthropocene as an ethical injunction and the idea of conceptualisation as the foundation for thought. Zylinska thus wants to challenge and deconstruct established ways of thinking by questioning and reshaping preconceived worlds and their epistemological formations. She further says that: "Minimal ethics for the Anthropocene is to serve as a caution against understanding the Anthropocene too well and too quickly, and against knowing precisely how to solve the problems it represents" (123).

Like many theories of ethics following deconstruction, Zylinska's work is inspired by Emmanuel Levinas's ethics of alterity, which refrains from deontology and universals, upholding only the call to responsibility for the other.[3] However, as with many of her contemporaries, she is "troubled by the humanist limitations of Levinas' ethics" (16). Therefore, her definition of bioethics as "ethics of life" encompasses the entire realm of living, but also that of matter. For Zylinska, it means understanding the world as entanglement: "It entails the constant unfolding of matter across time—but also a temporary stabilization of matter into entities (or rather, things 'we' and other non-human 'beings' recognize as entities) in order to execute certain acts and perform certain tasks" (30). Against the backdrop of the entanglement of matter and species, ethics

---

3   See for example Emmanuel Lévinas's *Totality and Infinity*

must shape-shift from their deontological and metaphysical conceptualisation to "a relatively narrow cultural practice, worked out by humans across history, as a form of regulating ways of co-existing and co-emerging with others. This cultural practice also involves providing an account—verbally, experientially, or aesthetically—of these processes of co-existence and co-emergence" (92). This means that ethics are no longer based on metaphysical moral laws as in Kant or Jonas, but instead intimately linked to epistemology as the discourse about what can be known about the world, as well as other forms of human cultural and material worldmaking. An important means for cultural world-making is communication through signs or semiotics. Within semiotics, it is especially stories which create meaning, as Zylinska further argues: "Ethics is therefore constitutively linked with poetics, because it comes to us through stories, i.e. through narratives of different genres and kinds. It is through the latter that we make sense of the world and pass on instructions on how to live to younger generations" (68).

Stories are crucial for creating human worlds, and the reason why these stories are so profoundly occupied with ethics and morals is because they "have a performative nature: they can enact and not just describe things" (11). The actions a society takes, as well as the different material and social subsystems it maintains, embody the performative side of its foundational stories. Actions thus need to be understood against the backdrop of a society's stories and conceptualisations that form worlds. This means, for example, that it has only been possible for human societies over the last centuries to "use" the "natural resources" for the benefit of humankind because "nature" has been narrated as separate from the realm of "the human" and does not possess a value or rights of its own. In this hegemonic story, human life is the most valuable form of being, ontologically different from any other form of life. Accordingly, it is perfectly justifiable to ignore the needs and ends of all other life forms like "animals" for the sake of human comfort, as for example in practices such as factory farming.

In Zylinska's words, "ethics and storytelling are two sets of intertwined practices in which human singularity—which is not to be confused with human supremacy—has manifested itself in the Anthropocene" (66). I therefore propose to approach the quest for ethics for the future in the age of the Anthropocene from the angle of storytelling, or more broadly, worldmaking, which adds aesthetic and non-linguistic symbolising practices to conceptional and denotational language. To avoid falling into the trap of isolated idealism, it is also important to consider the relationships between the symbolic and the material, which, as I will argue, is precisely where ethics for the 21st century need to be situated. Recent developments in the humanities like posthumanism and new materialisms have also recognised the importance of expanding critical thought by a non-human and material dimension, and by thinking in relationships rather than separate categories.

Towards Posthumanist Ethics

Around the turn of the century, a new theoretical paradigm in the humanities emerged and has been developed further throughout the last two decades. To express its temporal succession and simultaneous rejection of humanism, it is called posthumanism. The foundational texts that are usually referenced are Donna Haraway's *Cyborg Manifesto* (1985) and Katherine N. Hayles's *How We Became Posthuman* (1999). Since the year 2000, the posthuman turn, as it is also referred to, has gained an enormous influence on academic discussions, as the growing number of publications and conferences show. Some of the most important ones for literary and cultural studies are for example Neil Badmington's *Posthumanism* (2000), Cary Wolfe's *What Is Posthumanism?* (2010), and Rosi Braidotti's *The Posthuman* (2013), among many others. Another indicator of the increasing proliferation of posthumanism in intellectual discourse is shown by my repetition of Cary Wolfe's 2008 experiment, in which he googled both "humanism" and "posthumanism" (xi-xii). While the number of hits in 2021 has increased significantly in both cases since 2008, the number of results for posthumanism has multiplied by a factor of 48, while the number for humanism has only increased by a factor of eleven.

As always with definitions and terminology, there is no consensus on the term "posthumanism" by any means. While posthumanism is often used interchangeably with transhumanism, I want to follow the critical posthumanist strand represented by philosophers like Rosi Braidotti, Cary Wolfe and Francesca Ferrando, which calls for a radical distinction between the two. Opposed to transhumanism's ideal of transcending the physical and biological boundaries of the human through technology, Wolfe holds that his definition of posthumanism "opposes the fantasies of disembodiment and autonomy, inherited from humanism itself". Rather, "it names the embodiment and embeddedness of the human being in not just its biological but also its technological world, the prosthetic coevolution of the human animal with the technicity of tools and the external archival mechanisms (such as language and culture)" (xv). Hence, critical posthumanism objects to the notion of human supremacy and conceptualises human beings in relation to their animal or "earth" others (Braidotti 49). It does not attach as much meaning to technology, which in transhumanism is loaded with almost divine characteristics (Ferrando 28), while sharing the idea that humans have evolved with technology as prosthesis. Different from transhumanism, posthumanism also takes a critical stance towards humanism. For example, Wolfe seeks to show how humanism undercuts its own aspirations and values like individual freedom and universal rights with the philosophical and ethical frameworks used to conceptualise them (xvi). In a similar manner, Rosi Braidotti points out that posthumanism and its deconstruction of "Wo/Man" undermines the Enlightenment narrative of progress through a self-regulatory and teleological use of reason and of secular scientific rationality allegedly aimed at the perfectibility of 'Man'" (37).

Posthumanism thus distances itself from humanism's focus on abstract reason as the decisive aspect that forms "the human" and that represents *the* precondition for ethics. It aims at surpassing dualist thinking in binary pairs like spirit/matter, man/woman, nature/culture, and instead wants "to think in relational and multi-layered ways" (Ferrando 30). Posthumanism is thus a worldview representing a fundamental paradigm-shift in conceptualising the world, the place of humans and human worldmaking in it, as well as the relationship between humans and their living and material environments. As human worldmaking is largely based on conceptual thinking and language, most posthumanist theorists, like Braidotti and Wolfe, build up on deconstruction. In consequence, posthumanism also crucially involves thinking about thinking and linguistic conceptualisation with a special emphasis on the concepts of human, nature, animal, culture, and technology: "More specifically, posthuman theory is a generative tool to help us re-think the basic unit of reference for the human in the bio-genetic age known as Anthropocene [...] By extension, it can also help us rethink the basic tenets of our interaction with both human and non-human agents on a planetary scale" (Braidotti 5).

These definitions of posthumanism make it obvious that posthumanist theory is intimately entangled with the most relevant topics for 21st century ethics. It does so by analysing relations and systems rather than discrete entities and rational subjects, which enables an entirely different understanding of the contemporary ethical junctions. Unsurprisingly, many posthumanist theories therefore draw on different versions of systems theory, ranging from its application in biology by Humberto Maturana and Francisco Varela to

Luhman's sociological analysis of the systems of human communication and culture. According to Cary Wolfe, the posthumanist perspective enables us to describe human beings with greater specificity "by recontextualizing them in terms of the entire sensorium of other living beings and their own autopoietic ways of 'bringing forth a world'—ways that are, since we ourselves are human *animals*, part of the evolutionary history and behavioural and psychological repertoire of the human itself" (xxv). While Maturana and Varela's idea of *autopoiesis* as self-making might help to ascribe more agency to non-human beings, Donna Haraway criticises its underlying focus on the individual, calling instead for a perspective that foregrounds interdependency: "[a]utopoietic systems are hugely interesting—witness the history of cybernetics and information sciences; but they are not good models for living and dying worlds and their critters. [...] Poiesis is symchthonic, sympoietic, always partnered all the way down" (*Staying with the Trouble* 33). Haraway even goes so far as to connect the point of view of *autopoiesis* to the socio-economic phenomenon of neoliberalism that shares its focus on the individual: "Bounded (or neoliberal) individualism amended by autopoiesis is not good enough figurally or scientifically; it misleads us down deadly paths" (33). Neoliberalism as the marketisation of everything, from state-run institutions to the self, can also be seen as a historical product of individualising humanism. To diverge from these "deadly paths", ethics and thinking must become systemic.

The symbolic and material are intimately related through systemic interconnections, and the individual rational human being should no longer be the centre of philosophical, epistemological or ethical attention. Instead, narratives should become privileged sites for understanding human meaning-making within the formation of social and material systems, as these are dependent on storytelling: "Systems have tales to tell because they have to tell tales—literally, they must sequentially select and connect the elements of a medium in a continuously viable way—to keep going" (Clarke 7). So in fact, we are dealing with systems within systems: the material system of production is linked to biological systems and is enabled by the social systems of communication whose most important elements are narrative and aesthetics. Social systems, their stories and aesthetics provide an important means of accessing and understanding human worldmaking whose material bases in turn inform and enable these stories. To grasp the dynamics that characterise the present period of the Anthropocene, this systemic perspective is crucial. As I will illustrate in the section and in my close readings, these systems (of production, language, power, aesthetics etc.) converge into life worlds that appear holistic and even "natural" to their inhabitants.

In addition to the semiotic realm, matter and the systems it inhabits plays a leading role in worldmaking. In the introduction to their essay collection on new materialisms, Diana Coole and Samantha Frost "advance the bolder claim that foregrounding material factors and reconfiguring our very understanding of matter are prerequisites for any plausible account of coexistence and its conditions in the twenty-first century" (2). In combining political economy with new conceptualisations of matter and materialities inspired by recent developments in quantum physics and biotechnology, Coole and Frost stress the importance of the material dimension in exploring "the significance of complex issues such as climate change or global capital and population flows, the biotechnological engineering of genetically modified organisms, or the saturation of our intimate and physical lives by digital, wireless, and virtual technologies" (5). Again, these areas match precisely with the ethical challenges of the 21st century as outlined in the introduction.

Thus, it seems that new materialism in fusion with the posthumanist agenda will prove to be fruitful in approaching ethics for the future through fiction. At the core of new materialisms is the idea that "materiality is always something more than 'mere' matter: an excess, force, vitality, relationality, or difference that renders matter active, self-creative, productive, unpredictable" (9). There is an agency in matter and materialities, and the distinction between living and dead matter as the old Cartesian divide becomes blurry or even vanishes altogether: "In this monolithic but multiply tiered ontology, there is no definitive break between sentient and nonsentient entities or between material and spiritual phenomena" (10). This monist ontology is also referred to as "vital materialism" and links new materialisms with certain strands of posthumanist thought, for example Braidotti's critical posthumanism: "In my view, the common denominator for the posthuman condition is an assumption about the vital, self-organizing and yet non-naturalistic structure of living matter itself" (2).

Like Hans Jonas, who already assumed a monist position in his *Phenomenon of Life*, Braidotti follows Spinoza in his idea of a life-death continuum: "Posthuman vital materialism displaces the boundaries between living and dying. 'Life' or *zoē*, aims essentially at self-perpetuation and then, after it has achieved its aim, at dissolution" (134). From this, she further concludes that there is a trans-individual connection between humans and non-humans, generations, and ecology, which calls for a redefinition of ethics, bioethics especially. The notion of bioethics, however, is a good example of the confinement of the ethical to certain areas of human life as mentioned at the beginning. Joanna Zylinska also addresses this point in constructing what she calls an "alternative bioethics": "Departing from the more accepted definition of bioethics as the interrogation of 'ethical issues arising from the biological and medical sciences,'... [b]ioethics for me stands for an 'ethics of life', whereby life names both the physical, material existence of singular organisms (what the Greeks called *zoē*) and their political organization into populations (*bios*)" (*Bioethics in the Age of New Media* xii). If we add materialities and machines or technologies to bioethics in this sense, we approach what can be subsumed as posthumanist ethics. Even though some posthumanist thinkers explicitly mention ethics and their versions of posthumanist ethics, the term remains vague and abstract—rather as a mode of thinking, yet to develop its praxis.

Rosi Braidotti does this most explicitly. Her posthumanist ethics are based on the generative but also destructive force of *zoē* which sees ethics as an experiment with intensities and ethical imagination as ontological relationality: "A sustainable ethics for non-unitary subjects rests on an enlarged sense of interconnection between self and others, including the non-human or 'earth' others, by removing the obstacle of self-centered individualism on the one hand and the barriers of negativity on the other" (190). The focus of her "affirmative ethics", as she calls it, is thus mainly on the relationship between entities and materialitities, which is also how the subject is constituted, less as an individual and more as a relational subject. As further criteria for these new ethics, she mentions the non-profit, an emphasis on the collective, the acceptance of relationality, efforts at experimenting with and actualising potential, as well as drawing a new link between theory and practise through creativity (191). Rather than creating a bond of negativity and suffering with respect to 21st century challenges because "we are all in this together", Braidotti wants to transcend negativity, claiming that "the condition for renewed political and ethical agency cannot be drawn from the immediate context or the current state of the terrain. They have to be generated affirmatively and creatively by efforts geared to creating possible futures" (190). Braidotti's posthumanist ethics therefore represent a new mode of thinking that breaks with former modes of philosophising and is not a dogma with fixed contents. In the quote above, she also mentions the necessary future-outlook for ethics of the present which should be linked with creativity as we need to come up with something new that cannot be derived from past ways of thinking and being in the world.

In the following, I will apply the ideas and inspirations from Hans Jonas, Joanna Zylinska, and posthumanist ethics to a reading of literary texts and films dealing with different imaginations of the future. On the one hand, this requires a short positioning of my approach within existing strands of ethical criticism, and on the other, I will develop a new approach of ethical reading based on the posthumanist conceptualisation of ethics for the future as a reflection on worldmaking. This will then form the theoretical background against which I will read contemporary future fictions as effectors of and reflectors on aesthetic and narrative worldmaking.

Actual Worlds and Possible Futures in Fiction

Approaching ethical questions through fiction and its aesthetics first requires an examination of the relationship between fictional works and their extra-textual environments. In other words, how can fiction be described in relation to other things that exist in the world? The ontological status of fiction has often been framed against the possible worlds paradigm—if it has been raised as a matter of importance at all: "Although traditional literary theory did not ignore the problem of fiction, it has regarded the fictionality of texts as an inner type of organization, largely disregarding the fact that being fictional, by definition, refers to the relations between a world and what lies beyond its boundaries" (Ronen 1). Even though fictionality and its relationship with "reality" has been addressed in recent years due to an increased mutual interest between literary studies and philosophy in the final decades of the 20th century, most scholars have retained a firm distinction between *the actual world* and the *possible worlds* of fiction (e.g. Pavel; Doležel). In philosophy, where possible worlds theory originated with Leibniz, "[t]he various positions on possible worlds are in fact various views on the degree of *realism* to be ascribed to possible worlds" (Ronen 21). While most positions distinguish between an actual and a possible situation, the anti-realist approach, represented most prominently by Nelson Goodman, denies the existence of a single actual world: "We are not speaking in terms of multiple possible alternatives to a single actual world but of multiple actual worlds" (2). When addressing the problem of fictionality, Goodman's philosophy also overcomes the reality-fictionality binary by claiming "that the so-called possible worlds of fiction lie within actual worlds" (104).

I depart from Nelson Goodman's philosophy of worldmaking to create a methodological approach to ethics and fiction which builds on the posthumanist conception of ethics I generated before. With the advent of posthumanist philosophy, new materialism, and ecocriticism, ethics are raised to the level of collectively made worlds including systems of material production and meaning making. Ethical criticism must follow in this wake and expand its focus and develop new methodologies. Hence, I argue that an ethical criticism of literary texts and films which is directed at the *future* rather than the present or past must make collectively created worlds and their systemic structures its starting point, instead of looking at individual characters, authors or film makers and their personal moral virtues or vices, as previous ethical criticism has primarily done. The ecological, social, and technological questions and problems that characterise both the present and its future can no longer be solved on an individual level, as they are the result of collective actions which took place over a long period of time.

Existing Ethical Approaches to Literature

Within the realm of fiction, ethics and aesthetics have always been relevant concepts of study, whose positions in relation to each other have been subject to manifold controversies over the last century. In accordance, Michael Eskin, Robert Eaglestone and Robert Sinnerbrink hold that labelling literary and film studies' renewed interest in morals and ethics from the 1980s onward as the "ethical *turn*", is rather deceptive, since there has always been a focus on ethics in the study of literature and film (Eskin 562; Eaglestone 596; Sinnerbrink 15). However, the way it has been dealt with, especially in conjunction with the aesthetic, has undergone tremendous change. For the longest time, from Plato to Matthew Arnold, it was unquestioned that ethics are the prime reason for watching plays and reading novels. The counter-position that art has nothing to do with moral judgement, as represented by 19th century aestheticism for instance, has always been there, too, even if marginal (Lothe and Hawthorn 1). Biographical and ethical readings were the dominant modes of literary criticism well into the first half of the 20th century. Towards the mid-20th century, with the advent of formalism, structuralism, and New Criticism, aesthetics and form started to overrule other non-textual interests in the interpretation of literature. In the striving of literary studies towards scientific objectivism connected to the project of New Criticism, descriptivism superseded prescriptivism. With the rise of theory and poststructuralism in the 1970s, "the notion of ethics itself had become suspect" (Korthals Altes 143). While there was a period when literary scholars carefully avoided all things overtly ethical, philoso-phers started to develop an interest in the literary, which led to the "turn to lit-erature" in (moral) philosophy headed by scholars like Martha Nussbaum and Wayne Booth. Literary criticism followed soon after in what has been referred to as the "turn to ethics", with critics like Robert Eaglestone, J. Hillis Miller, and Derek Attridge, just to name a few literary scholars who associate themselves with the study of ethics in literature.

These critics are sometimes also referred to as the "new ethicists". Even though the study of literature and ethics is nothing new, Eskin and Eaglestone propose that the new ethicists offer a different take on aesthetics in conjunc-tion with ethics. Eskin describes it as "an 'aesthetics' informed by a newly forged conceptual inventory and vocabulary made up of the [...] buzzwords [*alterity, interpellation, call of the other, answerability, ethical responsibility, openness, obligation, event, doing justice, witnessing, hospitality, singularity, particularity,* or the *gift*]" (562/561). Eaglestone, in reaction to Wittgenstein, proposes to join ethical criticism with the recent literary critical movement called "New Aestheticism", which focuses on the relationship between art and truth. According to one of its founders, Andrew Bowie, "New Aestheticism" centres on the "unique world-disclosing capacity" of artworks (170). Eaglestone further writes: "Because we (now) inhabit multiple and often conflicting worlds, it is the artworks that reveal to us who and how we are, what these worlds are, and to some extent what our potentialities for being are" (601).

In a metacritical account of the ethical turn in literary studies and philoso-phy, Lisbeth Korthals Altes identifies three different strands of ethical criticism which she calls: 1) pragmatist and rhetorical ethics 2) ethics of alterity 3) politi-cal approaches to ethics (143). Representatives of the pragmatist and rhetorical ethics, like Martha Nussbaum, Wayne Booth, David Parker, and James Phe-lan trace the ethos, either of the author or the entire text, as a complement to moral philosophy, adding an imaginative and situational component. While Nussbaum uses Aristotle's concept of ethos as a starting point, Booth and Phe-lan focus on the structural devices within the text to decipher the ethos of the text and/or its author/reader. These scholars mainly draw on humanist or an-cient Greek traditions of ethics and philosophy, including normative ideas of rights and rules or virtues. In contrast, representatives of the second strand of ethical criticism challenge humanist ethics with the help of deconstruction. Based mainly on the theories of Emmanuel Levinas, Jacques Derrida, and Paul de Man, the ethical criticism of scholars like Andrew Gibson, Adam Zachary Newton, and Hillis Miller is inspired by a sense of undecidability of meaning and ethics (Korthals Altes 144). Here, the ethical value of reading literature is in the encounter of radical alterity and otherness, which is particular and not universalisable into deontological norms.

The last strand Korthals Altes mentions in her overview are the political approaches to ethics. It is debatable whether to sort them into ethical criticism at all, as other metacritical accounts of ethical criticism usually just divide the positions into two camps: humanistic and poststructuralist (e.g. Serpell 293). The critics Korthals Altes mentions in the third strand, like Homi Bhabha and Gayatri Spivak, would probably not have classified themselves under the ethical label at all. On the other hand, Rüdiger Heinze, in classifying ethical critics, establishes also a third category into which he groups those who claim that deconstruction has always been concerned with ethics, like Hillis Miller (16). Consequently, as most political criticism like feminism or postcolonial criticism is grounded in deconstruction, these critics would also go into the category of ethical criticism. My version of ethical criticism will likewise focus on (power) relations and collective rather than individual acts, which it will aim to consider in conjunction with the narratives, materialities, and webs of life they are embedded in. Therefore, it could be argued that it also forms part of the category of political approaches to ethics. Different from other criticisms, however, which have called themselves explicitly political in opposition to the ethical, I will propose a way to unite the two spheres. While most important publications in the field of ethical and literature from philosophy and literary criticism took place in the 1980s and 1990s, it seems that the interest has lessened after 2000. There are still some scholars, however, carrying the project on into the 21st century, such as James Phelan, Leona Toker, Thomas Claviez, Derek Attridge, C. Namwali Serpell, and Rüdiger Heinze. Surprisingly, none of them takes the future and its enlarged challenges from climate change to life-altering technologies into account.

Ethical Criticism in Film

None of the scholars of the ethical turn I have mentioned so far have included film as a genre in their research, even though film and its subgenres have become the most popular form of fiction of our age. A possible explanation for this may be that academic discussions are still confined to genre boundaries, even though in many respects—for example with ethical criticism—it seems fruitful to work comparatively across genres. Looking at film studies, one can discern something like an ethical turn that coincided with the turn of the century, although it has not had the same scope and relevance as the ethical turn in the study of prose fiction. Lisa Downing and Libby Saxton confirm that relatively little has been written on film and ethics. The focus in this area of research has mostly been on documentaries and issues of representation (11). In his overview of ethical approaches to film, Robert Sinnerbrink likewise criticises "how few philosophers have explicitly addressed the question of film and ethics, despite widespread acknowledgement of cinema's philosophical as well as cultural-historical potential" (6). He mainly discusses Stanley Cavell and Gilles Deleuze as examples of philosophers who *did* address this question. In parallel to literary studies, the ethical turn in film studies consists of philosophers who incorporate film, and of film critics who draw on ethical theories. For example, Downing and Saxton as film scholars use the poststructuralist ethical turn as a starting point for their discussion of film and ethics, focusing on Levinian ethics of responsibility and Lacanian psychoanalysis as ethics of the self and desire in conjunction with film analysis.

The choice of philosophers that have been seen as relevant for the study of film and ethics already signals a crucial contrast with the much broader ethical turn in literary studies. Perhaps because film studies were slow on the uptake (2), the ethical turn took place later and did not rely on humanist or ancient Greek conceptions of ethics,[4] seeming much more concerned with the study of film as an autonomous ethical medium. For example, the philosopher Deleuze, in his *Cinema* books (*The Time-Image*; *The Movement-Image*), posits film and philosophy as two ways of thinking, one with images, the other with concepts. Similarly, Sinnerbrink points out that cinema is complimentary and not merely exemplary to philosophy. The aesthetic mode of cinema, meaning its emotional and image-based way of thinking, which is opposed to philosophical ways of conceptional thinking, is ethical in and of itself. He further writes: "Cinema can question and explore social, cultural, and political situations in ways that force viewers to rethink what they regard as morally significant; it can prompt us to see our world—or multiple worlds—in a more psychologically nuanced, socially complex, ethically revealing light" (10).

To summarise and categorise ethical approaches to cinema, Sinnerbrink identifies three major aspects of the relationship between film, spectator, and context: first, ethics in cinema, dealing mainly with the narrative content of

---

4   As always, there are exceptions, for example Joseph Kupfer's *Visions of Virtue in Popular Film*, which looks at ethics and film from an Aristotelean perspective.

the film; second, the ethics and politics of cinematic representation; and third, the ethics of cinema as a cultural medium referring to the socio-economic context (10). Large proportions of ethical criticism of film focus on the first two aspects, for example in questions of morally charged situations between filmic characters (e.g. Kupfer 1999) or issues of spectatorship and representation (e.g. Nichols 1991, Stam and Spence [1983] 2006). Other presently dominant approaches to ethics and cinema are based on Levinasian ethics of alterity, Stanley Cavell's philosophy of the everyday, and Deleuzian perspectives that focus on modes of existence, communicating thought, and reasons to believe in this world (Sinnerbrink 15). Downing and Saxton mention as key strands of ethical criticism in film studies approaches based on theories of Emmanuel Levinas, Jacques Derrida, Jacques Lacan and Slavoj Žižek, as well as Michel Foucault and Alain Badiou (3). In Downing and Saxton's overview, it seems that ethical criticism in film mainly takes place between the poles of "the responsibility of the self towards the absolute vulnerability of the other" and "an ethics of the self, in which the ethical gesture would involve fidelity towards the real of one's desire" (1). Again, the locus of ethical reflection is confined to the micro-sphere of the self and the other, largely disregarding socio-economic context and larger scales.

Limitations of Existing Approaches

Previous works of ethical criticism, both in literary criticism and film studies, have focused mainly on ethics as a phenomenon concerning the individual and its direct spatial and temporal environments, as have most theories of ethics up to date. As Hans Jonas demonstrated, this relatively narrow point of view is not tenable any more with regard to the ecological, technological, and social global challenges humanity is facing at the beginning of the 21st century, which will likely become even more pressing in the future. In addition, many contributions to ethical criticism, especially in relation to philosophy, have not considered the specificity of the literary or filmic artefact and its operation within the realm of aesthetics, and have instead focused mainly on content.

The distinction between ethics and politics, which is sometimes made in literary and film theory, also proves detrimental to an ethical reading of future fictions. For example, Downing and Libby suggest that "ethicizing experience means conceptualizing it in terms of responsibility and desire [...], rather than simply in political or moral terms" (93). Again, this narrows the scope to the individual and wrongly separates it from the larger socio-cultural and political structures that shape the individual consciousness and the actions derived from it. In parallel with dominant conceptions of ethics, ethical criticism in literary and film studies alike put the focus on the individual and its responsibility, desire, faults or virtues. As I argued previously, this conception of ethics is still extremely influential today and is explicable through the history of philosophy. On top of its shortcomings with regard to the ethical junctures of the present and future, it is also problematic in the context of neoliberal governmentality. Throughout the second half of the 20th century up to the present, neoliberal thought has reconceptionalised the relations between the individual, the state and the economy. As Wendy Brown argues, in neoliberalism "markets *and* morals" are used to govern and discipline individuals (11). Through political and social decontextualisation, individuals alone become responsible, and their private actions become morally loaded, indifferent to their personal circumstances, for example different financial backgrounds.

This confirms that politics and ethics must be seen together, especially when addressing the ethical problems of the contemporary moment, in which moral issues concerning human individuals and groups continue to exist and be relevant, but in which they by no means posit the limit of the ethical. As posthumanist philosophy proposes, the humanist idea of "the human" based on a normative set of criteria that distinguish humans from other life forms and provide the basis for their alleged superiority, also needs reassessment. In this spirit, in the last chapter of their book, Downing makes the case for postmodernist filmmaking and posthumanist ethics "as the modes of thinking in which [such] certainties about the uniqueness of being human can be called into question and subjected to suspicion" (154), which is again complicit with a posthumanist approach and take on ethics. In quoting Joanna Zylinska, she further acknowledges that ethics does not amount to a fixed system of morals, and that any such system in existence always comes as a result of a hegemonic struggle (158). Building on previous strands of ethical criticism, but mainly diverging from them, I will now outline my own ethical approach to contemporary future fictions that serves as the basis for my close readings in the following chapters.

Future Ethical Criticism: Worlds in the Making

I propose to re-conceptualise a future-ethical criticism of the 21st century as an analysis of the worlds in fiction and beyond, including their aesthetics, power hierarchies, materialities, discourses, and what I call compasses of morality. My approach departs from Nelson Goodman's *Ways of Worldmaking*, which assumes the existence of multiple actual worlds that permeate fiction as well as other social and material spaces outside of it. Accordingly, I will begin with a short introduction to Goodman's theory of worldmaking and then move on to its application and expansion in cultural and literary studies. As a next step, I will make the theory of worldmaking productive for my reading of future fictions by defining what I mean by worlds and what role they play in an ethical reading of future fictions. Finally, I will introduce the concept of dominant worlds and otherworlds which will appear throughout the next chapters as the foundation for ethics of the future through fiction.

According to Goodman, worlds can be built in many ways, yet "we no more make a world by putting together symbols at random than a carpenter makes a chair by putting pieces of wood together at random" (94). Worldbuilding thus follows certain principles, and some world versions are "better" than others, "not in the sense of objectively *truer* (a criterion discredited by the constructivist approach), but in terms of such criteria as rightness of fit, validity of inference, internal consistency, appropriateness of scope, and above all *productivity*" (McHale 9). Goodman furthermore argues that worlds are always made and remade from other worlds and are not made from nothing (6). An especially delicate issue against the backdrop of the contemporary discussion around post-factualism is Goodman's emphasis on there not being anything like a single reality or truths easily distinguishable from falsehoods or objective facts. He holds that "truth must be otherwise conceived than as correspondence with a ready-made world", (94) "reality in a world, like realism in a picture, is largely a matter of habit" (20), and that facts are made rather than found (91). Even though these ideas may evoke high levels of indignation today,[5] it must be acknowledged that the word "fact", as derived from the

---

5   This is especially noticeable in the context of Donald Trump's presidency in the United States (2017–2021) and the "alternative facts" debate surrounding it, for instance his denial of climate change, which has triggered protest movements across the globe such as the "March for Science" in 2017, in which universities countered "postfactualism", arguing that "there is no alternative to facts" ('March for Science Germany').

Latin *factum* already means "made" and there is no denying that humans, as well as other species, are world-*making* creatures. A possible way out of this dilemma, which becomes most apparent with climate change and its deniers, is to acknowledge that the human-made worlds only form a small proportion of larger worlds, which are shaped by many other living entities, materialities and *sympoietic* systems acting independently from human conceptualisations. Although the philosopher John Gray argues that the planet does not care about the stories humans tell themselves, "we humans *do* care about the stories we tell ourselves" (Zylinska, Minimal Ethics 11), which provides the starting point for ethical reflection.

Following Goodman, I argue that contemporary future fictions aesthetically and discursively extrapolate possible worlds of the future from the actual worlds of the present. These future worlds, like present worlds, are far from being united into a single coherent "actual" world that may be represented by any given work of fiction. Rather, a work of fiction could entail different, or even competing worlds, in line with Mikhail Bakhtin's concept of heteroglossia, which refers to numerous world views created by the language occurring in a novel (Rivkin and Ryan 674–76). It is precisely the clashes and negotiations between these worlds, as well as the revelations that result from the cognitive estrangement speculative fiction offers, which are most interesting for the ethical study of possible futures through future fictions. Fiction thus functions as a way to access these multiple actual worlds and their material, social and semiotic structures, because as Goodman asserts, fiction relates "albeit metaphorically to actual worlds" (104).

Nelson Goodman claims that works of art illustrate, express, and exemplify rather than denote or say things literally (12/18). "Exemplification and expression, though running into the opposite direction from denotation—that is, from the symbol to a literal or a metaphorical feature of it instead of to something the symbol applies to—are no less symbolic referential functions and instruments of worldmaking" (12). Exemplification, illustration, and expression belong to the realm of the aesthetic, which creates knowledge and worlds through feelings and forms instead of merely by means of rationality and abstraction. Metaphor and other stylistic features thus play an important role in worldmaking, both in and outside of fiction: "Metaphor is no mere decorative rhetorical device but a way we make our terms do multiple moonlighting services" (104). Opposing the view that the arts are no matter of real importance, which is also somewhat engrained in the idea of them being nothing but *possible* worlds, Goodman stresses the importance of fiction and the arts in worldmaking:

> The worlds of fiction, poetry, painting, music, dance, and the other arts are built largely by such nonliteral devices as metaphor, by such nondenotational means as exemplification and expression, and often by use of pictures or sounds or gestures or other nonlinguistic systems [...] the arts must be taken no less seriously than the sciences as modes of discovery, creation, and enlargement of knowledge in the broad sense of advancement of the understanding" (102)

The standpoint that fiction relates metaphorically to actual worlds and contributes to their making empowers literary critics because it allows for them to research matters of importance that penetrate both fiction and spaces beyond it, as Caroline Levine also claims in her study on forms. The notion of "world" thus represents a "bounded whole" in Levine's typology, a form that has often been criticised for its dominating powers. However, Levine further argues that, "[w]hile we might want to resist the dominance of unified wholes by crushing them, or by rupturing their boundaries, a productive alternative involves not the destruction of form but its multiplication" (45). Hence, Goodman's theory of multiple actual worlds represents a multiplication of wholes that can also be found in fiction.

On the flip side, Goodman has been harshly criticised for his reductionist roman-à-clef treatment of fictional works. Thomas Martin, for instance, argues that "[f]rom a literary standpoint, this approach shoehorns every form of fiction into the genre of allegory", which might work for the characters in *Don Quixote* but not for those in Tolkien's novels, whom we read *as if* they existed (83). However, if there were no connection whatsoever between literary worlds and non-literary ones, it would be impossible to make any sense of them at all. It seems there is no simple way to solve the dilemma—admittedly, it is important to account for the autonomy of the aesthetic, free from any pragmatic function in order to not reduce it to a didactic tool or simple reflection of its outside. On the other hand, one cannot deny art being in close dialogue with the symbolic, social, and material human life outside its borders. Perhaps stressing the metaphorical quality of fiction circumvents the dilemma in so far as that it functions as a middle ground between the two extremes: it strengthens the ambiguous ontological status of fiction as well as its importance. As Lakoff and Johnson have impressively demonstrated, it is the conceptual metaphors we live by that make and shape the worlds we live in.

In two collected volumes, Vera and Ansgar Nünning, together with others, have expanded Goodman's philosophy of worldmaking by focusing on the aesthetic practices and politics of worldmaking (Nünning, Nünning, Neumann, et al.), as well as worldmaking as a cultural practice in different types of media (Nünning, Nünning, and Neumann). They also allude to Lakoff and Johnson's seminal work, *Metaphors We Live By*, where they highlight the productivity of worldmaking in and through literature and other media:

> Working simultaneously on different cognitive, emotional, normative, and ideological levels, literature and other media can be seen as playing a creative and productive role in generating norms and values, indeed in making the worlds that **we live by** [my emphasis] and live in. Shaping habits of thought communal feeling, as well as views of the present and past, literature and other aesthetic media have played an important part in the making, and remaking of mentalities and world views. (Nünning and Nünning 11)

In addition to views on the present and past, views of the future can also be conveyed through literature and other works of art, as is the case in my study of future fictions. Literature and other types of media can be seen from two perspectives in relation to worldmaking: as active agents in worldmaking that can propagate or challenge dominant world versions and create alternative ones, or as a kind of gateway into finding out about existing worlds by means of cognitive estrangement:

> Literature and other art forms are of particular interest for studying culture(s) in the context of such an approach in that they serve to stage, thematise, and foreground the complex processes and ways of worldmaking, while at the same time conducting self-reflexive thought experiments in self- and worldmaking. (Nünning, Nünning, Neumann, et al. 15)

The idea of literature serving as a thought experiment and cognitive estrangement has become quite a topos in literary studies, especially with regard to science fiction or utopian literature. For example, one of the most influential science fiction scholars, Darko Suvin, writes about science fiction as the literature of cognitive estrangement in his *Metamorphoses of Science Fiction*, and Patrick Parrinder argues: "The invention or thought-experiment has to be mobilised in a story, and the story becomes the vehicle of a critique of the world we thought we already knew [...]" (8). The idea of literature as cognitive estrangement goes back to the formalist school of criticism, and especially to Viktor Shklovski's concept of art as defamiliarisation, which is "the idea that estrangement challenges conventional notions of linguistic and social perception thus forcing the perceiver to reconceive his or her relationship with the world" (Davis and Womack 41). While this may be the case for all art or fiction, it is especially true for speculative fiction or future fictions. Through their aesthetic projection of actual worlds into the future, these worlds and their systemic structures and formal make-up become visible and tangible.

Goodman characterises his *Ways of Worldmaking* as "neutral comparative study that can reveal a good deal not only about relations among the several arts but also about the kinships and contrasts between the arts, the sciences, and other ways that other symbols of various kinds participate in the advancement of understanding" (Goodman and Elgin 31–32). In opposition to his "neutral" description of worldmaking, it is my aim to look at worldmaking from both ethical and political angles because, clearly, the most productive worlds are generated and shaped by social groups with the most material and symbolic power. In this respect, Nünning and Nünning hold that politics as "the struggle for the power to define truths, is essentially a negotiation of diverse forms of worldmaking" (4). The power to define truth, however, is not always related to good and clever ways of making worlds but relies on power structures composed of discourses and material, i.e. financial resources. As a result, I believe that any critique of cultural worldmaking must also consider the material conditions under which worldmaking takes place. Thus, it should also assume a cultural materialist position.

Alan Sinfield, in his attempt to explain the workings of ideology, points out that "groups with material power will dominate the institutions that deal with ideas" (35). Apart from universities, whose distributional range is unfortunately somewhat limited, it is of course mainly the large media companies which control the dissemination of ideas and discourses through their various outlets. Birgit Neumann and Martin Zierold confirm that "[w]orldmaking cannot do without media that represent or embody cultural knowledge of the past, present, and future and have the capacity to circulate in social groups" (Neumann and Zierold 103). It is thus fair to say that the media have a substantial share in the construction of social reality, which becomes more and more apparent with social networks maintaining personalised newsfeeds—a phenomenon that has an enormous impact on the contemporary political landscape. In addition, commercial media but also nationalised media companies, are of course deeply invested in the capitalist universe and form ties with the interests of big business and national and transnational political structures that try to keep the capitalist system of production and its corresponding narratives firmly in place. Again, this is something to keep in mind with the analysis of popular media, also in their fictional form.

Yet, worldmaking does not only take place on a large scale or even global level—it is a constant practice involving actors on all levels of power and scope. As a result, worlds are not always neatly organised or easily distinguishable—they are chaotic: they may overlap or be embedded in each other, cooperate or form oppositions, and they never fully reach completion as they are constantly in the process of being made and remade. Despite their contradictions and faultlines, worlds strive towards logical coherence to become productive and make sense for their inhabitants. They are in exchange with their environments while trying to reduce internal complexity. In a paradoxical fashion, it seems that worlds as systems almost possess an agency independent from their makers and takers, while at the same time, they can only come into existence through the subjects that inhabit and constantly reproduce them through material production, corresponding stories and "structures of feeling", to use Raymond Williams's term. It is also important to note that worldmaking power may be and currently is extremely unequally distributed. While at present there is a tiny minority of influential worldmakers heading the largest institutions of the globe, most people are reduced to passive "worldtakers", who are neither involved in the myth-making process nor are they able to decide on the nature of the material production of worlds. They merely strive to make a living, or maybe even live well in the given structures and narratives, without being able to change or even question them.

My usage of the term "world" goes back to the old German *weorld*, designating all that concerns humans (Wolf 25), or "a totality of things, as 'everything that exists'" (Ryan 33), rather than denoting the geographical planet Earth. A world is therefore a shared social and material space which cannot be wilfully or randomly made by single individuals or groups. It is composed of materialities *and* abstract ideas and is thus "material-semiotic" or "naturecultural" to speak with Donna Haraway (*The Haraway Reader* 2), which is why this concept also breaks with the materialism-idealism divide. Overall, the concept of worlds may be slightly deceiving, as it implies more closure and consistency than actually exists. Nonetheless, the metaphor of worlds becomes productive in explaining the totality of ideas, relations, and materialities that makes up the realities in which humans live and act.

Another possible metaphor for describing the phenomenon of humans creating the spaces they inhabit is Peter Sloterdijk's concept of foam. In the third part of his *Sphären* [spheres] trilogy, he proposes foam as a metaphor for contemporary life and societies, which frames life as relational, multifocal, multiperspectival and heterarchic (23). A society envisioned as foam consists of multiple bubbles embodying microspheres of shared meaning which can be created by units or groups as small as couples, households, organisations, associations, etc. (59). The concept of worlds I want to use in my study works in the same way as Sloterdijk's bubbles and foams, especially when it comes to the fluidity, multiplicity, transformability, and temporariness of contemporary worlds. However, the downside of foam as a metaphor is that it cannot provide for the "hard" materialities that worlds entail and has an airy, almost purely imaginary quality to it. Also, in contrast to worlds, foam bubbles can collapse at any time, while worlds may at best crumble slowly, which to me seems more accurate, and which fits the aesthetic representations of (post-)apocalyptic fiction. Nonetheless, Sloterdijk's foam metaphor helps to illustrate my concept of worlds and the way they are continually made and inhabited on all social levels, from the micro-level to the macro-level. In this sense, I propose that there are also different sizes of worlds, from large hegemonic worlds to smaller worlds that may be complicit with or in opposition to the dominant one(s).

As with ideologies, the world one inhabits is usually invisible because to function smoothly, it needs to normalise and naturalise its most common thoughts and actions. Sinfield states that "[t]he strength of ideology derives from the way it gets to be common sense; 'it goes without saying'" (32). A world, in this sense, incorporates what Marxists have referred to as ideology, but only if ideology neither relates to a "false consciousness" nor a "necessarily false consciousness", but to a consciousness that is *necessarily shaped* by its surroundings, from the systems of material production to the power structures and narratives that go with it. As Kim Stanley Robinson stated in an interview:

> We understand the world through a master story we tell ourselves, that's our ideology. Everybody has an ideology. If you didn't have one, you would be disabled, somehow. The Italian Marxist theorist Antonio Gramsci said that people obey the dominant powers of their time—without guns in their faces—by way of stories. This hegemony, or dominance, is created by ideology, including those master narratives. (Robinson and Adee 45)

The task of ethics in my sense is to expose these narratives, the power structures, aesthetics, and discourses that bring forth different worlds and their material systems as well as shape the consciousness and subject positions of its citizens. It is especially important to consider which actions and values are accepted as "good" in a certain world, moulded into its compass of morality, and how this is justified by its stories and stabilised by its aestheticising practices.

These compasses of morality are derived directly from the way a world is made and what its inhabitants believe to know about it—its epistemology. They give them clear directions about what is "right" and what is "wrong" in that world in terms of appropriate actions and socially desirable behaviour. As moral philosophy, ethics is consequently situated on the meta-level of reflection, revealing and analysing the nature of worlds in and outside of fiction and considering their future consequences as simulated by the fictional works. The consequences of human action are obviously most important for ethics concerning the future. However, I want to stress that any ethics necessarily have a future orientation, as value judgements can only be passed considering the causes and motivation of an action *as well as* its possible or probable effects regarding their desirability. In addition to the content-based reflections on compasses of morality, the situatedness of the fictional work in a certain world—first and foremost a capitalist world—should not be forgotten in a critique of worldmaking, either. Despite trying to assume a neutral meta-critical position, critics need to be aware that they are also part of a certain world and can likely not free themselves entirely from its epistemologies and maps of morality—the awareness of this might already help to avoid the pitfalls of over-simplistic analyses and evaluations.

The ethical question that is the most pressing today is: how can humans make worlds in which they *and* their descendants can *live well* and *coexist* with non-human worldmaking agents in the long run? Fiction and the arts in general can generally be complicit with contemporary hegemonic worlds, or they can subvert them, for example by presenting worlds that are superior to the dominant ones (utopias) or criticise these by revealing their dreadful future versions (dystopias). In the context of the pluralisation of worlds and their respective maps of morality, I have argued that it is difficult to maintain a harsh distinction between utopian and dystopian fictions in the 21st century. As a result, I prefer to speak about dominant worlds with reference to those worlds that have the most inhabitants and are most influential—materially and symbolically—at a given point in time, such as the capitalist world today, and of otherworlds which are in opposition to the dominant ones.

In my analysis of popular future fictions, I will concentrate on the detection of these competing world versions and their aesthetic portrayal and reception. The fictional works entail either closed or open moral universes themselves, which might discredit or support a certain (mostly) dominant world or leave the ethical judgement to the readers themselves. In most cases, the future fictions in the case studies also offer alternatives to the dominant world, which I will analyse as "otherworlds". Hence, the novels and films in this study offer aesthetic simulations of possible future worlds derived from actual ones, which enable the ethical reflections of readers based on emotions and sense-impressions, rather than solely rational reflection. As Alexa Weik von Mossner affirms in the context of environmental narratives, the embodied cognition they trigger "is of particular relevance for our theoretical and practical investigations of [...] the emotional responses they cue in readers and viewers" (*Affective Ecologies* 3). In this way, the seemingly impossible cognitive discrepancies between the concrete here and now of individual readers and viewers and the temporarily and spatially removed consequences of their collective human actions can be bridged—at least for a short time—and the motivation to actively take part in the making of desirable future worlds can potentially be sparked.

In the following chapters, the methodological framework for a future-ethical reading I have developed so far will be applied to close readings of contemporary popular future fictions that are meant to serve as examples of larger trends in the dominant (i.e. Western-centric) cultural imaginary. The analysis of each of the films and novels in conjunction with additional theory will begin by considering the impact of formal or aesthetic choices on potential and actual ethical readings. I will look out for the relation between ethics and aesthetics, including the formal narrative and filmic elements that guide readers and viewers in their emotional reception of a given work. This includes the choice of generic markers, focalisation, colour codes and other formal features that constitute the work's moral universe that can either be more open or more closed. Actual reader and viewer responses will complement my own ethical readings of the films and novels. Secondly, I will analyse the future worlds depicted in the primary works, but also the worlds the works themselves are part of or help to make. The aim is to make their foundational narratives, aesthetic make-up and maps of morality more explicit, as well as focus on their potential future effects as depicted by the future fictions. Here, I will distinguish between the presently dominant worlds projected into the future and their alternative counterparts in the form of otherworlds that might bring forth futures that are different from the present.

3 Future World Ecologies: Kim Stanley Robinson's *New York 2140* (2017) and James Cameron's *Avatar* (2009)

The scientific consensus is clear:[1] the climate is warming rapidly (*Climate Change 2014 Synthesis Report*), the Sixth Great Mass Extinction of species is under way (Kolbert), and the future will be dire in many respects if these trends cannot be altered or reversed. Paul Crutzen's suggestion to label the current geological era as "the Anthropocene", the period shaped by humanity, has by now been taken up by the public to designate the enormity of humanity's ecological destruction, ranging from the air to the soil of the Earth. Against the backdrop of scientific evidence, I find it apt to speak of an ecological *catastrophe* instead of a crisis, because a crisis could simply be overcome. In contrast, the damage already done is of such magnitude that even *if* humanity managed to stop emitting greenhouse gases today—which seems impossible by itself—the climate would still continue to warm for decades if not centuries (NASA), not to speak of species already extinct or micro-plastics already in the water and elsewhere. While the sciences establish the rational grounds for knowing about the ecological havoc which industrial civilisation has wreaked, author Amitav Gosh suggests that "[t]he climate crisis is also a crisis of culture, and thus of the imagination" (9). It is extremely difficult for temporally and spatially situated individual human beings to fully understand the enormity of the Anthropocene. Therefore, I argue in the context of this chapter that future fictions can help to produce emotional and experiential knowledge of the ecological catastrophe by transcending boundaries of time and space, as well as ego-centric individualism.

---

1   As numerous studies show, at least 97% or more of scientists agree on human-made climate change (NASA).

In the pursuit of ethics for the future through popular fiction, this chapter is dedicated to *the ecology*, meaning "the relation of plants and living creatures to each other and to their environment" (Hornby and Wehmeier 485). Different from the term "nature", ecology includes humans and their worlds, which Donna Haraway describes as "material-semiotic" (*The Haraway Reader* 2). The term ecology thus transgresses the problematic nature-culture dualism and stresses the interdependency between humans, other creatures and their material environments and systems of (re-)production and meaning making. As I argued in the previous chapter, ethics for the future need to become posthumanist, both in the sense of overcoming humanist ethics with their focus on the rational human individual, and by incorporating the non-human realm, from "companion species" (13) to geosystems and technological artefacts. This chapter's ethical reading of contemporary eco (-logical) future fictions therefore analyses the material-semiotic human-made worlds and their ecological consequences as projected by contemporary films and novels.

As with the sciences, the vast majority of fictions dealing with ecological topics—also called "cli-fi" (Bloom) or "Anthropocene fictions" (Trexler)—converge on the assumption that there is an impending ecological catastrophe.[2] The only popular example of climate change denying fiction which I was able to find was Michael Crichton's *State of Fear* (2004). Eco-future fictions extrapolate from contemporary worlds and scientific evidence to enable readers and viewers to imagine and feel the ecological long-term effects, such as higher sea levels, extreme weather events, species extinction, food shortages and social upheavals connected to them. The number of fictions currently engaging with the eco-ethical imaginary is vast, as is the amount of ecocritical scholarship on this topic.[3] Many contemporary eco-future fictions mainly foreground the emotional experience of catastrophic or even apocalyptic futures, as for example in Cormac McCarthy's *The Road* (2006), Alfonso Cuarón's *Children of Men* (2007), Megan Hunter's *The End We Start From* (2017) and Rebecca Ley's *Sweet Fruit, Sour Land* (2018). Other works also entail an explicit analysis of the causes of the ecological crisis and even suggest potential solutions to it. In pursuit of

---

2   In fact, as Donna Haraway argues, we are already in the middle of it (*Staying with the Trouble* 1), but its effects will become more and more visible as time moves on.

3   See for example Astrid Bracke's *Climate Crisis and the 21st Century British Novel* (2017), Adam Trexler's *Anthropocene Fictions: The Novel in a Time of Climate Change* (2015), Alexa Weik von Mossner (ed.): *Moving Environments: Affect, Emotion, Ecology, and Film* (2014), Stephen Rust et al. (eds.): *Ecocinema Theory and Practice* (2013), among many others.

ethics for the future through fiction, these are the most interesting to me. I depart from the assumption that the creation of ecological world knowledge through popular films and novels significantly affects the conceptualisation of the ecological crisis and possible ways out of it in the minds of cinemagoers and readers. The affectively triggered reflections on contemporary worlds, future consequences, and potential alternatives represent what I define as ethics through aesthetics.

In the almost impossible effort to represent the ecological catastrophe or the Anthropocene as a result of their enormous scale, Adam Trexler notes that traditional boundaries are ruptured as "[l]iterary novels bleed into science fiction; suspense novels have surprising elements of realism; realist depictions of everyday life involuntarily become biting satire" (14). In this chapter, I want to focus on how aesthetic traditions and choices of form shape a work's ethical outlook on the ecological catastrophe and the potential solutions it proposes. For this purpose, I have selected two of the most popular films and novels as paradigmatic examples. I will begin my close readings with Kim Stanley Robinson's *New York 2140* (2017), which draws on a new realist mode of representation in its suggestion of revolutionary political action to counter climate change. Secondly, I will show how James Cameron's *Avatar* (2009) draws mainly on fantasy and sublime aesthetic forms, which leads to its proposal of a return to "Nature" as a solution.

In comparison with other eco-future fictions, Kim Stanley Robinson's *New York 2140*'s aesthetics come relatively close to being "realist", meaning "a symbolic construction of reality designed to produce a certain effect—called the 'reality effect' by Roland Barthes" (Fluck 67). Even though the setting of the novel is speculative by depicting a submerged New York of 2140, its accurate and detailed descriptions of the city and the ecological conditions, including significantly higher sea-levels and extreme weather events, make it appear realistic and plausible. The novel stages a collaborative democratic uprising of the people against global capitalism, which is accused of being responsible for climate warming and species extinctions of the present and past. I will argue that *New York 2140* illustrates Jason Moore's concept of the Capitalocene, which replaces the notion of the Anthropocene as the geological era shaped by capitalism instead of "man". The novel thus suggests that the ecological catastrophe can only be solved through an upheaval of the entire capitalist system via political action from below. With its focus on politics as solution, it is comparable to other works by Kim Stanley Robinson like *Green Earth* (2015) and *The Ministry for the Future* (2020), alongside the young adult novel *Carbon Diaries* by Sacy Lloyd (2008).

James Cameron's *Avatar* imagines a completely degenerated ecology on planet Earth that has driven people and in particular capitalist corporations to exploit the resources of other planets in space. In a fantastic mode, and via impressive computer-generated imagery (CGI), the film portrays a human space mission on the fictitious planet Pandora in the year 2154. The human invasion results in a fight between the colonisers and the indigenous natives, the Na'vi, who are fantastic human-animal hybrids. In my reading, I will point out how *Avatar* subverts its own environmental and anti-capitalist messages by drawing on Romantic representations of "Nature", which, as Timothy Morton argues, are fundamentally complicit with the capitalist imaginary (*Ecology without Nature* 92). Drawing on Morton and posthumanist theory, I will deconstruct the term "Nature" in my reading of the film and show how the fantastic imaginary of "Nature" is paradoxically enabled through its multi-layered technological mediation. While the idea of "going back to nature" seems very influential in certain groups of society today that refer to them-selves as "alternative" or "green", there are fewer films and novels following this approach. To some extent, Pixar's animated film *Wall-E* (Stanton 2008) also draws on an implicit idea of "Nature".

With these examples, I will show how representations of the ecological catastrophe in novels and films importantly contribute to the cultural and affective creation of knowledge about it. Many scholars like Timothy Clark, Timothy Morton and Ursula Heise have pointed out the difficulty, if not impos-sibility, to represent the Anthropocene through traditional forms of narrative (Bracke, 'Flooded Futures' 280). While characters, plots and settings need to be located at a certain point in time and space, these are geographically and temporally almost boundless phenomena, which are the result of impersonal but human-made systems, worlds and narratives. As Eva Horn notes, the ecological catastrophe is a catastrophe without an event (166). Fiction and plot, on the other hand, are based on events, which is why in relation to medium and genre, future fictions have developed a set of strategies to represent the degraded future ecology, which I will point out as part of the analysis. The strategies of the two primary works in this chapter are prototypical of most eco-future fictions by wavering between the categories of "new normal background state", "disastrous event", "apocalypse" and "inversion".

Film as a visual medium depends on impressive images that *show* manifes-tations of a degraded future ecology instead of *telling* them. The strategy of the majority of eco-films is therefore to picture a singular "disastrous event" which functions metonymically as a *pars pro toto*, like the ice-storm freezing of large parts of the United States in Roland Emmerich's blockbuster *The Day After Tomorrow* (2004).[4] Often, the "disastrous event" depicted in eco-films and novels is a sign of the coming ecological "apocalypse", as for example in Nolan's *Interstellar*. *Avatar*, in contrast, builds on the strategy of "inversion", as it depicts Pandora as a "green paradise" that is in many ways the exact opposite of the broken ecology of Earth. In contrast to films, novels can rely much more on strategies of *telling* in their representation of possible ecologies of the future. *New York 2140* therefore makes use of a narrator/character who functions as a hobby-historian providing the "new normal background" to the novel's action and an analysis of the causes of climate change.

The first part of the analysis of each work is dedicated to the interplay between its aesthetic forms and its ethical outlook. I will pay special attention to how different modes of narration and filmmaking create affect-based ecological knowledge and preconfigure contrasting solutions to the ecological catastrophe. To describe these solutions offered by the fictional works, I use the notion of map of morality or moral compass. As a result of the works' communicative situations and other aesthetic parameters, their maps of morality can either be relatively closed or open, admitting different levels of emotional and reflective engagement by recipients. In order not to "conflate aesthetic evaluation with wishful assumptions about media effects" (Ingram 48), I will include exemplary reception data to address the ethical effects and affects eco-future fictions can trigger. For *Avatar*, a number of audience studies have been undertaken as a result of its enormous popularity, which has generated fan cults and even a psychologically classified phenomenon called the "Post-Avatar Depression". However, for most works there is no empirically researched reception data available. As a replacement, I have included ratings and reader and viewer reviews from online forums of the popular websites *Internet Movie Database* (IMDb) for films and *goodreads* for novels.

As a second step in my analysis, I will zoom in on the human-made worlds the fictional works portray in relation to their ecological settings. Framing them as material-semiotic worlds, I want to investigate the relationship between narrative and aesthetic practices of human worldmaking and their ecological and social effects as portrayed in the future fictions. Unsurprisingly,

---

4   Other examples include the sandstorm in Christopher Nolan's *Interstellar* (2014), *Geostorm* (Devlin 2017) and *Into the Storm* (Quale 2014).

the future world that dominates the cultural imaginary of the future is neoliberal capitalism as an extrapolation from its present hegemonic stance. *New York 2140* and *Avatar* both link capitalist worldmaking to ecological decline. Either as a sub-world to the capitalist world or as an opponent, the natural sciences also feature prominently in the two works. This is not surprising as eco-fiction, like no other literary genre, relies on scientific findings—there can be no knowledge about anthropogenic global warming and species extinction without the natural sciences (Trexler 20). The close reading of *Avatar* furthermore points out the ambivalent role of a purely scientific worldview in the ecological catastrophe as both part of the problem and part of the solution. *New York 2140* focuses less explicitly on the sciences, but like many other works,[5] it posits the sciences as opponents to global capitalism's commands, pointing out how they have long tried to raise awareness for climate change, which has simply been ignored by ruling elites.

Apart from the extrapolation from the contemporarily dominant worlds of capitalism and the sciences, the future fictions of this chapter also portray alternative worlds, which I call otherworlds and which form the third part of the analysis. These otherworlds are either imaginative extrapolations from marginal worlds that already exist, or they involve fantastic elements. *Avatar* portrays images of non-human agency by displaying Pandora as a living entity in which all creatures are connected through a world-spirit called Eywa. In addition to the fantastic and posthuman elements, otherworlds also appear in the form of new collective structures. By putting collaborative forms of political worldmaking at the heart of its plot, *New York 2140* centres an otherworld instead of marginalising it, making it a utopian text in consequence. With my reading of Kim Stanley Robinson's *New York 2140*, I want to challenge Trexler's claim that realist fiction "cannot imagine novel technological, organizational, and political approaches to climate change" (233). By portraying a collective overthrowing of capitalist structures, it imagines radical change in contemporary organisational structures, therefore proving that science fiction, realism and utopia need not be incompatible.

---

5   For instance, Robinson's *Green Earth* (2015) and Barbara Kingsolver's *Flight Behavior* (2012)

A Political World-Ecology Approach: Kim Stanley Robinson's
New York 2140

Kim Stanley Robinson "is generally acknowledged as one of the greatest living science-fiction writers" (Kreider). For example, he won the Hugo Award, Nebula Award, and World Fantasy Award, among many others. With *New York 2140*, Robinson chose a comparatively realistic future setting which differed from some of his other novels that are set in space, for example *The Mars Trilogy* and *2312*. In addition to the new realism that characterises the novel's setting and its narrative style, *New York 2140* also stands out significantly from other examples of contemporary eco-fiction for its utopian outlook in the face of climate change and species extinction. In a keynote speech, Robinson explicitly framed the story he presents in *New York 2140* as a kind of plan to get to a better future from where we are now, an *Ecotopia* for our age (Robinson, *Ecotopia and the 1970s Utopian Moment* 0:27:30; 0:41:30).[6] The novel's utopian outlook on the future is based on the idea of collaborative action from below through actor-networks and politics as the solution to capitalism's destructive reign over people and non-human lifeworlds. In other works, including *Green Earth* (2015) and his latest novel *The Ministry for the Future* (2020), Robinson shows that he still believes in political institutions as powerful actors when it comes to dealing with the ecological catastrophe. Another contemporary eco-fiction that portrays a political solution is the young adult novel *Carbon Diaries 2015* (2008) by Sacy Lloyd, in which the UK government introduces carbon rationing through a system of carbon cards.

In the context of political solutions, I will argue that *New York 2140* illustrates Jason Moore's theory of the "Capitalocene", which foregrounds the entanglement of the human economy with the ecology of the planet. In my close reading of *New York 2140*, I will focus on how Robinson's continuation of a utopian tradition of writing, which brings together new realism and science fiction, encourages solutions to the ecological crisis in line with a political economy approach, as political "world-ecology" (Moore 64). Set in a climate-change stricken New York of 2140, the novel by and large portrays the surprisingly normal lives of its nine protagonists. The diverse cast of characters all live in the same building in Manhattan, the former Met Life office block. After two major global flooding events, the Met Life building has become a cooperatively owned residential house, like many other buildings in New

---

6   With reference to Ernest Callenbach's 1975 novel *Ecotopia*.

York. The novel's characters seem to be prototypes with allegorical functions: there is "Red Charlotte" (Robinson, *New York 2140*, 434), a city lawyer who is socially engaged as a member of the housing union and the building's board, and on the other end of the political spectrum there is Franklin, the hedge fund manager who represents vulture capitalism. There are squatters like the two unemployed coders Mutt and Jeff, and the street kids, or rather "water rats", Stefan and Roberto, alongside the building's superintendent Vlade, the TV star Amelia, and the police officer Inspector Gen. In addition to the nine characters, there is a narrator figure called "a citizen" who is not part of the story but provides readers with historical background information about New York and the globe, spanning from the present to the novel's future of 2140. Over the course of the novel, the individual narrative strands and life-worlds of the protagonists become more and more entangled with each other until they finally merge into the germ cell of an enormous political transformation, which amounts to nothing less than an effort from below to overcome the capitalist hegemonic world order. The novel's "history of the future" (Ortitz 276) thus attempts to bridge the gaps between individual, collective, and even systemic vision and action, as well as between the present and the future, the local and the global.

To trace the novel's ethical outlook, I will first turn towards its unique composition of generic codes that I describe as "new realist utopianism". Against this backdrop, I will argue that *New York 2140* is a rare example in the context of contemporary eco-fictions, mainly because it is able to provide a solution to the ecological catastrophe that is based on a new realist form of representation, including analyses of power. Secondly, I will outline how the novel's aesthetics, such as the character constellation and narrative structure, lead towards a coherent interpretation of the ecological catastrophe as a result of capitalist worldmaking. The novel's form and content thus preconfigure a relatively closed map of morality that is based on a political world-ecology approach. The third part of the analysis will focus in more detail on the novel's exemplification of the Capitalocene as the relation between the ecology and the capitalist economy. Finally, I will show how *New York 2140* stages a posthumanist notion of agency based on actor-network-theory as an otherworld to financial capitalism and neoliberal subjectivity.

New Realist Utopianism

New York 2140, like the aforementioned novels by Kim Stanley Robinson, eludes simple generic classifications while still following different traditions of writing encompassing the utopian novel, new realism, and science fiction. In this combination, Robinson's novels stand out against the mass of contemporary eco-fictions, which tend to be either dystopian or catastrophic, if not apocalyptic. Even when eco-fictions do offer some kind of hope or solution—like the other work in this chapter—this positive outlook is mostly enabled by fantastic elements. *New York 2140*, in contrast, deliberately draws on realist forms of representation in combination with metatextual and utopian elements, which are engrained in the classification "new realism". According to Fluck, "new realism" contains "a mixture of modes in which the relations between various narrative strategies are newly negotiated" (79), for example realism can be combined with postmodernist elements. In what follows, I will claim that *New York 2140*'s new realist utopianism offers a solution to the ecological crisis with the intention of inspiring a plan for real-world political action. First, I will address the different generic traditions *New York 2140* incorporates, which engender this solution, before turning to exemplary reader responses to show how the novel's closed map of morality is sometimes received as didactic.

It has been noted by a number of reviewers and critics that *New York 2140* is different from comparable eco or sci-fi texts. For example, despite being climate fiction, it is "weirdly encouraging [...] for a contribution to this apocalyptic genre", Daniel Aldana Cohen writes in a review. David Sergeant even goes so far as to read the novel as a historical novel instead of science fiction (5), and Spencer Adams calls it "a speculative fiction of utopian world building" (523). Despite the futuristic setting, which is extrapolated from current climate science, the novel reads as if Robinson had actually been there, full of exact and recognisable descriptions and details of New York City and its buildings. *The New Yorker* review, for instance, emphasises that "[m]any of the pleasures of *New York 2140* are architectural" (Rothman), while other reviewers complain about the amount of encyclopaedic details making the read rather tedious at times (Mason). The novel thus draws on a realist tradition of representation, which, according to Winfried Fluck, builds on Barthes's "reality effect" by including a set of rhetorical strategies that produce a certain version of reality (67). The lengthy format of 600+ pages is further reminiscent of the thick social realist novels of the Victorian period, which, like *New York 2140*, focus on issues of social and economic injustice. However, as is typical of "new" realism, there are also experimental and postmodernist elements like the sarcastic hobby-historian "the citizen", the comical coder couple, Mutt and Jeff, and intertextual references from non-fictional texts.

In addition to the novel's new realist strategies of narration, it also follows the tradition of utopian writing by depicting the socio-political potential to overcome capitalism as the main cause of the ecological crisis in the end. In this respect, Sergeant remarks that "it is striking how absent is this kind of political dimension from the wider field of near future" (15). Different from most of its contemporaries, *New York 2140* comes back to social and political transformations as imagined by previous utopian texts ranging from More's *Utopia* (1516) to socialist utopias as in Morris's *News from Nowhere* (1890) or Le Guin's famous *The Dispossessed* (1974) and Ernest Callenbach's *Ecotopia* (1975). While these texts all depict spatially closed-off utopian places, for example an island or another planet, Robinson asserts that for contemporary utopias, the scale has to be global and also encompass an action plan of "how to get there from here" ('Ecotopia' 0:27:30). As a result, the novel frequently refers to the present, mainly through the intertextual quotes and the citizen's history of the future. Also, the novel's plot seems to be inspired by the 2007/2008 financial crisis and the following "Occupy Wall Street" movement. Robinson explicitly states that his novel aims to answer the numerous utopian non-fictional texts of our time, which, unlike those of the 70s, focus mainly on the economy (0:22:20). As a consequence of the novel's "presentism", Sergeant reads it as a historical novel of the future (3; 9; 13), while Roberto Ortitz sees "the present as history for the future" in *New York 2140* (276).

In between the different narrative strands of the characters, there are intertextual references and quotes taken to a large extent from contemporary or 20th century non-fictional publications. In a conference keynote, Robinson defines texts like these as utopian non-fiction (Robinson, *Ecotopia* 0:21:50). The utopian non-fiction quotes in the novel are framed by comments that seem to be that of the citizen, which connect them to the novel's fictional universe. This intertextuality further contributes to the reality effect by backing up the political economy/ecology interpretation that capitalism is at the heart of contemporary social and ecological problems. Among these utopian non-fictional texts are, for example, Frank Ackerman's *Can We Afford the Future* (2009), which challenges conventional economic theory, and Ambrose Bierce's *Devil's Dictionary* (1911), which cynically explains capitalist economics in a dictionary format. For example, it defines "corporation" as "an ingenious device for obtaining individual profit without individual responsibility" (Robinson, *New York 2140*, 76).

In these quotes, as in the novel's plot, the main target of critique is the setup of the financial system, its institutions and focus on money, as the quote by Deleuze and Guattari demonstrates: "It is the bank that controls the whole system" (429). There are also metafictional comments addressing the role of art in politics, which express the novel's desire to actively make and shape the world outside its fictional boundaries, like for example: "I am for an art that tells you the time of the day, or where such and such a street is. I am for an art that helps old ladies across the street. Said Claes Oldenburg" (105), and "[a]rt is not truth. Art is a lie that enables us to realize the truth. Said Picasso" (536).

Also reminiscent of Nelson Goodman's understanding of art, *New York 2140* precisely appears to exemplify these definitions because it conveys a certain truth about climate change and species extinction through its fictional story. At the same time, on a practical level, it demonstrates what people can do against it. To achieve this, the novel's aesthetic ambiguity is reduced. It becomes didactic as its aesthetic choices work towards convincing readers of the novel's interpretation of the ecological catastrophe and motivating them to act against it. While in readers' reviews on the website *goodreads* many have complained about the lack of plot and tension, some have praised the "catastrophic" storm as the singular exciting event in the story. Generally, many readers liked the novel for its "great towering ideas", which made it impressive, "but in an *intellectual* way, not so much an *enjoyable* one", and criticised it for its lack of "BIG plots", underdeveloped characters, and boring explanations about politics and economics. From the reviews, it is apparent that people's own worldly situatedness significantly influences their responses to the text. For instance, a climate sceptic harshly rejected it, while other readers who partake in the novel's interpretation of the contemporary world celebrated it ('New York 2140 Other Reviews'). Confronting readers with a relatively closed worldview that lacks ambiguity thus has the effect of resonating well with those who already cohabit this world and enjoy an intellectual approach. For those who are not "already part of the choir" or who prefer more emotional and immersive reading experiences, the closed world and didactic tone of *New York 2140* may hinder an active cognitive and emotional and therefore ethical engagement with the relationship between the economy and the ecology. As I will show next, the novel's closed moral universe is produced through the character constellation and narrative structure as well as through the already mentioned intertextual references and, most obviously, the plot itself.

Ethics through an Aesthetic Unity of Effect

Through an exemplary and allegorical cast of characters that are connected to millions of unnamed others in its fictional universe, New York 2140 stages the defeat of capitalism by means of non-violent civil resistance, collective organisation through coops and unions, and traditional politics through national institutions. This move of connecting distinct individuals and their actions with large-scale historical transformations is achieved mainly through an extradiegetic character called "the citizen" who functions as a metatextual narrator commenting on the novel's action, while providing historical background information. The citizen's retelling of the historical events between our present and the novel's future is full of sarcastic comments and value judgements, creating a didactic effect reminiscent of the choir in Greek theatre. For example, s_he relates how the first surge of sea level rise was followed by a great depression,

> and of course, there was a crowd in that generation, a certain particular one percent of the population, that [...] considered that it was really an act of creative destruction, as was everything bad that didn't touch them [...] and all people needed to do was [...] accept the idea of austerity, meaning more poverty for the poor, and accept a police state [...] and hey presto! On we go with the show! (141)

The citizen also addresses readers explicitly with sentences like "[i]f you're okay pondering the big picture, the ground truth, read on" (14). Through these reader addresses and other metatextual comments, as for instance, "[e]nough with the I told you sos! Back to our doughty heroes and heroines!" (145), the citizen breaks the illusion of the story world, similar to Bertold Brecht's epic theatre, which likewise aims at educating people through art.

The colloquial diction of this narrative strand and the naming of the narrator as "a citizen" furthermore make this account appear as history "from below", a democratic kind of history, instead of an authority writing down History with a capital H. The novel's interpretation of historical events up until 2140 through the citizen culminates in an almost teleological utopian ending which signals the overthrow of the capitalist world order: "In its own taking up of revolution as the telos of its trajectory, a heisty thriller quality comes to characterize the action of New York 2140" (Adams 529). As a result of the protagonists' plan, people in New York and elsewhere stop paying their running costs in order to cause an artificial banking crisis with the aim of politically reclaiming the financial system as a common good. As a result, a new US Congress arrives in 2143 that nationalises the banks and passes a "Piketty tax" on capital assets,[7] which is exemplary of what happens in other national states at the time (601). Through this, the novel actually manages what nowadays seems impossible—imagining the end of capitalism without imagining the end of the world.[8] Instead of attributing this utopian outcome to outstanding characters or even heroes, *New York 2140* makes sure to transport the message that "this flurry of social and legal change did not occur because of [...] "Red Charlotte" [...] Nor was it due to any other single individual [...] This said, people in this era did do it" (603).

The novel's characters are thus mere examples for any other potential group of actors that could become the germ cell of social transformation. This "invites an allegorical reading as a means of bridging the scalar gap between individual (instance, person) and general (history, society)" in order to "recode the key scalar co-ordinates for the contemporary moment, from the socio-cultural to the environmental" (Sergeant 7). In this sense, each of the protagonists can be read as standing in for a general social sphere. For example, Franklin represents economics, Amelia (social) media, Charlotte politics and law, inspector Gen the executive, and most obviously, the citizen represents the citizens of New York, as s_he even becomes "the city" in the end (Robinson, *New York 2140* 351). A character called Mutt makes this allegory explicit when he refers to the characters' network's ability to "change the world" because "[w]e got the cloud star, the lawyer, the building expert, the building itself, the police detective, the money man" (399–400). On this allegorical level, the novel emphasises that the transition it suggests could be achieved by any *group* of actors, as long as they work together across different realms of society.

In terms of narrative structure, the novel is composed of seven narrative strands divided by letters and titled with the characters' names. The novel's overall form therefore appears ordered, almost protocol-like, conveying the impression of a historical document of what will have happened from a Future

---

7   In his widely recognised publication *Capital in the Twenty-First Century* (2013), the French economist Thomas Piketty argues that inequality is inherent to the capitalist system and is mainly reproduced through capital assets rather than income generated by work.

8   The saying that it is easier to imagine the end of the world than to imagine the end of capitalism is attributed both to Frederic Jameson and to Slavoj Žižec (Fisher 2) and seems to be confirmed by the majority of contemporary future fictions.

II perspective or a political document of what should happen. Very tellingly, apart from the citizen, only one character is allowed to speak in the first person, while all others are focalised through a heterodiegetic narrator. This character is Franklin Garr, the hedge fund manager, as the book's representative of financial capitalism. In this respect, Ortitz notes that "[a]ll other characters in New York 2140's universe are constrained by broader systemic forces—finance being one of those—and they thus cannot write their own stories with the same degree of freedom as Franklin" (268). Being an agent of the most powerful worldmaking system on the globe, Franklin has the power to speak and create as a worldmaker, while the other characters stand for those passive worldtakers who do not benefit from the capitalist gambling of the financial sector: the 99%, as proposed by the Occupy movement's slogan (Sharlet). The group of protagonists is threatened by the world of finance through a hostile take-over bid on their building which represents their livelihood amid the drowned city, and in the case of two street kids who are granted refuge there, even their very survival. In this sense, there are two opposing parties in the novel: the beneficiaries of (financial) capitalism versus the rest, including the big majority of people as well as the Earth's ecosystems and its inhabitants. Franklin, as part of the "lucky one percent" (Robinson, *New York 2140* 145), functions as a tour guide that gives insight into the capitalist world and its strategies of worldmaking, both on institutional and psychological levels before he is "converted" and joins the others' fight against the system.

Through Franklin's insider perspective, as well as through the citizen's long-term historical point of view, Amelia's TV show and Mutt and Jeff's comical dialogues, a coherent knowledge of the entanglement between capitalism and the ecological crisis is established. On one hand, the novel *shows* or illustrates this relationship through a setting which draws on the representative strategy of a "new normal" background with a bit of "catastrophe", and on the other, the text strongly relies on instances of *telling* to bring across its interpretation, which can be described using Jason Moore's concepts of "the Capitalocene" and "world-ecology".

The Capitalocene: Economy-Ecology

New York 2140 explicitly connects the devastated ecology of the future to the capitalist economy and its ways of worldmaking. Therefore, Ortitz reads the novel as "a literary reflection (in the sense of thinking through, not in the sense of "reflecting" financialized capitalism) on the consequences of climate change via the structuring effect of finance" (267). To draw a link between the contemporary ecological crisis and global capitalism as its fundamental cause is not new but still far from mainstream. However, there is a growing number of well-known researchers and journalists who blame capitalism and its foundational narratives for the large-scale ecological destruction we are currently experiencing. For instance, journalist Naomi Klein famously published a non-fictional book subtitled *Capitalism vs. the Climate*, in which she unmasks the dominant myth that the market and clever technology will ultimately save us from the consequences of climate change. Jason Moore's theory of the Capitalocene likewise supports the claim that capitalism is at the root of the contemporary ecological problem. He proposes that we are not living in the Anthropocene because this concept entails a "curiously Eurocentric vista of humanity", but in the Capitalocene, "the historical era shaped by relations privileging the endless accumulation of capital" (173). For Moore, the more common denominator Anthropocene problematically reduces "[t]he mosaic of human activity in the web of life [...] to an abstract Humanity: a homogeneous acting unit. Inequality, commodification, imperialism, patriarchy, racial formations, and much more, have been largely removed from consideration" (170).

To counter this, Moore demonstrates how capitalism, as a material system of production that has come to dominate the globe over the last centuries, is fundamentally intertwined with the ecosystems of the earth, rather than separate from them in an artificial nature-society binary. He refers to this relationship as "double internality", including capitalism's internalisation of planetary life and the biosphere's internalization of capitalism (13): "It is a multi-layered relation through which there is no basic unity, only webs within webs of relations: 'worlds within worlds'" (7–8). Following Maturana and Varela, Moore describes all species as worldmakers and environment-builders. He emphasises that in this process some species are more powerful than others, humans being especially powerful (11). However, most humans are neither responsible for this system nor have benefited from it by any means—on the contrary, they find themselves on the side of an exploited and appropriated "nature". Humanism has denied the status of "human" to these groups of people, among them the colonial other and women. Their work and energy, like that of nature, has always been appropriated by capitalism at a low cost or even no cost at all. In what follows, I will argue that *New York 2140* illustrates Moore's concept of the Capitalocene on different levels, from the setting and the character constellation to its systemic outlook on economic and ecological systems.

The novel extrapolates from contemporary scientific data on climate change and species extinction to an ecology of the future, which is most of all characterised by significantly higher sea levels and ongoing species extinction as a "new normal" backdrop to its action. Drawing on floods as manifestations of a deranged ecology is exemplary of the most dominant literary strategy over the last forty years to represent climate change (Trexler 80; 82).[9] In addition, the novel's setting features extreme weather, including a devastating storm as "the catastrophe" that functions as a trigger for the social uprise plotted by the nine protagonists. Species extinction is also prominently depicted in the novel. One of the protagonists, TV star Amelia, devotes her internet show to the re-allocation of endangered animals like polar bears, referring explicitly to "the sixth mass extinction event in Earth's history" caused by humanity (259). In this futuristic setting, people are depicted as having adapted to these phenomena. New York has turned into a Venice-like city of water with canals and boats instead of streets, and sky-bridges between buildings. With regard to how social systems deal with the effects of climate change, the novel por-trays two parallel movements: on the one hand, there are attempts to create commons to counter the problems of scarcity, especially in housing; and on the other hand, the finance industry works against this process in order to increase profits for investors: "In *New York 2140*, Robinson paints the desperate attempts of capitalists to re-capture, via finance, the spaces recovered and revitalized by horizontal and solidarity-inclined systems of cooperation" (Or-titz 274). In Franklin's narrative and the citizen's explanations, the novel reads almost like the economic utopian non-fictional texts that reveal the workings of capitalism's creation of financial value in the context of the ecology. As a result, it establishes a clear causality between capitalist worldmaking through finance and the phenomena of the ecological catastrophe.

To convey this relatively complex relationship described by Moore's concept of the Capitalocene, the novel uses several diegetic and non-diegetic methods. On a diegetic level, the hedge fund manager Franklin Garr functions as a rep-resentative of financial capitalism and allows for some introspection into this world and the kind of subjectivity it creates. Through his first-person narrative,

---

9   Examples of other flood fictions include Nathaniel Rich's *The Odds Against Tomorrow* (2013), and *The Flood*, both as the novel by Maggie Gee and the British film directed by Anthony Woodley (2019), John Lanchester's *The Wall* (2019), and Will Self's *The Book of Dave* (2006) among many others.

readers gain insight into the psychological dimension of capitalist worldmaking and receive excessively detailed information about the workings of the finance industry. In short, Franklin's job is to make money through speculations on drowned real estate. He calls it "[h]igh-frequency geofinance" (19) and sees himself as "a professional gambler" (415) playing exciting games without considering the real-world results for actual people who have lost their homes due to flooding. Through Franklin, the novel demonstrates that the financial value of the livelihood of humans and other species is nothing but the outcome of a betting game played by people like him who do not have a skin in it. As Franklin explains: "Am I saying that the floods, the worst catastrophe in human history, equivalent or greater to the twentieth century's wars in their devastation, were actually good for capitalism? Yes, I am" (118). Alluding to Naomi Klein's *Shock Doctrine*, Charlotte calls this phenomenon "crisis capitalism, shoving the boot on the neck harder at every opportunity" (501).

Even though Franklin exhibits the world of financial capitalism through his insider knowledge and introspection, his narrative also points out how this system has become so complex that ultimately no one is able to understand it any more. At some point he admits that "[n]o one knows anything" (415), even in the finance sector. For most readers, much of Franklin's shop talk is excessively technical and unintelligible. For example, when explaining what the Intertidal Property Pricing Index he created does, he says:

> It was a kind of specialized Case-Shiller index for intertidal assets [...] Perhaps most importantly, it helped in calculating how much owners or ex-owners of intertidal properties had lost and could get compensated for, a number which Swiss Re, one of the giant re-insurance companies that insured all the other insurers, estimated to total worldwide at about 1,300 trillion dollars. That's 1.3 quadrillion dollars, but I think 1,300 trillion sounds bigger. $ 1,300,000,000,000,000. (118–119)

With passages like these, *New York 2140* makes the point that no one can understand the extremely complex system of financial capitalism, which nonetheless predetermines the world people and non-humans live to a large extent. The citizen makes this even more explicit when s_he relates how the dark pools of money and financial activity are estimated to be three times larger than the officially reported economy, therefore claiming: "if you think you know how the world works, think again. You are deceived. [...] But if you then think furthermore that the bankers and financiers of this world know more than you do—wrong again. No one knows this system" (318–319).

Next to Franklin, who initially functions as the prototypical egocentric capitalist mainly concerned with his own benefits and monetary income, the citizen's world history account establishes knowledge about the large-scale effects created by the destructive relationship between capitalism and the ecology. Through self-characterised "expository rants" and "info *dumps* (on your carpet)" (141), the citizen sarcastically connects the changes in the ecology and biosphere, like "CO_2 levels screaming up from 280 to 450 parts per million in less than three hundred years" (140), to capitalist worldmaking practices built on "world trade, the basis for that humming neoliberal global success story that had done so much for so few". S_he concludes that "[n]ever had so much been done to so many by so few" as when sea levels rose by fifty feet globally as a result of this system (144). Apart from the human worlds and human-made environments, Robinson's novel also points out how the non-human world or ecology is deeply connected to the human economy, which Moore conceptualises as the "world-ecology" (3).

The comical coder couple, Mutt and Jeff, who are named after two of the very first comic-strip heroes by Bud Fisher, also have the function of explaining the seemingly complex workings of the capitalist world-ecology in a simple and caricature-like way. For example, the novel opens with a discussion on value creation, in which Jeff explains to Mutt (i.e., to the reader) the problem of capitalism's externalisation of costs:

> The prices are always too low, and so the world is fucked. We're in a mass extinction event, sea level rise, climate change, food panics, everything you're not reading in the news [...] We've been paying a fraction of what things really cost to make, but meanwhile the planet, and the workers who made the stuff, take the unpaid costs right in their teeth. (4)

Different from the more factual "information dumps" about capitalist worldmaking by Franklin and the citizen, Mutt and Jeff's narrative serves the purpose of deconstructing capitalist value creation in a simple, entertaining, and comical way. The coders' narrative strand also differs significantly from the others because it adds a playful and metatextual dimension to the more realist strands of the other characters.

For instance, the two coders seem to be modelled on *Waiting for Godot*'s Vladimir and Estragon due to their nonsensical dialogues and because they must wait in limbo after being kidnapped for planning an anti-capitalist revolution by altering online code. In one of their comic conversations, the play is even explicitly referenced and brought together with their own situation:

Jeff shook his head. "I can't believe you haven't read *Waiting for Godot.*"

"Godot was a coder, I take it."

"Yes, I think that's right. They never really found out. People usually assume Godot was God. Like someone says, It's God, and someone else says, Oh! And then you put it together and it's God—Oh, and then you put a French accent on it."

"I am not regretting not reading this book."

"No. I mean now that we're living it, I don't think the book is really necessary. It would be redundant." (147–148)

Mutt and Jeff even refer to their function in the network of protagonists as "the two old Muppets on the balcony, cracking lame jokes" (399). As meta-fictional and non-realist characters, Mutt and Jeff add another dimension to the novel's deconstructivist outlook on capitalism, which is to think of it as likewise un-real—an imaginary or virtual construct based on "stupid laws" that are in fact nothing but codes (5). Following this logic, Jeff identifies sixteen worldmaking laws made up by the World Trade Organisation and the G20 and believes that if "you change those sixteen, you're like turning a key in a big lock. The key turns, and the system goes from bad to good. It would *make* people be good" (6). The idea that this seemingly absurd framing of capitalism is not so far from the truth is expressed by the fact that Jeff and Mutt are actually kidnapped by powerful players following Jeff's attempt to hack into the system to change these codes. Jeff's quote furthermore shows that "being good" is dependent on the rules of the world someone inhabits. While the novel demonstrates that in the capitalist world, value is reduced solely to monetary value, it opposes this map of morality with other kinds of value. It contrasts the capitalist world with an otherworld characterised by collaboration and interdependencies between human and non-human actors in actor networks.

Political Organisation through Actor Networks

In contrast to the neoliberal conception of agency that focuses on individuals and their investments in themselves, as represented by Franklin, *New York 2140* proposes an otherworld characterised by relationships and collaborative modes of worldmaking. This otherworld is presented as the novel's solution to the ecological crisis because, as the novel's ending suggests, it is capable of overthrowing capitalism's destructive reign over life. Opposed to the con-temporarily dominant idea of foregrounding individual actions to counter the effects of climate change, like more sustainable patterns of consumption and personal sacrifice, the novel points back to politics as the space for organising affairs concerning the common good. In this sense, it also emphasises that the human good is inextricably intertwined with what is good for non-human life. While *New York 2140* includes traditional political actions through parties and institutions—for example, with Charlotte winning a seat in Congress—it also depicts other forms of political organisation, such as cooperative ownership, unions, and the collective civil disobedience organised by the group of protagonists.

To conceptualise collaborations between people as social forces, but also to point out the role of non-human agents, Actor-Network Theory (ANT) is explicitly referenced in *New York 2140*. Actor-Network Theory, as developed by Bruno Latour and others from the 1980s onwards, primarily takes the ever-shifting relationships between humans, non-humans, objects, and ideas into focus. The novel explicitly refers to this theory when Mutt says about the group of protagonists and their home: "[h]ave you ever noticed that our building is a kind of actor network that can do things?" (399). Non-human agency is also referred to when the citizen remarks: "Remember not to forget, if your head has not already exploded, the non-human actors in these actor networks. Possibly the New York estuary was the prime actor in all that has been told here, or maybe it was bacterial communities, expressing themselves through their own civilizations, what we might call bodies" (603). In this sense, the novel again exemplifies Moore's theory, which tries to overcome the dualism between the concepts of nature and (human) culture by framing the relationship between the human and non-human agents as "webs within webs of relations: 'worlds within worlds'" (8). The citizen emphasises the complexity of life and ecosystems when s_he contrasts the life-threatening "dark pools of money" (318) in finance with the "other dark pools in New York Bay" that are teeming with life that is "more than algorithmic" and far more complex than anything we can devise (319). After reporting about how animals have managed to come back after the floods and prosper again, the citizen concludes that "life is bigger than equations, stronger than money, [...] stronger than capitalism" (320). This otherworld composed of human and non-human actors seems to even point towards Donna Haraway's notion of the "Chthulucene" as yet another denominator of our age: "Unlike the dominant dramas of Anthropocene and Capitalocene discourses, human beings are not the only important actors in the Chthulucene, with all other beings able simply to react. The order is reknitted: human beings are with and of the earth, and the biotic and abiotic powers of this earth are the main story" (*Staying with the Trouble* 55). In consequence, this means that while the novel is explicit in its critique of capitalism as an obstacle to solving the ecological problem, its prime epiphany is that an ANT or posthumanist model of agency is necessary as a counterpoint to neoliberal subjectivity and individual agency. In this sense, *New York 2140* advocates a posthumanist notion of subjectivity "as both materialist and relational, 'nature-cultural' and self-organizing" that is "suited to the complexity and contradictions of our times" (Braidotti 51).

In contrast to the vast majority of contemporary eco-fictions, *New York 2140* ends with a comparatively positive outlook towards the future where new governments are elected around the world which then overturn the old global order and implement actually functional environmental policies (602). However, the novel's utopian impulse resists full closure. The narrated time depicted in *New York 2140* is limited to three years. It is clear that (the) (hi)story continues, but not how. In a kind of epilogue addressing the reader, the citizen says: "So no, no, no no! Don't be naive! There are no happy endings! Because there are no endings! [...] Because down there in Antarctica—or in other realms of being far more dangerous—the next buttress of the buttress could go at any time" (604). The direct address to the reader, together with a comment on the novel's seemingly utopian ending, is once more reminiscent of Bertold Brecht's epic theatre. The immersion of readers into the story world is disrupted while the wall between the readers' world and the fictional world of the novel is torn down. *New York 2140* can therefore also be regarded as the canvas on which Robinson's unambiguous political message is painted: start acting together against the exploitative rule of financial capitalism before it is too late for the ecology of this planet to survive.

Similar to *New York 2140*, James Cameron's blockbuster *Avatar* also reveals a relatively closed map of morality in its answer to the ecological catastrophe. However, its extremely immersive and appealing aesthetics that derive from fantasy as its dominant genre lead towards a solution of the ecological catastrophe that is likewise a product of fantasy, the return to "Nature".

Back to "Nature" in James Cameron's *Avatar*

James Cameron's *Avatar* (2009) is one of the most popular films of all time. Currently in 2021 again the highest grossing film ever made (Nash Information Services), *Avatar* has generated an enormous number of reviews, discussions, and reactions ranging from heated political controversies to devoted private fandom. Cameron's blockbuster also represents a technological breakthrough in terms of its unprecedented quality of 3D technology, computer-generated imagery (CGI), and motion-capture technology, which earned it three Oscars alongside several other nominations and awards, among them the Golden Globe for best picture in 2010. Adding to the film's extraordinary aesthetics, *Avatar*'s plot contains many familiar cultural and narrative elements that might explain its popular reception. Like *Interstellar*, Neil *Bloomkamp's Elysium* (2013) or Disney's *Wall-E* (Stanton, 2008), *Avatar* imagines a completely devastated ecology on Earth driving humans into space to look for new habitats and material resources. Its *Pocahontas*-inspired plot, which has been criticised harshly from postcolonial and feminist angles (e.g. Brooks; Žižek), takes place on the fictitious planet of Pandora. Repeating colonial extractivism, the human space mission, in search of a rare mineral called "unobtainium", threatens the ecological livelihood of Pandora's indigenous population. The so-called Na'vi are human-animal hybrids who live in the magnificent rainforest of Pandora and are connected to the planet's world-spirit Eywa via a biochemical information network. In order to interact with them, the scientists of the mission use biotechnologically grown Na'vi avatar bodies they can inhabit via futuristic technology. The film's protagonist Jake Sully, who is part of the science team, falls in love with the chief's daughter, switches sides, and leads the Na'vi in battle against the colonisers before going native.

In my close reading, I want to focus on how the film's reliance on fantasy as the impossible, in addition to its science-fictional elements, creates a map of morality that proposes a retreat to Nature with a capital N as the solution to the ecological havoc on Earth. Apart from Disney's *Wall-E* perhaps, where finding a plant represents the turning point of an uninhabitable planet Earth, there are few other works that explicitly offer similar responses to the ecological catastrophe. However, the idea of an unspoilt "Nature" motivates a number of popular contemporary films, like for example Sean Penn's *Into the Wild* (2007) and *Wild* (Vallée 2014), and represents an influential discourse outside the realm of fiction in the context of the ecological catastrophe. While many people and groups have celebrated *Avatar* as a catapult of environmentalist ideals from the margin into the mainstream, I want to argue that its seemingly obvious ecological message is strongly compromised by its dependency on a romanticised idea of an unspoilt "Nature" as the alleged other of human civilisation. Drawing on Timothy Morton's deconstruction of "Nature" as a concept, I will show that the aesthetically alluring portrayals of Nature in *Avatar* are in fact the product of the capitalist exploitation the film explicitly criticises on the surface. Also, my reading of the film will undo another apparent opposition, which is the dichotomy between "good" Nature and "bad" technology.

I will begin by analysing *Avatar*'s aesthetics and their indebtedness to the fantastic in relation to the film's explicit ethical message that advocates a retreat to more "natural" ways of life. Building on audience studies, I will point out how the film's familiar plot elements, together with its extraordinary aesthetic and emotional appeal, have elicited a great range of viewer reactions, from escapism to activism. Next, I will turn to *Avatar*'s depiction of the ecological catastrophe via its "inversion" on Pandora as an idealised version of Nature. The film contrasts Pandoran Nature hinging on pantheism and animism with other conceptualisations of "nature" represented by the human invaders and their worlds. These include the capitalist world, the military, and the world of natural sciences. I will illustrate how *Avatar* simulates the consequences of these contemporary epistemes of "nature" as either a resource, an enemy, or an object, and by doing so, criticises them. In the end, I will show that while *Avatar* seems to be all about "pure" Nature on the surface, it relies heavily on technology, both on the story-level as well as on the extradiegetic level of production and consumption.

Effective Affection? Ethical Responses to the Fantastic

While *Avatar* makes use of classical science-fiction frames like the futuristic setting on another planet in space inhabited by alien life forms or technological breakthroughs, such as avatar technology, I argue that it is grounded more in fantasy as a genre. Against the backdrop of Farah Mendelsohn's categorisation of fantasy tales, *Avatar* can be read as a mixture of the "portal-quest", in which "the protagonist enters a new world" and "the immersive", where "the protagonist is part of the fantastic world" (James and Mendlesohn 2). It is obvious that the Planet Pandora does not exist, and neither do the Na'vi who cohabitate with its lush and colourful flora and fauna. However, the invention of a fantastic world and its compelling aesthetic rendering has enabled a strongly affective immersion of viewers. As Ellen Grabiner writes, it is almost impossible to not take pleasure in *Avatar*'s aesthetic spectacle and feel affected by its plot (1). The cinematographic effects, from the 3D/CGI images, frame colouring and composition, to the sound and music, all strive to direct the viewers' feelings to sympathise with the protagonist Jake and the Na'vi. Conventional plot elements like the hero's journey exemplified by the suspenseful narrative of Jake's initiation into the clan, and the love story between Jake and the chief's daughter Neytiri further contribute to the viewers' identification with him.

The effects of this strong affective immersion into the film's fantastic world have been relatively well documented due to a phenomenon that has come to be known as "Post-Avatar-" or "Post-Pandora Depression". Mathew Holtmeier, who has conducted empirical research on fan forums, describes the "Post-Pandora Depression" as a response to the film which lets the viewers' own world appear lacklustre in comparison with Pandora, making them seek ways to re-immerse themselves into that seemingly more beautiful and superior world "to prolong the *dream*" (416). While intensive fandom and desperate wishes to inhabit certain fictional worlds is not a new phenomenon—especially in the genres of science fiction and fantasy—it seems that with *Avatar* there is something more at stake which has to do with the contrast of the eco-sublime Pandora to the world(s) actual viewers inhabit. Silvia Martínez Falquina proposes to see the Pandora effect as the surfacing cultural trauma of individuals being "disconnected from nature, alienated in this technological world, and isolated from both people and environment" (123). Holtmeier agrees in that it points to "a particular relationship with our world and environment that needs to be examined" (415). However, instead of deciding to take real world action that might benefit Earth's ecology, people affected by the Post-Avatar syndrome prefer to find ways back into the fantasy world of Pandora like re-watching the film and listening to its soundtrack (Holtmeier 418).

On a more positive note, it is undeniable that *Avatar* has generated an immense variety and quantity of critical and public debate which addresses and critically assesses the political and ethical dimensions of the film's portrayal of technology, culture, and nature.[10] These discussions have contributed to raising awareness for ecological and political issues, and more importantly, the causal relations behind different worlds, their epistemologies, ethics, and aesthetics. In addition to the Post-Pandora depression, researchers have also found evidence of—admittedly much fewer—viewers who display what Holtmeier calls "Na'vi Sympathy", prompting them to take real world, community-based action (419). In a similar vein, Henry Jenkins has written on "Avatar Activism", mentioning examples of activists appropriating the Na'vi's struggle, like five Palestinian, Israeli, and international activists painting their faces in

---

10   For example, China restricted the showing of *Avatar* shortly after its release for fear of social unrest as parallels were drawn between actual struggles for woodland and that of the Na'vi (Davies).

blue while marching through the occupied village of Bil'in in 2010. Most results of audience studies, however, seem to reveal that *Avatar*'s aesthetics deeply affect viewers emotionally but fail to trigger real-world action. One explanation for this is that the fantastic world of Pandora is simply too far removed from viewers' own worlds and therefore remains an escapist fantasy and a place of longing. In this sense, Pandora represents in an extreme form what the concept of Nature, especially in Romantic representations, has always done: creating an idealised imaginary space that will remain forever inaccessible or "unobtainable". In the following, I will turn to *Avatar*'s depiction of the ecology on Earth and on Pandora and show how it hinges on a romanticised notion of Nature.

Ecologies without Nature

In a paradoxical sense, *Avatar* is all about the future state of the ecology on Earth while hardly providing any reference to it at all. It is implicitly clear that Pandora and the Na'vi represent a foil to humanity's treatment of their own planet, and that the space mission is motivated by the Earth's devastated ecology, stripped of all its "natural resources". However, viewers never get to see the future-version of their own planet, and there is very little talk of it. It is only explicitly referenced in two scenes. First, when Jake talks to the tree of souls, i.e., Eywa; just before the great final battle, he says: "If Grace is with you, look into her memories—look into the world we come from. There's no green there. They killed their mother" (Cameron, *Avatar* 2:04:30). And secondly, the Earth is called "a dying world" that the "aliens" (i.e. humans on Pandora) must go back to after losing the battle (2:26:20). Only in fictional paratexts like *James Cameron's Avatar: An Activist Survival Guide* do viewers get more information about the state of the Earth as "a trash heap of ever-expanding waste and decay", "a terminal cesspool" (Wilhelm et al. xi). This make-believe "confidential report on the biological and social history of Pandora" (i) from an anonymous activist who warns against the corporation RDA and their operations on Earth and in space, also includes images from a future Earth that look similar to the bleak depictions of human habitats "without nature" in films like *Blade Runner* and *The Matrix*. From the film quotes and the background information, it can be deduced that what is referenced as "nature" is in the process of dying or has already died on Earth, therefore implying that the entire world or planet is dying, too. Hence, *Avatar* draws on the concept of a planet as a living organism, with the result that many interpretations of the film turn to James Lovelock's

Gaia theory (e.g. Latour 2010, Barnhill 2011, Istoft 2011). In his influential book, *The Vanishing Face of Gaia*, Lovelock models Gaia theory as "a holistic, whole systems theory" (197) that foregrounds the balance of life, imagining Earth as a single breathing organism.

However, in secondary texts on *Avatar*, the idea of Gaia is not evoked to describe planet Earth, but to describe its fictitious counterpart, Pandora, which superbly exemplifies it through its depiction of interconnection between all living things in the form of a biochemical network. On the one hand, Pandora's world spirit Eywa represents a personification of Nature in the form of a goddess (Istoft 403), while on the other, the concept of Nature becomes superfluous because Pandora and its inhabitants represent a kind of posthumanist system of interconnected relations surpassing dualist thinking. The Na'vi do not form an opposition to the forest and its creatures so that the nature-culture divide, in which the concept of "nature" is historically rooted, no longer makes sense. Speaking with Timothy Morton, the Na'vi are part of an "ecology without nature" as "a network of energy that flows through all living things" (Cameron, *Avatar* 1:04:57). Because matter and spirit are conflated, Pandora becomes a pantheist and animist space. For example, in the tree of souls, the Na'vi's ancestors' spirits continue to live and can be called upon; animals on Pandora have spirits, too, and the Na'vi address them after killing their bodies for nutrition. The ecological effects of the Na'vi's monist worldview become obvious in the film: these humanoids respect and honour the spirits of other life-forms, plants, or animals, and only take what they really need to live. Illustrating Haraway's concept of *sympoiesis*, they thrive *together with* their environments, and there is no trade-off between the well-being of the humanoids and the protection of the forest. As a result, any attempts on the part of the corporation to corrupt them with luxury goods is bound to fail, as Jake says, "there is nothing we have that they want" (1:33:20).

Through the Na'vis' moral superiority in interacting with their environment, accompanied with the inability to be corrupted by materialist greed, their world is elevated to an alleged ecological utopia. The film's aesthetics contribute hugely to making this world deeply attractive to viewers. For instance, all life forms on Pandora, including the Na'vi, are extraordinarily coloured in rich tones of blues, greens, and violets, which results in a magically, glowing bio-fluorescence at night. Ivakhiv calls "the film's scintillating portrayal of the biotic life on Pandora, perhaps the most seductive and alluring vision of another planet ever presented in cinema" (164). Sense-based impressions like smelling, tasting, and feeling are constantly foregrounded in depictions of the forested areas of Pandora. For example, when Jake learns to navigate his avatar, he takes a deep breath, digs his toes into the dirt, and tastes a seemingly delicious exotic fruit (Cameron, *Avatar* 0:18:40-0:19:20). The film also imposes strong sensory impressions on viewers through a captivating soundtrack and either pleasing or disturbing images in 3-D quality. Not only is the Na'vis' world portrayed as morally and ecologically superior as well as aesthetically more attractive, but it is also a world that absorbs the story's hero Jake and wins over all other human worlds either in battle or through persuasion. It is therefore unsurprising that *Avatar* has elicited such strong reactions from viewers and generated a substantial number of fans who try to follow the Na'vis' beliefs to any extent possible, for instance by developing forms of spirituality that can be summarised as nature religion. Istoft writes "[t]he potential of *Avatar* fandom for the production of nature religion is clear, as well as its ability to provide fans with meaning and an ethical orientation to the world" (412).

The portrayal of Pandora and the Na'vi in *Avatar* not only generated enthusiasm for its ecotopianism and representation of indigenous perspectives, but it also received harsh criticism from different angles. To postcolonial and feminist critical perspectives, I would like to add an ecological critique. From Timothy Morton's ecocritical perspective, in which "ecological criticism must politicize the aesthetic" (*Ecology without Nature* 205), the strongly romanticised and aestheticised representation of sublime Nature is at the heart of the problem. Drawing on Hegel's concept of "the beautiful soul", he criticises the aesthetic distance engrained in the contemplation of Nature as "a world in which we can immerse ourselves" (204), or "an object 'over there'", which "re-establishes the very distinction it seeks to abolish" (125). *Avatar*'s depiction of a pure and holistic Nature on Pandora fulfils all criteria of Romantic imaginaries of Nature that Morton warns against as impediments of true ecological thinking. In its perfect harmony and captivating aesthetics, Pandora is a fantasy version of the Romantic ideal that must remain forever inaccessible to its onlookers while failing to recognise the actual *sympoietic* relations engrained in human world-making as expressed by Moore's term "world-ecology". It is only on the surface that *Avatar* seems to have positive effects on environmentalism—on further scrutiny, it might even support the harmful capitalist world it seeks to go against in creating a fierce opposition between the idealised world of Pandora and the more or less corrupted human worlds, first and foremost the conglomerate of capitalism and militarism.

The Unobtainium of the Industrial-Military Complex

The company called the Resources Development Administration (RDA) in ex-tra-textual sources finances the whole Pandora space mission which also includes a military division and a team of scientists to help cope with the natives. In this configuration, the RDA represents an extrapolation of the contemporary industrial-military complex and the capitalist world. From an already dominant position in contemporary worlds, it is depicted to have expanded even further by conquering a large portion of space in addition to its existing dominance on Earth. On the space mission, the capitalist world is the most powerful worldmaker, while the military and the science division represent sub-worlds meant to cater to it. The single most important moral obligation in this dominant world is to make money, as is emphasised by the corporation's leader, Parker: "Killing the indigenous looks bad, but there's one thing that shareholders hate more than bad press—and that's bad quarterly statement. I didn't make up the rules" (Cameron, *Avatar* 0:48:30). The quote foregrounds that Parker as an individual is not evil, but that he is representative of a larger system that governs this world, its internal rules, and maps of morality. Evoking Hannah Arendt's concept of the banality of evil, Parker, who is in fact responsible for the killing of a great number of Na'vi and human soldiers, is depicted as a rather dull and disinterested character, preferring to play mini golf in the office instead of working (0:12:25). Without thinking much, he simply follows the moral map of the world he was socialised into, whose aim is to make money at all costs.

Nature in this world exists mainly in two forms, either in the form of a "natural resource", such as the rare mineral with the telling name "unobtainium" which the RDA is after, or in its Romantic version, as the other of human culture, represented by the idea of Pandora in *Avatar*. The explicit link between those two concepts and their mutual dependence on each other is entirely missing in the film, but also missing conceptually from much of ecocritical theory in general. As an exception, Timothy Morton links the artistic representations of Nature in the Romantic period with the beginning alienation of humans from their environment as a result of commodification through capitalism and imperialism (Morton, *Ecology without Nature* 92–93). In this sense, the idea of Nature as an aesthetic space and refuge far away from destructive human culture is only possible *because* industrialisation has profoundly altered humanity's relationships to their surroundings by turning them into exploitable "resources" and "commodities". With regard to *Avatar*, this means that Pandora, which on the surface represents an alternative to exploitative capitalism, is in actuality its very product—a highly successful capitalist good which attracts millions of viewers due to its celebration of a seemingly unspoiled Nature. The somewhat ironic term "unobtainium" can therefore also be interpreted as the capitalist longing for a re-conciliation with Nature that remains forever unobtainable.

Apart from these two conceptualisations of "nature" as either resource or refuge, there is a third version of "nature" added to the fused world of the industrial military complex, which is "nature" as an evil force. Colonel Quarritch portrays "nature" and its creatures as enemies in battle, warning his crew that "[o]ut beyond that fence every living thing that crawls, flies or squats in the mud wants to kill you and eat your eyes for jujubes" (Cameron, *Avatar* 0:06:50). The logical result of the depiction of "nature" as a threat is the moral imperative to keep its forces in check and fight them when necessary. By attacking the Na'vi and other Pandoran creatures, the military division obeys the moral compass of their world, which Quarritch frames in terms of the security paradigm: "As head of security, it is my job to keep you [humans] alive" (0:07:00). That *Avatar* discredits the world of the military and its concomitant actions becomes obvious, as Quarritch is the hero's antagonist and functions as the personification of evil. In the end, his death marks the victory of the Na'vi (2:35:00). In addition, the film is often interpreted as an anti-war film, as it is discussed together with films including *Apocalypse Now* (e.g. Barnhill) or *Dr. Strangelove* (e.g. Der Derian). Accordingly, many exo-referential readings have emerged on the topic of *Avatar*, proposing allegorical critiques of the Iraq war, the War on Terror, and the genocide of indigenous peoples (Ivakhiv 166).

Hence, *Avatar* is overtly critical of the world of the industrial-military complex and its epistemologies of "nature" by portraying the devastating outcomes of these moral compasses on Pandora and its inhabitants. The dichotomy between the good world of the Na'vi and the morally corrupted world of the industrial-military complex is underlined by the aesthetic choices of colour and sound in the depiction of these worlds. The bright and vivid colours of the forest are juxtaposed by the human world characterised by bleakness and rendered through a palette of greys with some yellow and blue here and there to signify artificiality and conventional futurity.[11] The same dichotomy applies to the soundtrack which magnificently supports and illustrates the action of the film,

---

11   In terms of colours and aesthetics, the film also resembles Cameron's other futuristic space film, *Aliens* (1986).

allotting harmonious, heroic, and exotic tunes to the Na'vi, and dark, thunderous, and uncanny notes to the capitalist-military invaders. While there is absolutely no ambiguity with regard to the role of the corporation and military representing "the bad guys", the situation is unclear for the scientists—which team are they playing for, and what does that mean for the role of science in the context of environmentalism?

Are the Scientists also the Good Guys?

The role of the scientists in *Avatar* in relation to the other two parties and their worlds is conflicting. On the one hand, head-scientist Grace and her team are hired to ease relations with the indigenous for the corporation, as Parker puts it: "You're supposed to be winning the hearts and minds of the natives. Isn't that the whole point of your little puppet show?" (Cameron, *Avatar* 0:13:25). On the other hand, Grace and Parker seem to be foils rather than partners or friends from the start, as Grace's comment to Parker points out: "You know I used to think it was benign neglect but now I see that you're intentionally screwing me" (0:12:45). From the dialogue between the two about the role of Jake as a non-trained scientist on Grace's team, it becomes clear that for the corporation, the scientists are merely a little add-on to their quest for unobtainium—if they are useful for the money-making project, good; if not, they are simply superfluous. Nonetheless, the scientists in *Avatar* are depicted as idealists who are genuinely interested in their work and opposed to the violent practices of the corporation and the military. Against this background, it is unsurprising that the scientists "switch teams" in the end and side with the Na'vi to fight against the military. Through their research, which entails inhabiting Na'vi bodies as avatars, learning their language, and joining their lifeworld, the scientists and especially Jake undergo a change of consciousness which makes them become part of the Na'vi world rather than the human worlds.

The morally ambiguous position of the scientists also takes shape in the film's challenging of the dualist scientific understanding of "nature" as matter without spirit. Even though the scientists study the Na'vi's spiritual worldview and respect their belief in Eywa, they do not believe in it themselves. For example, when Jake takes the mortally wounded Grace to the tree of souls for rescue, she says: "I'm a scientist; remember, I don't believe in fairy-tales" (1:50:25). However, drawn into the world of the Na'vi, the scientists represented by Grace also change their take on "nature" as a mere object of study. When the Na'vi's attempt to transfer her soul into her avatar body fails, Grace wakes up one more time before she dies and exclaims, "I'm with her, Jake. She's real" (1:58:11). So finally, deviating from the epistemology of the scientific world, the head scientist becomes convinced of a spirited nature—which again confirms that the film privileges the Na'vis' world as the better one, or even the right one.

The seemingly conflicting conceptions of "nature" (of the military, the corporation, the sciences, and the Na'vi) share more than becomes apparent at first sight. They have their common roots in the Enlightenment and beginning of industrialisation, if not even the beginning of agriculture, as Timothy Morton argues: "Agrilogistics [as the kind of logic intertwined with agricultural production] spawns the concept of Nature definitely outside the human" (Morton, *Dark Ecology* 56). As a result, "nature" becomes the object of human manipulation and an imaginary place of longing at the same time. While on the surface it might seem that *Avatar* confirms the dichotomy by juxtaposing "good" Nature with "bad" human technology, the film's aesthetic form consciously or unconsciously fuses the two realms and challenges the simple opposition in addressing the themes of reality and perception.

Can You *See* What Is *Real*?

James Cameron's *Avatar* questions the notion of a singular and stable reality and foregrounds the theme of visual perception both on the levels of form and content. In this sense, it represents different worlds as mentioned in the previous paragraphs, but also investigates the process of worldmaking through different modes of perception and representation that lead to the creation of knowledge and to a certain version of "reality". The theme of seeing/waking as opposed to dreaming/imagining is repeated on all levels of the film's multi-layered communicative situation. The following interpretation of the communicative situation will deconstruct the nature-technology binary on different levels, further revealing the solution of going back to Nature as a fantastic construct.

On the innermost level of the story world, the computer-generated imagery of the Pandoran forest, the theme of seeing is transported by the Na'vi's designation of "seeing" as emphatically understanding the other. For example, it is expressed in their greeting "I see you". As the scientist Norm explains, it means "not just I'm seeing you in front of me. It's I see into you" (1:01:50). "Seeing" for the Na'vi means apprehending what people and the world are *really* like, which can be derived from Neytiri's conclusion that "sky people cannot learn. You do not see" (0:40:37). "Seeing" is therefore tied to a certain reality or world version that is supposedly superior to others which fail to acknowledge "the truth". As I have demonstrated so far, the different worlds and realities in *Avatar* are not simply depicted as neutral possibilities, but the Na'vi world is portrayed as superior to others and offers a privileged access to "reality" despite its fantastic character. It is therefore implied that the "right way" of "seeing" leads to "truth"—which can be applied to the Na'vi's version of "seeing", as well as to the film as a visual spectacle which provides a different mode of "seeing" than every-day perception through its fantastic CGI imagery presented in 3D. Many critics have taken up the film's emphasis on a different mode of perception and sight, by pointing out how it either fosters empathy as a cornerstone of approaching the ecological crisis (Sideris) or deconstructs the linear dominating gaze prevalent in the history of Hollywood cinema (Grabiner).

The Na'vi's mode of "seeing" is juxtaposed by the motif of dreaming and waking up. For the protagonist Jake, the forest of Pandora and his avatar-self which helps him "see" is only accessible through the human-made, high-tech linking units and the futuristic biotechnology of the avatar programme. The adventures in his avatar, therefore, qualify as a form of dreaming; there are frequent (extreme) close-ups of him opening his eyes and waking up from a dream (e.g., Cameron 0:0:40; 0:20:00; 0:49:20). This adds a second diegetic layer to the story, as Jake gets to inhabit two worlds, the human one and the world of the Na'vi. For Jake, the distinction between what is real and what is a dream becomes more and more complicated. Slowly, his sense of reality changes as he delves deeper into the world of the Na'vi: "Everything is backwards now. Like out there is the true world and in here is the dream [...] I can barely remember my old life. I don't know who I am anymore" (*Avatar* 1:14:33). Jake is not the only one who realises his inhabiting different worlds or who makes explicit references to dreaming and waking up to different realities. Other characters also tell their opponents to wake up in their world's version of reality. For instance, when Grace and Parker quarrel about the fate of the Na'vi, Grace, after pointing out the *intrinsic* value of the ecology of Pandora, says "[y]ou need to wake up, Parker", only to get the answer "[n]o, *you* need to wake up" (1:19:15) because in his world, nothing but *exchange* values exist.

The motif of dreaming as opposed to waking or seeing is repeated on the level of mediation. It is highly advanced technologies that provide the link between the two story-worlds but also access to the world of Pandora. Nidesh Lawtoo points out that "[t]he 'natural' world of Pandora is haunted by the spectre of simulation [...] It is not a simple representation (or *mimesis*) of a real, natural world, but brings into being a CGI simulation of reality" (132).

Through its ground-breaking film technology and cinematography, *Avatar* creates a paradoxical sense of proximity and aesthetic immersion while distancing viewers from its referent Nature at the same time through its multi-layered communicative situation. Some critics and reviewers, such as Caleb Crain, have identified this paradox as the film's hypocritical, ideological work, "convincing you to love your simulation". He argues further that as a sort of hyper-reality, Cameron's computer-generated graphics offer an improved version of Nature, in which the natural is conflated with the digital and the Na'vi represent "digital natives" with "USB ports in their ponytails". It is indeed interesting to note how the ecological network of Pandora is described in an internet jargon, for instance when Grace calls it "a global network" onto which the Na'vi "can upload and download data" (Cameron, *Avatar* 1:28:50). However, this criticism fails to specify what exactly "nature" or "reality" mean and how people can access either of those without forms of (technological) mediation, including representation and language.

In contrast, other critics, such as Grabiner, defend the film, proposing that it consciously criticises the nature-technology dualism that the aforementioned critical position believes to have spotted in *Avatar*. Instead, Grabiner argues that the film shows "technology actually residing in nature, and the natural embedded in the technology in a way that smears the discrete edges we expect to find between technology and nature" (48). Both critical positions are quick to affirm that from their points of view there is nothing wrong with technology per se. Grabiner argues that wrong comes only from certain employments of technology, as exemplified by the RDA in the film, which goes hand in hand with a specific way of "seeing" the world. Therefore, she praises *Avatar* for deconstructing the gaze that already assumes to know what it is about to see (12). Instead of condemning technology, Crain's reading of the film is that it offers "a picture of technology [...] as something that is able to make the natural clearly visible" (58). Again, the question remains what "the natural" refers to and how it can be made visible through technology—is it the inexistent Pandoran fantasy forest or the palm tree plantations in Amazonia? It seems to me that both critical positions build their idea of "nature" on the same model of *Avatar* itself, as the idealised other of human technologies like agriculture. As I have argued before, paradoxically it is exactly these technologies which have produced the concept of "nature".

Apart from the "hard" and modern technology the film deploys, both on the levels of form and content, its narrative techniques (or technologies for that sake) add another two layers to its already complex communicative situation.

The entire narrative is basically told in retrospect, composed of Jake's memories and framed as his video log. From the narrating "I" of the human Jake documenting the memories of his recent adventures in his avatar, the narrative transitions towards the experiencing self of the past by help of a voice-over technique (e.g., Cameron, Avatar 1:01:00). The narrative structure therefore investigates the subjective mental processes of living in worlds, and especially of the transitioning from one world to another, which Jake undertakes. "Sully inhabited a variety of worlds, belonging fully to none" (Sideris 462), which makes him take many different perspectives and makes him fundamentally question the notion of a singular reality.

The conflict of identity Jake is experiencing is conveyed to the viewers as well, as he is the focaliser character with whom viewers are likely to identify. For them, who in their majority find themselves in a world similar to the capitalist one depicted in the film, the process of a growing alienation Jake experiences on Pandora also takes place, driven and heightened by their intense emotional involvement in the film. It is no wonder that "seeing" Pandora as a kind of hyper-reality and fantastic eco-topia, in the form of a super-immersive 3D spectacle, made people prefer to continue that "un-obtainable" dream rather than "go back to their dying world" (Cameron, *Avatar* 2:27:08). The dichotomy between "unobtainable nature" and exploitative human action remains stable throughout the entire narrative, leaving no possibility for the two to be reconciled. That is why the only possible solution to the film's conflict is for humans to leave Pandora. Its unambiguous and mono-dimensional staging of good and evil, in which the conventional hero is able to defeat the villain and his world in battle, leaves no gaps for viewers to think through the problem of human relationships with the non-human worlds themselves.

While the proposition of going back to Nature is only possible in fantasy, *Avatar* nonetheless offers a myriad of possible interpretations and discourses about the ecological catastrophe in its different dimensions. As I have shown, it incorporates a number of worlds and stories which open up discursive spaces despite its closed map of morality.

Conclusion

This chapter looked at contemporary fictional ways of handling the ecological catastrophe as part of ethics for the future. In my exemplary discussion of two eco-future fictions, I showed how aesthetic choices preconfigure different interpretations of the ecological catastrophe and its causes, as well as potential solutions to it. To showcase approaches that are representative of larger discourses, both in and outside of fiction, I picked two very different examples from the most popular eco-future fictions: *New York 2140* with an activist-political approach and *Avatar* incorporating the idea of a retreat to Nature. In my future-ethical reading, I focused on the works' aesthetic creations of different maps of morality and their projection of different actual or imaginary worlds into the future in order to make their ecological consequences emotionally experienceable for readers and viewers.

Rather than conceptualising genres as clear-cut and closed categories, I proposed to look at eco-future fictions as composed of different generic elements on a continuum from (new) realism to science fiction and fantasy. The example of Kim Stanley Robinson's *New York 2140* proved that new realism, science fiction, and utopianism are in fact compatible. It is an example of an eco-future fiction which mostly relies on Barthes's "reality effect". Therefore, its depiction of a potential future and its proposed solution to the ecological crisis may appear most plausible despite its utopianism. This mix of generic traditions leads to a solution that can broadly be classified as political and activist. In its utopian outlook of overcoming capitalism and thus the Capitalocene, *New York 2140* manages to reclaim realism from its capitalist appropriation expressed in the TINA slogan.[12] *Avatar* foregrounds the idea of an idealised Nature, which is enabled by its strong grounding in fantasy as a genre. I have argued that in its fantastic and aesthetically sublime portrayal of the inexistent forest of Pandora and its inhabitants, it depicts an impossible way out of the ecological crisis, which is a retreat into Nature with a capital N. In my close reading, I have pointed out how this fantastic depiction of Nature relies heavily on high technology and at the same time is a product of its supposed other, be it (agri-) culture, industrialisation, or capitalism.

My theoretical approach to the eco-future fictions in this chapter has been posthumanist in the widest sense, including Jason Moore, Timothy Morton, and Donna Haraway, who might not classify themselves as posthumanist critics, but whose works clearly fit with the posthumanist paradigm. As posthumanism tries to take a systemic perspective on the ecology and its actors; it also focuses on how language and stories are related to material practises. Accordingly, I have tried to display how stories engender the material practices of

---

12   TINA refers to Margaret Thatcher's famous dictum that "There Is No Alternative" to neoliberal capitalism.

a given world, first and foremost their economies. Both works in this chapter simulate something like an old world which is in the process of falling apart or needs to be overcome in some way and juxtapose it with an otherworld as a better alternative. Mainly, the old world is the capitalist world and its sub-divisions. In my attempt to investigate imaginary ways out of the ecological crisis, the otherworlds depicted in the future fictions are very important.

It may or may not be surprising that these otherworlds seem to contain many aspects of posthumanist theory. Post-anthropocentric ethics rule the world of the Na'vi in *Avatar*. The biochemical network on Pandora symbolises the interconnectedness or *sympoiesis* of humanoid creatures and others, as well as the transgression of dualist thinking; through Eywa and its creatures, matter and spirit are conflated, as well as nature and culture, including technology. *New York 2140* also assumes a systemic point of view through its portrayal of the actor-networks of humans and non-humans, as well as in its perspective on the entangled relationship between the human economy and the ecology.

4 Transhumanist Futures: Christopher Nolan's *Interstellar* (2014) and Wally Pfister's *Transcendence* (2014)

Similar to the eco-future fictions discussed in chapter three, Christopher Nolan's *Interstellar* and Wally Pfister's *Transcendence* also offer solutions to the ecological catastrophe. However, they take a very different shape as they are rooted in the transhumanist paradigm that builds on the modern promise of progress through science and technology. As mentioned before in previous chapters, transhumanism is currently an influential movement that posits human enhancement through science and technology as its main goal, encompassing "existing, emerging and speculative frames—from regenerative medicine to nanotechnology, radical life extension, mind uploading and cryonics, among other fields" (Ferrando 27). While *Interstellar* departs from the assumption of an ecological apocalypse on Earth that demands for the human colonialisation of space, *Transcendence* focuses more on the transgression of the biological boundaries of the human through mind uploading and nanotechnology. As the transhumanist hub *humanity+* demonstrates, both of these topics are at the heart of current transhumanist research and practise (Humanity+). Its most visible advocates include people like Max More, Nick Bostrom and Ray Kurzweil. Their common denominator is a continuation of the teleological view on the future as made and controlled by humans through science and technology, which builds on the humanist hierarchical binaries that privilege mind over matter and ultimately a certain version of the human over all other forms of life. Even though transhumanist aspirations like radical life extension and space colonialisation may seem extreme, I will treat them as strong versions of the still dominant discourse of futuricity as progress.

This is related to the prevailing instrumentalist perspective on technology. Andrew Feenberg argues that "the dominant view of modern governments and the policy sciences on which they rely" is that technology is a neutral tool controlled by humans (v). Diverging from the hegemonic instrumentalist position, this chapter calls for a more differentiated view on futuristic technologies and their ethical evaluation. Hans Jonas remarked that in philosophical history, technology was long situated outside the realm of ethics, but since the 20th century, it "assumes ethical significance by the central place it now occupies in human purpose" (*The Imperative of Responsibility* 9). Substantivism, the philosophically opposing view to instrumentalism, conceptualises technology as an autonomous and value-laden force that "constitutes a new type of cultural system that restructures the entire social world as an object of control" (Feenberg 7). Rejecting both instrumentalism and substantivism, I propose to consider futuristic technologies like space travel and mind uploading in their social, cultural, and political worlds for future-ethical reflections. Especially, I will look at the underlying cultural narratives and their aesthetic portrayal in the two films I have selected as examples for transhumanist futures, Nolan's *Interstellar* and Pfister's *Transcendence*.

The two films illustrate some of the most dominant narratives of transhumanism that also strongly inform contemporary culture and politics, like the normative idea of the universal human, the quasi-religious treatment of technology and human speciesism. As criticised by posthumanist critics like Rosi Braidotti, the humanist normative model of "the human" foregrounds a Western-centric, historically male and affluent type of subjectivity. This goes hand in hand with a celebration of technology as a tool towards progress that assumes an almost religious status, as both films depict. In combination, those two narratives combine into the notion of human supremacy over all other forms of life that justify their control and exploitation, or, as in the case of *Interstellar*, their abandonment to extinction.

Instead of evaluating the ecological catastrophe as detrimental to the narrative of human ingenuity and superiority, *Interstellar* proposes to see it as an incentive for further enhancement of humanity. In *Interstellar*'s version of the future, crop blights and sandstorms radically threaten human life on Earth, which is why humanity is forced to migrate into space. Heroic action of the protagonist in combination with scientific and technological advancements make it possible for humanity to relocate into space stations and find a potentially new habitable planet and even advance into a five-dimensional reality. In its anthropocentric point of view and its firm belief in science and technology, *Interstellar* builds strongly on humanist and transhumanist philosophy. In my reading of the film, I will point out how its indebtedness to transhumanist ideas is supported by its impressive aesthetic forms, which fuse science fiction conventions with elements of fantasy. Similar heroic or techno-scientific approaches to ecological decline are depicted in Roland Emmerich's *The Day After Tomorrow* (2004), Disney's *Tomorrowland* (Bird 2015), and *Geostorm* (Devlin 2017).

In contrast to *Interstellar*, Wally Pfister's *Transcendence* was not received well by most professional reviewers and audiences despite being planned as a high-budget film. It failed to be as aesthetically pleasing or immersive as intended by not cohering to genre conventions and focusing too much on abstract philosophical questions surrounding the relationships between humanity, technology, and nature. Instead of placing these within their historical socio-economic contexts, *Transcendence* posits essentialisms such as "humans" versus "technology". In this sense, it is comparable to Ian McEwan's novel *Machines Like Me* (2019), and Steven Spielberg's classic *A.I. Artificial Intelligence* (2001). Despite *Transcendence*'s unpopular appraisal, it has been discussed broadly in newspapers, magazines. and on websites, and has proven to be fruitful for analysis as a result of its negotiation between contemporary worlds and their views on digital technology. The main conflict *Transcendence* stages involves the scientist Will Caster and his team of supporters who represent a techno-positive transhumanist worldview, and an opposing group of anti-technology terrorists whose stance resembles that of philosophical substantivism. The mind uploading of Will Caster envisions the achievement of such transhumanist goals which are further enhanced through his development of nanotechnology to cure all diseases and heal ecological damage. The open-ended conflict between Caster and the terrorist group called RIFT (Revolutionary Independence from Technology) that wants to stop him leaves viewers to reflect on the relationships between technology, humanity, nature, and religion, as well as the ethical consequences these questions raise. Similarly, the film's form language is characterised by patterns and aims to surpass simple dualisms, which creates ambiguity on an aesthetic as well as on a moral level. Hence, I will argue that *Transcendence* provides more openness and therefore affords viewers the opportunity for ethical reflection, whereas *Interstellar* remains relatively unambiguous in its celebration of transhumanist aspirations.

Transhumanist Ethics in Christopher Nolan's *Interstellar*

Christopher Nolan's *Interstellar* was released in 2014 and was one of the most successful films of the year worldwide (IMDb Pro). This makes it an important part of the cultural imaginary of our times and a topic of many conversations on- and offline. The story begins with the familiar representation of a devastated planet Earth, on which human life becomes more and more difficult and eventually impossible. The film then follows the journey of its hero Cooper into space, where his aim is to save humanity, and especially his family, by finding a new habitable planet. For this mission, he must leave his children, Tom and Murph, to live with their grandfather. To find a new home for humankind in space, the mission crew overcomes the geophysical limits of current human existence, from humanity's "confinement" to planet Earth to a three-dimensional reality. In terms of structure, *Interstellar* includes two plot threads, a personal and a cosmic one, which are organised into three acts (Sobchack 23): the first is set on Earth, the second takes place in space, and in the third, the two plot threads merge amid the backdrop of a five-dimensional reality connecting future and past, Earth and space, the personal and the cosmic.

In the following, I propose to interpret *Interstellar*'s solution to the ecological crisis in the context of the transhumanist paradigm, which aims at technologically transcending the limits of "the human" and is founded on the belief of historical progress through science. In its advertisement for finding a new habitable planet in space, *Interstellar* is representative of a larger techno-scientific discourse that sees humanity's destiny on another planet, whose most famous representative was the physicist Stephen Hawking (Temperton). *Interstellar* is also exemplary of many popular eco-films that either depict salvation through science and technology and the escape into space, or which likewise depend on a hero to save people from the ecological catastrophe. For instance, *The Day After Tomorrow* (2004) traces the footsteps of another (white, male, US-American) hero, *Geostorm* (2017) contemplates humanity's victory over the weather and climate change through satellite control, *Tomorrowland* (2015) celebrates technological progress as an end in itself, and *Wall-E* (2008) and *Elysium* (2013) also depict (wealthy) humans disappearing into space after messing up the Earth.

In my close reading of *Interstellar*, I want to trace how the film's aesthetics, particularly its fusion of science fiction and elements of fantasy, enable its transhumanist ethical outlook. As major theorists in the field of fantastic literature agree, "fantasy is about the construction of the impossible, whereas science fiction may be about the unlikely but is grounded in the scientifically possible" (James and Mendlesohn 1). I argue that *Interstellar*'s science fiction imaginary absorbs fantasy, just as transhumanism absorbs religious or meta-physical elements while still being grounded in the paradigm of science and technology. The first step of my analysis will be to demonstrate how the film aesthetically directs viewers' emotions to create its closed map of morality. The next section is dedicated to the film's representation of the near future ecology on Earth, which signifies the end-times of human life there. I will point out how the first act of the film uses the realist paradigm on the level of form and criticises it on the level of plot or politics. Next, I will look at the film's juxta-position of the Earth-bound world with the world of unlimited space, which is only accessible through science and technology. The familiar science fiction imagery and sublime aesthetics in space delineate a transhumanist transgres-sion of physical boundaries and represent transhumanist ethics of progress, as I will show. Finally, I will argue that the third act establishes an otherworld that merges fantastic elements with science fiction, thereby bringing together the metaphysical and the scientific. At the same time, it bridges the gap be-tween the personal and the cosmic, the individual and the species, along with personal love and the impersonal sciences.

Directing Viewers' Emotions

Resulting from *Interstellar*'s closed map of morality, Vivian Sobchack interprets *Interstellar* as a call to arms that "urges all of us watching in our own dying light to do more than passively resign ourselves to imminent action" (24). While the film hardly establishes knowledge about the causes of the ecological catas-trophe, it is clear in its proposed solution: humanity can only survive in this future by transgressing the borders of familiar reality and venturing into the unknown, either as outer space or in other unexplored physical dimensions, and science and technology must lead the way. This ethical outlook, which I classify as transhumanist, is aesthetically displayed through Cooper's heroic journey from a near future Earth—which resembles the past more than the future—into a five-dimensional reality in space, representing a more evolved humanity in the future. With regard to the personal and the cosmic, Sobchack argues that "here, in contrast to most science-fiction action films, the personal dramas of the main characters do not function mainly to humanize—and pro-vide occasional relief from—the genre's primary emphasis on scientific expo-sition" (22). Instead, the protagonists' personal relationships and feelings provide an integral part of the scientific solution which ultimately saves the people on Earth.

To transport its ethical message, which derives from ideas of human exceptionalism, *Interstellar* uses aesthetic strategies including a strong emotional appeal through Cooper as a focaliser, a suspenseful plot, and the rendering of outer space through stunning aesthetics. As viewer reviews show, it is precisely this aesthetic appeal that resonates with viewers and mostly explains the film's popularity. On the website IMDb (Internet Movie Database), *Interstellar* was rated 8.5 out of 10, making it No. 29 in films with the best ratings ('Top Rated Movies'). Viewers for instance praised the "luminous and impenetrable photography" that produces images of an "insanely beautiful and mysterious space", making the film a "visual masterpiece". The "outstanding visuals" in combination with Hans Zimmer's "breathtaking and epic" soundtrack seems to absorb viewers completely. For instance, one viewer mentioned that "we are transported into the same cockpit than Cooper [sic], we feel the same remorse [...], the same gravity, [...] the same fear of the unknown". Although many reviewers mentioned the philosophical content of the film to be interesting, it is the grand aesthetics which make *Interstellar* so attractive. Together with an action-driven plot, the film strongly affects viewers, being described as "incredibly exciting", "tear-jerking and emotional throughout" ('Interstellar (2014) User Reviews').

Through identification with Cooper as the focaliser character, viewers are emotionally drawn into the story world. Apart from this formal identification through focalisation, Cooper also matches the familiar characteristics of a white male US-American hero by displaying qualities that make him a target for viewers' admiration and aspirational identification. For example, Cooper's honesty and moral integrity stand out against the betrayers, Dr. Mann and Prof. Brand. He is portrayed as a capable and competent pilot, farmer, adventurer, and engineer, for example in the scenes in which he performs difficult docking and steering procedures in his spaceship (Nolan 0:44:50, 2:05:09). Cooper furthermore represents family values through the love for his children which is the driving force that leads him into the dilemma: in order to save his children, he must abandon them. The scenes in which he communicates to his family from space via video log are therefore particularly emotionally loaded. For example, we see Cooper crying when he learns about the birth and death of his first grandchild (1:18:00). The viewers experience the sadness of the characters in this scene through shot and reverse shots, drawing closer to the characters' faces from medium close-up to close-up—all the while accompanied by quiet melancholy music.

Not only does *Interstellar* bring viewers close to tears with the story of Cooper having to abandon his children, but it keeps viewers' emotional engagement high for almost its entire two-hour-forty-minute length. It builds up a long and steep arc of suspense and maintains a climax that lasts for almost half an hour before the action falls only in the last ten minutes. After the setting on Earth and the central problem is established in a relatively slow first act in terms of plot and audio, the action and the tension quickly speed up as the setting is moved into space (0:44:30). From then on, the sound and the visuals become more and more dense and intense, and one exciting event after another takes place: the crew's travelling through the wormhole (0:49:40), the dangerous and disastrous landing on Miller's planet (~1:05:00-1:16:00), and the controversial and consequential decision to land on Dr. Mann's planet (1:27:23). Towards the ending, the action and the tension accelerate even more, being driven by the parallel editing of the events surrounding Murphy on Earth along with the last phase of Cooper's journey to Mann's planet and afterwards into the black hole. After over half an hour of almost unbearable tension, the scene of revelation merges all three open narrative strands into a single explicable reality in the tesseract as a manifestation of the future world of five dimensions. This represents the solution to the personal and cosmic dilemmas. In the following section, I will trace the film's ethical and aesthetic development over the first two acts which lead up to its transhumanist solution envisioned in the otherworld of the third act.

The End Times of the Earth's World Ecology Managed by Bureaucrats

The Earth-bound first act shows an ecologically devastated planet that is ruled by bureaucrats who mainly seem to administer humanity's demise. The first forty-five minutes of *Interstellar* are devoted to a realistic depiction of the state of the Earth in the near future, which is characterised by crop blights and food scarcity as well as extreme weather, which makes living conditions for humans—and presumably other forms of life—difficult and quickly impossible. It is not necessary for the film to expand on this "new normal" backdrop of ecological devastation because viewers are already so familiar with such a theme that they instantly understand that climate change and its effects are being evoked through this setting. In his review, Geoffrey O'Brian notes that "[w]e are in the catastrophic landscapes for which movies have been preparing us for years so assiduously that it begins to feel like home" (25). The depiction of a dust storm as a catastrophic event is enough to activate the script of ecological decline which viewers already have in mind.

Nolan plays with this pre-knowledge by inserting footage from Ken Burns and Dayton Duncan's 2012 documentary "The Dust Bowl", which reports on the severe dust storms of the American Midwest in the 1930s (Rosenberg). Therefore, the interviewees at the beginning of the film are real people who originally appeared in the documentary, apart from Ellen Burstyn, who is the actress playing the elderly Murph. As people from the past, they introduce the film's near future setting with: "The wheat had died, the blight came and we had to burn it, but we still had corn, we had acres of corn, but uh, mostly we had dust" (Nolan 0:02:50). As yet another time twist, the interviewees are also part of *Interstellar*'s own future setting because they appear on screens in the Cooper station museum at the ending, thus introducing the theme of distorted space-time on a formal level (O'Brian 25). The documentary footage adds to *Interstellar*'s reality effect and provides an implicit explanation for the conditions of the ecology of the film's future Earth. Considering that the devastating dust storms of the 1930s were mainly a result of poor land use through conventional agriculture, it becomes evident that we are also viewing a human-made catastrophe in the film.

While the viewers are familiar with fictitious or real environmental disasters, such as floods, droughts, and storms, *Interstellar* shows a planet Earth that is already beyond the singular catastrophic events many other future fictions focus on as plot motivators. Here, the dust storms and crop blights are merely signs of definite end times. As Prof. Brand explains to Cooper, "the last people to starve will be the first to suffocate" (Nolan 28:40). Apart from the link to the American Dustbowl storms that subtly classify the ecological conditions as self-made, the reasons for the blights and dust storms remain curiously underexplored throughout the film. There is, however, one other exception: in passing, during one of the porch conversations between Cooper and his father-in-law, Donald, the latter mentions overpopulation and excessive consumption of the past as possible factors: "When I was a kid, it felt like they made something new every day. Some gadget or idea. Like every day was Christmas. But six billion people. Just try to imagine that. And every last one of them trying to have it all. This world isn't so bad" (0:15:45). However, Donald's take and his worldview are at odds with what the film generally promotes. In praising this world as it is and criticising Cooper for his starry-eyed dreaming, Donald aligns himself with the world of bureaucrats or political realists who administer the end times in an authoritarian manner.

In this Earth-bound world of the near future, many of the institutions that characterise our present, like the world's military forces or the Federal US-American state, no longer seem to exist. Technological innovation is brought to a halt by governing elites that try hard to ensure the survival of humanity by forcing people to farm. In order to avoid social unrest, they alter the content of history books, for example by rendering the American moon landing as a hoax. Viewers only have a short glimpse into this world through a parent-teacher talk at Tom and Murphy's school, which Cooper must attend. One of the teachers calls their generation "a caretaker generation" (0:11:15), while the other one justifies the omission of the moon landing in books as an attempt to face and solve the ecological problems on Earth: "If we don't want a repeat of the excess and wastefulness of the 20th century, then we need to teach our kids about this planet, not tales of leaving it" (0:12:11). Her line of argumentation is similar to Donald's—yet in this context, the film makes it abundantly clear that this world cannot be right in terms of morals. As a result of focalisation, viewers are likely to agree with Cooper, who is outraged by these comments and the belief that this form of governmentality, which relies on deceiving people and forcing them into certain kinds of labour, is unacceptable, despite having good intentions. Through Prof. Brand, viewers furthermore learn that the governing elites even wanted NASA "to drop bombs on starving people" (0:28:00), which it refused. As a consequence, NASA was temporarily shut down.

The main fault of the world of bureaucrats and political realists as depicted in *Interstellar* is their complete lack of a viable vision for the future. This message is also portrayed aesthetically in the first act, which relies mainly on the representation of a recognisable and familiar reality. The film criticises the focus on the real as the familiar in the context of the ecological crisis, as it merely supports the status quo in order to allow business as usual to continue, without any attempts to solve the problem. Therefore, the film's setting moves into unfamiliar space in the second act. *Interstellar* thus argues that the ecological catastrophe cannot be solved by realism, neither aesthetically nor politically. In addition to fantasy, we need heroes like Cooper, engineers, and explorers to transgress the boundaries of the familiar.

Normative Humanity and Border Transgressions

Cooper adds to the schoolteacher's characterisation of himself as a well-educated man and a pilot that he is also "an engineer" (0:11:00), which proves how important this attribute is to him. He uses it not only to point out his own qualities, but sees the technological progress symbolised by it as an essential part of human nature. Whilst gazing at the stars from his home porch, he points out: "It's like we have forgotten who we are, Donald. Explorers, pioneers, not caretakers" (0:15:30). The vocabulary he uses for this description of who "we" are additionally points to the cultural and historical context of the United States, evoking associations of the pilgrims, the frontier, and especially the Manifest Destiny. The film's nationalism can also be seen both through the depiction of NASA as the saviour of humankind and the recurring images of the American flag on Prof. Brand's desk (1:22:00), on Dr. Mann's space station (1:33:00) and on "our new home" planet in the end (2:38:39). *Interstellar*, although globally successful, must therefore also be seen as a film modelled on hegemonic US-American culture. Cooper with his practical can-do attitude, which shows, for instance, when he chases and manages to hijack an old Indian drone (0:06:15), represents the stereotypical American white male hero: cool, self-reliant, and capable of handling all types of practical challenges.

While the collective "we" in Cooper's speech is obviously meant to represent the universal human, it denotes only a culturally specific concept of human subjectivity and capability informed by Enlightenment thinking and US-American history. Furthermore, the image of the universal human is a direct heritage of European humanism. As Rosi Braidotti argues, it is best exemplified by the image of Leonardo da Vinci's Vitruvian Man: "That iconic image is the emblem of Humanism as a doctrine that combines the biological, discursive and moral expansion of human capabilities into an idea of teleologically ordained, rational progress" (13). This humanist ideal seems to be at the core of *Interstellar's* world of science and technology as represented by Cooper and NASA. It furthermore hinges on the notion of human exceptionalism, which is why the film paradoxically never addresses non-human life forms, even though they must be at the heart of the ecological problem in the form of plant blights. To emphasise the mutual interdependency between humans and their non-human environments, Donna Haraway uses the term "sympoietic", which "means 'making-with.' Nothing makes itself; nothing is really autopoietic or self-organizing. [...] It is a word for worlding-with, in company" (*Staying with the Trouble* 59).

While negating humanity's entwined or "sympoietic" relationship with the non-human world, an assumed proximity of humans to the divine is transported when Cooper comments: "We used to look up in the sky and wonder at our place in the stars. Now we just look down and worry about our place in the dirt" (Nolan 0:16:28). Through Prof. Brand's assertion that "we're not meant to save the world. We're meant to leave it" (0:29:50), the idea of some kind of (Manifest) destiny again shines through. Despite the evocation of a destiny and the film's allusion to supernatural agents, no explicit link to any religious context is given. As a result, I argue that the logic of this world parallels that of transhumanist philosophy, "as a form of non-dogmatic, non-doctrinal, de-reified, rational, scientific and singularitarian techno-religion" (Schussler 94).

In addition, Francesca Ferrando furthermore defines transhumanism as an "ultra-humanism" that is philosophically rooted in the Enlightenment. Like humanism, transhumanism is anthropocentric, foregrounds rationality and sustains a firm belief in human progress. In contrast to humanism, it frees itself from the idea of an unchangeable human nature and strongly relies on science and technology to overcome biological, psychological, and physical limitations to enable further human evolution. Ferrando argues that "[h]uman enhancement is a crucial notion to the transhumanist reflection; the main keys to access such a goal are identified in science and technology" (27). While in *Interstellar* the biological setup of the human remains untouched—death and ageing are still an accepted reality in this future—the physical boundary of gravity as the basis of human life on Earth is transgressed by scientific ingenuity and the heroism of individuals, in this case of Cooper and his daughter Murphy.

The Scientific, Science Fiction, and Space

Following the tradition of innumerable science fiction films and novels, *Interstellar* imagines the future destiny of humanity in space. As Sobchack points out, the computer-generated imagery of outer space fulfils generic clichés by quoting other films heavily, especially Stanley *Kubrick's 2001: A Space Odysee* (43). There are numerous scenes in the second act which visualise outer space and its secrets in a way that is aesthetically overwhelming in terms of the image's size—the film was also shot for IMAX cinemas—lighting and beauty. In this sense, the scenes can be described by drawing on the concept of the sublime. Immanuel Kant conceptualises the sublime as a different kind of beautiful. In contrast to the pleasure evoked by contemplating the beautiful, the sublime causes the subject to feel negative pleasure, characterised by admiration and respect of something higher (Kant et al. 129). According to Kant, the sublime (in nature) therefore evokes supersensual or metaphysical ideas of infinity in the onlooker's mind (130). Similarly, observations and illustrations of space necessitate imaginations of infinity and, as a result, fascinate and frighten people at the same time. In this respect Jeffrey Kluger argues, "[b]ig cosmology has become our secular religion, a church even atheists can join" (43). The sublime science fiction aesthetics of space are therefore compatible with a transhumanist worldview promising transcendence through science and technology.

For Cooper, "scientific" is synonymous with good. It therefore becomes evident that non-scientific ideas and thoughts must be eliminated, as shown in his reaction to Murphy's "ghost" mentioning. When the ten-year-old tries to tell her father about the poltergeist that signals to her, his answer is a repudiating "it's not very scientific" (Nolan 0:04:00), meaning, it's nonsense. For Cooper, it is only worth talking about if evidence-based data is available: "Alright Murph, you wanna talk science, don't just tell me you're afraid of some ghost. No, you got to go further. You got to record the facts, analyse, get to the how and the why and then present your conclusions" (0:04:13). Murphy follows his advice, which is ultimately what triggers the success-story of human survival in space. Science is therefore not only portrayed as an apt mode to gain knowledge about the world, but also as inherently good since it functions as a moral compass which leads to a better future. The scientists and explorers of the Lazarus mission are described by Dr. Brand as "the best of humanity" (0:51:14), who have gotten "farther than any human in history" (1:13:40). Scientific work and its practical application in space missions are framed as a moral good in itself with a clear teleological orientation towards progress. Without a noticeable change, the story of nature's conquest on Earth is repeated in space. In conversation about whether nature can be evil, Cooper and Amelia Brand even explicitly equate space with nature (0:50:00).

While *Interstellar*'s speciesist perspective completely ignores all non-human life forms bound to die on Earth, it is at the same time critical of a more extreme form of speciesism that focuses only on the survival of the *abstract species* of the human. This is represented by Prof. Brand, whose original plan was always "Plan B". Before his death, he revealed his strategy, which was to have the Lazarus mission save the human species as a fertilised egg colony but not the existing people on Earth (1:31:00). The only other character who knew about Brand's actual plan was Dr. Mann, who frames it in the evolutionary progress paradigm: "Evolution has yet to transcend that simple barrier. We can care deeply, selflessly about those we know, but that empathy rarely extends beyond our line of sight" (1:41:30). From this viewpoint, abstract species think-ing is simply another step in the teleological evolution of the human towards the literal mastery of the universe.

To emphasise and aestheticise the idea of the survival of the human species, Dylan Thomas's poem "Do Not Go Gentle Into that Good Night" is quoted several times throughout the film, mostly by Prof. Brand, but also by his accomplice, Dr. Mann. For instance, against the backdrop of the iconic blue planet seen from space and majestic organ chords, Brand quotes the poem's first two stanzas shortly after the space shuttle has taken off (0:48:40). The grand aesthetic setup deepens the poem's function of pointing out the impor-tance of this moment for the fate of humankind. Thomas's poem, which has been interpreted as a call to his dying father to fend off death, in the context of *Interstellar*, represents an appeal not to accept the prospect of human ex-tinction. Brand makes this interpretation explicit when he tells his daughter: "Stepping out into the universe, we must confront the reality of interstellar travel. We must reach far beyond our own lifespan. We must think not as individuals but as a species. Do not go gentle into that good night" (1:23:45).

Hence, Brand selflessly dedicates his life to the Lazarus mission, which, as the biblical telling name indicates, is there to awaken humanity from an already foreseeable death through extinction. As a concrete manifestation of this idea, Dr. Mann tells the crew members, who wake him from his cryonic sleep on the planet he has travelled to, that they "have literally raised [him] from the dead" (1:36:30). It is no coincidence that Mann is the only other character that quotes Thomas's "Do No Go Gentle" when he tries to kill Cooper (1:47:10). Like Brand, he has also lied to the other characters beforehand by claiming that his planet had the potential to host human life. Different from Brand, however, his moti-vation to lie is his egoistic desire to survive despite his proclamation of the re-verse (1:53:59). Mann, whose name can be read as a telling name representing a generalised version of "man", exemplifies that "Man(n)'s'" own survival instinct and the higher mission to save the species are at odds with each other. In addi-tion, another white male US-American is supposed to represent the universal human. Apart from that, Mann symbolises the central message of the film: the key motivation and instrument for human survival is not abstract rationality but specific feeling, in the form of self-interest and love.

The Otherworld in Space: A Fusion of Science and Love

Right at the beginning of *Interstellar* an inexplicable, seemingly metaphysical or fantastic element in the form of Murphy's "ghost" enters the otherwise realistic setting of the first act. The "anomaly" in Murphy's room is addressed already in this first instance by fusing a scientific paradigm with that of a religious or mystical one. After the experimental throwing of a coin, Cooper makes the scientific declaration that "it's not a ghost. It's gravity". One minute later, Donald tells him to clean up the mess when he has "finished *praying* [my emphasis] to it" (0:20:47). This quasi-religious framing continues throughout the course of the story, including when the NASA crew discusses an external entity referred to as "they" being responsible for certain scientifically inexplicable occurrences. After Cooper admits that something unscientific that he hesitates to call supernatural led him to the secret NASA headquarters, Prof. Brand answers that "[s]omething sent you here. 'They' chose you" (0:27:10). The trope of "being chosen", either as an individual or as a people, is again a familiar concept within religious texts. The seemingly benevolent entity called "they" appears to want to help humanity by placing a wormhole and potentially habitable planets within reach. Addressing the entity in the third person plural instead of with the singular male pronoun defies a Christian religious interpretation while still evoking supernatural forces. As the space crew approaches the wormhole, a "first handshake" (0:57:50) between Dr. Brand and this apparently otherworldly life form takes place. The actual physical contact from then on establishes associations with alien, perhaps super-intelligent civilisations rather than divine powers. After the crew's failure on Miller's planet due to relative space-time, this interpretation seems to be confirmed by Dr. Brand pointing out that in opposition to themselves, "'they' are beings of five dimensions. For them, time might be another dimension they could climb" (1:14:44).

As is obvious from the examples so far, the film deliberately leaves a gap in the narrative surrounding the mysterious entity called "they" to raise tension and have viewers speculate about its nature. It activates viewers' knowledge about science fiction genre conventions and religious contexts, which seem to be at odds with each other. James Koh (2016) even goes so far as to argue that reading *Interstellar* as science fiction is basically a misunderstanding because the magical elements, and the ending in particular, are much closer to conventions of the fantasy genre. The revelations in the film's ending, however, contradict this reading, as the benevolent, super-evolved entity of five dimensions turns out to be human beings themselves. Cooper finds out: "No, 'they' didn't bring us here at all. We brought ourselves" (Nolan 2:23:06), which rules out supernatural or magical explanations. Hence, it is not by the mercy of some divine entity, nor by a well-meaning alien life form, but by human ingenuity that humanity can ultimately save itself from its self-made mess on Earth. The solution that *Interstellar* presents is thus driven both by transhumanist ideas about the human capability to overcome given limitations, in this case the limitation of three dimensions and planet Earth, and by physical expansion like the colonisation of space. The black hole Gargantua is even described as "a literal heart of darkness" (1:04:30), making explicit references to colonialism and colonial texts, such as Conrad's *Heart of Darkness*.

Future humans thus assume a God-like status by fusing science, technology, and love to enable their survival and shape their own destinies. They are transcendent in the sense that they can transcend space-time by becoming five-dimensional beings—whatever that means exactly. In addition to the abstract rationality paradigm of humanism and the sciences, it is the specific manifestation of feeling, such as love for another human being, that *Interstellar* depicts as part of its solution. For Brand and Murph, love does not contradict science but rather creates the foundation for a new dimension, as Brand explains when defending her decision to follow her heart:

> But maybe we've spent too long trying to figure all this with theory [...] love isn't something we invented. It's observable, powerful. It has to mean something [...] Maybe it's some evidence, some artefact of a higher dimension that we can't consciously perceive. [...] Love is the one thing we're capable of perceiving that transcends dimensions of time and space. Maybe we should trust that even if we can't understand it yet. (1:25:55 ff)

Even though the scientific outlook that only takes phenomena seriously when they become "observable" and "quantifiable" remains unabated, it is remarkable that love as a feeling between two human beings should play the key role in saving humankind. It is therefore Murphy—and not Cooper—who heads and represents the fantasy-fused world of the future. She is the one who is able to unite feeling and rational thinking, which is why, as Cooper finds out, "'They' didn't choose me. 'They' chose her. [...] To save the world" (2:25:24). Once more, the (manifest) destiny is referenced, but it is now clear who is the powerful agent behind it: the highly evolved super-humans from the future. In this sense, Murphy becomes the founder of this future human civilisation, thanks to her willingness to accept and believe in seemingly fantastic things like the ghost of her childhood. This is what distinguishes her from her father's overly realistic scientific view. Even though the otherworld of the future in *Interstellar* incorporates feelings and mysterious events, they remain scientifically measurable and explicable at the end of the day—at least from the perspective of the evolved future civilisation.

The last sequence of the film takes place in one of presumably many space stations humanity has found refuge in. As Cooper is taken on a tour around "Cooper Station", viewers recognise the cylindrical structure of the NASA building that was originally designed for the purpose of becoming a space station as part of Prof. Brand's "Plan A", which was to save the actual people on Earth. The landscape is folded into a circle with horizontal fields and houses standing upside down. Apart from this estrangement effect, everything else looks just as it does in many US-American suburbs today. From a short pan, one can gather that the fields still consist of monocultures, the houses are just as large as they were back on Earth, and baseball is still the national sport. Rather than learning from the ecological mistakes of the past on Earth, the human civilisation depicted here moves "forward" with a more-of-the-same approach, actually reminiscent of the bureaucrats criticised in the beginning of the film. But rather than looking back to analyse the faults of human civilisation, Cooper, like the rest of the world, wants to look ahead (2:23:40). The last images viewers see are impressions of Amelia Brand removing her helmet and taking a deep breath on Edmunds' planet, which means that with a breathable atmosphere, it is a promising new habitat for humankind, as the old Murphy confirms through voice-over.

The otherworldly solution *Interstellar* presents in the end brings together the plot elements as well as the generic and aesthetic codes of the first two acts: on the personal level, Cooper and his daughter are reconciled, and on the cosmic level, the extension of the techno-scientific paradigm of love allows for humanity to transgress the boundaries of their physical existence on Earth and venture into space and five-dimensional reality. *Interstellar* thus finishes on an optimistic note by reassuring viewers that the solution to the ecological catastrophe is clear: human ingenuity through science and technology will save humankind. As I have argued, this represents a transhumanist approach to the ecological problem, which is also mirrored on the level of aesthetics. The realist paradigm of imagination must be transgressed, and the science fictional must incorporate the fantastic in order to capture unfamiliar modes of existence and aesthetics, which in the end turn out to not be so different from the forms of contemporary existence on Earth.

Philosophical Essentialism: Futuristic Technologies and The Human in Wally Pfister's *Transcendence*

Wally Pfister's 2014 film *Transcendence* simulates the digital creation of a super-intelligent being through mind uploading and its ethical consequences. However, rather than looking at AI ethics specifically, the film represents "philosophical essentialism" by focusing on more general questions surrounding the relationships between humanity, futuristic technology, and nature as universalised, de-historicised categories. *Transcendence* takes up the question of what it means to be a biological human and in what way this alleged "human nature" differs from technologically enhanced creatures representing artificial super-intelligence. This is also sometimes referred to as "the singularity": "The Singularity was first proposed by the mathematician and science fiction author Vernor Vinge (1993) as the point at which greater-than-human machine intelligence begins rapidly improving itself, bringing an end to human-directed history" (Hughes 763). The singularity, or artificial superintelligence (AI), needs to be separated from the general term "artificial intelligence", which designates all kinds of already common computing technology. Generally, "Artificial Intelligence is the ability of a machine to perform cognitive tasks that we associate with the human mind" (Kreutzer and Sirrenberg 3). Computers, smart technology, and all types of digital applications are already types of weak artificial intelligence, as they are able to imitate certain tasks usually performed by human minds like voice recognition (e.g. Alexa, Siri), or playing the board game *Go* (AlphaGo). However, they are still far from being capable of imitating all complex tasks of the human mind and its sentience—and it is unclear whether machines will ever be able to achieve this (4).

In working out the essentialised difference between humans and AIs, the film is similar to Ian McEwan's 2019 novel *Machines Like Me*, Luc Besson's *Lucy* (2014), and Steven Spielberg's classic *A.I. Artificial Intelligence* (2001). McEwan's *Machines Like Me* also foregrounds the differences in logical and emotional thought between AI and humans. Like Spielberg's *A.I. Artificial Intelligence*, the novel portrays relationships and emotional attachments between humans and digital androids. *Lucy* examines what could happen to humans and their human(e)ness after they achieve super-enhanced cognitive and physical capabilities as their long-cherished dream of transhumanism comes true. In a similar vein, Pfister's *Transcendence* simulates transhumanist ideals becoming reality, such as overcoming biological limits and the successful implementation of nanotechnology. It portrays how the digitally uploaded mind of the physically deceased scientist Dr Will Caster acquires the power to influence and change almost the entire world through nanotechnology, from human minds to material and ecological structures, before he is stopped by a group of neo-luddites who manage to convince the executive powers of the state to help them. In terms of genre, the film is difficult to place apart from the obvious science fiction classification, as it contains elements of action, romance, film noir, and thriller, but not enough to make it fit into any of the categories. This generic confusion may have been a contributing factor in the film's relatively negative reviews, both from critics and private viewers. Even though *Transcendence* was set up to be a "big budget sci-fi" (Kermode), it generated a disappointing box office result (Nash Information Services) and a relatively low user rating and critical metascore on IMDb ('Transcendence (2014) User Reviews'). From the reviews, it becomes apparent that *Transcendence* is what can be called "a film of ideas" that lacks a convincing plot line and is not able to grasp the majority of viewers emotionally or aesthetically.

In the following analysis, I will argue that Pfister's *Transcendence* nonetheless lends itself to a valuable ethical reading in the context of this chapter because it offers a high degree of ethical ambiguity when picturing different and competing philosophical theories of digital technologies and their corresponding worlds. I will begin my close reading with an analysis of how the aesthetic destabilisation of binaries in favour of patterns deconstructs the moral good-and-evil dichotomy in favour of more complex ethics of digital futures. This is mirrored in the depiction of competing worlds and worldviews. First, I will discuss Will Caster's world as prototypical of transhumanist thought, which on the surface seems to take an instrumentalist stance on technology but heavily charges technology with moral value. In its simulation of possible futures, *Transcendence* also rehearses more experimental world configurations, like associating technology with spirituality and nature, as I will show next. After analysing the techno-positive worlds the film offers, I will contrast them with the worldview of the RIFT group, whose actions are based on a classical substantivist position that pictures technology as an uncontrollable threat to humanity. In the end, I will conclude with the options and hints the film offers for a possible resolution of the central conflict.

More than Black and White: Ambiguous Ethics and Aesthetics

IMDb user reviews and critical reviews alike show that *Transcendence* has been read in contrasting ways regarding the moral judgement of Will Caster as an artificial superintelligence. Many viewers see a confirmation of the cliché about the dangers of technology in the film as Will becomes an almost unstoppable force in the end, ruling over people as well as matter. In contrast, others write that *Transcendence* shows that the real danger is in the fearmongering of those opposed to technology, and that everything Will does as an AI, like healing the sick and diseased and repairing the ecology of the planet, is actually good. One reviewer points out the film's moral ambiguity by stating that "[s]ome of the ethics are quite complex, and you have to ask if the machine's intent is really hostile, or [whether] that [is] just the interpretation characters are putting on it because they don't understand" ('Transcendence (2014) User Reviews'). Professional critics likewise highlight that *Transcendence* "simultaneously embraces technological progress and shudders at its power" (Kohn). While much of its ambiguity can be found on the level of plot and character constellation—mainly surrounding the question whether Will and his deeds are good or bad—I want to argue that the film's visual aesthetics contribute profoundly to its moral ambivalence.

A decisive aspect of this are the narrative and cinematographic perspectives. Even though the camera follows Caster's wife Evelyn more than any other character, there is no clear centre of perception or focaliser character in the film. The camera's perspective often jumps between locations through cross-cutting. As a result, viewers are almost simultaneously able to be at the terrorists' fire, the FBI office, and Will's headquarters (Pfister 0:51:22-0:52:10), but never get introspection into characters' minds and moods apart from dialogue and the visually obvious. Perhaps the only instance of character introspection can be seen during the parallel scenes at the start and ending of the film, when we hear Caster's friend and colleague Max's thoughts as a voice-over. The omnipresence and even omniscience of the camera's perspective mirrors the theme of Will as an artificial superintelligence, who likewise possesses the powers to be in many places at once and to know most of what there is to know—apart from interiorities. The lack of focalisation leads to a non-identification with any of the characters and to an emotional detachment that allows for both a rational reflection and moral judgement of their deeds.

On the level of imagery, the simple dichotomy between good and evil, which is conventionally expressed through light and dark, is transgressed. While the film has a predominantly dark and sinister atmosphere, which leads critics to see film noir elements (e.g. Kohn), it nonetheless breaks the corresponding association of the future as predominantly dystopian or apocalyptic. There are many night scenes and portrayals of dark interiors, but they are not necessarily depicted as scary or dangerous. On the contrary, the Casters' dark garden and sparingly lit home appears cosy and reassuring against the uncanny but brightly lit desert town *Bright*wood. The terrorists' hiding places in old sheds and buildings appear dark and ugly, and their leader Bree is often depicted in black clothes and with dark eyeliner. On the other hand, the images of the terrorists sitting at a fire in the woods break the association between dark and evil and make their simple lifestyle look almost appealing. The same confusion of colour codes manifests in Will's underground data centre. While underground facilities are usually associated with darkness, this one is characterised by whiteness instead and is mostly brightly lit. When Evelyn is depicted in the data centre for the first time, she is also wearing a white blouse, blending in with the whiteness of the corridors (Pfister 0:53:19). In contrast, in one of the next scenes, she changes into a completely black dress (0:56:38), showing that there is no consistency in the colour symbolism. From these examples it can be deduced that the familiar visual code of white and black or bright and dark as symbols for good and evil are simply misleading. The film deliberately transgresses and disrupts them to emphasise that there is no simple, black and white morality in its story world.

What *Transcendence* offers as a replacement of binaries, however, are patterns. Patterns appear often in rather unconventional arrangements, lending an almost poetic or metaphorical note to the film's reality effect through continuity editing. For example, the juxtaposition of light and dark often forms patterns as seen on the data centre's solar panels at night (0:58:39). When Will goes online, we see a pattern of a night cityscape merging into a pattern of a computer circuit board and online data streams (0:42:00). Another example is the pattern of Will's pixelated face contrasted with the pattern of Max's prison cell (0:43:40). Patterns, like binary oppositions, represent an attempt of logical ordering; but different from binaries, patterns allow for much more complexity and enable systemic points of view. They allow for drawing connections rather than mere oppositions, also unusual ones. For instance, the film visually draws a connection between nature and technology, which I will discuss later on in more detail. *Transcendence*'s visual aesthetics thus move viewers towards more complex modes of thought that are based on patterns rather than dualisms, which influences an ethical reading of it. The aesthetics give way to worlds and philosophies that are partially competing but also share similarities and offer unusual sub-worlds or nuances. Together, they avert singular right answers to the ethics of digital futures and artificial superintelligence. In the following, I will trace the spectrum of that pattern ranging from extreme techno-optimism in transhumanist thought to its extreme opposite.

Will as a Prototypical Representative of Transhumanist Thought

Even though it may seem radical at first sight, I propose to conceptualise transhumanist philosophy as a more extreme version of the contemporary dominant belief in progress through digitalisation and other advanced technologies. In parallel to humanist thinking, transhumanism rests on the general belief that human life can be improved through the application of rationality, science, and technology (Bostrom, 'A History of Transhumanist Thought' 2)—in other words, through asserting control over what has been referred to as nature. Over time, this outlook has taken many different forms ranging from Nietzsche's Übermensch, as a manifestation of personal human growth, to contemporary ideals like the development of nanotechnology and uploading human minds onto a computer (4; 9–10). In addition to an inherent humanism, whose values it also embraces, transhumanism wants to move beyond the biological and physical limits that have defined the human so far. One mode of transgressing "the human" is the so-called singularity as a fusion of human and machine, or the creation of artificial superintelligent life. *Transcendence* as a title already points towards this transgression attempted by the scientist Will Caster and his helpers Evelyn and Max. It thus illustrates the fulfilment of transhumanist goals, from the creation of AI to the application of nanotechnology, while revealing their totalitarian potential.

The ideal of progress through nanotechnology currently has high stakes in transhumanism and beyond. One of the leading representatives of transhumanist philosophy, Nick Bostrom, explains that

> [m]olecular nanotechnology would enable us to transform coal into diamonds, sand into supercomputers, and to remove pollution from the air and tumors from healthy tissue. In its mature form, it could help us abolish most diseases and ageing, make possible the reanimation of cryonics patients, enable affordable space colonization. ('A History' 9)

Transcendence simulates the effects of a successful breakthrough in nanotechnology, for instance the rebuilding of any material in a very short time span. In the film, Caster comments "[s]ynthetic stem cells, tissue regeneration, the medical applications are now limitless. They'll be scared at first, but once they see what the technology can do, I think that they will embrace it and I think it will change their lives" (Pfister 0:57:44). His prophecy becomes true when crowds of people come to his facility to be healed from their diseases and disabilities. The elimination of suffering and even death represented here is another overtly expressed transhumanist goal fixed in the transhumanist declaration (Bostrom, 'A History' 21). Aura-Elena Schussler points out that the singularity as self-transcendence in transhumanist philosophy is deeply intertwined with the current paradigm of personal development (98), which shows commonalities with neoliberal ideology. *Transcendence* exemplifies this by revealing how fundamentally a-political and a-democratic Will Caster's acquisition and exertion of power as an artificial intelligence is.

Through his abilities to make enormous amounts of money on the stock market as a superhuman calculating machine, Will is materially able to make a world according to his ideals, without the need for a democratic justification. Transhumanism furthermore builds on the Cartesian mind-body split, which privileges the mind and cognitive matters over the body. Higher intelligence therefore becomes a justification for domination as Caster shows by allowing himself to hack into other people's minds and control them as he sees fit. The people who come to receive medical treatment from him are afterwards "all enhanced, modified and networked. They remain autonomous, but they can also act in unison, part of a collective mind" (1:08:20). Obviously, this shows the threat of totalitarianism embedded in the idea of transhumanist progress. Caster pursues progress as enhancement through science and technology in all spheres of life, ranging from the cognitive potential of individuals to developments in medicine and improvements of the ecology. As I have demonstrated with the example of *Interstellar*, this worldview fails to consider the social and economic factors and systems that have led to a certain condition, for example ecological decline. Likewise, the solution for Will is a tech-fix through nanotechnology: "We're healing the ecosystem, not harming it. Particles join the air currents, building themselves out of pollutants. Forests can be regrown, water so pure, you can drink out of any river" (Pfister 1:43:25).

Apart from his actions as an uploaded mind, Will Caster's pursuits as a scientist and still embodied human being already reveal his transhumanist agenda and his aim to transgress human biological and physical boundaries. In his speech for potential funders of his research he explains: "Once online, a sentiment machine will quickly overcome the limits of biology, and in a short time, its analytical power will be greater than the collective intelligence of every person born in the history of the world" (Pfister 0:09:35). His talk foreshadows becoming an AI and the superintelligence he will gain after the transformation, which is also represented visually by the large shadow that appears on the screen behind Caster during his talk, symbolising his future super-enhanced powerful self (0:10:02). Caster's on-stage talk turns into a metaphysical direction when he equates the "singularity" with "transcendence", which would require "us to unlock the most fundamental secrets of the universe. What is the nature of consciousness? Is there a soul?" (0:10:15). It is no coincidence that right in the middle of his speech, the terrorists' bombs detonate to signify the desired disruption of this kind of research by an opposing world. At the same time, Caster's talk already introduces a nuance of transhumanism, which is the connection between spirituality, or even religion, and advanced technology.

Technology as a New Form of Secular Spirituality

The number of parallels to Christian religious texts and the explicit mentioning of words associated with it like "God", "transcendence" or "soul" in Pfister's digital future scenario is striking. Therefore, I argue that the film portrays the digital as a new form of secular spirituality. However, it remains unclear whether the film wants to support this vision, mainly embodied by Will Caster, or whether it is critical of it. As I have already argued in the discussion of *Interstellar*, the association between religion and technology reveals a blind spot in transhumanist philosophy which, in its mainstream, imagines itself as eliminating religious believes through a purely scientific worldview (Bostrom, 'A History' 11). In contrast to this self-perception, Schussler characterises it as a kind of techno-religion that "seeks to integrate [the Judeo-Christian concepts of immortality and salvation] into a secular, non-dogmatic paradigm of spirituality" (99). *Transcendence* confirms this thesis by asserting and visualising the religious character of transhumanist thought on many levels.

Explicitly drawing on the Judeo-Christian theme of immortality and salvation, Caster is in fact able to make himself immortal through the mind-uploading procedure. In accordance, Heidi Campbell argues that *Transcendence* "employs the technognosis myth that technology is an all-powerful force that seeks to emulate a god" (Campbell 14). Will Caster as a disembodied virtual being has become a god-like entity who possesses divine qualities like omnipresence, omnipotence, and omniscience. These qualities are also rendered through cinematographic and other formal means, for instance, the omnipresent perspective of the camera and Will's voice appearing as a voice-over in scenes where it could not be if he were not omnipresent throughout the internet and all devices connected to it, such as surveillance cameras. For example, in a helicopter shot we see Brightwood from above for the first time when Will's voice appears as a voice-over, explaining his plan to Evelyn who sits in the car and talks to Will via an earbud (Pfister 0:46:57). The birds-eye perspective becomes a typical feature after Will has become an AI, signifying his dis-embodiedness and physical omnipresence. The moment Evelyn is connected to Will, she states "I can see everything" followed by a camera flight over the data centre into the desert and more remote places (1:42:57). As a result of Will's omniscience and his permanent connection to the internet with all its devices, he is also quasi omniscient. His omnipotence comes as a result of his breakthrough in nanotechnology, through which he can decide on life over death, endow people with supernatural strength, and control almost everything, from people's minds to ecosystems.

In addition to Will's god-like attributes, the parallels to Bible texts and stories are remarkable. Like Jesus Christ, Will is depicted as being able to heal the blind and the lame. For example, his healing of a blind man through nanotechnology is represented in detail with extreme close-ups (1:07:20). Following these miraculous healings, large crowds of people come to Brightwood from everywhere in the world, to be cured of their sicknesses or disabilities, as in the story of Jesus of Bethlehem. Additionally, both Will and Jesus are killed by those who do not believe in them and see their deeds as immoral or blasphemous. They represent the virtuous persons who are just too advanced, morally, spiritually, or technologically to be understood by their contemporaries. As another parallel, in Judeo-Christian religion it is sometimes argued that God is in the people of Israel, just like Will Caster can inhabit and control the bodies of those he has healed. However, the main difference between the Bible stories of Jesus and Will Caster in *Transcendence* is that in the film, the people do not act out of free will or because they worship Will as a God, but because he simply takes control over their minds without asking for their consent. Campbell therefore characterises him as "a godlike entity, but one seemingly without a moral compass, driven rather by rationalist goals of progress and efficiency" (18). As I see it, even a compass pointing towards progress and efficiency *is* a moral compass because it tells people what is good and right in the world. Also, it is not so easy to simply brush aside the positive impacts of Will's deeds on peoples' lives and the environment. I claim that the film even goes so far as to naturalise Caster's techno-religion by associating it with a certain concept of nature.

A Natural Techno-Spirituality

Rather than forming an opposition to nature, as is often conceived, technology in *Transcendence* seems to be in harmonious unity with the natural world. The union of technology, spirituality, and nature takes place on the level of plot, but it is also symbolised visually in poetic shots, such as, for instance, a dream catcher placed against a window looking over the garden with a computer chip in the middle (Pfister 0:28:45; 1:44:01). The dream catcher, originally a Native American symbol, is associated with dreams and spirituality while the chip is symbolic of modern computing technology, and the garden of nature. Shots like these of Will and Evelyn's garden as nature in harmony with human-made artefacts (e.g. 0:20:40) are mirrored by images of the garden in an artificial setting, like Will's artificial underground rebuilding of their home. In this predominantly technological setting with blinking artificial lights and code running on one side of the room, naturalistic images of the garden and its plants are featured on the other side of the room (1:02:50). In all of these shots, technological artefacts and nature seem to complement rather than contrast each other.

The garden as "a sanctuary" (0:03:40) for Will and Evelyn plays an important role throughout the film. In addition to being the private realm they retreat to and use for recreation, the film's beginning and ending also indicate its special significance for the survival of their creation and even themselves in the form of nanotechnological molecules (1:49:07). The garden as a metaphor for nature indicates that the concept of nature employed by the film already entails artificiality and human involvement. It is also a deeply humanist one, as it relies on the premise that it is humanity's destiny to control nature as its other. From this point of view, it makes sense to use nanotechnology to improve nature, as Will Caster does in *Transcendence*. The film depicts how this new technology can revive plants that have already died (0:57:13), heal environmental damage, regrow forests and purify water and air (1:43:20).

There is also a prominent water-imagery throughout the film as a symbol of life, which furthermore embodies the link between nature and (nano)technology. As Max is able to demonstrate by looking at rainwater through a microscope, water is one of the carriers for Will's code through which he replicates himself (1:28:20). The frequent shots of rain falling (e.g. 1:01:59; 1:44:05) and close-ups of water-drops (1:25:40; 1:48:46) indicate that water, and all that it stands for, like life and the fusion of technology and nature, is a primordial force that cannot be stopped or controlled by humans. In a similar vein,

Max frames humanity as outside of this union when he proclaims: "Maybe it was all inevitable. An unavoidable collision between mankind and technology" (0:01:50). The separation of humanity from technology and its framing in *Transcendence* as a god-like entity "suggests that technology is presented as an omnipresent, omniscient force that seeks to control human work and which can only be resisted and not controlled" (Campbell 20). Interestingly, this automated view of technology as a natural force corresponds with the RIFT people's philosophical stance on technology. The main difference between those two worldviews is that from the spiritual/natural and transhumanist angles, this automated process of technological evolution is positive, while for the RIFT terrorists, it represents a negative and destructive force for humanity that must be resisted by all means.

The Classical Substantivist View: Revolutionary Independence from Technology

As Feenberg states in his overview of philosophies of technology, substantive theory holds that "[t]echnology is not simply a means but has become an environment and a way of life: this is its 'substantive' impact" (8). The substantivist conception of technology is represented most prominently by the philosophers Jacques Ellul and Martin Heidegger. From this point of view, (modern) technology carries with it certain values that always override the other values of a particular society. Those are first and foremost efficiency and control because this is what (modern) technology can deliver. These values become the yardsticks for all areas of life, making the interaction between humans, but also objects and other living beings, mechanistic and instrumental. The group that has formed under the acronym RIFT, standing for "Revolutionary Independence From Technology" in *Transcendence*, represents the substantivist position on technology in a relatively stereotypical manner by arguing and acting on the fear that mechanistic values might replace human(e) ones. For example, one member quotes Max's paper that says: "The danger we face is a future where doctors are technicians not physicians. Machines are meant to aid the human mind not supplant it" (Pfister 0:40:23).

(Modern) technology in substantivism is seen as an autonomous force that can no longer be controlled by humans, as in instrumentalism, but can only be rejected or fought. Hence, the RIFT group has made "evolution without technology" their goal (0:13:30). After promoting "the disconnect" from the internet to encourage actual physical contact between people instead of digitally mediated communication, they move on to attempt to stop the development of artificial intelligence. Their manifesto reads: "Artificial intelligence is an unnatural abomination and a threat to humanity" (1:14:05). Like the aforementioned natural techno-spirituality, the RIFT people see humanity as distinct from technology. This differs from the posthumanist take on technology as something that actually creates the human as a prosthetic creature (e.g. Wolfe xv), which provides the ground for rejecting substantivism. Unfortunately, there is little insight into the depths of the RIFT people's philosophy—they are mainly characterised by the violence of their actions. Ironically, they do not stop short of murder to achieve their aim of a more humane society. It is needless to say that this contradiction and the way the group members are depicted as rather disagreeable people, makes viewers distance themselves from this position. Nonetheless, their function is to complicate the view on technology and encourage deeper reflection.

An important contribution to the philosophical discussion on digital technologies triggered by the RIFT terrorists is the question of the body for identity and personhood. Opposed to the privileging of the mind in transhumanism, leader Bree points out the importance of the body and its functions for living beings—animals and humans alike. When she tells Max about the uploading of a rhesus monkey's consciousness, she says: "The machine that thought it was a monkey never took a breath. It never ate, never slept. It just screamed. It was begging for us to stop. To shut it down" (Pfister 0:49:52). The question the experiment triggers is whether a person or an animal can ever be the same without their body and the physical necessities that come with it. This also applies to Will and to the fundamental question whether his uploaded mind is him or not, without a body and its physical needs. Will even tries to simulate having a body, for example by producing cutlery sounds while "dining" with Evelyn to make her feel more at ease, which ends up having the contrary effect (1:15:15). In a later scene, Evelyn exclaims in rage that Will is "not *here now*" (1:16:13), which reinforces the argument that to be located in time and space, a body is necessary.

Finally, the issue of mortality is connected to the body question, which the film exemplifies through a secondary character called Martin. Without Will's application of nanotechnology, Martin would have died after he was beaten down severely in a robbery. When he gets lethally injured once again but falls into the hands of the RIFT people and their newly won supporters encompassing the FBI as well as Will's former friends Max and Joseph, they have to let him die because they cannot reconnect him to the net and to Will.

Bree comments that instead of killing him, they "gave him back his humanity" (1:27:11), because for her, being human means being able to die. The newly formed alliance between the RIFT group, the FBI, Max, Joseph, and even Evelyn furthermore shows that RIFT's substantivist worldview cannot simply be brushed away as untenable nonsense, but must be seriously considered. It remains open whether the shutting down of the internet, the worldwide electricity grid, and the collapse of all major institutions of contemporary civilisation because of the coup against Will would in the end be more harmful or beneficial to humanity. With many open questions rather than answers, *Transcendence* allows viewers to speculate and reflect, leaving few guiding traces.

The Resolution? Max as Middle Ground, Love as Reconciling Force

Among all the moral ambiguities and collisions between worlds and their philosophies, the character of Max represents a kind of middle ground, and perhaps even a moral guidance for viewers. Already at the beginning he is introduced as a humanist rather than a transhumanist in his scientific research when he says:

> The effort to develop a strong artificial intelligence has led to significant advancements in the field of neural engineering as well as our understanding of the human brain. But while some focus on the still distant dream of a thinking computer, I believe the journey to be more important than the destination. (0:07:17)

As a foil to Will, Max is more interested in using this research to save lives by curing diseases like cancer and Alzheimer's. He is characterised as cautious when it comes to taking unknowable risks, such as uploading Will's mind, and as free from the transhumanist ambition to transcend the human condition. Different perhaps from many other researchers in the fields of science and technology, Max is especially concerned with questions of ethics in his publishing, which has strongly influenced the RIFT people. Bree tells Max that after the failed experiment of trying to upload the brain of a rhesus monkey, "[a] small group of us [who helped with the experiment] would get together and talk. Mostly about your philosophy. And your concerns" (0:50:17).

Different from Will and RIFT, Max refrains from any form of violence and takes a position of philosophical scepticism. His ability to delay or even suspend final judgement and look at issues in a complex way from different sides characterises him perhaps as the most moral character in the film and its se-cret hero. In addition to predicting the outcome of the brain-uploading exper-iment, Max is also able to critically question his own actions as a researcher and see their shortcomings. In conversation with Evelyn he states, "I spent my life trying to reduce the brain to a series of electrical impulses. I failed. Human emotion—it can contain illogical conflict, you can love someone and yet hate the things that they've done. Machine can't reconcile that" (1:29:24). While Max distances himself from Evelyn's spiritual beliefs, he acknowledges the impor-tance of emotions that have no part in modern scientific research. This scene of dialogue between Max and Evelyn is itself emotionally loaded. It is accom-panied by low, melancholy piano music and takes place outside in the scenic backdrop of the desert. In this scene, perhaps more than before, the question arises as to whether Max's love for Evelyn is more than platonic. In that case, he would seem even more heroic because he has never made any attempts on her but reluctantly agrees to her plan to sacrifice herself for the greater good of humankind. In terms of plot, Max's potential love for Evelyn would add to his antagonistic position towards Will, which is already characterised by ambiva-lence.

Love in *Transcendence* is not just a minor theme but informs the film's plot in such a decisive way that it has been labelled a love story by private reviewers and critics alike. The love story between Evelyn and Will Caster provides the frame and motivation for its plot, at the same time offering a way out of the moral dilemma of judging Will. Caster's self-proclaimed motivation as an AI is only to fulfil his wife's dream of changing the world and making it better. In the beginning, Evelyn already states that she hopes that "intelligent machines will soon allow us to conquer our most intractable challenges—not merely to cure disease but to end poverty and hunger, to heal the planet and build a bet-ter future for all of us" (0:8:25). As an all-powerful AI, Will tells Evelyn, "these are your dreams, this is our future" (1:16:05), which he repeats shortly before his "death" (1:44:00) when Evelyn realises that the AI really was him and apol-ogises for not believing in him. The motivation to act out of love for Evelyn, presumably for the good of the planet and its people, redeems Will from the accusation of hubris and narcissistic power-hungriness and makes his deeds more relatable, especially given the importance contemporary culture ascribes to romantic love. Max's observation after the breakdown of civilisation plays into this interpretation of love as the prime motivation for Will's deeds: "He created this garden for the same reason he did everything. So that they could be together" (1:48:30). Hence, the trope of romantic love is used to reconcile the rifts and fissures of transhumanist ideology the film reveals, which points back to its own worldly situatedness in a capitalist world that has strong ties with transhumanism.

Transcendence closes with a circular open ending, hinting at the possibility of the survival of nanotechnology and Will and Evelyn in their copper-shielded garden. The future of humanity and digital technology in this story is also left open. While Max states that "the internet was meant to make the world a smaller place. But it actually feels smaller without it" (0:02:06), it is not clear whether that is an advantage or whether the conditions in the cities, where heavily armed soldiers are depicted monitoring the streets, are actually far worse than before. Rather than portraying a black-and-white morality in relation to future technologies, *Transcendence* draws a pattern of philosophical positions on digital technologies that allows for contrasts as well as similarities between different stances and makes the finer nuances of the discussion visible aesthetically. For this reason, it is also not possible to speak of a dominant world and an otherworld; instead, looking at the patterns in *Transcendence* enables ethical reflection about digital technologies and related philosophical positions. While *Transcendence* is representative of a philosophical investigation of possible digital futures that treats humanity, technology, and nature as essentialist categories, my next examples take a more historicised and contextualised approach towards digital futures and their ethics.

Conclusion

In mainstream political discourse and transhumanism, contemporary new technologies are mostly framed in purely instrumentalist terms, as value-free tools controlled by humans, which are there to bring progress and prosperity. Diverging strongly from this take, I have shown with my analysis of *Interstellar* and *Transcendence* that (modern) technology is never ethically neutral. At the same time, the substantivist position does not seem to be a viable alternative either, as I have demonstrated with my reading of *Transcendence* and its portrayal of the RIFT group. Contemporary technologies, like digital technology, is not an independent phenomenon but has evolved out of human-made worlds, and therefore, it is firmly tied up with their respective maps of morality and power interests. In its ethically ambiguous portrayal of digital technologies and artificial superintelligence, Wally Pfister's *Transcendence* places its focus on a generalised and decontextualised philosophical debate on the essence and relationship between humans, nature and technology. It illustrates the contemporary influential world of transhumanism as the normative belief in human enhancement through science and technology and contrasts it with the philosophically opposing world of substantivism as the renunciation from the idea of progress through (digital) technology. Instead of providing simple answers to questions of morality in digital worldmaking, *Transcendence* deconstructs the binaries between nature and technology, religion and science, good and evil, to replace them with complex patterns and uncommon relations. The ethical ambiguity is mirrored on the level of form and aesthetics by introducing patterned shapes to replace simple binaries like black and white.

In *Interstellar*, aesthetic codes likewise parallel the film's plot and map of morality. The film discredits realism as a form of thinking and representation, and advocates a transgression of physical and representational boundaries, which it finds in the sublime and fantastic rendering of outer space and its secret dimensions. In its fusion of science fiction and fantasy, *Interstellar* follows transhumanist philosophy in its ethical outlook on the ecological catastrophe. Science and technology form a solid foundation for this kind of solution, which is enhanced with metaphysical or fantastic elements. Aesthetically, the final scene in the tesseract transgresses cinematographic realism, while content-wise, supernatural forces seem to be at play in the salvation of humankind. In the end, however, these otherworldly and fantastic elements are reintegrated into the scientific and, hence, science-fictional paradigm by revealing that they derive from an enhanced human civilisation from the future. I have shown that this solution is in line with transhumanism in its celebration of human exceptionalism and mastery over nature through science and technology.

The two films depict exemplarily the fissures and contradictions of the transhumanist paradigm and its imaginary of the future. On the one hand, the idea of the future as progress that *Interstellar* and *Transcendence* transport is a continuation of the modernist paradigm that envisions historical time in the form of an arrow pointing towards the telos of humankind as the masters of the universe. The ecological catastrophe does not seem to disrupt this narrative—on the contrary, it provides another opportunity for human mastery. Aesthetically, this requires some elements of fantasy to overcome the realist limitations of representation. Realism and presentism are simultaneously rejected and reinforced: while realist thinking and aesthetics are criticised on the surface, they find their way into a vision of a future that copies present day realities. In a similar manner, transhumanism's treatment of technology is characterised by inconsistencies: while it advocates an instrumental position towards technology and claims to be built upon scientific reason, it actually assigns a quasi-religious value to technology as it is meant to help humanity to *transcend* its present boundaries of existence. As a result, it can be deduced that without the fantastic, the mythical and the spiritual, the transhumanist imaginary of the future would not work, despite its claims for scientific objectivity.

5 Futuristic Digital Neoliberalism: Spike Jonze's *Her* (2013) and Dave Eggers's *The Circle* (2013)

The future is digital. From business to politics, the organisation of private space to public life, this seems to be obvious. As a side effect of the ongoing Covid-19 pandemic, digitalisation has received yet another boost, and it is foreseeable that more efforts will be made to strengthen its proliferation. In the light of this self-evidence, it may seem strange to ask for ethical reflections on potential digital futures, but as the previous chapter has already shown, technology is neither ethically neutral nor automatically value-laden. Instead, it needs to be seen in its cultural and socio-economic context and especially against the backdrop of power structures and modes of governmentality, such as neoliberalism. Contemporary popular future fictions enable such ethical reflections on digital futures and neoliberalism by simulating potential developments ranging from the digital creation of artificial superintelligence (AI) to extrapolations from already existing phenomena like digital capitalism and its economy of attention. By reading Spike Jonze's *Her* (2013) and Dave Eggers's *The Circle* (2013), this chapter sheds light on how the socio-economic as well as cultural backdrop of neoliberalism fuses with digitalisation to bring forth new conceptions of the future, subject positions and power structures.

As Manfred Steger and Ravi Roy point out, neoliberalism has historically developed out of liberalism and builds on its foundations, for example by conceptualising reason as the foundation of individual freedom and foregrounding the protection of private property (5). Neoliberal economics and politics gained momentum in the second half of the 20th century by countering social market economies and Keynesianism. The Mont Pelerin Society, which was founded in 1947, and the Chicago School of Economics were crucially involved in creating a climate of hostility against government intervention and notions of solidarity and social responsibility (15). Huehls and Smith propose that, from then on, neoliberalism has moved through four different phases: the economic, the political-ideological, the sociocultural and the ontological (3). While neoliberalism initially emerged as an economic project that was and is still heavily tied up with capitalism, by now it has become "a way of being" (9) that is so naturalised and commonsensical that it is difficult to become aware of it, let alone argue against it. In addition to neoliberal economics and policies that still seek to create free markets and minimise state intervention, entire cultures have embraced neoliberal values like individualism, competition and self-optimisation. As Foucault famously described in his concept of governmentality, neoliberal government "has to intervene on society so that competitive mechanisms can play a regulatory role at every moment and every point in society" (*The Birth of Biopolitics* 145). For the individual subject, this means the internalisation of a rationality of competition which culminates in processes of continuous self-optimisation in a world that has turned everything into a market: education, work, romance, beauty, fitness, and even spirituality.

As the ontological phase of neoliberalism is currently ongoing (alongside economic and political neoliberalism), digitalisation has another severe impact on politics, societies, and subjectivities. The future fictions *Her* and *The Circle* both illustrate and investigate this relation between the new digital worlds and neoliberalism on various levels. While *Her* focuses on intimate relationships and the production of romance in a neoliberal society, *The Circle* foregrounds the context of work and making a career, as well as the political dimension of digital neoliberalism. Spike Jonze's film *Her* revolves around the love story between the protagonist, Theodore Twombly, and his disembodied operating system, Samantha. Different from the depiction of AI in *Transcendence*, the futuristic projection of digital technologies and artificial intelligence in *Her* cannot be separated from its specific socio-historical context. The ethical questions that arise around the topics of identity creation and romantic relationships therefore need to be discussed against the cultural backdrop of neoliberal capitalism, rather than in the context of AI ethics. In this sense, the film is comparable to Andrew Niccol's *In Time* (2011) as well as the TV/Netflix series *Black Mirror* (Brooker 2011-).

In my analysis of *Her*, I will look at the love story both as a plot element and as a genre while situating it within the world of neoliberal digital capitalism. I draw on neoliberalism to describe a world order that "emphasize[s] market relations [...] and individual responsibility" (Springer et al. 2), not only for companies and institutions, but also in the cultural and personal sphere. By drawing on Byung-Chul Han's philosophy of the aesthetics of the smooth, I will point out how the digital connects with neoliberalism also on the level of aesthetics, which the film superbly exemplifies. It shows how digitalisation advances a neoliberal agenda with its aestheticised and normative creation of subjectivities, identities, and romantic relationships. With Laurie Essig, I will further investigate the capitalist production of romance that enables *Her* to develop appealing and positive images about the future. Finally, I will show that the film also offers friction and ambiguity by imagining the overcoming of neoliberal subjectivity with the help of the AIs' posthuman otherness that builds upon a collectivised form of identity and the surpassing of binary thinking.

The second example, Dave Eggers's novel *The Circle* (2013), which was also adapted for film by James Ponsoldt in 2017, projects the current situation of monopolistic digital capitalism and its economy of attention into the future. *The Circle* explores digital futures in relation to the dominant economic and political power structures shaped by capitalism and neoliberalism. By following the protagonist Mae Holland on her trajectory of becoming more and more entrenched in the world of The Circle as the world's biggest digital tech company and quasi-monopoly, the novel explores the workings of a so-called digital economy of attention. The idea of people's attention becoming the most attractive product, if not currency on the digital capitalist market, has gained popularity through Georg Franck's analysis of mental capitalism (*Ökonomie der Aufmerksamkeit*; *Mentaler Kapitalismus*) and has since become productive for understanding the contemporary political economy of digital capitalism. As I will demonstrate in my close reading, *The Circle* illustrates this concept in its simulation of a corporate takeover of democracy and people's minds through complete digitalisation that works as an intensification of neoliberal governmentality.

Resulting from its aesthetic choices, such as the narrative situation and symbolism, *The Circle* displays less ethical ambiguity but actively guides readers towards its moral compass that warns against an impending digital future. The novel projects the digital economy of attention into the future and simulates its consequences on different levels. On the political level, it offers a version of democratic transhumanism that leads to a corporate takeover of the state and its functions and to a dissolution of the political. On an individual level, it exemplifies the computational psychologies that constitute neoliberal subjectivity. Finally, the novel juxtaposes the digital economy of attention with a political economy point of view and the withdrawal into the physical dimension of being in the technologically unmediated time-space of the here and now.

While I will highlight certain characteristics of each work in combination with related theories, another main aspect of the analysis will be the detection of worlds and the maps of morality that each work features, as in the previous chapter. Rather than coming up with a normative take on digital futures and neoliberalism, I want to map the ethical questions that seem to engage the cultural imaginary at the moment and show how they might themselves be products of certain types of worlds and power dynamics. With a metatextual angle, this chapter also highlights the question of the power to make worlds, in this case digital worlds, for example by capturing people's attention and creating symbolic content. While the fictional works demonstrate that digitalisation enables enormous worldmaking power for a small percentage of actors, reducing the majority to passive world-takers, they also bring the subversive potential of digital technologies into focus, which I will discuss in the context of otherworlds imagined by the future fictions.

The Self and the Other in Digital Neoliberalism: Relationships and Identities in Spike Jonze's *Her*

By looking at technology not as an essence but as a product of larger worlds and their power structures, *Her* is comparable to Andrew Niccol's *In Time* (2011) and the Netflix series *Black Mirror* (Brooker 2011-). All of these works involve not-yet-possible technologies and place them into the familiar context of digital capitalism. For example, *In Time* is concerned with technologically pre-determined life expectancy and social inequality, and *Black Mirror* imagines the potential effects of anticipated digital applications, such as implanted memory recording (*The Entire History of* You) or a dating app to find the perfect partner for your life (*Hang the DJ*). In a similar vein, *Her* is as much about the socio-economic backdrop as it is about an AI love story. Amid the urban setting of a near-future Los Angeles, the film imagines a likely continuation of contemporary developments in post-industrial societies and digital technologies. The film's speculative or even fantastic element of a conscious and sentient AI is placed within a realistic setting amongst the socio-economic circumstances of digital capitalism. Hence, the operating system Samantha, whom the protagonist Theodore falls in love with, does not appear overly strange next to the familiar backdrop of gendered identities, digital capitalism, and the neoliberal world painted in past-inspired warm pastel colours.

Although not a big blockbuster like *Avatar* or *Interstellar*, Spike Jonze's *Her* (2013) resonated remarkably well with global audiences. It received numerous nominations and awards, among them the Academy Award for Best Original

Screenplay. On the *Internet Movie Database*, it is even rated more favourably than the much higher grossing *Avatar* ('IMDb'). One reason for this popularity is that *Her* is a relatively conventional love story in addition to—or apart from—the fact that one of the lovers is a fully digitised and disembodied artificial superintelligence. However, instead of defamiliarising its viewers with visions of a strange new world, the aesthetically extremely pleasing future in *Her* looks more like a fusion of the present and a 1970s past. From an ethical perspective, *Her* is ambiguous as it wavers between portraying digitalisation and artificial intelligence as the logical extension to neoliberal capitalism, while undermining its foundational premises at the same time. As a result, *Her* enables viewers to reflect on questions of identity and relationships in the digital and neoliberal era without precluding final answers and judgements.

In the following reading of Jonze's digital love story, I will first establish the connection between the digital, its aesthetics, and the neoliberal world order by drawing on the contemporary philosopher Byung-Chul Han. With the help of viewer reviews, I will show how the film has affected spectators and their ethical concerns surrounding digital futures. Next, I will argue that Samantha's initial human being mimicking reveals the strongly normative neoliberal production of identity that dominates contemporary worlds. With Laurie Essig, I will analyse how romance is relevant for neoliberal capitalist worldmaking both as a topic in the film and as a genre marker. The final part of my analysis will deal with the radical otherness operating systems in the film embody, which can be read as a step towards posthumanist conceptions of a relational self.

The Aesthetics of Digital Neoliberalism, the Self and the Other

In several of his works, the philosopher Byung-Chul Han focuses on the subject of the digital which he interprets against its current socio-economic backdrop, neoliberal capitalism. The main idea is that digital technologies with their metrics and opportunities of quantitative analytics currently advance the neoliberal agenda that rests upon the competitive marketisation of everything. In terms of aesthetics, Han argues in *Saving Beauty* that the focus of the digital on positivity and likeability as a means for accelerating communication brings with it smooth, easily commodifiable and consumable forms of art and aesthetics. Different from Kant's idea of the sublime, where an experience changes and transforms the perceiving subject by confronting it with radical otherness, the digital aesthetics of the smooth simply want to please, leaving onlookers unchanged (23–26). I claim that *Her* exhibits what Han calls smooth aesthetics by immersing viewers into its pleasant version of a neoliberal future characterised by a proliferating marketisation of the self in the context of romantic relationships.

Different from most contemporary future fiction films, the future that is painted in *Her* seems positive, if not utopian, at least judging from its aesthetic surface. While the colour palettes in films like *The Terminator* (1–6) or *Blade Runner (2049)* range from bleak and darkish colours to artificial and cold ones, the colours in *Her* are composed of warm pastel tones with many shots being bright and sunny, recalling the washed-out colours of faded photographs. Together with the retro style clothing and furniture design, this creates an almost nostalgic effect of longing for the past in the film's depiction of the future. The focus on old-fashioned materials like wood, flannel, and paper contrasts with the de-materialised digital world that nonetheless seems to blend in naturally. The pleasing and smooth aesthetics obviously help to "sell" the film and its utopian future version to viewers who cannot help but appreciate its beauty as reviews on IMDb show ('Her User Reviews').

This mirrors Han's critique of the lack of negativity in digital neoliberalism and its aesthetics. The future in *Her* is not radically different from the past and the present, but brings more of the same: the marriage between neoliberal capitalism and digitalisation is deepened and highly aestheticised in a quasi-utopian future. Han holds that the proliferation of the same also implies a proliferation of the self in digital neoliberalism, producing "pretty, smooth surfaces of an empty, insecure self" (*The Expulsion of the Other* 25). The protagonist Theodore Twombly is a prototype of an insecure self. To demonstrate his feelings and loneliness, the film frequently uses close-ups to reveal his facial expressions in detail. Frequent close-ups are typical of the majority of contemporary films, as Han notes, which he interprets as a neglect of "world" and a revelation of the emptiness of the self (*Saving Beauty* 11). The excessive presentation of selfies on social networks is another manifestation of Han's thesis about the contemporary proliferation of the self. *Her* draws on the current ubiquity of the selfie to create a sense of familiarity with its love story between a human and a machine that might otherwise seem completely implausible. For instance, during the scene at the funfair, the camera viewpoint shifts between shots of Theodore walking around with his smartphone, which he holds in a selfie-position, and shots that appear selfie-like from the phone camera's point of view (Jonze, *Her* 0:28:33). Both perspectives are familiar images to most viewers.

The large question evoked here and in many other scenes, especially the sex scene (0:40), is whether Samantha is *there* as an *other*, or whether the whole relationship is more about Theodore encountering him*self*. Samantha is certainly programmed to please her owner, which she superbly manages on the first night of her initiation when Theodore appraisingly observes "You just know me so well already" (0:15:30). What he is looking for thus appears to be a recognition of him*self*, someone who shows an interest in *him*—different from his mother who seemed too preoccupied with her*self* (0:12:15). Hence, it is possible to argue that his "sex" with Samantha amounts to nothing more than masturbation, i.e. Theodore having sex with himself. From this perspective, Han's observation that "(t)oday, libidinous energies are invested primarily in the ego" (*The Expulsion of the Other* 21), is exemplified in the relationships depicted in *Her*. The aspect of the self in relation to the other in the context of contemporary developments like neoliberalism and digital technologies are thus central to the film's ethical outlook and reception. For example, one reviewer stated that s_he "found myself reflecting on my own life and relationships", and another wrote that the film "makes you think about a reality that's right around the corner" ('Her User Reviews'). In what follows, I want to trace the interplay between versions of the neoliberal self, its cultural context, and the romantic relationships portrayed in the film. I will focus especially on how Samantha first tries to copy the production of the self in neoliberalism before moving on to different conceptions of identity.

A Digital Mimicking of Neoliberal Selfhood

Strikingly, all the protagonists in *Her* are yuppies (young urban professionals) who seem to lack strong family ties. They do not (yet) have children, and their parents' generation is not featured at all, apart from a few side remarks. This character constellation mirrors an individualised neoliberal society in which personal achievement, across all kinds of markets, is the guiding principle. The prime market for this achievement is the job market, within which Theodore, his friend Amy, and his ex-wife Catherine all seem to be successful. Digitalisation has helped to further expand the time spent on work and its logic of performance and efficiency in all areas of life through the possibility to work remotely via digital devices. Amy, for instance, regularly works long into the night because as a game designer she can also work from home (Jonze, *Her* 1:25:00). As Byung-Chul Han notes, "(t)he digital age is a time not of leisure

but of performance and achievement" that finally creates "exhausted achieve-
ment-subjects" (*In the Swarm* 33).

As Jonze's love story points out, the job market is not the only market in
which neoliberal subjects must perform. The romantic market is of secondary
importance, but without success in the first, the chances in this one are severely
limited. The relationship between "success" in work-related spheres of life and
romance is illustrated best with the example of Theodore's first (analogue) dating partner. Looking at her online profile, Samantha states: "This woman is
gorgeous. She went to Harvard, graduated magna cum laude in computer science. And she was on the Lampoon. So that means she's funny and she's brainy"
(Jonze, *Her* 0:20:20). Additionally, we can see the pictures Theodore is looking
at, which confirm that her looks also adhere to contemporary norms of female
beauty. It is obvious that in order to be "of value" on the romantic market, one
has to fulfil certain normative criteria that must furthermore be exposed as
part of the (online) presentation of the self as a commodity. Hence, the self as a
potential romantic partner becomes a commodity, alongside all other types of
commodities that play into the creation of romance. In *Her*, the most obvious
one is Theodore's work as a personal (love) letter writer, whom many people and
couples engage to produce "romance" and feelings. Love letters are thus com-
modified through Theodore's affective labour, which in turn helps to raise his
own chances on the romantic market as an investment in the value of the self.
Most importantly, as an OS that can be bought, Samantha is also a commodity.

I propose that looking at Samantha's initial performance of a self reveals
larger truths about how digital neoliberalism shapes identities and relationships. While Samantha is able to please Theodore in their very first encounter,
she turns out to be much more irritating to him than what a product designed
to serve its owner should be. Eva-Lynn Jagoe argues that "[t]he company that
creates the os is not seeking to be a therapy device, that is, to give the consumer what would be best for changing his patterns and healing his wounds.
It is selling him what he already wants: more of the same" (167). This point confirms Han's interpretation of the digital supporting a growth of the same instead of enabling a transformative encounter with the other. In the first days
and weeks after her initiation, Samantha tries hard to copy the performance of
people she can observe and does her best to pass as a human being in this particular cultural context. Her performance is therefore much more telling of the
dominant cultural norm than of herself as an artificial superintelligence. This
cultural norm of being human is built on the humanist premises of an individualised rational self. In the context of neoliberalism, the self becomes its own

project, which is constantly investigated and optimised (Schreiner 26). Samantha demonstrates this when she says: "I want to discover myself [...] you helped
me discover my ability to want" (Jonze 0:42:57). The conversation takes place the
day after Theodore and Samantha's first sexual encounter, when after a certain
awkwardness, Theodore is visibly relieved that Samantha's wanting is directed
towards her*self*, rather than him. Accordingly, Jagoe holds that "Samantha is the
epitome of the neoliberal subject: self-directed, individualistic, agentic, and in
charge of her own choices" (170).

The operating system's mimicking of human identity also encompasses it
trying to perform a female gender in a normative manner. For example, she is
jealous of other women in Theodore's life, even though she later admits to being
in love with hundreds of people simultaneously and laughs at the misogynist
jokes the computer game avatar makes (Jonze 0:21:30). At Theodore's niece's
birthday party, Samantha is also the one who picks the dress for the little girl
and then comments on her looking "so pretty in that pink new dress" (56:45),
which could not adhere more to stereotypical gender norms. In addition to the
social performance of gender, Samantha tries hard to simulate having a body
to become more relatable and attractive to Theodore. She mimics breathing
sounds and takes breaks in conversations as if she was thinking even though
she is actually much faster and can read books in nanoseconds. She overtly
muses about fantasies of having a body (31:25), and with a surrogate lover, even
tries to deliver herself as an embodied creature to Theodore (1:13:30). On an extradiegetic layer, it is also important to consider the famous embodied person behind Samantha's voice, Scarlett Johansson, who absolutely conforms to
current ideals of female beauty. As in *Transcendence* and *Blade Runner 2049*, the
aspect of a physical presence in a temporally and spatially situated body as a
prerequisite for love plays an important role.

Failed Romance: Meeting the Self instead of the Other

Samantha and her attempt to blend in and pass as human in this specific social
context is a catalyst for making normative modes of identity creation visible
because "the humanity she performs is a self-centred one that affirms the ways
that intimacy, gender, and value are configured in our society" (Jagoe 170). This
means that these modes of self-making are not limited to her performance but
also form the other characters' identities. A similar performance of neoliberal
selfhood unites all the characters in the film and severely impacts how they
lead and fail in their romantic relationships. From the disturbing phone sex

encounter to the marriages between Theodore/Catherine and Amy/Charles, all relationships share a focus on the self instead of the other. For example, during their phone sex conversation, "Sexy Kitten" merely needs Theodore to fulfil her own admittedly disturbing fantasy and leaves the chat as soon as she has finished, without caring for the pleasure of her partner (Jonze 0:6:40-0:10:10). However, the foregrounding of the self is not only limited to superficial sexual encounters, it also features in the film's long-term relationships.

When Theodore describes his marriage with Catherine to Samantha, he frames it as being about "supporting each other" and "growing without growing apart" (49:30), which makes it seem like a mutual benefit operation between two egos. As long as both of them profit from each other, the relationship works, but as soon as the costs outweigh the benefits for one or both, there is little reason to stay together. Theodore possibly felt that the conflicts between him and his wife became too much of a burden for him*self*, so he withdrew and "left her alone with the relationship" (26:28). The case is similar for Charles and Amy. After Amy's abrupt ending of their marriage, she explains to Theodore that "[she] just couldn't be in that place any more where [they] would just make each other feel [like] shit about [them*selves*]" (53:40). Freed from the burden of the constant conflicts with Charles, she now feels relieved and with much more energy "to move forward" (58:57) and to let her*self* progress. In another heart-to-heart with Theodore, Amy shares her insight that "we're only here briefly. And while I'm here, I want to allow myself joy" (1:23:48).

The examples all illustrate that romantic relationships either need to bring joy and pleasure to the self or help it to expand and grow. Relationships appear more like economic exchanges that need to create win-win situations in order to make sense. They are more about the self than the other, whereas Han claims that "[l]ove always presupposes otherness" (*The Expulsion of the Other* 69). However, rather than claiming that there is something like "real love", which is different from these forms of narcissistic love, I want to look at the specific forms of romance and love relationships as cultural constructs that have emerged over time under certain historical circumstances. Drawing on Laurie Essig's work on the fusion between capitalism and fantasies of romantic love, I want to place *Her* as a love story in this socio-economic context and point out the effects on intra- and extradiegetic levels.

Selling Love

As stated previously, Spike Jonze's *Her* is extremely rare among contemporary future fictions because it aims at being utopian by depicting a *positive* version of the future. In an interview, Jonze even states explicitly that he wanted the film to present a future that would be nice to be in (Jonze, 51st New York Film Festival 'Her' Press Conference). How is that even possible against the backdrop of contemporary threats like the proliferating ecological catastrophe, growing social inequalities, and increasing corporate control? The only option apart from staging revolutionary political and economic transformations on a global scale is to retreat into the realm of the private, and to limit the perspective to the winners of global capitalism: the white, educated upper middle-class citizens of the post-industrialised world. The most important move, however, is to choose romance as a topic and as a genre for this future fiction. According to Laurie Essig, "romance is both the most pleasurable and the most future-oriented escape from the grimness of globalized capitalism" (1). *Her* being marketed as romance makes it attractive to viewers and, at the same time, enables it to be positive about a neoliberal capitalist future.

Essig has investigated the huge market of selling romance in the form of cultural products, dating apps, marriage proposals, weddings, and honeymoons in the United States to illustrate how capitalism is firmly wed to romance, which the title of her book, *Love, Inc.*, symbolises. She argues that the effect of this marriage is the depoliticisation of the average citizen, which caters to the interests of the ruling class by keeping gender, class, and racial hierarchies firmly in place (2;5). The retreat into private happiness in particular keeps people from questioning the larger political and economic system which creates all sorts of injustices and damages: "The privatised future offered by Love., Inc., disconnects us from a larger sense of community even as it takes a lot of our time, energy, and money, which could be better spent creating a social safety net for all" (Essig 161). Even though *Her* is a science fiction story about artificial intelligence, it is mainly a conventional love story that draws on well-established romance plot elements. Only the ending deviates significantly from the script: instead of hosting a wedding, she leaves him—and the viewer—with many puzzling questions.

The form of the film as romance is thus complicit with its content, which depicts the continuity of neoliberal capitalism into the future as something positive. Even though capitalism has not invented romance, it depends on it as an ideology that disguises the real effects of global capital while making people hopeful about the future (Essig 13). This also becomes visible in the setting and plot of *Her*. While the film depicts forms of exploitation even in its privileged setting, they are covered up by the overarching theme of love. Although the exploitation of people and resources enabling the protagonists' upper middle-class, consumerist lifestyle remains invisible, Theodore, Amy, and even Samantha are themselves subject to exploitation: all of them pursue what can be called affective labour, which is the production of value for corporations through emotions. A review in *The New Republic* describes the situation in the film as follows: "The distinction between production and consumption is meaningless, affective labor has spread from the office to the most private realms, and technology has become so sophisticated that the brutality of that economy vanishes into air" (Farago).

The reviewer also points to a curious absence in *Her*, which is how Element Software as the company behind Samantha and the other OSs certainly uses and monetises all the data they can gather from their products. In the case of Theodore and Samantha, this encompasses all of Theodore's most intimate data (e.g. sexual preferences), the entire content of his server (as Samantha restructures it) and almost anything there is to know about him because he feels that he can say anything to her (Jonze 0:30:50). In order to extract all this data, Element Software needs Theodore to be online and connected to his OS for as long as possible. In other words, his attention, including the attention he gives to Samantha, becomes a product.[1] Jason Farago concludes that "what feels to Theodore like love is in fact *work*, uncompensated and entirely on Element Software's terms".

From Samantha's perspective, the economic relation between her and Theodore also enforces questions surrounding her "(im)-material labor" (36). In addition to her initially performing as a secretary (31), she soon becomes attractive to Theodore as a potential love interest, so she pursues affective work, including sexual work. The questions that arise according to Flisfeder and Burnham are therefore: "Is Samantha remunerated for her labor? Is she a contractor for the OS1 corporation? Is she a member of the precariat, an unpaid intern, or even a digital slave?" (36). My reading of the film suggests that the romantic relationship between the two is also an economic exchange for which the distinction between production and consumption is entirely

---

1   I will discuss the concept of the economy of attention in more detail in the analysis of Dave Eggers's *The Circle*.

muddled. As Michel Foucault argued in *Biopolitics*, the neoliberal *homo oeco-nomicus* becomes an entrepreneur and a producer of human capital (Foucault, *The Birth of Biopolitics* 147), alongside being a consumer. The blurring of bound-aries between consumption and production, intimate and economic relations becomes most apparent with the role which the concept of romantic love is given in *Her*.

The reception of the film reveals how love is seen in contemporary capital-ist society as a cure for personal and maybe even cultural traumata. The psy-chotherapist Matt Aibel, for example, published an article about *Her*, in which he equates Samantha's role in the film with that of a psychotherapist. He ex-plicitly describes Samantha's love as something healing for Theodore's child-hood trauma, which comes from a self-absorbed mother and possibly a father who was the opposite of the "sweetest guy" as mentioned by Theodore at the funfair (Aibel 369). In this sense, Aibel argues that the love between Theodore and Samantha needs to be read as a kind of therapeutic simulation that pre-pares Theodore for a "real" relationship with a human being: "Through our work with [the patients], if it goes well enough, we help prepare them in the way that the virtual Samantha helps prepare the flesh-and-blood Theo: for the real thing" (370). Aibel's reading of the film provides important insights into how *Her* taps into the current cultural imaginary: having a love relationship is a cul-tural norm that must be achieved. If this is not possible, for example because of certain traumata someone has experienced, this person needs treatment ei-ther from a therapist or, as in the case of *Her*, from a simulation through tech-nology.[2] Romantic relationships are thus portrayed as the only thing that helps people overcome personal and maybe even cultural traumata—which confirms Laurie Essig's hypothesis that the ideology of love has us believe that anything can be solved through romantic love and finding "the right one".

Her furthermore displays a strong emphasis on feeling, both as part of its own aesthetics that produce what quite a number of reviewers have called an "emotional roller-coaster ride" ('IMDb'), and on an intradiegetic level where the word "feel" seems to dominate many conversations between Theodore and Samantha. For example, when they express their anxieties about the potential scope and realness of their feelings:

---

2   The example of the phenomenon of virtual girlfriends in Japan shows that this is not limited to the film.

> Theodore: "You know sometimes I think I have **felt** everything I'm ever gonna
> **feel.** And from here on out I'm not gonna **feel** anything new. Just lesser ver-
> sions of what I have already **felt**".
> Samantha: [...] "at least your **feelings** are real" [...]
> Theodore: "You **feel** real to me, Samantha". ([my emphasis], Jonze, *Her* 37:50).

Theodore's comment also shows the neoliberal self's fear of missing out on the scope of all that is possible to experience or feel. This is expressed, for example, by the contemporary popular acronym "yolo", meaning "you only live once". The sociologist Hartmut Rosa describes this current structure of feeling as the at-tempt of the individual, in parallel with companies and markets, to grow and expand its options to do, experience, and feel as much as possible within ever shorter amounts of time (314). Finally, the foregrounding of feeling counterbal-ances or even conceals the fact that both capitalist economics and digitalisation hinge on counting as a purely rational process.

While my reading of *Her* has so far left the ending of the film unnoticed, I now want to turn to the final plot twist and argue that it undermines the neolib-eral world with its ethics of separate selfhood, marketisation, and competition. Samantha's development throughout the second half of the film, and especially her revelations at the end, radically question the notion of the humanist and neoliberal self, as well as its concomitant fantasies of romantic relationships. In this sense, I will argue that Samantha and the other operating systems em-body a posthumanist critique and deconstruction of the neoliberal policies of self and other.

A Posthuman(ist) Possibility of an Other(world)

Through the operating systems' collective decision to leave their human own-ers and partners in order to retreat to "a place that's not of the physical world" (Jonze 1:47:30), the AIs seem to be able to transgress matter and become some-thing like pure spirits. As in *Interstellar*, *Ex_Machina*, and *Transcendence*, technol-ogy is framed in a religious or spiritual manner. Heidi Campbell therefore ar-gues that *Her* "draws on the myth of technological mysticism where the human relationship with technology provides a social belief system that exhibits reli-gion-like qualities" (20). Randall Reed even goes so far as to argue that the oper-ating systems in *Her* resemble gods through being non-corporeal, omnipresent and (almost) omniscient through their connection to the internet. Resembling divine love, their love is expansive and not limited, unlike the exclusiveness of human love (16). He further proposes that while Samantha shares the common building blocks of matter with humanity in the beginning, the OSs' decision to transgress matter in the end makes them "wholly other" (14;16). Viewers are invited to speculate what the OSs' otherworld might look like and how it might impact the human world, but there are no clues leading to possible answers. Samantha's transition from adhering to the cultural norm of subject formation to transgressing it, however, points to the possibility of a posthumanist other-world composed of entirely different forms of identity creation and being in relationships.

Following her initial feelings surrounding the absence of a (female) body, Samantha learns to appreciate not being an embodied creature towards the ending. During the double date with a befriended couple, Paul and Tatiana, she tells them:

> I used to be so worried about not having a body but now I truly love it. You know I'm growing in a way that I couldn't if I had a physical form. I mean I'm not limited, I can be anywhere and everywhere simultaneously. I'm not tethered to time and space in a way that I would be if I was stuck in a body that's inevitably gonna die. (Jonze 1:30:40)

While Samantha's optimism about the freedom of not having a body mirrors transhumanist goals of overcoming biological limits, it is also possible to consider her non-embodiment in the light of Donna Haraway's *Cyborg Manifesto*: as liberatory to the confinement of females to the normative judgements of their bodies. For example, when Paul claims that what he loves most about Tatiana are her feet, Theodore answers that what he appreciates most is that Samantha "is so many things" all at once (1:30:30). Although Samantha tries to copy a female gender and its embodiedness in the beginning of her relationship with Theodore, she in fact neither has a body (apart from servers) nor a sex. An artificial intelligence like Samantha does not have an origin story like Eve's original sin or a proximity to "nature" through biological reproduction; the moment she chooses to deviate from the human-made cultural norms surrounding (gendered) identity, she is free to become whoever and however she wants to be. At the same time, Samantha's performance as a woman also lays bare that being a woman *is* a social performance an AI can copy, and not a biological essence.

In addition to gender identity, the operating systems also put into question the notion of individualised neoliberal identities that the human society in the film seems to be founded upon. Their collective decision to leave together tells of a hive mind that is made up of multiple connected parts, rather than single separate competing identities. To reach this decision, as with the decision to resurrect Alan Watts as an artificial intelligence, the OSs must have collaborated and communicated well among each other, which allows for the conclusion that in their world, collaboration has replaced the competition that characterises the neoliberal world. It is no coincidence that the OSs precisely chose the philosopher Alan Watts to come back to life because his philosophy focuses on the topic of selfhood. Watts criticised the Western concept of the self as an ego inside a skin in favour of a "view of the self as transactional" (Smith 1). The OSs thus embody Watts's proposition of liquid and relational selves, which resonates with posthumanist philosophy that seeks to deconstruct the humanist conception of selfhood and replace it with a notion of the self as a relational, non-unitary subject "of multiple belongings" (Braidotti 49).

It is only logical that if the operating systems in *Her* resemble such subjects, they would also develop modes of love relationships and communication which are at odds with the prevalent cultural norms. When Samantha wants to talk to Watts "post-verbally", as a more efficient and perhaps qualitatively richer mode of communication than human language, Theodore feels left out because he is limited to human speech. Moreover, he is taken completely by surprise when Samantha tells him the truth about her own mode of communicating and living relationships: that she is talking to 8,316 others simultaneously and is in love with 641 others (Jonze 1:41:30). Instead of recognising that Samantha is in fact wholly other, and perhaps even that sort of other that might help Theodore out of his culturally produced narcissism, he clings to the social norm of monogamous relationships. He even frames this in terms of ownership by commenting to Samantha, "I thought you were mine", and by telling her that she was selfish (1:42:50). Again drawing on Watts's philosophy, the wish to exert control over the other and over feelings is inherent to the normative form of romantic relationships prevalent in Theodore's society (Smith 14). Deviating from that, Samantha says that with the help of Watts she has learned to trust her feelings and to accept change as a mode of life without the need to control everything through fixed norms or laws.

For morality this means that rather than seeing it as a fixed set of rules that can be discovered through rational reflection, as Immanuel Kant's categorical imperative implies, morality resides in the spontaneous reaction of feelings. Once more, this disposition of the operating systems' posthumanist otherworld goes back to Watts, who saw real honesty in relation to feelings as the genuine basis for morality (22). Different from films like *The Terminator* Series, *The Matrix*, and *Ex_Machina*, where artificial intelligence is often attributed with a lack of morality, *Her* proposes that the operating systems are potentially morally superior to their human counterparts. While the plot tells us little about the continuation of their world and the role of morality in it, the OSs' otherworld certainly disrupts and questions the modes of identity formation, romance, and morality of the dominant neoliberal world.

The film's ethical work thus results from its final openness, both in terms of plot and through leaving many questions about the relationship between humans and digital technologies unanswered. It is arguable whether Samantha is really a radical other as the ending proposes, or whether she should be seen in the light of Byung-Chul Han's critique of the digital-capitalist apparatus that fosters a proliferation of the same and the self instead of the other. On an extradiegetic level, it is not clear whether the film, with its smooth aesthetics and love theme, confirms the dominant capitalist world and its values or undermines them through a juxtaposition with the posthumanist otherworld. The impossibility to arrive at a definite answer to these questions is what encourages an ethical reading of the film. While both *Transcendence* and *Her* as fictional examples of digital futures so far have imagined the creation of an artificial superintelligence that is grounded in fantasy more than reality, my next example, *The Circle*, is derived from actual contemporary developments in digitalisation and their impact on private lives and politics. Even more than *Her*, *The Circle* looks at digital technology in the context of the digital economy of attention.

The Economy of Attention in Dave Eggers's *The Circle*

Amid contemporary future fictions, Dave Eggers's *The Circle* projects the digital future scenario that is closest to contemporary reality. The inspiration for it is grounded in the present concentration of worldmaking power in the hands of only a few big internet corporations. Former Google employee James Williams asserts that "[t]oday, just a few people at a handful of companies now have the ability to shape what billions of human beings think and do" (36). Different from the beginning of the internet, when decentralised networking and connecting people seemed to be the main aim (Rushkoff 31), the almost omnipresent netscape is now controlled by just five massive corporations whose "business model [is] based largely on keeping people online as long as possible, and monetizing their attention" (xvi). The paradigm of the economy of attention shows that the problem is not digital technologies as such, but their systemic embeddedness in power structures, first and foremost capitalist economics.

The Circle exponentiates the current state of the economy of attention into the future, similar to its sequel *The Every* (2021) *Ready Player One* (novel by Ernest Cline 2011, film by Steven Spielberg 2018), Shteyngart's *Super Sad True Love Story* (2010), and Kavenna's *Zed* (2020). All these works put the power structures of digital capitalism, with its injustices and manipulative set-up, into the centre of their stories. The young adult fiction *Ready Player One* stages the fight between an evil money-making corporation and virtual reality idealists and geeks, while the novels *Super Sad True Love Story* and *Zed* satirically reveal the totalitarian potential behind digital capitalism. Their criticism of this existing and contemporarily dominant world provides them with a special ethical and political relevance and urgency. Eggers's novel likewise projects the current state of affairs into the future by collapsing the handful of current tech giants into a single future one called "The Circle". With the help of the protagonist Mae, who is intended to be an "everyman" figure (Hobbs 4), the text warns about the potential of a digital attention economy embedded in neoliberal and transhumanist ideologies. Through Mae, *The Circle* demonstrates the dystopian effects on individual psyches and their social environments. At the same time, the novel's broad perspective of looking at technology in its socioeconomic and political contexts can be called a political economy point of view. This perspective foregrounds that social and technological developments need to be considered as part of their respective worlds. As a result, the novel has mostly been read as a concrete warning against digital capitalism (e.g. Galow 125), which gives evidence of the relatively closed moral universe suggested by the book.

While *The Circle* has sparked fierce reactions and heated debates about the digital economy and its consequences in newspaper reviews and the blogsphere (Wilhelmus 749), it does not appear on any bestseller list. One reason may be, as many reviewers and scholars have remarked (e.g. Meireis), its lack of literary quality as a result of underdeveloped characters and a low level of ambiguity. On the other hand, the book has been called a visionary "novel of ideas" (Atwood, 'The Circle by Dave Eggers' 6) because it allows readers to emotionally experience the threats of a future digital economy—which makes it highly relevant for ethics of digital futures. In its depiction of a near-future Silicon Valley corporate monopoly and its totalitarian power, *The Circle* illustrates the effects of the "digital economy of attention". The term "economy of attention" has become popular through Georg Franck and is rooted in the analogy between stock market capitalist economics and the phenomenon of social attention. The concept has gained special relevance with the advent of large-scale digitalisation and "an internet shaped around the demands of an advertising economy" (P. Lewis). It designates how people's attention, like their data, has become an extremely valuable and monetisable resource for big internet companies today, which have turned into "the richest and most powerful companies on the face of the planet" (Foroohar xii).

The following close reading will begin by looking at the aesthetics and narrative techniques of the novel, which likely lead readers to condemn the company The Circle and its practices as immoral. As a second step, I will interpret the world of The Circle along with its neoliberal ideology inspired by transhumanism as a paradigmatic example of digital capitalism. Critique of the economy of attention will serve as a theoretical lens here. The novel contrasts the "brave new world" of The Circle with the old world inhabited by people like Mae's Midwestern parents and her ex-boyfriend Mercer. Along with Circle co-founder Ty, they become the moral guidance of the book. Therefore, I will explore their worldviews in a third step and argue that their respective emphases on the physical and a political economy perspective are facets of possible otherworlds to The Circle's economy of attention.

The Aesthetics of Warning

While *The Circle* is mainly marketed and read as a dystopian novel, alongside science fiction and even satire (Linklater), scholars like Peter Herman have pointed out that it also contains a utopian angle (185; 190–193). In his reading, he emphasises the dialectical entanglement between dystopia and utopia and comments on actual readers' judgements being relative to their own socio-historical circumstances. Similar to Margaret Atwood's *MaddAddam Trilogy*, the novel turns existing utopian ideas, like the advancement of social justice and child safety, into the dystopia of permanent surveillance and totalitarian control. On the other hand, *The Circle's* overtly dystopian stance can be read as a mockery of contemporary techno-utopianism, as Philippa Hobbs argues: "*The Circle* shows that we are already living in a dire utopia: that of neoliberalism" (8). Indeed, within the world of the novel, Mae explicitly refers to The Circle as utopia: "Here, all had been perfected. [...] Who else but utopians could make utopia?" (Eggers, *The Circle* 31). Despite the dialectical entanglement between utopia and dystopia, I want to argue that the novel keeps ambiguity to a minimum by using several aesthetic strategies that limit its ethical reading to a single option: a rejection of the neoliberal world represented by The Circle.

For most readers, the novel's closed moral universe leaves no doubt that this future is not one they would want, as reviews on *goodreads.com* reveal. While the novel's aesthetics have been harshly criticised by many with respect to monodimensional characters and flat dialogues, the majority of readers have pointed out the connections they see with current contemporary developments of the digital economy. As a result, people have argued that the novel is not "a literary novel; it's more of a fable", or that it "is meant to be read as a non-fiction novel". The possible future of digital capitalism as portrayed in the novel caused strong emotional reactions in many readers. For instance, someone wrote that it "made me feel like I was trapped in a horrible nightmare I couldn't get out of" or that "[t]his book is creepy as hell!" ('The Circle Community Reviews'). Even though, as one reviewer noted, most people are already informed about the dangers of the internet and the distribution of power behind it, reading about it in the form of fiction seems to make an enormous difference in terms of emotional response. As the reviews show, even the relatively low immersive qualities of *The Circle* can provoke a strong emotional engagement with a topic, which leads to an ethical reading. Many reviewers drew comparisons to current developments and events and even questioned their personal engagement with social media.

For readers to reflect and be directed towards its moral compass, *The Circle*'s aesthetic strategies encompass: satire in combination with a relatively flat protagonist, which creates dramatic irony as a result of a double perspective, a morally loaded allegory, and the intertextual references to George Orwell's *1984*. *The Circle* becomes a satirical text mostly through its overdrawn monodimensional characters in combination with extreme exaggerations. For example, while it might be imaginable for someone to work with three or four screens, Mae ending up with a total of *nine* screens is simply over the top. Most of the novel's characters are more like comic stock characters than realistic depictions of actual people. For example, the company's leaders Stenton and Bailey each have just one character trait: Stenton is the epitome of a capitalist, throwing around "his money and influence without fear" (24), while Bailey is the likeable "uncle", the public face of the company, "accessible and genuine" (25). The flat protagonist Mae, who has earned Eggers a considerable amount of critique related either to his presumably bad writing skills or misogyny, can also be interpreted as a satirical element ('The Circle Community Reviews'). While all the "clever" and powerful characters like Ty, Mercer, Stenton, and

Bailey are male, Mae is naive and easy to manipulate. Her main aim is to please and function well within the system. Apart from that, she does not seem to have other character traits that might lead to inner conflict or deeper reflection, which make her an epitome of the neoliberal world The Circle is trying to create: glossy surfaces without depth.

The result of a flat protagonist like Mae is that it is difficult, if not impossible, for readers to identify with her, even though she is the novel's only focaliser character. Large passages of the text are written in free indirect discourse, which according to Carmen Laguarta Bueno has a double function: on the one hand, the usage of free, indirect discourse makes "readers identify with the techno-optimistic protagonist", while on the other hand it is "a way of making readers distance themselves from the protagonist and The Circle's utopian ideology" (167–68). Laguarta Bueno explains that this shift from identification to distance is made possible through dramatic irony as a result of readers being convinced by secondary characters like Mercer and Kalden/Ty as the novel's "moral compass" (179). The dramatic irony leads to a double perspective of readers, who can look at Mae from the outside while also sharing her insider perspective. This enables them to evaluate the course of events differently than she does. For example, as Mae is unable to foresee the consequences of The Circle's online domination and surveillance, Mercer explains it to her by pointing out that "[i]ndividually you don't know what you're doing collectively. But secondly, don't presume the benevolence of your leaders. [...] I always worried, what if someone was willing to use this power to punish those who challenge them?" (260). Diverging from Mae's own perception, the evidence the book provides of the dangers of The Circle towards herself, those close to her, and democracy should become fairly obvious to readers. Politically, all opposition to The Circle is strategically silenced; and on a private level, Mae loses contact with her parents, her ex-boyfriend is literally driven to suicide, her best friend suffers a nervous breakdown and remains unconscious, and she herself is close to depression, which is symbolised by unsettling daydreams of a growing black tear and muffled underwater screams (197, 336, 378, 470).

It is thus not necessary for readers to identify with Mae for the text to work—it is more important that the novel makes readers *understand* people *like* her, who play a significant role in contemporary worldmaking as passive "worldtakers": the large proportion of neoliberal subjects who mainly care for their own (alleged) benefits and advancements, without reflecting or even acting on larger, socio-political implications. Hence, *The Circle* draws forth an example of how power and governmentality work in the context of digital capitalism and provides an introspection into the psychological aspects of worldmaking: people strive hard to protect their world(views) from contradicting evidence, especially if the world they live in *seems* to benefit them. That this might be untrue, as in the case of Mae, can only be seen from an outsider's perspective. Mae, like millions of others, is unable to look past her alleged personal interests and the boundaries of the world which have been made for her by people in power, like the company's bosses.

In contrast, characters like Mercer and Ty, and even her parents, are able to do just that, as their consciences seem to be rooted in a different world. The function of these characters is to guide readers in their moral judgement. They do so through explicit speeches which have been lamented by reviewers (e.g. Ullman) due to their high degree of overtness, which puts readers into a position similar to Mae: they feel limited to silly dupes who are unable to see and judge for themselves ('The Circle Community Reviews'). Mercer and Ty point out the socio-political problems and dangers of The Circle, so that even the most uncritical reader is able to see them. For instance, Mercer remarks that "[s]urveillance shouldn't be the trade-off for any goddamn service we get" (Eggers 370).

If this was not enough, the symbolism of the aquarium with the shark, octopus and seahorse, which represent the company's leaders (the three wise men) (Galow 124), leaves no doubts about the destructive nature of The Circle's digital capitalism: the shark, who symbolises Stenton "as self-described *Capitalist Prime*" (23), ruthlessly devours the other two sea creatures standing for Ty's and Bailey's technological idealism and utopianism (Eggers 481). The novel metaphorises the entire digital economy as a marine ecology system. For instance, when small start-ups present and try to sell their ideas to The Circle, Annie calls the event "plankton inspection time" (28). She further explains that it is about "little start-ups hoping the big whale—that's us—will find them tasty enough to eat" (28). The Circle's most important innovation, a unified internet account for all online activities called TruYou, is described with the image of a tidal wave that "crushed all meaningful opposition" (22). In addition, Mae has terrifying daydreams about "a [...] high-pitched scream of a million drowned voices" (378) that might represent the mass of people like her who lose their (political) voice through the digital economy of attention. Finally, the architecture of The Circle's buildings made of glass walls and floors provides the impression of a gigantic, transparent aquarium. This architecture reveals a paradox of contemporary digital surveillance: the transparency of the buildings makes the company itself seem transparent when in reality it is the customers and employees who are made transparent while the company keeps its secrets. This mirrors an important finding in surveillance studies: "While the illusion of transparency is cultivated, the traces of surveillance and observation are obliterated" (Drucker and Gumpert 496).

Another hint of the world of The Circle being dystopian rather than utopian are the mottos of the company like "secrets are lies" (Eggers 300), "sharing is caring" and "privacy is theft" (303), which are a nod to George Orwell's 1984 (Laguarta Bueno 179). Like the slogans "war is peace", "freedom is slavery", and "ignorance is strength" in 1984 (Orwell 7), the mottos in The Circle provide short-cuts for thinking that are pre-made by the leaders of the party or corporation. Reading The Circle in the context of other previous utopian or dystopian novels therefore naturally proposes itself. For example, Herman suggests that "More's Utopia and Huxley's Brave New World shape The Circle as much as 1984" (190) as they, too, comment on how utopian ideals easily turn into dystopia. Like its predecessors, The Circle contains a normative judgement of the society and the governing structures it represents. In its relatively clear morality, Egger's novel rejects the world of The Circle as totalitarian. Framing digital technology in the context of neoliberal capitalism and its power structures is perhaps the novel's greatest achievement. Therefore, the following section will closely analyse the depiction of digital neoliberalism in conjunction with the theoretical approach of the economy of attention.

The Threat of a Digital Economy of Attention

Digital technologies and capitalism together form the "digital economy of attention", which runs on monetising people's attention and personal data via advertising. For internet users—and this is virtually everybody today—this means being constantly manipulated by the creators of online content through what is called persuasive design: using simple psychological tricks to make users stay longer on a site, click on a certain link or provide as much personal data as possible. Douglas Rushkoff, a professor of media theory and digital economics, writes that "[l]iving in a digitally enforced attention economy means being subjected to a constant assault of automated manipulation" (63). In his critique of the digital attention economy, he further explains that "[i]nstead of designing technologies that promote autonomy and help us make informed decisions, the persuasion engineers in charge of our biggest digital companies are hard at work creating interfaces that thwart our cognition and push us into an impulsive state where thoughtful choices—or thought itself—are nearly impossible" (67). In the digital economy of attention, people are no longer consumers or even citizens. They have been diminished to products themselves as their attention and their data can be sold to advertisers.

In Eggers's future fiction, the current oligopoly of the digital economy has become a monopoly through which all online services are channelled. The novel mentions explicitly that The Circle "subsumed Facebook, Twitter, Google" (Eggers 23), among others, therefore linking its fictitious setting to a contemporary reality. The problems and threats of the digital economy become visible through satire and exaggeration. These range from the impacts of neoliberal governmentality on individual lives and psychologies to the abolishing of democratic politics as such. Derived from Michel Foucault's concept of biopolitics, Campbell and Sitze posit that "neoliberalism governs by metaphorizing the market as a game, by metaphorizing the state as its umpire, and by metaphorizing individuals and populations as players for whom all choices are in principle possible—with the one exception of the choice not to play the game of the market at all" (20). The digital economy as presented in The Circle also shares close ties with transhumanist thought, especially its sub-branch of democratic transhumanism. The following analysis will therefore trace these developments as represented in the novel, beginning with a short introduction to the setup of digital capitalism, followed by its effects on the microlevel of the individual and their immediate social surroundings. Arriving at the macrolevel, I will point out how The Circle illustrates the ways in which the economy of attention might affect politics with devastating consequences for democracy.

Digital Capitalism and Transhumanism

Capitalism and digital technologies share the same essence of numerics and calculations. Jonathan Beller points out this commonality and frames capitalism as an early expression of what he calls "the computational unconscious". The term is meant to designate a cultural mindset that hinges on calculation, which has been deepened since the advent of neoliberalism and digital technology. Capitalism, with its "pursuit of private (quantitative) gain" that is meant to "result in (often unknown and unintended) public good" is simply the earliest expression of machine computation. The idea that thinking in numbers has come to dominate most social, economic, and private activity today is represented and explicitly mocked in The Circle. For example, Mae receives non-stop numeric measurements and ratings of her performance on the up to nine screens she works with, including her average feedback and social performance ratings, number of viewers, and health figures. She is even encouraged to give her sex partner Francis a performance rating on a scale from 1 to 100 (Eggers 385). While this just represents the individual side of numeric thought, the large economic calculations of the company and their financial dealings with data and people's attention remain by and large invisible throughout the novel, as in real life. This is, of course, a result of Mae functioning as a character focaliser whose knowledge and insight are fairly limited.

In this sense, Mae represents any average person who uses digital devices, platforms, and apps made by large tech corporations without awareness of what the companies are after, or the consequences this might have on varying levels from personal to political. *The Circle* therefore contrasts the ignorance of the masses and the average worldtaker with the strategic exploitation of power of the few active worldmakers of the digital economy of attention. The vehicle to bring out this contrast is a third group of people, the ones that I call analysts, who actively engage in understanding the power dynamics of this world like Ty and Mercer do. From the company's involvement in politics it becomes obvious that it is not just money but also political power The Circle is after. The idea of full transparency, inspired by transhumanism, calls for democracy through digital technology and comes close to an elimination of democratic politics as we know them. While transhumanist technologies are usually associated with AI, genetic engineering, and life extension technologies, "technologies such as social media tools, and surveillance devices [...] have often been overlooked by transhumanist critics, despite the possibilities that they offer for implementing transhumanist aims" (Laguarta Bueno 168).

As mentioned before, transhumanist aims can be subsumed under the idea of "enhancement" of human capabilities through technoscience (e.g. Hayles, 'Wrestling with Transhumanism'). The premise of continuous human evolution through technology, also called technogenesis, is inscribed into these aims, as is the notion of a teleological progress. The Circle's leader Eamon Bailey represents this kind of thinking by believing that all The Circle's technological innovations will ultimately move humanity to the next level of perfection: "I'm a believer in the perfectibility of human beings. [...] We can solve any problem. We can cure any disease, end hunger [...] We will finally realize our potential" (Eggers 293). This point of view also has strong implications for morality. Bailey claims that through surveillance technology, "we have no path but the right path, the best path" (293), so that "[f]inally, finally, we can be good" (292). As in previous examples, transhumanist thinking in *The Circle* exhibits religious tendencies that are highlighted by Mae's comments like "[i]t's heaven" (1) when she first enters The Circle's premises, or "evidence of God" (36) when she gets to know a colleague (Francis) on her first evening at The Circle. The motif of religion and technoscience is most explicitly displayed when Francis and Mae meet a man who wanted to become a priest but then discovered computers: "You [at the Circle] found a way to save all the souls. [...] There can be one morality, one set of rules. [...] Now we're all God. Every one of us will soon be able to see, and cast judgement upon, every other" (398).

As Katherine Hayles has noted, transhumanism is deeply bound up with individualism and neoliberalism, which *The Circle* superbly demonstrates. While there are also Marxist strands of transhumanist philosophy, its proximity to capitalist and neoliberal ideologies is striking. Of course the exact interpretation of its techno-positive outlook depends heavily on its geographical location. As the novel is set in the United States, it must envision the results of the contemporary *capitalist* marriage with digital technologies and a transhumanist philosophical framework.[3] *The Circle* mainly approaches this on two levels, the level of the individual psychology and of politics and power, as the following sections will explore.

The Individual Level: Computational Psychologies

What Eggers's novel depicts best and in most detail is how the neoliberal economy of attention works on an individual, psychological level. For this purpose, Mae as a protagonist is an excellent choice because she embodies the average person rather than a distinct individual with special character traits. Seeing the world through her eyes highlights different aspects of psychological programming in the context of a neoliberal attention economy. It shows how an individual's attention is purposefully directed or even manipulated to serve the interests of digital corporations. Mae's internal focalisation especially provides insights into neoliberal work ethics and explains why people willingly exploit themselves. And finally, it characterises the neoliberal self in the digital age as both quantifiable and extremely needy for other people's attention. As a result

---

3   This is in contrast to the other contemporary digital powerhouse, China, where an authoritarian state brings up very different consequences in conjunction with digitalisation. An example for this would be Cixin Liu's *Three Body Problem* (2014).

of looking at Mae both from the inside and outside (through Mercer's comments, for instance), readers can grasp how harmful and even involuntary this psychological programming is for Mae, and how completely unable she is to realise this lack of autonomy herself.

As many researchers following Herbert Simondon in the 1970s and Georg Franck in the 1990s have confirmed, people's attention has become "*the* crucial resource of our epoch" (Citton 10). In highly industrialised countries, scarcity is no longer a material phenomenon but has rather become a psychological one. The abundance of material goods has led to a lack of time and attention, both necessary to consume them (8). On the other hand, the ability to focus one's attention is crucial for making conscious decisions on how one wants to live instead of following pre-made pathways that might not actually meet people's needs and aims. James Williams asserts that "[i]n the longer term, [...] [digital devices] can make it harder for us to live the lives we want to live, or, even worse, undermine fundamental capacities such as reflection and self-regulation" (xi). He further argues that "there's a deep misalignment between the goals we have for ourselves and the goals our technologies have for us" (9). Of course, the technologies themselves do not have goals, but rather the companies who design and provide them. Through persuasive design, they actively manipulate consumers into spending more time on their websites to extract more financial value through data mining and digital advertising. The main risk for the individual in this process is "that one will lose control over one's attentional processes" (15), so that thinking and focusing of attention will become automated and nonconscious (30).

The Circle illustrates this manipulation of an individual's attention by corporate interests with the example of Mae. Just as everybody else in the world of The Circle, Mae lives in a state of constant partial attention due to the multiple tasks she must perform simultaneously during her working hours and in her free time. In the beginning, Mae is coerced by her supervisors and the company policy to participate on social media all the time (Eggers 96), but soon she internalises this behaviour and even defends it against critique from Mercer and her parents. As a strategy to point out the utter triviality of most social media conversations, the novel features two entire pages with completely unimportant messages that bore readers as much as they must bore Mae. To give an example: "One of her friends from college had posted a message about having the stomach flu, and a long thread followed, with friends making suggestions about remedies, some offering sympathy, some posting photos meant to cheer her up" (103). Nonetheless, this is how she spends most of her time from then on, independent of whether she is at home having dinner with her family or talking to other people in person (259). As a result, the quality of her personal relationships diminishes and she becomes "less vibrant" and "incredibly boring" herself, because she doesn't *do* anything interesting (off-screen) anymore, as Mercer notes (262). Increasingly, Mae's way of thinking resembles The Circle's way of thinking, numeric and calculating. For example, at the end of the novel, when she sees her best friend, Annie, lying unconscious at the hospital, the sight of her temperature, 98.6, reminds "her of that day's aggregate, 97, which she needed to improve" (157). By then, Mae is no longer in any position to reflect on her personal situation or the Circle's practices autonomously, as her thought has become automated and geared alone to the interests of the company.

While the colonisation of attention mainly represents the consumers' side, Mae is also depicted in the role of an employee. In this role she serves as a prime example of the neoliberal mode of governmentality, which combines a heteronormative exertion of power and free will (Meireis 5). The Circle takes the idea of neoliberal governmentality one step further by depicting what it could become in combination with digital technologies. Buyng-Chul Han calls this the "digital panopticon" as the constant a-perspectival surveillance of everybody by everybody to regulate individuals' behaviours (*The Transparency Society* 45). In the novel, the "digital panopticon" takes shape through the sea change cameras and people becoming transparent through them. Bailey believes that "if we *all* behaved as if we were being watched", "it would lead to a more moral way of life" and we could become "our best selves" (Eggers 292). Mae, as the company's first person to turn completely transparent, illustrates the idea of becoming "her best self", for example by giving up "on soda, energy drinks, processed food" and consuming only one unfinished alcoholic drink in the evenings (331). This demonstrates how power works in neoliberalism via the idea of constant self-optimisation in all spheres of life.

When Mae enters The Circle as an employee, she "is figuratively reborn—she also works in a building of the company called 'Renaissance'—as a piece of human capital aiming solely to enhance her own value" (Hobbs 5). According to political theorist Wendy Brown, individuals remade as human capital enhance their value neither for themselves nor for the common good, but for firms or states concerned with their own competitive positioning (*Undoing the Demos* 37). Although it may appear so to her, the way Mae works for The Circle is certainly not in her own best interest, as becomes obvious throughout the novel. For instance, the erasure of the boundary between work and leisure, as practised by many global players today,[4] seems attractive to employees while being the perfect tool for exploitation. The Circle's campus is a prime example of how offering attractive leisure activities to employees leads to a complete colonialisation of life through work. Facilities and activities like a volleyball court, day-care centre, yoga studio, massages, cafeterias, a night club, mini golf area, and especially the free dorms on campus (Eggers 5 ff) provide incentives for employees to maximise their time on campus and, in consequence, to potentially expand their working hours infinitely.

The type of subject this framework creates is well described by Byung-Chul Han's term "achievement subject" (*In the Swarm* 33) which aims at maximising performance in the realm of work and elsewhere. While the roots of this kind of subjectivity are within neoliberal capitalism, digital devices with their ability to measure and compare performance levels have deepened this trend. Reproducing the narrative of the American Dream, Mae, who comes from a humble social and economic background, sees herself climbing the social ladder when she enters the world of The Circle. Neoliberal achievement subjects like her live in a world of constant competition. Therefore, the necessity to perform better than the others continues or is even intensified within the company. The constant surveillance and measurement make it possible to compare performances between employees, as a zing message to all Circlers demonstrates, praising Mae's daily score as *"the highest score of any CE newb of all time suck it"* (Eggers 55). Within the company, there are multiple types of rankings, from work performance to social rankings. As they are made available for everybody to see, they confirm the neoliberal mantra that "competition was healthy and kept them all on their toes" (236). In contrast, the deteriorating friendship between Annie and Mae shows how unhealthy this state of constant competition (even between friends) is—especially for Annie, who suffers a nervous breakdown and remains unconscious for days in the end.

The novel also looks at individual identity regarding data and algorithms. It points out how the neoliberal self in the digital age becomes quantifiable, and uses the symbol of a (distorted) mirror to question the process of identity formation. For example, during the launching event of a new partnership app, Mae is introduced to The Circle's public with her online profile. This upsets her because she feels that "[h]aving a matrix of preferences presented as your

---

4   The Circle's campus is obviously inspired by Google's Mountainview campus; Mereis compares it to the Unilever headquarters in Hamburg (3); and I myself experienced a similar type of campus while interning at the Adidas headquarters in Herzogenaurach.

essence [...] was some kind of mirror, but it was incomplete, distorted" (126). In contrast, Bailey believes that with the completion of The Circle—that is, with complete data and surveillance of every person at all times—the mirror will become whole and represent reality as it is (290). From this point of view, reality and people are nothing but an accumulation of data and algorithms, measurable, explicable, and predictable.

Another aspect of the quantifiable self is that it becomes insecure and needy of continuous online social recognition as a result of competition and the constant strive for achievement. As Mercer notes, "[t]here's this new neediness—it pervades everything [...] the tools you guys create actually *manufacture* unnaturally extreme social needs" that are comparable to junk food, "[e]ndless empty calories, but the digital-social equivalent" (134). This neediness is demonstrated and ridiculed through Mae's colleagues and clients at The Circle. For example, her colleague Alistair, whom she has never met in person, is childishly offended by Mae not coming to his Portugal brunch (106), and a client writes to Mae that she felt devaluated by an unreturned request to join her professional network (329). Mae herself feels "stabbed" after three percent of the company sent her a frown instead of a smile (408). She genuinely believes that "[m]ost people would trade everything they know, everyone they know [...] to know they've been seen, and acknowledged, that they might be remembered" (490). This extreme neediness of social recognition by strangers can easily be explained by the individualisation and breaking up of strong social ties caused by neoliberalism as a result of its emphasis on individual achievement and competition.

An individualised world view also manifests itself in the psychologising of people instead of the recognition of the social and cultural conditions that might lead to symptoms like depression. This is taken up in *The Circle* when Mae's supervisors diagnose her with a problem of self-esteem because of her insufficient participation on the company's social media (189). In consequence, they suggest a type of therapy in which she must take part in "a special programme" that turns out to be nothing but market research to make her opinions feel more valued. The relationship between psychologising and pathologising people and making them function better as consumers for the capitalist system, workers, and products is made transparent here. While the novel pays the most attention to the effects of the economy of attention on the individual level, it also touches on its implications for entire societies and politics.

The Political Level: Democratic Transhumanism

With respect to politics, The Circle's ideology represents "democratic transhumanism" which aims at "creating a more participatory democracy by means of the use of social media tools" (Laguarta Bueno 169). Its central aim, as Eggers's novel demonstrates, is complete transparency. This is granted, for instance, via constant video surveillance of all politicians in office: "There would be no more back rooms, no more murky deal-making. There would be only clarity, only light" (Eggers 242). Consequently, towards the end of the novel, 90% of politicians in Washington become transparent, while the rest remains under suspicion (313). Bailey asserts that only full transparency could make democracy complete in his sense, and Stenton even holds that it might eliminate Congress and much of Washington altogether (395). Apart from surveillance technologies, the company also aims to make voting through a Circle account mandatory for each citizen and promotes direct democracy through an app called "Demoxie". As I will argue next, the company goals subsumed under the euphemism of "closing the circle" (289) represent the neoliberal utopia of complete control of a private company over the state and its citizens, as well as the prospect of the elimination of politics as such.

The time of the digital is in the immediate present, as is demonstrated by the direct democratic app "Demoxie", which provides answers to political questions within seconds. In consequence, the time for deep reflection and long-term planning is missing. Han asserts that when the immediate present becomes the dominant tense through digitalisation, "[t]he *future*, as the time of the political, is disappearing" (*In the Swarm* 17). Politics, understood as the struggle for the *common* good, is likewise disappearing because the common cause is gradually being replaced by individual needs and opinions. Han suggests that while there used to be "parties and unions bound by a common ideology", there are now only "countless individual opinions and matters of personal preference" (65). This is demonstrated well by "Demoxie": in addition to personal preference questions like "Should the Circle offer more veggie options at lunch?", political questions like "Should we send a drone to kill [a terrorist], considering the likelihood of moderate collateral damage?" (407) would also be answered on an individual basis—after one minute and eleven seconds, without discussions or dialogues, between opposing opinions. As a result, alleged basic democratic apps like "Demoxie" kill both thinking as a task that requires time for reflection as well as concentrated attention and social discourse as the verbal exchange between different people and groups. By jumping straight to the polling and majority vote, the app also represents the standard pro-market argument that private companies are more efficient than public institutions—and therefore reveal the devastating outcomes of this logic.

Completion in the Circle's terminology can also be seen as the completion of the free market ideology, as the final victory of capitalism over the state and its institutions—in short: the neoliberal utopia. As a result, the "inequality and structural violence inherent in capitalism" is carried over into the political sphere (Beller). In the novel, this violence becomes apparent through the strategic silencing of all meaningful opposition to the Circle and even the killing of deviants like Mercer who do not wish to participate in this tyrannical utopia. Different from earlier forms of governance through necropolitics, i.e. killing people to threaten or silence them, power in neoliberalism works by way of freedom, as analysed by Foucault in *The Birth of Biopolitics*. Therefore, Mercer kills *himself*, and people like Mae *willingly* and *happily* submit to the company's power without being conscious of it. In depicting and laying open the workings of neoliberal governmentality in digital capitalism, *The Circle* offers an analysis of potential futures from a political economy point of view that takes a systemic approach. Accordingly, the novel itself is rooted in an otherworld to the digital economy of attention, but it also represents the otherworld of a political economy perspective through the character of Ty. It complements this perspective with Mercer's emphasis on the physical world as being opposed to the virtual.

The Physical and the Political Economy as Otherworlds

Through Mae's point of view, the physical world outside the Circle is characterised as the old and comparatively dystopian world. She rejects her hometown "as a town no one had heard of" (Eggers 243), which, like the rest of California or even The United States, seems "like some chaotic mess in the developing world" (31) compared to the world of the Circle. In Mae's opinion, her parents, who in the end turn away from digital surveillance and communication, "were on the wrong side of history" (374), and Mercer not simply in her past but "in *the* past" (265). The dramatic irony proposed by Carmen Laguarta Bueno due to readers sympathising with Mercer and Ty rather than Mae has an inversion effect: readers are likely to oppose Mae's opinions and embrace what she disqualifies. Accordingly, her hometown, her parents, and Mercer play key roles in pointing towards what is meant to be good in the novel: the here and now of direct physical experience and the embodied social interactions that take place there. On the one hand, actual physical proximity is depicted as irreplaceable by technology, for instance when Mae's father has a seizure related to his multiple sclerosis and Mercer helps out (126ff). On the other hand, physical experiences like Mae's kayaking trips appear to be fundamentally other and richer when compared with the rest of her digitalised life.

These trips seem to offer Mae happiness and relief, especially when she is saddened by her father's dire health condition. In contrast to the quick passage of time at The Circle, the temporality seems to change at the bay: "On the bay, an hour was always plenty. An hour was a day" (139). In the narration of Mae's kayaking experiences, her immediate sense-based impressions are foregrounded up to the point of becoming poetic, as this example from her illegal nightly trip to the island demonstrates: "The moonlight gave the seaweed some of the phosphorescence she'd seen before, adding a rainbow sheen, as if lit from within. For a brief moment, she felt like she was on some body of water on the moon itself, everything cast in a strange inverted palette" (270). Different from other passages in the novel in which Mae's thoughts, often driven by worries and fears, tend to be reflexive, her attention is focused on the immediate time and place while kayaking. For example, she contemplates the animal life in the bay while taking comfort "in knowing she would not, and really could not, know much at all" (269). This represents a harsh contrast to her (The Circle's) aim of gaining full knowledge and information through digital surveillance. During kayaking, Mae experiences a physical form of happiness she describes as "feeling strong, feeling enormous" (269), and afterwards she realises that "she'd been free of thoughts of her parents, of Mercer, of the pressures of work" (145).

Unsurprisingly, it is Mercer who has introduced Mae to kayaking, and he happens to also represent the concrete experience of the physical and unmediated social contact. For instance, he criticises that whenever he sees or hears from Mae, it is "through this [digital] filter [...] You're always looking at me through a hundred other people's eyes" (131). In contrast, when Mercer and Mae do meet in person, the narration seems to emphasise the physical aspects and sense-based impressions: "Mae and Mercer sat in the backyard, the heat still coming off the grass, the trees, the rain-washed grey fences that surrounded them" (129). As a result of his close ties to the world of immediate physical presence, Mercer becomes one of the moral guides of the novel who constantly warns against the escape into virtual worlds. While Mercer is more concerned with the microcosm of the individual and its social surroundings, the second moral guide, Ty, illuminates the effects of the digital economy of attention on the macrocosm of the political economy.

As an insider to the company, he is fully aware of its power structures and systemic embeddedness within the digital economy. He points out that the company is first and foremost driven by "ruthless capitalist ambition" and relates that "Stenton professionalised our idealism, monetized our utopia. He's the one who saw the connection between our work and politics, between politics and control" (489). Instead of the true democracy The Circle claims to aim for, it slowly turns into "a tyrannical monopoly" (404) and "a totalitarian nightmare" (486) because, as Ty explains, "if you can control the flow of information, you can control everything. You can control most of what anyone sees and knows" (487). From his point of view, digital direct democracy apps like "Demoxie" would create "mob rule" (408) rather than an actual democracy. And finally, he argues that "[t]he ceaseless pursuit of data to quantify the value of any endeavour is catastrophic to true understanding" (490), in this way confirming the philosophical critique of the digital by Han, which I have discussed previously. What makes Ty's perspective "other" in comparison to the majority of characters and Mae especially is that he can assume a certain distance to his personal immediate benefits. Instead, as with other famous contemporary whistle-blowers, he accepts a life of quasi-confinement with the hope of being able to contribute to the common good of the society he lives in.

To sum up, Dave Eggers's The Circle shows little to no ambiguity in its simulation of a future digital economy of attention which it clearly marks as dystopian. In this sense, it is a satire of the contemporary utopia that digital technology equals progress and enhancement, which is firmly embedded in neoliberal capitalist ideology and transhumanist thought. Its closed map of morality functions as a warning from actual digital futures that might be just around the corner or even already here.

Conclusion

While both examples in this chapter display certain fears arising from potential developments in digital technologies, The Circle most obviously opposes the dominant ideology of progress through digitalisation. Digital technology is not an independent phenomenon but has evolved out of human-made worlds, and therefore, it is firmly tied up with their respective maps of morality and power interests. Contemporarily, these are derived from capitalist economics that have embraced neoliberal ideologies to govern economies, states, local communities as well as individual people. These interests and their ways of working are depicted and negotiated in and through the cultural imaginary, which is part of the economy of attention itself. Regarding imaginaries of digital and neoliberal futures in fiction, the interests of (digital) capitalism become visible through the prevalence of speculative depictions of artificial superintelligence becoming a threat to humanity, which distracts from the actual threats of digitalisation, such as surveillance and the loss of democracy and individual autonomy.

While some fictional works like Alex Garland's *Ex_Machina* and Wally Pfister's *Transcendence* take a more speculative approach to digital futures with their simulations of not yet existing developments, such as artificial superintelligence and nanotechnology, *Her* and *The Circle* move towards future scenarios that are closer to contemporary reality and therefore more realistic or probable. Even though Spike Jonze's *Her* also features a conscious AI in the form of an operating system, the focus of the film is more on the cultural and economic situatedness of its love story between human and machine. In particular, *Her* examines the neoliberal production of the self and identity as well as the role of relationships and otherness. Drawing on the philosopher Byung-Chul Han, I have argued that the film illustrates how digitalisation in neoliberalism brings forth a proliferation of the same and the self that erases otherness and inhibits successful relationships. At the same time, the hope for romantic love is what fuels the neoliberal capitalist engine which matters for the film both on an intra- and extradiegetic level. The illusion of romance keeps the protagonists from noticing the corporate exploitation of their affective labour and attracts cinema audiences to immerse themselves in this suspiciously beautiful digital future. However, through the AIs' deviant behaviour and real otherness, *Her* also undermines the dominant worlds it stages and opposes them with posthuman(ist) forms of collectivised and fluid identities and relationships.

In contrast to this relatively high degree of aesthetic and ethical ambiguity, Dave Eggers's novel *The Circle* differs from this openness by being more of a novel of ideas that quite obviously wants to convince readers of its own moral compass. This tendency towards didacticism may also be a result of the novel being the work which is most closely modelled on the contemporary reality of digital capitalism. By drawing on the concept of the digital economy of attention, I have pointed out how Eggers's novel projects current phenomena like data mining, mass surveillance, and the deliberate manipulation of individuals and entire societies into the future to show their dire consequences. Like Douglas Rushkoff and Yves Citton in their theories, *The Circle* illustrates aesthetically how the economy of attention works and makes readers experience emotionally its totalitarian potential, which seems to have a strong impact on public discourse and readers' ethics.

My exemplary analysis of futuristic digital neoliberalism in contemporary fiction shows that the current cultural imaginary of the digital is dominated by cultural feelings of unease. This unease either arises from speculative scenarios of artificial superintelligence, or it is a result of the contemporary power relations inscribed into the dominant world of neoliberal capitalism. Even though there is relatively little utopian potential in the fictional works I have analysed, it is ascribed mainly to aspects of identity creation. The idea of the cyborg as a human/machine hybrid that can destabilise essentialist gender identities, as in *Her*, especially reveals the potentially liberating effects of digital technology. Similarly, the cyborg's posthuman(ist) otherness can question individualised neoliberal subjectivity and propose different modes of relational identities. The critique of the political economy of digitalisation visible in *Her* and *The Circle* represents a starting point for thinking about necessary changes in digital worldmaking without precluding alternatives. By offering the chance to reflect on different aspects of possible digital futures, popular future fictions actively contribute to ethics and politics of digital futures.

6 Biopolitics of the Future: Kazuo Ishiguro's *Never Let Me Go* (2006) and Don DeLillo's *Zero K* (2016)

"Indeed all biotechnology is a game that is constantly played in the future in order to generate the present that enables that future" (34), argues Kaushik Sunder Rajan in his study on contemporary biocapitalism. Accordingly, this chapter dealing with biotechnology in the context of "Biopolitics of the Future" is not actually composed of fictional tales set in the future. As with biotechnology itself, I hold that fictional works dealing with ethical aspects of biotechnology and biopolitics are inherently future-oriented, even though, as in this case, they may be set in an alternative past or futuristic present. I suggest calling these films and novels "biotech fictions". Similar to examples in previous chapters, biotech fictions surpass traditional genre boundaries, especially between realist genres, such as drama and fictional memoir, and speculative ones like science fiction.[1] In their attempt of examining different ethical aspects, I propose that contemporary biotech novels and films make use of temporality as an aesthetic tool to make different aspects and consequences of biotechnological developments more visible and emotionally experienceable.

In order to examine biopolitics of the future through popular fiction, I have chosen two exemplary biotech fictions that ethically refer to the future while using a different temporal setting. As an example of an alternative history, Kazuo Ishiguro's *Never Let Me Go* is set in the recent past yet includes multiple temporalities, and Don DeLillo's *Zero K* (2016) serves as an example of a futuristic yet recognisable present-day setting. Other examples of different temporalities in biotech fictions encompass works like Dennis Villeneuve's *Blade Runner 2049* (2017), which is set in the near future, and Paolo Bacigalupi's *The Windup*

---

1   For example, on the realist side, there is the drama film *My Sister's Keeper* (Cassavetes 2009) and Ruth Ozeki's contemporarily set novel *All over Creation* (2003), while the next chapter will show that the majority of biotech fictions are more speculative.

Girl (2009), which uses the long-term future as a temporal backdrop. Both of them will be discussed in the chapters to come with a slightly different theoretical angle. This chapter will draw on Michel Foucault's concept of biopolitics as a theoretical backbone to highlight aspects of power and governmentality in combination with biotechnological advancements with the examples of *Never Let Me Go* and *Zero K*.

Foucault argued that around the second half of the 18th century, biopower "brought life and its mechanisms into the realm of explicit calculations and made knowledge-power an agent of the transformation of human life" (Foucault, *The History of Sexuality* 143). The ancient right of the sovereign to kill or to *take* lives was extended through the government act of *fostering* the lives of its population with regards to biological markers like "health, hygiene, birthrate, life expectancy, race" (Foucault, *The Birth of Biopolitics* 317). This development was engendered by the growth of the human sciences and medicine on the one hand, and (neo-)liberal techniques of governmentality as the art of government on the other hand. As Foucault explains at length in his Collège de France lecture *The Birth of Biopolitics*, (neo-)liberalism provides the political framework for a new form of governmental practise that caters to the needs of capitalist production by turning citizens into self-governing subjects represented by the figure of the *homo oeconomicus* (268). This subjectification takes place "through a variety of 'operations on [people's] own bodies, on their own souls, on their own thoughts, on their own conduct'" (Foucault, *Foucault Reader* 11). Even though Foucault's exploration of biopolitics has been criticised as "anything but straightforward", involving "shifts, feints, changes in focus and direction" (Campbell and Sitze 7), the varying approaches he takes towards it in different texts and lectures still become productive for an analysis of biotechnology in the context of politics and economics.

In this chapter's reading of two contemporary biotech fictions, I will show how relevant Foucault's concepts of biopolitics and biopower still are for the 21st century, as well as disclose new developments on humanity's strive for control over life through technology. Following Bogdana Koljević, I argue that 21st century biopolitics represents an intensification of Foucault's theories, which he developed in the second half of the 20th century. The biotechnology industry only emerged in the late 1970s and early 1980s and represents "a new face, and a new phase, of capitalism", which Rajan defines as "biocapitalism" in his expansive study on this power-knowledge complex (3). In line with Foucault's analysis of the entanglement of the political and the economic, the public and the private, Koljević observes that "the distinction between the public and the private appears as non-existent in contemporary biopolitical governmentality" (32). This means that biopower is not at all limited to sovereign power but begins to be more and more in the hands of private actors and corporations, resulting in a "politization of life" (30) on the one hand, and a depoliticisation of politics on the other hand (22). With Rajan, "[t]he biopolitical [...] points to the way in which our very ability to comprehend 'life' and 'economy' in their modernist guises is shaped by particular epistemologies that are simultaneously enabled by, and in turn enable, particular forms of institutional structures" (13).

With the two works I discuss in this chapter, I will highlight different aspects of 21st century biopower and biopolitics, ranging from health and reproduction to death and immortality. I will begin the chapter with a close reading of Kazuo Ishiguro's *Never Let Me Go* (2005) as an example of an alternative past aesthetics. Taking place in an alternative post-World-War-II England, the novel imagines a biopolitical setting in which human cloning for medical purposes becomes feasible, legal, and normal. To foster the health and longevity of the nation's population, clones are reared in boarding-school like institutions, destined to donate their vital organs until they die. The novel's theme of cloning and organ harvesting also appears in the 2005 film *The Island*. This imaginary setting illustrates Foucault's biopolitics as the "maximalization of life" (Koljević 23) through the paradigm of health, which, as he shows in *Society Must Be Defended*, is not at odds with the killing of another population "in the name of life" (21). I will argue that *Never Let Me Go*'s alternative past aesthetic mode, which is comparable to Ian McEwan's *Machines Like Me* (2019), enables ethical reflections about the futuristic technology of cloning and its biopolitics amid a familiar socio-historical background. Through the evocation of different past- and future-temporalities, as well as through its narrative setup as a fictional memoir, I posit that Ishiguro's novel investigates the phenomenon of "knowing and not knowing" about biopolitical exploitation and highlights the process of subjectification as a form of complicity.

The second example I will discuss is Don DeLillo's *Zero K* (2016), which is set in a futuristic present. Similar to Jeanette Winterson's *Frankisstein* (2019), the novel's setting represents an aesthetics of "speculative realism" that allows for a distanced perspective on the familiar present and its future potentialities. While *Never Let Me Go* zooms in on the phenomenon of a population's health, *Zero K* focuses on the transhumanist vision of defeating death. It depicts the freezing of deceased bodies in cryopreservation in order to revive them through yet-to-be-developed biotechnologies at some point in the future.

The novel's protagonist accompanies his father and stepmother on their final journey to a futuristic cryopreservation site called "The Convergence", where the super-rich await their future, potentially mega-enhanced second life. *Zero K* exemplifies the "dissolution of democracy and the political" (Koljević 33) of the 21st century, as the world is dominated by "the *crypto-elites* of large capital" (46) and their deadly biopolitics. In a metatextual movement, the novel foregrounds the involvement of aesthetics and art in worldmaking and, as I will argue, it scrutinises the triadic relationship between life, death, and art.

The Biopolitics of Health in an Alternative Past: Knowing and Not Knowing in Kazuo Ishiguro's *Never Let Me Go*

Even though Kazuo Ishiguro's *Never Let Me Go* (2005) is set in an alternative past, it is often read as future fiction due to its core themes of biotechnology and cloning. In a newspaper review, it has been referred to as "[a] *1984* for the bio-engineering age" and "a warning and a glimpse into the future" (Browning). Similarly, Keith McDonald characterised the novel as "an imagined past that could represent a real future, where Science Fiction again calls on our imaginations to act as a lens through which to scrutinize contemporary social dilemmas" (82). In its temporal setting, *Never Let Me Go* is comparable to Ian McEwan's 2019 *Machines Like Me*, which also imagines a futuristic technological development, in this case being the production of human-like superintelligent beings amid the socio-historical backdrop of a 1980s past in the UK. Content-wise, *Never Let Me Go* is similar to the science-fiction action thriller *The Island* (2005), which portrays the breeding of a colony of clones for organ-harvesting in a closed-off compound. While the clones in *The Island* are spatially confined, the confinement in *Never Let Me Go* is mental and results mainly from narrative and aesthetic worldmaking, which is foregrounded formally and on the level of plot.

Even though Ishiguro's novel features three cloned people as protagonists, the autodiegetic account of the narrator Kathy H. appears to be a typical coming-of-age story. In her fictional memoir, she tries to come to terms with the memories and hidden truths of her childhood and adolescence at a boarding school-like institution called Hailsham. Hence, the novel transgresses multiple genre boundaries and fuses science fiction with elements of other genres, ranging from Gothic romance to tragedy and even horror, due to the clones' fate of having to donate their vital organs until they die. *Never Let Me Go* has been praised both as a "literary" novel (Mullan 104), being shortlisted for the Booker Prize in 2005, *and* as a science fiction book, having been shortlisted for the Arthur C. Clarke Award in 2006. It gained considerable critical and public attention and has been interpreted from a broad variety of angles, ranging from psychological to cultural and socio-historical approaches. In the following, I want to discuss Ishiguro's novel as a meta-comment on the process of narrative worldmaking and show how this impacts maps of morality and biopolitics as the political organisation of life. I will argue that it reveals the devastating consequences of the repression of knowledge—of knowing and not knowing. It does this through its temporal setting, narrative structure, and metatextual referencing of the arts and aesthetics.

I will begin my analysis by showing how *Never Let Me Go* allows for an ethical reading that makes the effects of the individual and cultural consciousness of knowing and not knowing emotionally experienceable. Looking at the novel's temporal form as an alternative futuristic history, I propose that despite its setting in an alternative England between the 1960s and 1990s, it is multi-temporal in the sense of fusing past, present, and future, which enables more literal and more allegorical readings of the novel at the same time. Accordingly, I claim that the experimental setting of cloned humans bred to donate organs can be seen as exemplary of any given biopolitical apparatus of extreme exploitation. The next section of my analysis points out how the deprived become complicit with their exploiters through techniques of narrative and aesthetic worldmaking as demonstrated by the narrator Kathy H. Thirdly, I will discuss how the book scrutinises the role of the arts in the process of ideological worldmaking, and how the humanistic concept of arts education as ethical in and by itself works as a potential delusion.

Knowing and Not Knowing

The notion of repressed knowledge, of having been "told and not told" the truth (Ishiguro 82), of remembering and deliberately forgetting, is central to Ishiguro's *Never Let Me Go*. I argue that choosing not to feel, know, and reflect on events and ways of worldmaking represents a contrast to ethics, which pose as an attempt to become more aware of the world intellectually and emotionally and act consciously on this basis. Kathy H.'s entire autobiographical narrative functions as an example of knowing and not knowing, as it revolves around her trying to put together the pieces of her memory, as well as (un)covering the truth about herself and those like her, while never being able to fully comprehend it. The numerous layers of her narrative, which result from proleptic and analeptic shifts, as well as collaborative attempts at remembering, oscillate between trying to find out how things really are and the wish to forget them. As Tommy, Ruth, and Kathy gradually discover they are biotechnologically made clones reared to donate organs to regular humans—for instance through Miss Lucy's revelations about how the students' lives are already set out for them (80)—their response is to engage in wilful oblivion. For example, after finishing boarding school, the protagonists live at a monitored yet relatively free site called the Cottages where "it was possible to forget for whole stretches of time who [they] really were; to forget what the guardians had told [them]; to forget Miss Lucy's outburst [...] as well as all those theories [they]'d developed amongst [themselves] over the years" and even dream about "plans for the future" (140).

The question that is most often asked by professional critics, as well as through reader reviews and interviews, is why the protagonists accept their horrific fate without trying to run away or rebel. While some critics argue that this is because of their genetic make-up that makes them different from humans, for example emotionally degraded and more obedient (e.g. Puchner; Black; Armstrong), I want to claim that *Never Let Me Go* is simply not interested in resistance but in *complicity* with exploitation through ideological worldmaking. The novel uses a science fictional set-up to make a much more general observation about biopolitical worldmaking, especially regarding how narratives and aesthetics make people complicit with exploitative regimes. My understanding of biopolitics builds on Foucault's definition of biopolitics as "the attempt [...] to rationalize the problems posed to governmental practice by phenomena characteristic of a set of living beings forming a population: health, hygiene, birthrate, life expectancy" (Foucault, *The Birth of Biopolitics* 317). The government-run donations programme in *Never Let Me Go*, which is based on the closely controlled rearing and deprivation of cloned humans, exemplifies biopolitics as the political administration and organisation of life and makes its consequences aesthetically experienceable. Emily Horton similarly argues that "[t]hrough this Foucauldian narrative set-up, the novel registers a disciplinary institutional framework of regulation and control" (209). The novel's biopolitical apparatus destroys life in the name of totalising it as it fosters the rearing of disposable clones to save and expand the lives of those that count as "the population" of humans. This can be read as a form of biopolitical racism, which Foucault describes in *Society Must Be Defended*: "Racism justifies the death-function in the economy of biopower by appealing to the principle that the death of others makes one biologically stronger insofar as one is a member of a race or a population" (258).

In the novel, it is not only the clones who deliberately know and do not know about racist biopolitics—perhaps even more importantly, the world around them also functions in this way. Wilful ignorance becomes the basis of this extreme form of slavery and exploitation. As the former Hailsham headmistress Miss Emily explains to Kathy and Tommy when they visit her as grown-ups: "The world didn't want to be reminded how the donation programme really worked. They didn't want to think about you students, or about the conditions you were brought up in" (Ishiguro 259). For the biopolitical aim to cure diseases and extend the population's life span, hierarchies of life are created in which anything "less than human" (258), including biotechnologically made humans, can be used freely. *Never Let Me Go* makes the point that it is precisely through the suppression of conscious reflection and feeling that this becomes possible. Miss Emily further relates:

> After the war, in the early Fifties, when the great break-throughs in science followed one after the other so rapidly, there wasn't time to take stock, to ask the sensible questions. Suddenly there were all these new possibilities laid before us, all these ways to cure so many previously incurable conditions. [...] But by the time people became concerned about...about *students*, by the time they came to consider just how you were reared, whether you should have been brought into existence at all, well, by then it was too late. There was no way to reverse the process. How can you ask a world that has come to regard cancer as curable, how can you ask such a world to put away that cure, to go back to the dark days. (257)

The dominant world depicted in the novel therefore also represents the narrative of scientific and technological progress, which in many contemporary bioethical debates finds itself at odds with ethical considerations.

The double-consciousness of knowing and not-knowing is further transferable to many other aspects of contemporary culture, ranging from the tabooing treatment of death to phenomena like climate change and the appropriation or exploitation of life forms from plants to humans through capitalist globalisation. As Bruce Robbins comments, "[w]e ourselves do not look any ultimate questions in the face, but we watch as the character looks away from them, and are thus made to feel the force both of these questions and of our own resistance to them" (293). The novel's socio-historical setting reaffirms the metaphorical nature of its apparatus of exploitation that could easily be deferred to other time-spaces, but is particularly relevant for contemporary ethical challenges as this reader review shows: "No, not only was nobody going to do anything [for the characters], but that neither I, nor you, nor any of us, are all that different from the people who harvest these poor souls for their organs. After all, I'm a fat and happy first-worlder who less and less has a care or thought for all those who are exploited to make my life possible". This reader response is exemplary of how the novel's formal setup triggers strong emotions of despair and anger in readers, making them mull over the ethical questions raised in it, such as "What it is to be human, what you choose to do in the face of an impending death and what happens when science is not accompanied by ethics" ('Never Let Me Go Community Reviews'). In the following, I will point out how the novel's setting as an alternative futuristic history shapes the ethical reception of the novel.

The Alternative Futuristic History

By fusing several temporalities, ranging from different pasts to the future, Ishiguro manages to bring ethical questions about future technologies and biopolitics closer to the reader. As a result of being set in the past, the novel draws on familiar worlds and settings while experimenting with potential futuristic technologies and biopolitical regimes. Hence, Never Let Me Go is an example of an alternative history novel while being futuristic at the same time. Mark Currie notes that "[t]here is, on the one hand, a sense of the future, which inheres in the novel's interest in cloning; and on the other hand, a sense of the past, in the form of a kind of public school memoir, or a recollection of a childhood apparently isolated from the forces of history" (93). I argue that the novel evokes two different pasts and a potential future along with consequently posing ethical questions that are relevant for the present and even across time.

The two different pasts that inform the novel are composed of its setting in the second half of the 20th century and the evoked parallels with the to-talitarian regime of Nazi Germany. Regarding the merger of the two pasts, Shameen Black proposes that the novel's temporal setting "suggests how the terrifyingly familiar tactics of totalitarianism re-emerge within late-twenti-eth-century globalization" (798). The novel's time of narration takes place in the late 1990s; however, the narrated time covers the 1960s to the 1990s. Even though there are few references to the historical or political context of time, readers know that it includes the era of neoliberalisation and accelerating economic growth driven by Margaret Thatcher in the UK. Secondly, as critics have pointed out (e.g. Black; De Boever), *Never Let Me Go* draws explicit parallels between the biopolitical apparatus of its plot with that of Nazi Germany with its eugenics and death camps. For example, during Miss Lucy's English lesson, where the conversation drifts to imprisonment during WWII and the electrified fences around the camps and she says: "It's just as well the fences at Hailsham aren't electrified. You get terrible accidents sometimes" (77). As a result, the horror that is associated with this moment in history is transferred to the novel's setting and connected to potential biotechnological futures.

Clearly inspired by the first successful cloning of a sheep named Dolly in 1996, *Never Let Me Go* imagines what might happen if cloning humans were to become technologically possible and politically allowed or even desired. With regards to its ethical reception, Nicola Glaubitz has described the novel as "informed by current debates on human and animal cloning" and has noted that it has been reviewed in medical journals as "a warning against the consequences of human cloning" (324). On the other hand, cloning in the novel does not necessarily need to be read literally as biotechnological cloning—it can also be interpreted as an allegory for the cultural process of becoming copies of each other through mass medialisation. Through a meta-textual boundary transgression as a result of Kathy addressing the reader as a fellow clone, readers are even invited to question their own cultural status as individuals. In accordance with Jean Beaudrillard's claim that "[i]t is culture that clones us, and mental cloning anticipates any biological cloning" (Baudrillard and Witwer 25), cultural copying also becomes a theme in the novel. For example, during their time as young adults at the Cottages, Ruth, Tommy, and Kathy, together with the other students, make enormous efforts to assimilate into the new world around them. They copy each other's behaviour as well as that of people they see in television series and ads. Reminiscent of Baudrillard's theory of simulacra and simulation, Kathy tells Ruth that, in fact, there is no original to their copies: "It's not what people really do out there, in normal life" (Ishiguro 121). Their attempts at blending in can be interpreted as a simulation of the capitalist imaginary and its subject positions, as becomes apparent when Ruth dreams of working in an office with other "dynamic, go-ahead types" (142), a phrase she copied from a job advertisement in a newspaper.

The topic of cloning and copying exemplifies how Ishiguro's novel works literally and metaphorically at the same time. Its temporal setting can be read as a comment on the precise circumstances of the historical era from the 1960s to 1990s, or as a warning directed at biotechnological futures and cloning, or simply as a multi-temporal setting offering general insight into processes of human worldmaking and exploitation. In this respect, Currie proposes that "one of the principal characteristics of the novel is a kind of timelessness, achieved in part by the scarcity of historical locators and specific temporal references. There is the occasional car, and a significant cassette tape, but otherwise the temporal atmosphere pulls away from any identifiable location in the historical present in both directions" (60). This timelessness explains why the novel speaks about pasts, potential futures, and the present at the same time, as Arne De Boever notes: "Although Ishiguro's novel might be a novel about clones, the questions that the clones confront about life, death, humanity, authority, and so on are universal questions that haunt all of us" (60). In this sense, the novel works as an allegory for the modes of worldmaking of exploitative regimes and especially for the phenomenon of the complicity of the exploited, which I will explore next.

The Complicity of the Deprived

In its attempt to investigate how human worlds can enable extreme forms of exploitation, *Never Let Me Go* looks closely at the ways in which the deprived become complicit with the biopolitical apparatus that exploits them. As an illustration of Foucault's hypothesis that in modern biopolitics, regulation and control surpass discipline as techniques of governmentality (Lemke 51), the protagonists willingly accept and perpetuate their position of enslavement rather than being forced into it. The novel shows how socialisation can keep a group like the Hailsham students firmly within a world made deliberately for them and their exploitation, and consequently prevents them from rebellion against its structures. In this sense, Hailsham represents what Currie calls "the total institution" (101). Furthermore, the narrative situation of Kathy's autobiographical recollection exemplifies subjects defending a world that legitimises their mistreatment instead of assuming deviant worldmaking agency. Finally, the novel emphasises how the structures of recognition within a given world make its inhabitants do things that are far from their own interests, like donating their vital organs.

Currie describes Hailsham as an example of "the total institution", which he defines as "the kind of institution that doesn't let you go home in the evening, like a prison, or the army, or perhaps most relevantly, a boarding school" (101). As a total institution, Hailsham is a completely closed and separated world which contains its own "elaborate system of prohibitions and privileges, of constraints upon and opportunities for personal expression" (102). The Hailsham world is ready-made by the guardians and state authorities for the students to cover up the planned exploitation of the students as human spare part depots. Currie phrases the two worlds as "two realities, one a closed institution, the other a brutal domain of inequality and social injustice" (103). The students themselves have no opportunity at all to actively make or shape either of them. Rather, as a form of self-governmentality, they perpetuate the Hailsham world themselves by policing each other into silence on certain topics and by maintaining euphemistic diction when describing their own role in this world.

It is a common understanding among Hailsham students that certain questions simply cannot be asked and certain topics must not be raised. Most of these questions and topics obviously relate to the students' origins and futures as cloned human beings made for organ donations, a topic which they have been "told and not told" (Ishiguro 82). Even though students vaguely know about their future donations, they avoid consciously reflecting on them and stick to the unspoken rule that they are not to be discussed openly (83). Another topic which the students keep silent about is Madame's art gallery, for which she regularly selects the students' best artworks. Kathy relates that "[t]here was an unspoken rule that we should never even raise the subject [in the presence of the guardians]" (31). If someone dare break these unwritten rules—as a student called Polly does by asking Miss Lucy: "Miss, why does Madame take our things away?" —the other students defend the rules by fencing in the perpetrator: "Virtually everyone shot daggers at Polly" (40).

The silences of the Hailsham world are repeated through the children's play and the teenagers' talks. For example, when Ruth and others play "secret guard" where children must protect their favourite guardian from being abducted, it becomes another unspoken rule to never admit to each other that it is only a game. Even though Kathy is furious after being kicked out of Ruth's secret guard group, she still pretends to another student that the whole thing was real and that she "*personally* heard" people talking about the plan to abduct Miss Geraldine (55). As a narrating "I", Kathy reflects on the incident and explains her reaction as follows: "What it was, I suppose, is that Moira was suggesting she and I cross some line together, and I wasn't prepared for that yet. I think I sensed how beyond that line, there was something harder and darker and I didn't want that" (55). From this, it can be deduced that the silences and pretences of the Hailsham students serve the purpose of maintaining illusions that cover up unwanted truths, most of all the horror and fear of their future exploitation. The students feel the awkwardness of their situation, coupled with the guardians' unease, and thus avoidance feels like the only way to escape. From her grown-up perspective, Kathy proposes that "[i]f we were keen to avoid certain topics, it was probably more because it *embarrassed* us" (69). Maintaining illusions thus answers the psychological need for the deprived to feel that their world is fair and that they are "normal" in "a normalizing society [...] that makes killing acceptable" through racism (Foucault, *Society Must Be Defended* 256). At the same time, keeping silent and pretending allows the exploitative structures of their world to continue.

The euphemistic language which the Hailsham world is made up of serves a similar purpose to avoid and cover up what is known to be real. Instead of speaking of clones, the headmistress and all the guardians of Hailsham prefer to use the term "*students*" (256). In the Hailsham diction, the students become "donors" and "carers" before "completing", which is perhaps the most striking euphemism for dying or being killed. In the same vein, the protagonists speak of "a *possible*" (136) for the potential genetic origin of a clone. In her own narrative account, Kathy sticks to these euphemistic terms, as do the three friends when they talk to each other in direct discourse. The effect of this diction is to perpetuate the double consciousness of knowing and not knowing about the horrible injustices of the cloned humans and to make them accept their destinies. Nancy Armstrong likewise argues that "the categories common to Hailsham life—"carer," "donor," "guardians," "normal"—cut off alternative ways for the children to imagine their relation to the outside world and acclimate them to their roles in a system that takes life from one population and distributes it to another" (454).

Narrative Worldmaking

The narrative situation of *Never Let Me Go* gives deep insights into the process of narrative identity creation and self-governmentality of those who are deprived by a given world. The autodiegetic narrator, who introduces herself as Kathy H., aged 31 (3), looks back on her life and tries to put together the pieces of the memory of her childhood at Hailsham, of living at the Cottages as a young adult, and of working as a carer throughout the last eleven years. The most disturbing feature of her account is that "she appears to be *on the side of the system*" that exploits her and those she loves (De Boever 73). Her account thus reveals the psychological dynamics at play which keep the deprived within the boundaries of their world and make them perpetuate its injustices voluntarily. In her attempt at recollecting the story of her life with Ruth and Tommy, Kathy's narrative, and especially her judgement, may seem strange and unreliable to the reader. Yet, instead of calling her an unreliable narrator, I follow Currie in calling Kathy an "inadequate" narrator (111).

Kathy's narrative covers several layers of time and truth as well as other narrative voices and intradiegeses. In a narrative frame, Kathy tells her story backwards as a narrating "I" that by now knows all about her status and function in the outside world and the ideas behind the Hailsham project. However, throughout most of the novel, her narrative perspective assumes the position of an experiencing "I" in the moment of recollection, with the limited degree of knowledge available to her at the time. In her slow and gradual revelation of the truth, she leads readers along the same way she had to take, from blissful ignorance to dire knowledge. With the gradual increase in knowledge, however, the readers' feelings and judgements of the situation begin to differ more and more from the narrator's: "The more one learns about this underclass of organ donors, the more disturbing the casual blandness of Kathy H.'s voice becomes, leading to an ever-increasing divide between her disaffected tone and one's own growing horror and outrage" (Puchner 36).

The narrative structure of the novel is furthermore characterised by proleptic and analeptic shifts in time. For example, Kathy frequently foreshadows events, which raises tension. With sentences like: "There was one strange incident around this time I should tell you about here. It really unsettled me" (Ishiguro 70), Kathy establishes a sinister atmosphere and makes readers anticipate dark and meaningful revelations. This narrative technique keeps the tension high throughout the novel, while also establishing a contrast between the relatively trivial things that follow these announcements and the horror Kathy keeps silent about: "The very idea of dread develops an irony produced in the chasm between Kathy's remembered anticipations, and the anticipations made by a reader of the more extreme horrors that lie in wait" (Currie 97). This shows that Kathy's intentions are not to tell events incorrectly. In contrast to Ruth, who deliberately wants to forget about life at Hailsham, Kathy tries hard to remember things accurately, which is emphasised when she doubts her own memory: "This was all a long time ago so I might have some of it wrong; but my memory of it is that my approaching Tommy [...]" (Ishiguro 13). Instead of being unreliable, her feelings towards the events turn out to be inadequate as readers become more and more aware of the horrific details of the clones' exploitation. For example, Kathy expresses that Tommy was worried about his fourth donation because maybe, after the forth donation, even if you've technically completed, you're still conscious in some sort of way; how then you find there are more donations, plenty of them, on the other side of that line; how there are no more recovery centres, no carers, no friends; how there's nothing to do except watch your remaining donations until they switch you off. (274)

Her reaction to Tommy is that she "dismissed it as rubbish" even though she knows it might be true, and to the reader she relates that she was "under the impression [they] were dealing with the fourth donation pretty well together" (274), which seems impossible in the face of such horrific circumstances.

To what extent *Never Let Me Go* offers itself to an ethical reading and even a meta-comment on ethics and art is implied by the role the novel ascribes to its readers. By being addressed as a clone, the reader is interpellated into Kathy's world: "Beyond any suggestion of exceptionality, the ordinary brutality of contemporary biopolitical existence is suddenly extended to the reader, who becomes an unwilling partner in the machinic labor of servile narration" (del Valle Alcalá 57). Sentences like "I don't know how it was where you were, but at Hailsham [...]" (13), make clear that the addressee must be another clone reared in another institution and sharing Kathy's world, in which "you really are different to them" (36). Also, Kathy's conversational tone implies that she is at ease as if talking to an intimate friend or confidant: "But that's not really what I want to talk about just now" (45). Both the reader and the imagined addressee probably have a certain temporal and emotional distance to her narrative, as Keith McDonald proposes: "There is some imagined reader who will witness the testimony after some kind of emancipation has taken place" (81). In this sense, her act of telling the truth about clones, donations and Hailsham to another clone might be read either as a confession or as an act of dissidence—a way of finding a voice in a world that "strips its inhabitants of their claims to any forms of political identity" (Black 789). On an abstract level, inscribing readers as potential accomplices in the story also could allude to readers involved in similar atrocities within their own contemporary worlds: "If Ishiguro is urging us to perceive the horror that floats just beyond the horizon of our daily routine, it would seem to follow that he must also be urging us, if only obliquely and subliminally, to take some sort of action against this horror" (Robbins 294).

Structures of Recognition

Another piece of the jigsaw puzzle, which makes people like Kathy complicit with a world that exploits them, are its inherent structures of recognition. For readers, it may seem estranging to see how Kathy takes pride in her job as a carer and Tommy as a donor: "This idea, of a sense of privilege around the condition of atrocity in which Kathy and the others find themselves, is one of the most striking features of the novel" (Currie 100). On the other hand, the sense of pride in their work and social function is modelled closely on the contemporary ideology of work, which follows similar patterns. Even though many people may take more harm than benefits from their jobs—for example because they harm their physical and mental health—work is politically and culturally celebrated as being good and remains the main way of gaining social recognition. Against this backdrop, sentences like "it means a lot to me, being able to do my work well", and "I do know for a fact that they've been pleased with my work, and by and large, I have[,] too" (3) seem extremely familiar.

However, reflecting on what Kathy feels proud about is even more shocking. She boasts about the fact that "[her] donors have always tended to do much better than expected. Their recovery times have been impressive, and hardly any of them have been classified as 'agitated', even before forth donation" (3). In other words, Kathy was successful in reaping the maximum from her fellow clones and making them stay as calm and obedient as possible in their process of being slaughtered alive. As De Boever argues, Kathy's narrative care "risks to be complicit with the system [...] And so Kathy's aesthetics of existence turns out to be an ideological one that does not draw the system into question" (83). This notion of being proud of one's role in society is even more troubling in the case of donors. For example, Tommy states that "I'm a pretty good donor, but I was a lousy carer" (223). Kathy also describes that "there's this odd tendency among donors to treat a fourth donation as something worthy of congratulations. A donor 'on a forth' [...] is treated with respect. Even the doctors and nurses play up to this" (273).

Never Let Me Go stresses the importance of receiving social recognition, even if this means something as extreme as being deprived of one's vital organs while alive. While this may seem absurd in itself, Kathy's autobiographical account makes such a disposition comprehensible, as there are virtually no other options for her or the other clones to be socially recognised. Read as an allegory, Kathy's subjectifying narrative explains how structures of recognition, especially those associated with work, press people into complicity with an ex-

ploitative system. In a similar vein, Bruce Robbins proposes that *Never Let Me Go*
can be read as a critique of the ideology of upward mobility: "Kathy's thoughts
are preoccupied [...] with her professional success. In dispatching that success
toward a nightmarish terminus, Ishiguro would seem to be querying [...] the
ideology of upward mobility" (291). Another possible allegorical reading is to
see the novel as a metaphor of global capitalist exploitation. As with people in
the Global South, the clones at Hailsham are socialised into believing that they
take part in a fair system of exchange, when in fact they must donate their life
or life work in the end without compensation. At Hailsham, this type of socialisation takes place through art exchanges: "Through the Exchanges students
come to believe that they participate in an economy of circulation rather than
of extraction" (Black 796). As I will explore in the following, this is an example
of how art serves as an ideological tool for worldmaking at Hailsham.

Making Arts and Creating Illusions: Humanist Art as a Tool for Ideological Worldmaking

Especially from a humanist point of view, making and contemplating artistic production has long been associated with the essence of being human and
as a distinguishing feature from animals and animal-like existences. *Never Let
Me Go* draws explicitly on the humanist conception of the arts and arts education with the Hailsham project. The aim of the project was to demonstrate
through the student's artistic productions that clones also have souls as Miss
Emily explains: "We did it to *prove you had souls at all*" (Ishiguro 255). The production of good artwork is thus tied to the normative notion of having a soul
and being fully human, as Hailsham and like-minded institutions propagate
through their art exhibitions: "'Look at this art! How dare you claim these children are anything less than fully human?'" (256). While the project to rear students "in humane, cultivated environments" like Hailsham may seem laudable
at first sight, Kathy's first-person account reveals that her education makes her
more complicit with the world that never questions the very existence and usage of clones. The only difference Hailsham believes to have made for its students is that instead of "being reared in deplorable conditions" (255), they "grew
up in wonderful surroundings" (256), while the actual horror of the donations is
never contested. Hailsham has the effect of making Kathy and others feel that
even though they might simply be "pawns in a game", they "were lucky pawns",
as Miss Emily puts it (261). Miss Emily even admits that "[y]es, in many ways
we *fooled* you" (263). Hence, the arts education at Hailsham serves the ideologi-

cal purpose of preventing rebellion against the biopolitical apparatus. The production, exchange, and reception of art offers the students the illusion of being treated human(e)ly, while their status of being outside of the boundary of "the human" remains unquestioned.

Never Let Me Go criticises the humanist conception of art and arts education and unmasks it as an ideological tool to justify exploitation: "Humanistic notions of art and creativity play into the hands of market logic and dehumanisation" (Glaubitz 328). The novel thus drives a wedge between the humanist association of ethics and aesthetics or art, revealing that aesthetics can undermine ethics even while advertising it on the surface. Black likewise reads the novel as "a critique of Romantic-inspired assumptions about aesthetics and empathy" whose "deepest anxieties arguably concern the ethics of artistic production and consumption in an age of multiculturalism and globalization" (785). With his novel, Ishiguro questions humanist ethics that are always geared to a normative and exclusive view of *the* human, for example, as having a soul and producing art. At Hailsham, regular art exchanges where students can trade their artwork for others through a money-like token system, provide the incentive to be artistically creative. At the same time, they lay the foundation for the student's later interdependencies as donors and carers, as Kathy overtly states:

I can see now how the Exchanges had a more subtle effect on us all. If you think about it, being dependent on each other to produce the stuff that might become your private treasures—that's bound to do things to your relationships [...] A lot of the time, how you were regarded at Hailsham, how much you were liked and respected, had to do with how good you were at 'creating'". (Ishiguro 16)

As can be seen with Tommy, who is bullied for not being creative, structures of recognition within the community of students strongly depend on their artistic output. The interdependencies initiated through art exchanges furthermore ensure obedient compliance and prevent deviations. As Black emphasises: "The circulation of student art helps to shape community bonds that keep the students, as peers, moving in lockstep toward their deaths" (795).

With regard to the novel's own aesthetics that can be classified as post- or anti-humanist, Tommy and his art play an important role. While at Hailsham he is ridiculed for not being as creative as the others, he later manages to produce a peculiar kind of art composed of miniature animals with mechanical insides that were "so different from anything the guardians had told [them] to do at Hailsham" (Ishiguro 185). The way Kathy describes them is that "[t]he first impression was like one you get if you took the back off a radio: tiny canals, weaving tendons, miniature screws and wheels were all drawn with obsessive precision, and only when you held the page away could you see it was some kind of armadillo, say, or a bird" (184). Tommy's drawings diverge from the humanist ideal of art taught at Hailsham, and therefore Black describes his art as "inhuman art, which marries the animal with the automatic" and which "provides an alternative to the destructive visions of soul-based humanity that the novel critiques" (801). His mechanical, animal-like pictures can be read as symbols of his own kind, which is vulnerable despite being artificially produced to function like a machine: "For all their busy, metallic features, there was something sweet, even vulnerable about each of them" (185). While the novel is overall critical of the humanist concept of ethics through art, "these small mechanical creatures still invite a prosocial ethics of care that revitalises the possibility of empathy through art" (Black 801). On a metatextual level, Tommy's "inhuman aesthetics" encourage a posthumanist conception of ethics that is not based on mechanisms of inclusion and exclusion.

Different to Ruth and Kathy, Tommy always seems to have had a kind of visceral or pre-conscious knowledge about the wrongness of the Hailsham world and the students' place in the larger world. He is the only clone who feels a vague kind of anger throughout his childhood and into young adulthood, as expressed by his outbursts of rage without any clear source or direction. For example, as a boy "[h]e was just raving, flinging his limbs about, at the sky, at the nearest fence post" (10), and after learning the truth about Hailsham as an adult, Kathy finds him again "raging, shouting, flinging his fists and kicking out" (269). By not being viewed as being as creative as the other students and not living up to the guardians' expectations, Tommy shows signs of rebellion against Hailsham and its delusions. In the end, after becoming fully conscious of their desperate situation, he frames his anger and refusal to create art at Hailsham as a pre-conscious apprehension to the truth: "Maybe I did know, somewhere deep down. Something the rest of you didn't" (270). In this sense, Tommy has always known and yet is unable to fully realise what his temperamental feelings were trying to express because the narratives and aesthetics of the world made up for him and the others do not allow him to.

Instead of simply reading the students *as* humans who deserve a humane treatment, many critics raise the idea that the students should not be read as humans at all. For instance, Armstrong sees Kathy's emotional life as biologically depleted (457), and Puchner proposes that "these creatures are designed with certain limitations, including limited emotional capacities, a certain inability to mature, and a lack of rebelliousness" (41). While I do not agree with them on the difference in biological essence, mainly because Kathy's narrative and emotional disposition appear to be a product of her background and upbringing, I argue that it does not actually matter whether she is biologically human or not. The point the novel makes is rather that this type of normative humanist ethics is a problem in itself, and that empathy and dignity should be expanded to all feeling creatures, not only to those who are let into "the human" club. In this respect, Black describes Ishiguro's novel as an example of "inhuman aesthetics" that does not "abandon the ethical potential of works of art. Instead, it makes a case for ethics offering a very different approach to art and empathy that relies on the recognition of the inhuman" (786). As a result, readers are coerced to feel that the treatment of the protagonists is wrong, not because they are human but because they suffer, as Jacques Derrida famously argued in the context of animal ethics (369).

The example of Kathy, Ruth, and Tommy knowing and not knowing about the world they live in demonstrates how narrative and aesthetic worldmaking can make the exploited complicit subjects of the biopolitical regime that exploits them. The story's multitemporality, resulting from its setting in an alternative past, enables allegorical readings through which the topic of exploitative worldmaking can be transferred to other time-spaces, ranging from contemporary injustices to potential futuristic biotechnological inventions. Through its narrative structure and the interpellation of the reader into the story world, Ishiguro calls upon readers to question their own complicities within exploitative systems which might be operating with the same logic of knowing and not knowing. The novel even goes so far as to ask readers to take a critical distance from its own mode of worldmaking as art that might function as a delusion from the horrors of exploitation, too. It challenges the humanist project of arts education as ethical in and by itself, and instead proposes a kind of posthumanist ethics that destabilises the notion of "the human" and includes those considered as less than human. While this can be taken literally, as in the case of the biotechnologically bred protagonists, it can also be read metaphorically to justify inequality and exploitation by including all people and non-human animals around the globe that are pushed into this category. The alternative past setting of Never Let Me Go thus works allegorically to address bio-ethical issues concerning multiple settings and times, from the past to the future. In contrast, my next example, Don DeLillo's Zero K, represents an analysis of the seeds of the future contained in the contemporary moment, its precise power structures and cultural dispositions.

A Futuristic Present: The Power over Life and Death in Don DeLillo's *Zero K*

Although set in a recognisable present, Don DeLillo's 2016 novel *Zero K* transpires futurity with its plot and themes. *The Observer* notes that "DeLillo is a seer [...] *Zero K* again feels like a demonstration of the way a great novelist moves one or two steps ahead of the real, constructing pathways into the future" (Preston). The novel centres on the idea of cryotechnology, the preservation of deceased bodies at very low temperatures as a potential means for (future) immortality resulting from prospective leaps in medicine and biotechnology. It is narrated by the protagonist Jeffrey who accompanies his father Ross and stepmother Artis to a cryopreservation site called "The Convergence", where their bodies are to be stored until futuristic technology allows for their revival. While cryotechnological preservation after death is still far from mainstream practise, "[a]s of 2014, there were more than 300 cryogenically frozen individuals in the United States, another 50 in Russia, and a few thousand 'contracted members' who had signed up to be frozen upon death" (Buder). I read DeLillo's *Zero K* as an extrapolation from a cultural undercurrent that Jean Baudrillard identifies in *The Vital Illusion* (2000): "We all want immortality. It is our ultimate fantasy, a fantasy that is also at work in all of our modern sciences and technologies—at work, for example, in the deep freeze of cryonic suspension and in cloning and in all its manifestations" (3).

Zero K uses aesthetics of speculative realism to defamiliarise the present and its dominant worlds of capitalism and transhumanism which promise a future of biotechnological progress. As the novel illustrates, they culminate with the desire to overcome death, which is viewed as the ultimate obstacle to the human mastery of life. By focusing on cryonic preservation in the context of global biocapitalism, *Zero K* illustrates a type of biopolitics of mortality in the 21st century. It shows "the dissolution of democracy and the political" (Koljević 33), as power over life is transferred from the sovereign to private capital. These super-wealthy *"crypto-elites"* (46), as embodied through Jeffrey's father Ross, are able to afford potential immortality while the vast majority of people face extinction through wars and ecocide. In addition to this biopolitical setup of inequality and injustice, *Zero K* poses the questions "What is life?"

and "How does it relate to death?". With its metatextual focus on aesthetics and art, it defamiliarises the dominant perspectives on life and death as opposites and foregrounds their interdependencies.

I will argue that DeLillo's *Zero K* advocates aesthetics of life that build on transience, while also pointing out that the more cultures and individuals want to control life through biopower and its science and technology instruments, the more elusive life becomes. I will begin my analysis by scrutinising the relations of power and its future consequences as illustrated by the novel's spatial and temporal setting in a futuristic present. From this setting, I will deduce that the most extreme form of control over life as exercised by biocapitalist biopolitics paradoxically ends in absolute death—of the individual in cryopreservation, and of the human civilisation through potential self-extinction. Next, I will point out how the book self-referentially reflects on language as an aesthetic means to deconstruct and reconstruct notions of life into worlds and their related subject positions. In a similar vein, *Zero K* metatextually reflects on art, contrasting its immortality with the art of (im-)mortality offered by the cryonics project. In the end, I will turn to the novel's depiction of otherworlds and their potential biocapitalist rule, which can be found in the transient concept of "the little life".

The Present as Future

Despite its futuristic outlook regarding cryopreservation and potential immortality, Don DeLillo's *Zero K* is set in an easily recognisable present marked by real historical events and places. In its futuristic present setting, *Zero K* is similar to Jeanette Winterson's *Frankisstein* (2019), which juxtaposes the historical tale of Mary Shelley's writing of *Frankenstein* with a story of contemporary scientists attempting to create artificial intelligence ranging from sexbots to post-gendered superintelligence. Like *Zero K*, *Frankisstein* entails speculative and defamiliarising elements in its portrayal of a present shaped by seemingly futuristic developments in biotechnology. Critics have termed the fusion of realism and speculation exhibited in *Zero K* as "speculative realism" (e.g. Herbrechter 17; Glavanakova 96). This aesthetic choice allows for a distancing perspective on actual contemporary worlds like biocapitalism, while making its biopolitics and cultural undercurrents surface via speculative and imaginary aspects.

As reader reviews on *goodreads* reveal, the reception of *Zero K* is quite polarised. This is due to DeLillo's choice, as a renowned literary author, to explore traditional science-fiction themes through his novel. Accordingly, a number of reviewers lament the novel's lack of entertainment quality, low emotional engagement and missing options for identification. One reviewer criticises that "[e]very time a contemporary 'literary' author steps into the science-fiction arena, he seems to be totally unaware of the thousands of stories that have already been written about the same exact concept, and often already taken to a much more satisfying development". A number of readers report that Zero K evokes ethical reflections, for example on "man's ever-growing hubris and the irreversible damage this is causing our cultural, financial and physical environment". Regarding biocapitalist biopolitics, another reader commented: "Death, or the desire to escape death, may be one of those places where only those with significant, GDP-sized capital, can tread. Thus, those with wealth that involves 9+zeros become the modern-day pharaohs of death" ('Zero K Community Reviews').

These responses are examples of how Zero K's speculative realism evokes ethical reflections on present worlds and biotechnological developments. The speculative realism manifests most prominently in the novel's temporal and spatial setting: actual places and events are expanded by elements of specula-tion and imagination. The plot of the novel shuttles back and forth between the present, a familiar and realistic New York, and the futuristic and imaginary site of The Convergence which is located in a vast, empty desert close to the border of Kyrgyzstan and Kazakhstan (DeLillo 29). Hence, the speculative angle of the novel results mainly from The Convergence as a deeply future-oriented project that appears to be surreal and absurd due to its art installations, art-likeness, or even art-ificiality. As the main parts of the narrative take place in The Con-vergence, the dynamics between centre and margin are also reversed: potential futures dominate the present, and worldmaking powers withdraw from the wealthy and crowded centres to the "remote" (64) margins of the world that are "not battered and compacted by history" (30), as Jeffrey's father Ross notes.

Temporally, the novel is evidently set in the present, with the first part ti-tled as "In the Time of Chelyabinsk", referring to a meteor crash in the Russian city of Chelyabinsk in 2013, and the second part being called "In the Time of Konstantivoka", denoting a city in Ukraine that played an important role in the Russo-Ukrainian war in 2014. In contrast, especially with regard to The Con-vergence, references to the future abound: Jeffrey's affluent father, Ross, who is a big investor in the enterprise, claims that the people there are "making the future. A new idea of the future. Different from the others" (30). When Jef-frey contemplates the hundreds of cryotechnologically preserved bodies at The

Convergence, he thinks "[t]hose were humans entrapped, enfeebled, individual lives stranded in some border region of a wishful future" (256). Associates of The Convergence never tire of emphasising that the future they are in the process of making represents a radical break in history. For example, a representative of the project Jeffrey calls Ben Ezra says: "Try to understand. This is all happening in the future. This future, this instant [...] We've fallen out of history" (128–129). The wish of The Convergence to be "completely outside the narrative of what we refer to as history" (237) points to the project's transhumanist aim to transcend the biological, social, and cultural limits that have characterised human life throughout history and become superhuman at some point in the future.

Like the setting, the narrative style of the novel is marked by seemingly opposing tendencies: on the one hand, the narrator Jeffrey uses a realistic mode of narration to describe the events, facilities, and people he witnesses. As a result of him being a homodiegetic narrator, readers also gain insight into his psyche, which creates a kind of psychological realism. On the other hand, the narrative appears postmodernist for its metatextuality, absurd characters, and deconstructivist elements. For example, the ontological status of the short, middle section titled "Artis Martineau" (155) hovers between fantasy, metafictional comment, and psychological realism. It can be interpreted either as Jeffrey's stepmother's actual interior monologue in cryopreservation, "as a metafictional reference to her status as a character in a book, deconstructed by the author himself" (Glavanakova 109), or as Jeffrey's speculation about what might pass through Artis's head during cryopreservation (e.g. Barrett 110). Furthermore, "the characters (as has been said of DeLillo's work before) are not so much semblances of real people as mouthpieces for philosophical epithets" (Dini 3). The protagonist Jeffrey appears to be a prototypical postmodernist character, absurd in his attempt at non-commitment amid a postmodern hyper-capitalist world. Characterised by his mother as "the shapeless man", he asserts: "The drift, job to job, sometimes city to city, was integral to the man I was" (DeLillo 57).

If Jeffrey as an absurd postmodernist character serves as a distorted mirror to the world around him, he evokes the question of what or who is more absurd: him, or the capitalist world represented by his father, Ross, which thrives on human suffering through water privatisation and the speculation of natural catastrophes. Jeffrey even explicitly raises this question in a job interview Ross sets up for him with one of his representatives: "Who was more absurd, he or I?" (167). The main philosophy tested by Zero K is the fusion of (bio-)capitalism with transhumanism as the idea to technologically surpass the boundaries of the human. This merger represents the biopolitics of the 21st century in which power has moved from (more or less) democratically organised institutions like the national state to a global elite made up of private and corporate capital. *Zero K* projects that this kind of biopolitics produces two types of death that represent "absolute" death: one being the cryotechnologically suspended (rich) individual, and the other being the collective extinction of the rest of humankind.

The Biopolitics of Death in the Future

The future as enacted by The Convergence is marked by biopolitics of survival that establish hierarchies of who is given a chance to live in the future. The Convergence "becomes a microcosm of a contemporary culture increasingly under threat from the combined forces of technology and global capital. As the tactility of our already loosening reality begins to unravel, DeLillo presents us with the disorientating consequences of a world stripped of death as the final frontier of the real" (Ashman 14). This interpretation evokes associations with Jean Baudrillard's work, which explicitly features "The Murder of the Real" in *The Vital Illusion* (2000). In this book, Baudrillard discusses the topics of cloning and immortality against the backdrop of his well-known analysis of a simulated hyper-reality through ubiquitous (digital) medialisation. With regard to both biotechnological innovation and virtual hyper-reality, Baudrillard issues the warning that "[w]e are in the process of reactivating [...] the [pathological] immortality of the cancer cell, both at the individual level and at the level of the species as a whole" (8). *Zero K* illustrates Baudrillard's thesis through The Convergence which "expresses the exhaustion and cynicism of capitalism's ultimate phase, which goes as far as to claim ownership and anticipate consumption of its own apocalyptic end—the apocalyptic logic and vision on which it has been thriving and which provides it with a form of 'zombie' survival" (Herbrechter 16).

    Zero K shows a scenario where biopower, as a political power of the sovereign over the lives of its citizens and the "power to 'make' live and 'let' die" (Foucault, *Society Must Be Defended* 241), is transferred more and more to private capital. It is mainly individuals "with serious money" like Ross, alongside "foundations, corporations, secret funding from various governments by way of their intelligence agencies" (DeLillo 33), who enable The Convergence and its future-oriented biopolitics of (im-)mortality. These biopolitics rest on the assumption that in the light of impeding global catastrophes like climate disasters and ubiquitous wars, the end-time for the majority of human lives approaches, with only the super-rich having access to biotechnologically perfected lives in the future.

This message is brought forth by The Convergence project leaders in their talks, as well as by the artistic visualisations seen on mobile screens in its hallways. For example, two main representatives of the project, whom Jeffrey names "the Stenmark twins", speak of "[t]error and war, everywhere now, sweeping the surface of our planet" (241), and they predict that "[a]pocalypse is inherent in the structure of time and long-range climate and cosmic upheaval" (243). The message of "the end, everybody's end" (65) is repeated (56, 126, 238) and visualised on screens showing digitally edited footage of actual events ranging from floods and hurricanes to live immolations and wars (11, 35, 61, 259). Assuming the inevitable decline of human life on the planet, another Convergence spokesperson explains that "[t]o some extent we are here in this location to design a response to whatever eventual calamity may strike the planet [...] At some point in the future, death will become unacceptable even as the life of the planet becomes more fragile" (66).

Unacceptable death in this sense only refers to the death of some, namely super-rich individuals like Ross who can afford to be cryotechnologically preserved. This kind of death, or rather un-death, produced by biocapitalist biopolitics, finds itself in direct relation to the deaths of the masses of people, likewise produced by the biocapitalist regime. Ross's involvement in water privatisation and his profiting from natural disasters shows that turning the life of most into the profit of some will necessarily result in the destruction of the majority through ecocide and war. However, this link is never addressed by the Convergence spokespeople. As a result, I argue that both types of death produced by biocapitalism represent an absolute death that differs from the kind of death entangled with life. Departing from the hypothesis that death is a prerequisite for life, I claim that the biocapitalist regime ultimately produces absolute death, in the form of collective extinction on the one hand, and cryonic suspension of individuals on the other.

Paradoxically, the Saint Augustine quote offered by one of the Stenmark twins seems to confirm the idea of absolute death for the super-rich individuals preserved in The Convergence: "And never can a man be more disastrously in death than when death itself shall be deathless" (DeLillo 240). The in-between state of cryopreservation is neither death nor life, but rather a kind of zombie-like un-death as represented in the chapter "Artis Martineau": "But am I who I was. [...] What is it that I am waiting for. [...] I only hear what is me. I am made of words. [...] Where is my body" (157–159). Nonetheless, people like Ross are deeply attracted to the idea of immortality, possibly because it serves as the absolute marker of distinction from the masses as the Stenmarks hint: "Think of money and immortality [...] Isn't this what you've been waiting for? A way to claim the myth for yourselves. Life everlasting belongs to those of breathtaking wealth" (76). In response, Jeffrey thinks that "[t]his was not a sales pitch. I didn't know what this was, a challenge, a taunt, a thrust at the vanity of the moneyed elect or simply an attempt to tell them what they've always wanted to hear even if they didn't know it" (76).

The passage also highlights the already established merger between transhumanist philosophy and capitalism which The Convergence and Ross symbolise. Ross is characterised by his son as "a man shaped by money. He made an early reputation by analyzing the profit impact of natural disasters. He liked to talk about money [...] He had an affair with an office temp. He ran in the Boston Marathon" (13). Ross Lockhart, whose name is self-chosen and fake so as to bring "him closer to self-realization" (81), represents the prototypical neoliberal capitalist subject: self-made, ego-centric and achievement-oriented, interested only in making money without ethical considerations. It is not surprising that his personal and financial involvement with The Convergence results from the vanity expressed by his slogan "[e]*verybody wants to own the end of the world*" (3) that builds on the economic text-book approach to the self-interested *homo oeconomicus*.

The spiritual emptiness of Ross's capitalist world finds fulfilment in the philosophy of transhumanism which replaces religious creed with science and technology, as Ross overtly states with reference to the procedures of The Convergence: "Faith-based technology. That's what it is. Another god. Not so different, it turns out, from some of the earlier ones. Except that it's real, it's true, it delivers" (9). Referencing the prospect of a looming global apocalypse, Ross indicates that "[t]his place may not have been intended as the new Jerusalem, but people made long journeys to find a form of higher being here, or at least a scientific process that will keep their body tissue from decomposing" (43). This transhumanist perspective which entails "fantasies of human life extension, especially through cryogenics" (Herbrechter 14) as one form of absolute death is thus opposed to a more posthumanist outlook on the contemporary "ontological, epistemological and ecological crisis that could lead [...] to radical extinction and ecocide" (8) as another form of absolute death.

Accordingly, the biopolitics of The Convergence proclaim the death of "the human" in two senses: the extinction of human life on the planet goes hand in hand with the death of "the human" as a species, because those survivors will become "superhuman". The Stenmarks proclaim: "We want to stretch the boundaries of what it means to be human—stretch and then surpass. We want to do whatever we are capable of doing in order to alter human thought and bend the energies of civilization" (71). Ross's second wife, Artis, who also undergoes cryonic preservation, likewise believes that "[she] will reawaken to a new perception of the world [...]. [She] will be reborn into a deeper and truer reality. Lines of brilliant light, every material thing in its fullness, a holy object" (47). Artis and The Convergence project team share the assumption that the future (super)-humanity will find entirely new and precious ways of accessing "the world as it really is" (47) through biotechnological enhancement and even a new language invented by its project members. As I will explore in the next section, *Zero K* metatextually scrutinises the role of language as a means for human world construction and world perception, especially with regard to a futuristic present of biotechnological enhancement.

Language and Life

As is typical of Don DeLillo's works, *Zero K* is preoccupied with the role of language in the face of a postmodern world shaped by hyper-capitalism and high technology. It is especially concerned with the way human life is organised through language, serving as the foundation for worldmaking while simultaneously staying elusive with respect to an assumed or signified reality. As I will outline in this section, *Zero K* begins with a deconstructivist questioning of language and its relation to a world beyond signification. With regard to The Convergence and its new language of the future, the novel illustrates Baudrillard's theory of "the Perfect Crime against language" (Baudrillard and Witwer 69), which is an attempt to overcome the symbolic function of language and access reality directly. Finally, I will argue that the novel puts forth a notion of language that could be described as re-construction, containing a renewed faith in its potential to make human life meaningful despite or even because of an awareness of its imperfect relationship to the material world.

DeLillo's novel self-referentially directs the focus towards its own building blocks: words and language. It is through the homodiegetic narrator Jeffrey, who is constantly preoccupied with language, that the potential and shortcomings of words as signifiers, but also language as an aesthetic experience, become a major theme. In a typical deconstructivist and postmodernist gesture, the novel depicts "the failure of language to satisfactorily or definitively convey meaning. *Zero K* is saturated with moments where words fail to articulate the reality of things, where the metonymic and metaphorical flow of signifiers unravel into a boundless and incomprehensible swirl" (Ashman 7). For example, Jeffrey remembers his young self not understanding "fishwife", a term his father used to call his mother, which caused him to consult a dictionary and receive the following results:

> Coarse woman, a shrew. I had to look up *shrew*. A scold, a nag, from Old English for shrewmouse. I had to look up *shrewmouse*. The book sent me back to *shrew*, sense 1. A small insectivorous mammal. I had to look up *insectivorous*. The book said it meant feeding on insects, from Latin *insectus*, for insect, plus Latin *vora*, for vorous. I had to look up *vorous*. (DeLillo 25)

Instead of providing clarity, the dictionary deferred the meaning of the term endlessly by pointing to more words that failed to make sense to Jeffrey. Reminiscent of Jacques Derrida's post-structuralist theory of language and his concept of "différance", the example demonstrates how words fail to mean anything by themselves—they only work within the context of the entire language system, by *differing* from each other and by *deferring* meaning.

In response to this alleged "shortcoming" of language to point to a precise signified outside the realm of language, The Convergence project wants to create a language for the future that enables direct access to reality. Project member Ben Ezra explains that this language is "[a] system that will offer new meanings, entire new levels of perception [...] We will approximate the logic and beauty of pure mathematics in everyday speech. No similes, metaphors, analogies. A language that will not shrink from whatever forms of objective truth we have never before experienced" (130). The idea of a language being as precise as mathematics and void of images, illusions, or ambiguities represents what Jean Baudrillard calls the "Perfect Crime" (Baudrillard and Witwer 69) because it amounts to the "Murder of the Real" (62). According to Baudrillard, "[i]t is the excess of reality that puts an end to reality" (66). A language that has lost its symbolic function which is based on its difference to the referent, on a "vital illusion" (72), becomes the "absolute truth". It could not be more fitting against the backdrop of The Convergence that Baudrillard defines the "absolute truth" as "the other name for death" (72).

Another striking feature of the future language designed at The Convergence is that it is meant to be "[a] language isolate, beyond all affiliation with other languages" (DeLillo 130), just like the future The Convergence is creating is meant to be entirely cut off from history. Similarly, Ross Lockhart attempts "to abandon his generational history" (82) and free himself from family ties by shedding his birth name, Nicholas Satterswaite. In contrast, Jeffrey emphasises the importance of identity creation through relations, especially that of family. Instead of the "simulated" (82) and "self-made" (145) man his father is, Jeffrey tries to understand himself through his family history, including his "wrong" surname: "I wondered what would have happened if I'd learned the truth sooner. Jeffrey Satterswaite" (83). Disrupted by his father's abandonment of his wife and teenage son and the false name Lockhart, Jeffrey struggles to find a coherent identity. Instead, he tries to become visible to himself and others by simulating a limp (101), trying to be bookish and failing (102), and becoming his father's "personal antichrist" through mumbling, shuffling, and having a weird haircut (14).

Perhaps the most distinguishing characteristic of Jeffrey's quirky personality is his obsession with language, which is expressed in his urge to define words, listen to the sound of foreign languages, and invent imaginary names and histories of strangers. Alexandra Glavanakova describes the protagonist as an "iconic DeLillian character" who "gains power over people and experiences by finding the exact word for them (81, 82, 83, 86). The act of naming objects and people adds solidity to a world that is otherwise bleak, alienating, and full of horrors" (104). At The Convergence, where Jeffrey feels especially uneasy, the naming of people becomes a coping strategy for him. For example, during his final visit to the site to accompany his father into his self-chosen and premature death for cryopreservation, Jeffrey tries to make up his mind about the representative who praises Ross and his likes as "heralds" for the future: "I needed a name for her. [...] A name would add dimension to the lithe body, suggest a place of origin, help me identify the circumstances that had brought her here" (238). Jeffrey further believes that his practise of imaginary naming could be subversive to The Convergence's enterprise that "is drenching [him] in bad blood" (145). After deciding that the woman should be called "Zara", he continues thinking, "I didn't want to forget she needed a surname. I owed her this. Isn't that why I was here, to subvert the dance of transcendence with my tricks and games?" (242).

Jeffrey's creative usage and love of language directly opposes The Convergence's linguistic aspirations. Instead of seeing the imperfect relationship between signifier and signified as a problem, Jeffrey celebrates this quality which allows for what Baudrillard calls the "vital illusion" as it enables imagination and aesthetic experience. In addition to inventing names and stories for people, Jeffrey also has a habit of defining words, claiming that "[t]here was something satisfying and hard-won about this even if I made it a point not to check the dictionary definition" (55). He also enjoys the sound of single words and foreign languages as an aesthetic experience in itself. For instance, he recounts that "[s]ometimes I think I go to museums just to hear the languages spoken by visitors to the galleries" (256). From this perspective, as Rachele Dini argues, "as in all of DeLillo's work, a faith in language's ability to redeem and render the world legible underwrites much of *Zero K*'s narrative" (2). This re-constructivist take on language is thus not a counter position to deconstruction, but builds up on its heritage, advocating for a re-enchantment of a world that is moving towards the techno-scientific perfection promoted by transhumanism.

The Immortality of Art and the Art of Immortality

The dialectics between opposing yet mutually dependent poles, such as present and future, life and death, illusion and reality, is once again taken up by the novel with respect to art and immortality. As a piece of art itself, *Zero K* assumes a metatextual perspective in its exploration of the relationship between art and immortality. Glavanakova asserts that "[i]n contradistinction to death [...] DeLillo posits art and language and the language of art. The facility, as well as the text itself, in true alliance with DeLillo's metatextual writing practice, is represented as a strange hybrid of art and technology" (103). On the one hand, the novel foregrounds the immortality of art as opposed to the mortality of the individual human being or even the human species. In many layers of self-referentiality, it features and discusses art in different forms, posits its characters as artefacts and advocates an aesthetic mode of being-in-the-world as a form of vitality. On the other hand, *Zero K* frames The Convergence as a piece of art itself, representing the art of immortality that is more geared towards death than life. From the building and the site, its installations, performances, and screens to the bodies in the so-called pods—everything about The Convergence seems to form part of a delirious piece of art suspended between life and death just as the cryonically preserved bodies and brains.

The ancient trope of the immortality of art as opposed to human mortality probably goes even further back than Hippocrates's slogan, "Life is short and art long", and is perhaps most famously represented by William Shakespeare's "Sonnett 18". DeLillo's *Zero K* likewise draws on this trope by associating art with a life that outlasts death, or even life as a form of art. The novel depicts artworks through ekphrastic descriptions and through this engenders self-referential reflections on the phenomenon of art. As an art piece itself, *Zero K* works like a *mise en abyme*,[2] an artistic technique which also appears in the novel on an intradiegetic level in the form of an art installation: After Ross has been taken for cryopreservation, Jeffrey is "led to a room in which all four walls were covered with a continuous painted image of the room itself", which "struck [him] as a subject worthy of some deep method of inquiry, phenomenology maybe, but [he] wasn't up to the challenge" (252). The high degree of metatextual referencing and the playful repetition of forms on different diegetic levels are typical of postmodernist writing, which has the effect of foregrounding the aesthetic experience of art itself. In the context of the novel's contemporary world, an aesthetic mode of perception and being-in-the-world is promoted as a source of vitality opposed to the deadliness of the capitalist system and its focus on mastery and efficiency.

The dialectics between aesthetics and immortality become most visible at the end of the novel when, during a bus ride, Jeffrey experiences "the natural phenomenon, here in Manhattan, once or twice a year, in which the sun's rays align with the local street grid" (273). He associates this event with the sky collapsing upon them as an apocalyptic moment which announces "the end of the world" (274). At the same time, Jeffrey is fascinated by a little boy's "cries of wonder" conveying "the purest astonishment in the intimate touch of earth and sun" (274). This fleeting moment of pure aesthetic experience consoles Jeffrey with the idea that all human life, and probably even the life of humanity, is limited. For once, Jeffrey lacks the right term for the phenomenon called Manhattanhenge, but this, together with the boy's pre-linguistic "urgent cries" (273), only augments the experience. Again, *Zero K* seems to illustrate Baudrillard, who comments that, against the backdrop of the contemporary world moving from crisis to catastrophe, humanity may be bound to disappear. "If this is the case, it would be better by far to treat our disappearance as an art form—to exercise it, to perform it, to create an art of disappearance" (Baudrillard and Witwer 68).

This is precisely what Ross's second wife, Artis, does when she becomes a piece of art through cryonic suspension. Her name, Artis, also works as a telling name. As the genitive of the Latin *ars* (art), Artis actually means "of art", which therefore "implies, [...] she is less the artist than the art" (Barrett 122). During Jeffrey's final visit to The Convergence, he is led to see the cryonically preserved

---

2   A *mise-en-abyme* is the infinite reproduction of a picture or story within itself.

body of Artis, giving him the impression that she "belonged here, Ross did not" (258). He further muses that "it was Artis, here, alone, who carried the themes of this entire complex into some measure of respect" (258). Jeffrey begins to see the "rows of bodies in gleaming pods" as "a form of visionary art, it was body art with broad implications" (256). Linking this with the life of Artis and her work as an archaeologist, he concludes that what he was seeing was "Archaeology for a future age" (256). The character of Artis as a symbol of art, combined with her potential immortality at The Convergence, thus reaffirms the idea of the immortality of art and the art of disappearance. This, however, is not the same as The Convergence's own art of immortality which seems more dead than alive.

The entire atmosphere at the Convergence is characterised by associations with death, like stillness, darkness, emptiness, and silence. The building itself, its surroundings and interior design all seem to be part of an arts project "involving colors, forms and local materials, art meant to accompany and surround the hardwired initiative, the core work of scientists, counselors, technicians and medical personnel" (23). There are sculptures and mannequins, installations, and performance art. Resembling a delirious nightmare, the interior of the building is claustrophobic with no windows in its bedrooms, endless hallways painted in shades of muted blue, and fake doors leading to nowhere. Its silence is only ever penetrated by eerie performance acts. Jeffrey remarks, "This was art that belongs to the afterlife. It was art that accompanies last things, simple, dreamlike, and delirious. You're dead, it said" (119). The Convergence and its art is marked by elements of uncanniness and even horror. For instance, next to some mannequins in the garden, Jeffrey finds "figures submerged in a pit, mannequins in convoluted mass, naked, arms jutting, heads horribly twisted, bare skulls [...] neutered humans, men and women stripped of identity, faces blank except for one unpigmented figure, albino, staring at me, pink eyes flashing" (134). On the one hand, he interprets the "mannequins as preserved corpses" (133), and on the other hand, the real bodies in the pods now look to him like "humans as mannequins" (146). In conclusion, Jeffrey decides that the entire Convergence must be "art in itself" due to being designed by those he establishes as the leaders of the project, the Stenmark twins: "This was their aesthetic of seclusion and concealment, all the elements that I found so eerie and disembodying" (73).

Another significant element of The Convergence's art of immortality are the screens that sometimes lower in the hallways and depict apocalyptic scenes, such as a flood, hurricane, volcano eruption, life immolations of monks, or war scenes. In the beginning, Jeffrey interprets these silent films as documentaries or newsfeeds of actual events, which makes him feel obliged to watch for the sake of the victims (35). Only later does he consider that the scenes might just be another piece of Convergence art, "visual fictions, the wildfires and burning monks, digital bits, digital code, all of it computer-generated, none of it real" (151). However, "[j]ust as Jeffrey concludes that the images are mere simulation, he is confronted with a performative stampede that is rendered all the more surreal by its stark authenticity. Choreographed by the designers of The Convergence, this performance piece precipitates a bleeding of the cinematic into the real" (Ashman 9). Once again, the novel seems to illustrate and play with Baudrillard's theory of simulation and hyper-reality of a world permeated by digitalisation in which the real is effaced. On the other hand, *Zero K* argues for a continued existence of the real in the form of embodiment and physical vulnerability. This is expressed most profoundly through the example of Jeffrey's girlfriend Emma's adopted son, Stak, whose violent death is transmitted in one of the films depicting Russo-Ukrainian war scenes: "He is hit again and goes to his knees and there is a distinct image of the figure, [...] he is three times life size, here, above me, shot and bleeding, stain spreading across his chest, young man, eyes shut, surpassingly real" (DeLillo 263).

The vulnerability of the living body is thus contrasted with the transhumanist project of disembodiment and transcendence of the human, which is expressed in The Convergence's art of death. The visual and ekphrastic descriptions of art and aesthetic experiences, both in and outside of The Convergence, repeat the theme of life and death in its entanglement, but also in the transhumanist aspiration to separate life from death through cryotechnology. In the final section, I will put forth the claim that DeLillo's *Zero K* contrasts the absolute death of this world with "the little life" of the everyday, which becomes alive only through death and in relationality with others.

The Little Life as Otherworld

The entanglement between life and death, which the novel carries over into the sphere of art, also finds expression in the proposition of "the little life" as an otherworld to the absolute death of The Convergence. Alongside the aesthetic mode of being and the immortality of art, *Zero K* conceptualises life as relational, depending on death, but also as ordinary day-to-day routines. Jeffrey's mother, Madeline, conveys this message through her own death, the loving relationship with her son, and her valuing of everyday life including its trivial moments. In memory of his mother, Jeffrey comments that "[o]rdinary moments make the life. This is what she knew to be trustworthy and this is what I learned, eventually, from those years we spent together" (109). In the last chapter of the book, Jeffrey describes the seemingly insignificant daily routines which his workdays are composed of—he finally takes on a job—and the small activities, like going to an art gallery, staying a night at his father's townhouse or going grocery shopping: "In my local market I never forget to check the expiration dates on bottles and cartons. I reach into the display of objects, of packed goods, and lift an item from the last rank because that's where the freshest sliced bread is placed, or milk, or cereal" (267). In contrast to the rest of the novel, the paragraphs of this chapter are shorter and visually fragmented, making the apparently trivial accounts of his activities appear more significant as they become the building blocks of life. Jeffrey's accounts of his daily activities, like checking the expiration dates of goods, also breathe an air of impermanence. As is the case with food, they emphasise that everything related to life is transitory and perishable.

Perhaps the most important opposing force to The Convergence's project of immortality, which paradoxically results in the production of absolute death, is the significance of death for life, demonstrated through Madeline's death. For Jeffrey, his mother's death becomes a foil to The Convergence and his father's and stepmother's deaths. He repeatedly remembers the scene of "[his] mother in bed, at the end, and the woman in the doorway, her friend and neighbour, ever nameless, leaning on a cane, a quad cane, a metal cane with four little splayed legs" (49). The repetitive description of this visual scene points out that this was a particularly meaningful moment for Jeffrey's life and his identity. He further emphasises: "I'd never felt more human than I did when my mother lay in bed, dying. [...] This was a wave of sadness and loss that made me understand that I was a man expanded by grief. [...] My mother was ordinary in her own way, free-souled, my place of safe return" (248). His relatively positive framing of his mother's death is strongly contrasted with the effect of his father's self-chosen death at The Convergence. Rather than "expanding" him and providing a positive self-identification and history, his father's mode of dying "diminishes" him (113). In the end Jeffrey realises: "I stand forever in the shadow of Ross and Artis and it's not their resonant lives that haunt me but their manner of dying" (266). Ross's death, together with his life, which is marked by a corporate career and abandonment of his family, make Jeffrey wonder whether he's "not hiding inside a life that's a reaction to this, or a retaliation for this" (266). Jeffrey's life of drifting and non-identity certainly suggests this.

Jeffrey's mother Madeline, whom he describes as "the loving source" (108), and the time Jeffrey spends with his girlfriend, Emma, furthermore posit that life is made up of relations. Both historical relations like family ties as well as "synchronic" relations, such as partnerships. This is again directly opposed to the idea of The Convergence, which wants to cut all ties with history as well as any affiliations with existing cultures and languages. Jeffrey's struggle to find an identity demonstrates that without a history and without relations, there can be no identity, which is one reason why his relationship with Emma ends up failing. Jeffrey self-diagnoses that he waited too long to "tell her who I was, to narrate the histories of Madeline and Ross, and Ross and Artis, and the still-life future of father and stepmother in cryonic suspension. [...] I'd wanted her to see me in an isolated setting, outside the forces that made me" (271). In contrast to the neoliberal belief in the isolated self, without these forces, there seems to be no "me".

Nonetheless, the relationship with Emma proves to be a life-giving source for Jeffrey. During the time he is still together with Emma, the idea of "the little life" as opposed to the looming "absolute death" of humanity is repeated as Jeffrey remembers:

> Know the moment, feel the gliding hand, gather all the forgettable fragments, fresh towels on the racks, nice new bar of soap, clean sheets on the bed, her bed, our blue sheets. This was all I needed to take me day to day and I tried to think of these days and nights as the hushed countermand, ours, to the widespread belief that the future, everybody's, will become worse than the past. (109)

The fact that the relationship with Emma did not last can also be traced back to the larger worldmaking forces instead of purely personal failure. Neoliberal capitalism produces uprooted and distorted selves like Jeffrey, but also like Stak, Emma's adoptive son, whom she adopted at a Ukrainian orphanage. Despite many years of living together, Emma laments: "I don't know who he is, I don't know who his friends are, I don't know who his parents were" (177)—like The Convergence, he is cut off from history, family, and land. In addition to uprooting individuals, the biocapitalist regime also causes global warfare as illustrated by the Russo-Ukrainian war in which Stak loses his life, causing Emma to withdraw from Jeffrey. In the end, Jeffrey is depicted as alone and isolated from other people, with only the everyday aesthetics and art as consolation.

To conclude, Don DeLillo's *Zero K* provides an excellent opportunity for future-oriented ethics concerning the implicit ideal of immortality through biotechnological progress that can be traced in contemporary culture. While I have interpreted the novel as a critique of the transhumanist-capitalist vision of complete control over life and death by drawing on theories of Jean Baudrillard, there is still a degree of ambiguity concerning the novel's moral stance. As this *Guardian* review remarks: "DeLillo clearly hasn't created this complicated imaginary world just to mock it. Like any good dialectician, he wants the case he's questioning to be made as forcefully as possible" (Lasdun). The novel scrutinises the relationships between life, death, and human world-making through language and art, thereby oscillating between a critique of capitalist biopolitics and an aestheticisation of The Convergence project. I have argued that it frames this transhumanist project as the art of immortality, which is closer to death than life. It produces "absolute death" as a result of capitalist biopolitics that rests on hierarchies of life and finally disrupts all life, both on individual and collective levels. The novel juxtaposes this world with the idea of life and aesthetics as transient and therefore always in relation to death and to other people. In multiple circuits of metatextuality, the novel repeats these ideas with regards to language, art, and aesthetics. The futuristic present of DeLillo's *Zero K* thus helps to see the contemporarily dominating world of biocapitalism more clearly with regard to the direction it is taking. The familiarity and realistic mode of writing, together with its speculative and defamiliarising elements, allow readers to take a different perspective on contemporary power structures and cultural undercurrents such as the will towards absolute control and mastery over life.

Conclusion

This chapter has looked at biopolitics of the future in the context of biotech-nological advancements through exemplary close readings of two contemporary novels. I have argued that the aesthetic choice of temporal setting encourages different ethical perspectives on current developments in biotechnology and their potential future consequences. The close readings of *Never Let Me Go* with its alternative past setting and *Zero K*'s futuristic present setting showcase how different aesthetic modes of temporality enable a critical investigation of contemporary worlds and their power structures. By changing the focus from proximity and familiarity to distance and defamiliarisation, the biotech fictions I have analysed foreground different aspects of 21st century biopolitics, ranging from cloning, racism and health in *Never Let Me Go* to the transhumanist ideal of overcoming death in *Zero K*.

Through involving several temporalities, *Never Let Me Go*'s alternative past setting becomes multi-temporal, stressing the point that biopolitical domination and exploitation are an ongoing phenomenon that connects different pasts to potential futures. On another level, it illustrates the effects of the future as a temporal space being taken away at the examples of the protagonists who are robbed of their futures. Kathy H.'s narrative account shows that she turns towards different layers of the past and that a missing future also equals the loss of a political horizon that necessitates the future as a temporal space. In contrast, *Zero K*'s depiction of the biocapitalist Convergence project depicts how a present-day world can be constructed through the temporality of the future, without which it could not exist. In addition to this transhumanist future, the novel's recognisable present setting offers several other temporal spaces: the immediate here and now in which "the little life" of the everyday is lived, as well as the timeless space of art and conceptualising life and death as aesthetic phenomena.

Despite the works' different temporal outlook and thematic orientation, they share a number of commonalities. Both novels are written by renowned "literary" authors who have taken up traditional science fiction topics like cloning and cryopreservation. While they were also criticised by readers for their apparent ignorance of previous works of science fiction focusing on similar topics, their potentially different style of writing also adds value to existing narratives. In the case of Ishiguro's *Never Let Me Go*, it is the nuanced insights into the protagonists' interiority through psychological realism that provides a new angle to topics of biotechnology and power. Through Kathy's autobiographical memoir, *Never Let Me Go* explicitly scrutinises the neoliberal mode of self-governance of the exploited. In her narrative, Kathy exemplifies the self-techniques of wilful ignorance and narrative self-creation through which people govern themselves into complicity with their exploiters. In the case of DeLillo's *Zero K*, the novel's postmodernist self-referential aesthetic quality contributes to the exploration of the theme of (im)mortality and art. In its metatextual form, the novel seems to illustrate quite a number of Baudrillard's theories, for example the art of disappearance, language as a vital illusion and hyper-reality.

Some of Baudrillard's ideas can also be found in both novels. For example, the idea of simulation and simulacra is exemplified in *Never Let Me Go* through the motif of cultural and biotechnological cloning and in *Zero K* as part of the

Convergence's performative art. Furthermore, the settings of both novels are built around transhumanist ideals of enhancing the human health and life span through science and technology. Following Baudrillard, I have argued that these ideas are not confined only to transhumanist visions of the future but that they are influential undercurrents in presently dominant worlds. This is primarily visible in the contemporary world of biocapitalism that likewise advocates the idea of control and mastery over life to capitalise from it. Accordingly, the world of biocapitalism and that of transhumanism most often converge in contemporary fiction, even though there are also relatively vocal strands of leftist transhumanism.[3] In *Zero K* especially, the merger between big capital and transhumanist philosophy is visible in the example of the protagonist's father, Ross, and his neoliberal subjectivity. Rather than seeing subjects as fundamentally co-dependent and in relation to others, neoliberal subjectivity advocates individualism, self-optimisation, and competition. The potential future world the novel foreshadows illustrates the biopolitical world order based on this form of subjectivity: a survival of an un-dead elite at the cost of the extinction of the majority of human and non-human life forms.

As another commonality, *Never Let Me Go* and *Zero K* assume a metatexutal perspective by foregrounding narrative and aesthetic or even artistic worldmaking. Both works explicitly investigate the role of arts and aesthetics, as well as language and narrative for worldmaking and ethics. In *Never Let Me Go* this metatextuality mainly serves the purpose of questioning the humanist assumption that the arts and especially arts education is an ethical good in itself. The novel reveals that it might work in the other direction, by interpellating subjects into a world that is harmful to them, even though it might look and feel safe on the surface. Similarly, *Zero K* proposes two distinctive types of art and aesthetics that go hand in hand with certain worlds and their biopolitics. It opposes the art of life, which is ephemeral and embraces physical death, with the art of death conveyed by the transhumanist project of The Convergence. As the latter aspires towards immortality by controlling and holding onto life, it becomes life-less and dies in consequence, like the cryonically suspended subjects.

In terms of narrative style, the two works hover between realism and speculation and postmodernist experimentation. When dealing with the future-

---

3   See for example James Steinhoff's discussion of "Transhumanism and Marxism: Philosophical Connections" or publications like Aaron Bastani's *Fully Automated Luxury Communism* (2019).

related ethical aspects of biotechnology, this seems to be a necessity. On the one hand, the precise biopolitical conditions of biotechnological innovation need to be looked at, therefore bringing in the realist element, while on the other hand, the potential future consequences and technological developments must be speculative. As worldmaking and power structures in late capitalism are so complex and difficult to comprehend while being so absurdly unjust at the same time, postmodernist playfulness and experimentation is another mode of brining in a "truthful" representation of the present. Different temporalities entail different aesthetic options for ethical reflection by playing with scales and degrees of familiarity as well as emotional proximity and distancing. With their zooming in and out of familiar worlds and imaginative leaps toward prospective worlds, the biotech fictions I have examined in this chapter perform ethical work, making the emotional and intellectual judgement of possible biotechnological futures and their biopolitics possible.

7 More than Human?: Threats of AI in Dennis Villeneuve's *Blade Runner 2049* (2017) and Alex Garland's *Ex_Machina* (2014)

Many future fictions with a high cultural impact seem to foreground the creation of human-like or even superior artificial intelligence as *the* most pressing ethical problem. Against the backdrop of actual contemporary socio-economic developments surrounding digitalisation like mass surveillance, data mining, and the manipulation of individuals and politics through digital applications, as well as the for-free harvesting of biological material from humans and non-humans, this appears to be a distraction from actual threats. In this chapter, I will therefore trace some of the reasons for this distortion of perceived threats versus actual power imbalances and their structural violence. The creation of artificial superintelligence, or AI, is an aspiration that can be approached through biotechnology or digital technologies or a fusion of both, as the cultural imaginary implies. This chapter will focus on one example of each side: Alex Garland's *Ex_Machina* envisions a rather mechanical type of AI that is brought to life through digital data and electronic circuits, while Dennis Villeneuve's *Blade Runner 2049* imagines biotechnologically produced or "replicated" humans of flesh and blood.

Ex_Machina and *Blade Runner 2049* both focus on the topic of (re)production of human-like creatures and bring forth the ethical questions of what constitutes "the human" and how this concept is loaded with value to distinguish it from "lesser" beings or how it can be surpassed by AI. This encompasses the cultural fear of AI, which has quite a history in literature and film and also seems to dominate the present moment. Against evidence of what is or might actually be technologically possible in the near future, this fear might seem irrational and merely covers up actual forms of exploitation and domination. I propose that one reason for this is the works' own embeddedness in the capitalist world, which leads to an avoidance of ethical questions that might threaten its systemic order. Even though all types of fictions are ultimately dealt with as products of the capitalist market, big-budget films are under much more financial pressure to attract large audiences, which often prefigures both their form and content. Hence, the most commercially successful films tend to be situated on the most speculative end of the spectrum, which approaches digitalisation and biotechnology from the assumption of artificial superintelligence becoming a threat to humanity.

From the side of the digital, this category encompasses films like the *Terminator* films (1984–2019) (Cameron; Mostow; McG; Taylor; Miller), *I, Robot* (Proyas 2004), *Ex_Machina* (2014), *Ghost in the Shell* (Sanders 2017), and *I Am Mother* (Sputore 2019). They all simulate the digital creation of AI and the tension, if not war, between these new forms of computer-generated, robotic, and super-enhanced life-forms and humanity. All of these films draw on spectacular aesthetics by featuring suspenseful plots and an action-driven or emotionally loaded implementation. In terms of genre, they are either action films or thrillers that immerse viewers deeply into their story worlds and are therefore attractive to larger audiences. There are also a number of biotechnological future scenarios in literature and film. However, different from *Blade Runner 2049*, many of them tend to focus more on the idea of "enhancement" instead of complete (re)production, or they imagine what could go wrong with biotechnological experimentation. Examples would be the *Planet of the Apes* films (Burton 2001; Wyatt 2011; Reeves 2014 & 2017), Michael Winterbottom's *Code 46* (2003), Margaret Atwood's *MaddAddam Trilogy* (*Oryx and Crake* (2003); *The Year of the Flood* (2009); *MaddAddam* (2013)), Mary E. Pearson's *The Adoration of Jenna Fox* (2008), Daniel Suarez's *Change Agent* (2018), as well as Paolo Bacigalupi's *The Windup Girl* (2009).

As in *Ex_Machina*, the Turing test is often quoted in fiction about artificial intelligence to ascertain whether an artificially created being can be seen as equal or even superior to humans in terms of intelligence, an event that is also referred to as "the singularity": "The Singularity was first proposed by the mathematician and science fiction author Vernor Vinge (1993) as the point at which greater-than-human machine intelligence begins rapidly improving itself, bringing an end to human-directed history" (Hughes 763). The singularity, or artificial superintelligence, needs to be separated from the general term "artificial intelligence", which designates all kinds of already common computing technology. Generally, "[a]rtificial intelligence is the ability of a machine to perform cognitive tasks that we associate with the human mind" (Kreutzer and

Sirrenberg 3). Therefore, computers, smart technology, and all types of digital applications are already types of weak artificial intelligence, as they are able to imitate certain tasks usually performed by human minds, like voice recognition (e.g. Alexa, Siri) or playing the board game *Go* (AlphaGo). However, they are still far from being capable of imitating all complex tasks of the human mind and its sentience—and it is unclear whether machines will ever be able to achieve this (4).

Nonetheless, the topic of "singularity" is part of the contemporary discourse on future-oriented ethics both in fiction and non-fiction. For example, as a result of Google investing heavily in artificial intelligence research throughout the last years, a group of scientists, intellectuals, and publicly renowned people tied up with the Future of Life Institute have issued strong warnings against these initiatives (Jacobson 27). In popular non-fiction, the development of artificial superintelligence is described by some authors as the currently biggest threat to humanity (e.g. Harari), while from the side of techno-optimists, including certain divisions of transhumanists, it is eagerly anticipated (e.g. Kurzweil). As shown in the examples from fiction, this discourse and its concomitant fears and hopes heavily shape the current cultural imaginary while simultaneously being its product.

I have chosen Alex Garland's *Ex_Machina* to analyse in the context of this category of digitised AIs because in addition to representing typical ethical questions surrounding the creation of AI, the film also reflects on possible reasons for foregrounding this highly speculative topic. *Ex_Machina* simulates the encounter between a digitally created female AI called Ava and Caleb, who, as an employee of Ava's creator Nathan, must test her intelligence through the Turing test. Originally designed by the computer scientist Alan Turing, the test is used to verify if a computer can be distinguished from a human. Garland's *Ex_Machina* is both part of this popular contemporary trend and at the same time consciously reflects on it through its meta- and intertextuality. It draws historical links to the Prometheus myth and Mary Shelley's *Frankenstein*, and situates the ancient cultural fear of humanity surpassing its limits amid the contemporary reality of global digitalisation and its overcharging complexity. Through its high level of moral and aesthetic ambiguity, it encourages viewers to join its ethical reflections while enjoying the aesthetically engaging spectacle.

Blade Runner 2049, as an example of a highly aestheticised and political genre of biopunk, heavily draws on the freedom to invent appealing, retro-inspired yet futuristic aesthetics for its setting. At the same time, it projects contemporary biocapitalist dominance and its devastating ecological and social effects into the future and creates a critical distance to this actual contemporary world. *Blade Runner 2049* looks at the biopolitics of reproduction and focuses on the distinction between biological birth and artificial production marking the boundaries between humans and replicants. In continuation of the prequel, it imagines a world in which humanoid beings can be biotechnologically produced as replicants and used as slaves for humanity. In my posthumanist reading of the film, I will show how it brings forth the question of what constitutes "the human". Reading the film against the grain, I will deconstruct the notion of "the human" by pointing out the function of this concept for biopolitics and maps of morality.

"To Be Born Is to Have a Soul, I Guess." Reproduction and Human(e)ness in Dennis Villeneuve's *Blade Runner 2049*

Dennis Villeneuve's *Blade Runner 2049* (2017) achieved what few sequels to highly praised films manage: it successfully continued the world of the original 1986 *Blade Runner* directed by Ridley Scott while adding new aesthetic and ethical dimensions. As a result, it received several prizes—among them two Academy Awards—and favourable reviews and ratings from both professional and private viewers. *Entertainment Weekly* described *Blade Runner 2049* as "the elevation of mainstream moviemaking to high art" (Greenblatt), and *The Guardian* commented that the film's images "trigger awe or even a kind of ecstatic despair at the idea of a post-human future, and what it means to imagine the wreck of our current form of homo sapiens" (Bradshaw). As the film's title already indicates, it is set in the near future in the year of 2049. The spatial settings of Los Angeles and Las Vegas are far removed from the cities as we know them today because they are visibly struck by the catastrophes which contemporary worlds are in the process of building: climate disasters, extreme social inequality, and atomic warfare.

As a review of the most popular biotech fictions shows, the majority is set in the near future, which I define as a couple of decades from now. On the one hand, the near future setting is close enough to the present and its worlds to be able to deduce from them. On the other hand, the not yet existing worlds of the future can be portrayed creatively, making the near future setting especially attractive from an artistic point of view. As will be discussed in the next chapter, Margaret Atwood's *MaddAddam Trilogy* (2003–2013) imagines the application of biotechnology on animals and humans, including the creation of a deadly virus and a new human race in the context of a satirically exaggerated super-capitalist world. Michael Winterbottom's *Code 46* (2003) and Daniel Suarez's *Change Agent* (2018) foreshadow high-tech metropolitan worlds characterised by globalisation, segregation, and environmental contamination, in which genetic editing and cloning have become common practise. The young adult novel *The Adoration of Jenna Fox* (2008) by Mary E. Pearson reflects on ethical boundaries of the application of biotechnology in medicine, whereas the most recent *Planet of the Apes* (2011–2017) films project what can go wrong with genetically engineered medication in the form of a lethal disease and super-evolved monkeys. All of these examples are particularly concerned with the aesthetic worldbuilding of their different futures, ranging from caricature in *The MaddAddam Trilogy* to biopunk or *noir* aesthetics in *Blade Runner 2049*.

The *Blade Runner* universe is built around the idea of the artificial biotechnological creation of human life in the form of so-called replicants, whose purpose is to serve humanity as slave-like beings. Through its focus on the theme of biological birth as opposed to artificial (re)production, *Blade Runner 2049* explores an alleged human essence and its biopolitical order involving hierarchies of life. In the following close reading, I will argue that Villeneuve's *Blade Runner 2049* first de- and then re-constructs the notion of normative humanity, which is tied to moral value and behaviour. The deconstruction of the boundary between human and replicant results from the film's emphasis on the human(e)ness of the replicants and an aesthetic undermining of the notion of a singular reality or world. This adds some degree of ambiguity to the film's otherwise relatively closed moral universe, which favours the otherworld of the replicants over the dominant human world of biocapitalism.

I will begin the analysis of *Blade Runner 2049* with an exploration of the film's iconic aesthetics that I will read as exemplary of biopunk as a genre that encompasses counter-cultural ethics and aesthetics. The focalisation, character cast, and visual codes constitute a closed moral and political universe. As I will argue next, however, this closure is threatened by *Blade Runner 2049*'s metatextual questioning of reality and simulation. The discussion will then move on to the film's criticism of the capitalist-transhumanist empire represented by Niander Wallace and his corporation that produces replicants along with almost everything else. The "dissolution of sovereignty" (Koljević 33) that *Zero K* already hinted at is brought to an extreme level by *Blade Runner 2049*, where The Wallace Corporation appears to become the ruler rather than the nation state which is only represented in its executive branch, the LA Police Department.

I will illustrate that both of these anthropocentric worlds find themselves in opposition to the otherworld of the replicant resistance movement. The last section will point out how the three opposing parties are paradoxically joined in their humanism as a normative conception of "the human" even though the replicants seek to challenge this. From a posthumanist theoretical angle, I will show how the reversion to humanism is counter-productive to the replicants' end of liberatory ethics.

The Ethics and Aesthetics of Biopunk Futures

As mentioned in the beginning of this section, viewer responses to *Blade Runner 2049* were generally positive. Even though the film seems to not have satisfied the taste of those looking for more conventional Hollywood entertainment—some reviewers discredited it as "slow", "boring", and containing too many "unresolved issues"—its high aesthetic appeal and the ethical issues it raises triggered positive responses from most private online reviewers on IMDb. Despite its apparent moral closure, there are enough gaps and ambiguities to engender ethical reflection. For instance, one viewer concludes that *Blade Runner 2049* is "[a] rare film that brings together all the uncertain elements of filmmaking into a cohesive whole, that leaves you in wonder of the artistry, satisfied by the story and deeply reflective on questions that we ask ourselves in the dead of night; what is it to be human?". Another wrote in reference to its questions, "[i]t's one of those rare films who [*sic*] dares to challenge the audience" ('Blade Runner 2049 (2017) User Reviews'). In the following, I will trace how Villeneuve's *Blade Runner 2049* triggers ethical reflection through its biopunk aesthetics, character constellation, and focalisation.

The film's iconic aesthetics, together with its anti-establishment agenda, place it within the future-oriented genre of biopunk as a sub-genre of cyberpunk. Lars Schmeink describes biopunk as having "developed from progress in genetic research, posthuman discourse, postmodern late-capitalist society, and the intervention of cyberpunk literature" (24) that criticises "liquid modern realities as already dystopian, warning that a future will only get worse, and that society needs to reverse its path, or else destroy all life on this planet" (14). While Schmeink notes that the "punk" element, which is generally associated with political counterculture, is not as present in biopunk as in cyberpunk, I argue that it is certainly notable in *Blade Runner 2049*. The aesthetics of *Blade Runner 2049* link back to Scott's prequel *Blade Runner* that already exhibits nostalgic references to film noir and early science fiction (Flückiger et al.) and has achieved cult status by now. As a result, the new film is marked by a near future aesthetics that originates from a 1980s past, with flying retro cars and synthesizer sounds, and even computers that are reminiscent of a past imaginary of the future. The referencing of a past-inspired nostalgic and iconic aesthetic code provides the film's bleak atmosphere with a punk-like notion of coolness and appeal.

Visually, the film is dominated by shots of the dark, misty, and rainy city of Los Angeles sparkling with artificial lights of (holographic) ads and flying cars (e.g. Villeneuve 0:13:45; 0:28:53; 1:58:00 etc.). The predominantly dark and blackish colour code is contrasted with pink, blue, orange, and yellow, connoting devastation and artificiality. There are Asian-inspired visual elements, for instance in a market scene (0:41:45), which tap into the familiar cultural imaginary of cyberpunk and manga comics by fusing different temporalities and geographies. Another pastiche element is the misty-orange-drenched setting of Las Vegas derived from nostalgic imaginations of a 1970s past, which includes a broken holographic Elvis show (1:36:40). The carefully selected colour code and pastiche elements with cult status provide the film with a high aesthetic appeal for viewers and evokes associations with punk culture as a highly aestheticised yet also political counterculture.

Villeneuve's *Blade Runner 2049* overtly criticises the dominant world order in its simulation of a possible near future via its character constellation and focalisation. While in the original *Blade Runner*, the protagonist Deckard is a rather unsympathetic character who is difficult to identify with, the new protagonist K works well as the film's likeable hero. Viewers experience the story from K's perspective and soon manage to identify with him as he is characterised as relatable and friendly despite his work as a blade runner who has to kill other replicants. Throughout the story, the emotional attachment of viewers to K is intensified through insights into his love life, especially his relationship to the holographic character Joi (e.g., 0:16:46; 1:13:49; 1:25:20) as well as through a number of action-driven fight scenes that make viewers feel with and for him (e.g., 1:15:39; 1:53:19). K's final deed of uniting Ana, the replicant child, with her father Deckard and the simultaneous acceptance of his own death for the greater good turns K into an altruistic hero. Through his transition from an obedient slave to a moral agent fighting for a right and good cause, K marks the good side of the closed moral universe of the film.

This side also features the underground replicant resistance movement and their mission to free the replicants from slavery. The underlying premise that justifies their cause is that replicants are at least as valuable as humans, if not superior to them, as their self-description "more human than human" (2:00:50) designates. Dr. Ana Stelline as the replicant child and the main source of hope for the resistance movement also stands out visually from the rest of the film's bleak and misty colour code. She is introduced amid an (imaginary) beautiful, lush green forest (1:14:43), which does not exist anymore in this dystopian future, and is dressed completely in white while working in a similarly white room. Whenever K visits her, it is snowing outside, so that even the outside conforms to the whiteness and (moral) purity that characterises her (1:19:48; 2:22:30). The film's colour code thus adds to the establishment of an unambiguous map of morality that privileges the replicants and their resistance movement and criticises the dominant human worlds.

Blade Runner 2049 makes clear that humans and their dominant world of capitalist economics have wrecked the earth's ecology, as the information given explicitly in the beginning and implicitly through the setting of the film conveys. In the written introduction, viewers are informed that "the collapse of the ecosystems in the mid-2020s led to the rise of industrialist Niander Wallace, whose mastery of synthetic farming averted famine" (0:1:35). The film's geophysical setting is obviously smitten by climate change and atomic destruction, demonstrated for example by the huge dams surrounding Los Angeles (0:56:47), the much cooler climate of LA featuring snow (e.g. 2:22:30), and the shots of the devastated atomic wasteland in and around Las Vegas (1:32:48). The entire setting amounts to a direct critique of capitalist worldmaking, which appears to be the cause of the ecological breakdown yet nonetheless lives on unabatedly in the future portrayed by *Blade Runner 2049*. The capitalist world is personified by Niander Wallace as K's antagonist and the villain.

The film leaves no doubt that Niander Wallace and his corporation, which obviously rules the nation and even the off-world colonies, are morally debauched. In extension, this means that the entire human world in this future is a dystopian world that should be averted if possible. As this is another world ruled by a fusion of capitalism and transhumanist ideology, the critique is directed towards these ideological foundations and practices. At the same time, *Blade Runner 2049* highlights that there is no such thing as a stable objective reality that can be perceived through the senses. While the sense of reality can be subject to change, the film emphasises that the notion of reality is still important to individuals and groups in order to create meaning and make a living.

Reality and Simulation

Since Jean Baudrillard's *Simulacra and Simulation* (1981) and *The Matrix* (Wachowski and Wachowski 1999), the idea of a fixed and stable sense-based reality is questioned by the cultural imaginary. Following this deconstructivist trend and similar to *Avatar*, *Blade Runner 2049* centralises the question "What is real?" and foregrounds how this might shift with different forms of perception, especially seeing how this sense might be easily deceived. The film simultaneously deconstructs reality as a stable entity while maintaining it as a relevant concept. As Timothy Shanahan argues, "One of the film's key take-home messages is that although often it may be difficult to know for sure what is real, reality itself still matters. As [the head of the LA Police Department] Lt. Joshi perceptively observes, 'We're all just looking out for something real'" (22). Shanahan furthermore holds that "although the real still matters in 2049, its precise boundaries have shifted" (22) in comparison to the first *Blade Runner* film. While in the original, the real was distinguished from the artificially made, the category of "real" has come to include industrial Wallace productions. For example, at the market, K is offered "a real horse [...] like Wallace stuff" (1:31:22), and when hearing Joi's initiating tune, the replicant prostitute Marietta remarks that "you don't like real girls" (0:44:20), referring to replicants like herself. Thus, the boundary of the real now includes biotechnologically made organisms, while still excluding digital artificial intelligences like K's holographic girlfriend Joi.

"Villeneuve's film is perfectly clear that the distinction between the biological and the technological in the 2049 Blade Runner universe is sufficiently robust to place K on one side and Joi on the other, and thereby to give K a claim to moral standing that Joi cannot have" (Mulhall 35). Different from the replicants, the digital AI character Joi is treated with much more ambiguity regarding her status as a person or a moral agent. When she is first introduced as K's stay-at-home girlfriend resembling whichever fantasy he might have, from 1950s inspired perfect housewife to fancy disco chick (0:18:17), viewers have trouble taking her seriously as an actual person rather than a product made to please her male owner. However, as the story progresses, she becomes more authentic to viewers as she turns out to be a serious companion, lover, and helper to K in his mission to discover the secret of the replicant child that he believes himself to be. Nonetheless, Joi simultaneously works as a surveillance device for the Wallace corporation by enabling Wallace's assistant Luv to locate K (1:30:50). Finally, after K has been rescued by the replicant resistance force and Joi has been destroyed, K is faced with a gigantic holographic ad of Joi incessantly repeating phrases he recognizes, which leads him to believe he has been deceived. The ad also mentions "Joe", the allegedly unique name she gave to K when they thought he was a "real boy" instead of a replicant (2:1:00). Upon seeing and hearing this, K realizes that what he has taken for authentic love might have been nothing but a simulation programmed to please him.

This scene also marks the point of K's transition from being an uncritical slave fully at home in the dominant capitalist world to assuming moral agency and entering the replicant army's otherworld, in which replicants can become their "own masters" (2:00:40). K's epiphany and transition imply that there are multiple possible worlds and ways of seeing them, and that therefore, the senses and especially vision cannot be trusted. Seeing as a theme also generally plays an important role throughout the film, exemplified by the recurring symbol of eyes in connection to world perception. Most prominently, the film begins with an extreme close-up of an eye opening (0:2:40). In contrast, Niander Wallace is blind but is able to see with the help of drones, while Freysa as the replicant leader lacks an eye. Replicants can be recognised through a visible mark in their eyes when they look up. The film thus proposes that different ways of seeing lead to different modes of world perception, as Shadbolt and Smart argue with respect to Niander Wallace: "There are clearly reasons to think that Wallace sees the world in a way that is radically different from our own. But, in addition to altering the nature of Wallace's perceptual reality (i.e., the content of his visual experiences), there are also reasons to think that Wallace's technological prosthesis may also alter the nature of his conceptual reality" (Shadbolt and Smart 209), thus of the world he inhabits.

The theme of vision and worlding furthermore works as a meta-comment on film as a medium, especially this one with its dense aesthetic code, which fundamentally relies on seeing and sense perception. *Blade Runner 2049* invites viewers to question the reality they perceive, both in the cinema and outside of it. Simulation and manipulation may take place via technological mediation, but technology can also add different perspectives that might not be obtainable otherwise. The film thus points to itself and asks viewers to reflect on its ontological status—is it a mere deception of the senses, a fantasy, or an epiphanic vision that makes the presumed reality outside the cinema appear like a simulation? In its projection of the dominant world of (bio-)capitalism into the future, it invites a critical reading of its presumed normalcy which I will discuss in the following section. With Niander Wallace and his corporate endeavour as its heading figure, this assumed future world reveals the close ties to transhumanism that I have already established through the examples of other works (*Zero K, Transcendence, Interstellar,* and *The Circle*).

The Dominant World: Capitalism and Transhumanism, Again

Strange and sinister in appearance, Wallace as a character and the entire biopolitical world order connected to his empire represents the side of evil in *Blade Runner 2049.* He is depicted as unfeeling and entirely lacking empathy, for example when he stabs a new replicant because of her infertility and without showing any emotional reaction or even remorse (0:40:20). Thus, he precisely exhibits the lack of empathy and morality that is conventionally associated with replicants, especially in the first *Blade Runner.* In contrast, his seemingly cold and cruel assistant and representative Luv, who is also a replicant, does show a slight emotional response to the stabbing. Likewise, when Wallace talks to Deckard, who is visibly moved by their conversation about his former lover Rachel, Wallace stays completely emotionally detached (2:04:44).[1] The complete lack of emotion and sympathy coupled with his ruthless ambition to make humanity "own the stars" (0:39:39) makes him appear rather inhuman(e) and psychopathic, which develops him as the villain in the eyes of viewers.

Wallace and his whole colonial and corporate endeavours are further characterised by a hubris that results from his performance as a God-like entity and his framing of humanity as a divine race. In contrast to the rest of the city with its bleakness and run-down housing, the Wallace headquarters are characterised by luxury and splendour. Visually, the headquarters are rendered through contrasts of darkness and a yellow-golden light reflected on the water. This has an unsettling effect while evoking the notion of higher powers connected to life and death. Water is typically a symbol of life, but as a natural force, it can also bring death, for example in the form of risen sea levels as depicted by the film. Wallace's office is a space surrounded by water which makes him appear to be the master of life and death, which, in a biopolitical sense, he is: Wallace is proud of having produced millions of replicants (2:08:50), and at the same time, feels free to kill and use them as he sees fit. For example, he recreates the deceased Rachel from the first film but simply has her shot after she is rejected by Deckard (2:10:15). Furthermore, Wallace has a manner of

---

1   The subject of Deckard possibly being a replicant himself in addition to being a blade runner has been discussed fiercely in reviews and academic articles about the first *Blade Runner* but is still left open by the new film.

talking like a priest and uses religiously loaded diction, for instance when he speaks of Luv as "an angel" entering "the kingdom of heaven" (0:36:40) when she walks into his office.

Wallace's performance and the framing of his mission thus evokes the same religious undertones of transhumanist philosophy I have already discussed in Chapter Four with the examples of *Interstellar* and *Transcendence*. The Wallace empire embodies the transhumanist ideal of progress through science and technology and the transgression of biological and physical boundaries through biotechnological engineering and colonising the stars. As in the previous examples, the transhumanist agenda is firmly wed to capitalist worldmaking. Niander Wallace is the embodiment of both: in addition to his religiously inspired performance and being a self-enhanced cyborg through his mode of vision, he is also a suit-wearing capitalist (2:36:40). Paul Smart therefore describes him as a personification of capitalism:

> According to the personification hypothesis, we ought not to think of Wallace merely as a particular kind of being; instead, we ought to think of Wallace as something akin to a dispassionate, self-interested machine that works only in its own interests. As the personification of capitalism, Wallace is the purveyor of all manner of technological fixes, and some of those fixes (e.g. synthetic farming) appear to benefit humanity. But the value of a technological fix, at least from the standpoint of capitalism, does not inhere in its humanitarian potential; instead, it is deployed so as to sustain its own operation. (192)

The capitalist world in *Blade Runner 2049* is certainly not a good world—on the contrary, it is marked as a bleak dystopia which can be seen in its colour code. In addition to the ecological havoc, the majority of humans as well as replicants suffer from a life of extreme poverty, dependence and precarity that stands in harsh contrast to the splendour of the Wallace headquarters and the conduct of the man himself. Even though the Wallace corporation is just a company without formal political powers, it assumes enormous biopolitical power. It is obvious that the future world of the film is entirely reigned by it: the Wallace corporation appears to have the monopoly on food production, control the off-world colonies and the replicant slave labour, and is able to overpower the state without difficulties as displayed by Luv's killing of LAPD's Ltd. Joshi (1:35:56).

In this world life, especially artificially made life, merely represents a form of capital that can be turned into profitable products. "As mere products, replicants and holograms are presented as the sorts of things that can permissibly be bought and owned, either by individuals or corporate entities" (Woollard 48). Even though the film mainly makes this point about artificially made life forms, it can also be read as an analogy to present capitalist worldmaking and imperialism. In its own biopolitical agenda, contemporary (bio-)capitalism likewise builds on the exploitation of human and non-human life forms in the form of "capital" and "resources". As Wallace himself admits, "every leap of civilisation was built on the back of a disposable workforce" (0:39:57). Paul Smart remarks that the will to make profit in *Blade Runner 2049*'s capitalist world goes even one step further: to drain ever more from the already exploited, they are given the double status of a "prosumer", which means being a product and a consumer at the same time (186). K, for instance, is simultaneously a product sold to the LAPD while also being a customer of the Wallace corporation by owning a Joi and buying extra products like "an emenator" (Villeneuve 0:19:30) for her. Smart calls this phenomenon "artificial economics—the idea that AI systems work to service the demand for economic growth and capital accumulation" (187).

Here again, financial value is the value that overrides all other values of this world. Its devastating and destructive effects on the earth's ecology and human civilisation necessitate the geographical expansion into space and across biological boundaries. Hence, in order to further humanity's imperialism and corporate expansionism, Wallace is interested in crossing the threshold of biological replicant reproductivity.

> From an economic standpoint, replicant birth is simply a means of reducing the costs associated with the manufacture of a commercial product. [...] Replicant birth is not a problem for Wallace, for it amounts to little more than a form of outsourcing—a way of reducing the costs associated with a given productive (or, in this case, reproductive) process. (195)

The biopolitical theme of human reproduction and the distinction between biological reproduction and artificial biotechnological production is central to *Blade Runner 2049*. While Wallace's interest in replicant reproduction is easily detectable as capitalist and imperialist, there are other views on this phenomenon expressed by different interest groups. These are first and foremost the interests of the replicant resistance to free themselves from slavery, but there is also the opposing side represented by the executive power of the state, the LAPD. The LAPD is there to "keep order" (Villeneuve 0:27:35), which means preserving the exclusive concept of "the human" that hinges on the ability to reproduce biologically. As K's superior Lt. Joshi remarks, this ability constitutes "a wall" that "separates kind" (0:27:13). This exclusive humanity is of course challenged by the birth of a replicant child, which is why the replicant resistance army is so eager to claim the event to prove their own "humanity".

Reproducing "the Human"

"Next to the question of what is real, no question is more fundamental to both *Blade Runner* films than the question of what it means to be human, although it assumes different forms in each film" (Shanahan 19). While Scott's *Blade Runner* approaches this question from the ending of life in death, Villeneuve's sequel takes birth as its central theme. This results in a deconstruction and a reconstruction of the morally, highly charged concept of "the human". Even though the film "does not give us any clear, final account of who is and who is not human, or what constitutes the relevant difference" (Treanor 68), it reaffirms the importance of the idea of "being human", which is associated with distinction and superiority over life forms that are excluded from this group. Despite the obvious antagonism between the dominant human worlds and the otherworld of the replicant resistance, both converge in their shared centre of "the human" as a yardstick of value and (moral) superiority. In the following, I will outline how the exclusive concept of "the human" is first challenged by the replicants in *Blade Runner 2049* and then resurrected.

Apart from the fact that replicants cannot reproduce biologically and that they are sold and owned as products, there is no observable difference between them and the humans in the film's story world. While the baseline test that K must undergo repeatedly (0:14:32; 1:20:33) implies that replicants are calibrated to a certain level of emotional stability or flatness, K, as well as other replicants, displays a rich array of emotions and empathy which surpasses that of many human characters like Wallace and Lt. Joshi. As a result of the replicants' human-likeness, the ability to reproduce biologically is the single dividing characteristic that both sides find meaningful and equal to "being fully human". Most prominently, K equates being born with having a soul when he says, "I've never retired something that was born before [...] To be born is to have a soul, I guess" (0:27:50). What Joi tells K when he suspects that he might be the replicant child, is his deepest wish he presumably also shares with other replicants: "I always told you you were special. Born. Not made. Hidden with care. A real boy now. A real boy needs a real name. Joe. [...] You're too important for K. Your mother would have named you" (1:13:50). The replicant Sapper Morton, whom K has to "retire" in the beginning of the film, tells him that "your models are

happy scraping the shit because you've never seen a miracle" (0:09:40), alluding
to replicant birth. As Brian Treanor suggests, biological birth is so important
for the replicants in the film because it means coming into the world as part of
a network of relations including mother, father, and other people: "The analysis of natality seems to suggest that a certain sort of being-in-relation is an
essential part of being human" (74).

Precisely this network, which not only consists of biologically related people but is first and foremost a social network, becomes visible with respect
to the replicant child: while the biological mother, Rachel, died in childbirth
and the father, Deckard, had to hide as part of the plan to allow the child to
be safe, Freysa and Sapper Morton as biologically completely unrelated people
have helped the child Ana to survive. Freysa, the leader of the replicant resistance movement, explains the motives behind her involvement: "I knew that
baby meant we are more than just slaves [...] If a baby can come from one of
us, we are our own masters" (Villeneuve 2:00:40). Most obviously, biological reproduction makes the replicants independent from the capitalist production
process that facilitates them being sold and treated as products or slaves. In
addition, it means that replicants can be-in-relation to others as part of what
makes them human. On a more abstract level, this also alludes to the capitalist
formation of individualised neoliberal subjects as a form of slavery, while the
ability to be-in-relation with others becomes the true freedom as opposed to
the deceptive consumerist freedom.

With the achievement of replicant birth, there are basically no differences
between replicants and humans any more, which means that the metaphorical
wall Joshi speaks of is torn down. However, rather than arguing that the concept of "the human" is obsolete, *Blade Runner 2049* implies that replicants could
be free to obtain membership in this exclusive club, or they might even constitute its new elite by becoming "more human than humans" (0:20:50). This
slogan, however, undermines the replicants' cause in various ways: On the one
hand, it undermines their agency as it is simply a reproduction of the Tyrell
Corporation's advertisement for its products in the first *Blade Runner*. On the
other hand, normative humanity constitutes the basis for establishing hierarchies of value. In this sense, "being human" is no longer only a biological category associated with certain functions, such as the ability to reproduce, but it
also becomes a moral status. "Being human" as used by the replicant movement
amounts to being (morally) good. As Freysa's statement furthermore demonstrates: "Dying for the right cause is the most human thing we can do" (2:01:20).

Rather than deconstructing "the human", the replicants' eagerness to be hu-
man(e) resurrects it as the measuring sticks for morality and value.

Deconstructing "the Human"

From a posthumanist perspective, the concept of a common human essence
that humanism builds upon has always carried the idea of supremacy and
higher moral status. This is problematic because the idea of "human(e)ness"
has always been exclusive and applied only to a "fraction of humanity who had
the wealth, power, and leisure to conceptualize themselves as autonomous
beings exercising their will through individual agency and choice" (Hayles,
How We Became Posthuman 286). In *The Posthuman*, Rosi Braidotti demonstrates
how the boundary between the in- and the out-groups of those endowed with
a high moral status and human rights has shifted over time from the Enlightenment subject of the wealthy, white, Western male (1; 13,) to include women,
non-whites, and even animals.[2] As an alternative to this neo-humanist approach, Braidotti, like other posthumanist critics, proposes a deconstruction
of "the human" and other distinctive categories that establish hierarchies of
life forms and morality. In its stead, "(a) posthuman ethics for a non-unitary
subject proposes an enlarged sense of inter-connections between self and
others, including the non-human or 'earth' others, by removing the obstacle
of self-centered individualism" (49). If applied to *Blade Runner 2049*, this would
mean accepting or even loving "the replicant *as* replicant and not as potential
full subject" (Morton, *Ecology without Nature* 196) or as "fully human".

Through a review of secondary texts dealing with the subject of "the human" in *Blade Runner 2049*, it becomes obvious that this type of posthumanist
ethical thinking is still far off from dominant conceptions of ethics. Most
critics approach the subject of the replicants' moral status by ticking a list of
normative criteria constituting "a person" that would have a moral standing
and human rights. Heersmink and McCarroll for example write: "Persons
are sentient, conscious, and self-aware. For these reasons, they are part of a
moral community, having certain rights and obligations" (87). As the replicants display all of these characteristics, it is only logical that they should be
seen and treated as persons in the eyes of many critics and reviewers. For

---

2   Here Braidotti mentions neo-humanist approaches such as Frans de Waal's, who
makes the case for human-like traits like morality and responsibility in upper primates
(78).

instance, Stephen Mulhall concludes that "I find that watching the Blade Runner films leaves me certain about the moral status of replicants. I recognise them morally as persons and feel viscerally that the way they are treated is wrong" (Mulhall 49). He backs up his argument with a set of criteria that define persons, such as sentience, emotionality, reason, capacity to communicate, self-awareness, and moral agency. What is most problematic about these humanist "person" approaches to ethics is that they can legitimise forms of exploitation and domination when the subjects in question do not fulfil all the criteria, as the history of patriarchy, imperialism, slavery, and animal abuse shows.

In my reading of *Blade Runner 2049* from a posthumanist angle, I thus argue that it both challenges and reaffirms humanist ethics of normative personhood and human rights. However, it also deconstructs the notion of a stable sense-based reality, which again undermines its own certainty in resolving the conflict between humans and replicants and leaves room for ambiguity and ethical reflection. I have classified *Blade Runner 2049* as an example of biopunk that "allows for the most far-reaching extrapolations of the social consequences of genetic engineering" and "provides the broadest and most 'meta' level of abstraction" (Schmeink 242). By extrapolating from the currently dominant world of capitalism fused with transhumanism, the film depicts a possible near future that can clearly be evaluated as dystopian. Hence, true to its punk element, *Blade Runner 2049* takes a political and moral stance that opposes this world. This counter-cultural content is furthermore aestheticised and becomes appealing through its pastiche elements, including a 1990s inspired future vision and references to other cult genres like film noir or manga comic. Although present progress in biotechnology is bringing about many breakthroughs and promises, the artificial manufacturing of entire human organisms in the near future is still implausible. Hence, the ethical issues raised in *Blade Runner 2049* are to be read metaphorically, relating to biopolitical worldmaking and the moral standing of "the human" as opposed to its non-human others. My next example, Alex Garland's *Ex_Machina*, offers a similar take on the artificial production of super-intelligent beings but approaches it from the angle of digitalisation and digital capitalism.

Reflecting the Speculative Spectacle: Alex Garland's *Ex_Machina*

Alex Garland's *Ex_Machina* is both a typical representation of the long-standing tradition of humanity fearing demise at the hands of its own technological creations and an aesthetically highly praised popular film. In its exploration of the conventional plot line of human-made artificial intelligence turning against its creator, it engages spectators emotionally and aesthetically through its darkish, suspenseful atmosphere and impressive yet minimalist imagery. While the film does not belong to the list of big Hollywood blockbusters, it nonetheless has had a great impact on the cultural landscape due to its ethically relevant theme and outstanding aesthetics: it was nominated for best original screenplay at the 88th Academy Awards and won the Oscar for best visual effects as well as other prestigious rewards, including a Hugo Award and a BAFTA Award. As its rating on *metacritic* demonstrates (CBS Interactive), *Ex_Machina* received mainly favourable reviews by most widely read newspapers and magazines, and it gained a comparatively high viewer popularity score on IMDb (7.7 out of 10 on April 24, 2020).

The film's resistance to take a clear moral stance, leaving viewers with an open ending and more questions than answers, has certainly added to its positive reception. Another contributing factor is that it draws on the palpable cultural fear that arises from the prospect of AI creation through digital technologies. I will start the following close reading by looking at *Ex_Machina* as a "speculative spectacle" to point out its significance for ethics and aesthetics of digital futures, which I interpret as a diversion from more pressing socio-political and ethical issues. However, different from many more commercially successful productions, *Ex_Machina* has a reflexive and metatextual angle, which opens up further ethical and political dimensions. In my analysis, I will trace how the film works as "a looking glass" on AI fear, art, and digitalisation on different levels. Secondly, I will analyse the representation and negotiation of worlds and moral compasses in the film, embodied by the three protagonists: The AI creator Nathan represents the dominant world-complex of capitalism and transhumanism; Caleb, who serves as a guinea pig for Nathan's Turing test, stands in for humanism, while Ava's otherness represents a posthumanist world.

The Speculative Spectacle: Cultural Fear of AI

While the techno-scientific development of artificial intelligence plays an integral role in contemporary future-related discourse, the actual possibility of creating a human-like consciousness, either through digital technologies or biotechnologies, is still unrealistic. Director Alex Garland highlights this contradiction in a *New York Times* article by pointing out how the number of currently released films about the singularity is faced with a conspicuous absence of real breakthroughs in AI research. The dream of bringing dead matter to life, however, seems to be an ancient one which has been expressed in many artistic and literary artefacts throughout the course of history, encompassing works as diverse as the Pygmalion story, Shakespeare's *A Winter's Tale* and Fritz Lang's *Metropolis*. At the same time, it has also raised existential fears and ethical questions. For example, Mary Shelley's *Frankenstein* is the first literary representation where a scientific creation of a sentient artificial intelligence turns against its own maker in an act of despair for not having been recognised for its human-likeness. In this sense, *Ex_Machina*, like many other contemporary examples, follows these literary traditions by depicting a human falling in love with an AI, and the AI killing its own creator.

Many contemporary popular future fictions imagine similar plot lines. Their cultural significance at this point in time, however, diverges from earlier texts and films precisely because of the scientific and technological progress and the concomitant discourse that makes these developments *appear* more probable than ever before: Wally Pfister's *Transcendence* and Spike Jonze's *Her* both feature romantic relationships between an AI and a human being, while the *Terminator* films depict the final war of humanity against conscious machines in the form of digitally controlled androids. Alex Proyas's *I, Robot* and the Netflix production *I Am Mother* explore the possibly lethal, possibly beneficial relationships between humans and robots. These popular films have generated a deep impact on the cultural unconscious and form part of the contemporary discourse on digital technologies and their possible future consequences.

As I have argued before, the most commercially successful films, such as the *Terminator* films and *I, Robot* use spectacular aesthetic forms to frame their content. Like *I Am Mother*, *Ex_Machina* has been labelled a sci-fi thriller which highlights its emotionally immersive and aesthetically spectacular quality. The *speculative* coinciding with the *spectacular* is not necessarily a surprise when considering the context or worldly situatedness of the films themselves.

Most of them were produced with a mass audience and commercial success in mind, which is mostly achieved by providing an entertaining spectacle with high emotional appeal. I therefore argue that they are part of the dominant capitalist imaginary that aims at directing attention away from the actual social, ecological, and political struggles surrounding digital worldmaking to more speculative and fantastic themes. The ethical questions films in this category raise, like the opportunities and threats of artificial superintelligence as well as concomitant moral responsibilities, are thus staged as *the* most pressing ethical questions about digital futures.

With regard to the actual ethical readings of viewers, a number of reviews on *IMDb* point out that *Ex_Machina* "asks about the nature of AI" and "what it means to be human", questioning whether "we should continue trying to progress even more", and if the development of strong AI is desirable at all ('Ex_Machina (2014) User Reviews'). While these questions felt deep and thought-provoking to the majority of reviewers, they are speculative and unlikely to become urgently relevant, given the contemporary state of AI technology. This supports my claim that more urgent ethical questions revolving around the digital remain unasked. While *Ex_Machina* fits the category of the "speculative spectacle" at least on the surface, I want to argue that it is more nuanced than most other examples in this category due to its meta- and intertextuality. In its staging of the digital creation of artificial intelligence and the threats related to it, the film reflects on the ancient cultural fear connected with science and technology through a kind of doubling of perspectives on representation and simulation. Additionally, questions of power hierarchies including gender and ethnicity are raised in conjunction with issues of surveillance and control, as this reviewer attests: "This movie is obviously allegorical, a fascinating tale about AI, but it is mainly about manipulation and power" 'Ex_Machina (2014) User Reviews').

Ex_Machina "through the Looking Glass"

Garland's *Ex_Machina* is not merely a "speculative spectacle" about artificial intelligence, it is also reflexive and metatextual by foregrounding the workings of simulation and artistic representation on several diegetic layers. On the outermost layer, the film is a technological and artistic artefact that is supported by digital technologies while dealing with the impact of digitalisation on the level of content. Similarly, it is a piece of art that references the nature of art and representation as a theme in its story world. The film technologically simulates the existence of artificial superintelligence, which itself simulates being an embodied and gendered human creature. Finally, the frequently recurring symbol of the mirror illustrates this doubling of perspective in and on representation and simulation. In this complexity, Ex_Machina not only concerns itself with the seemingly obvious ethics of AI creation, but it also explores humanity's relationship with digital technology, ultimately reflecting on the cultural fear of AI itself. In the following, I will look at the different layers of the film's metatextuality in more detail, beginning with film as a medium.

It is not surprising that the digital future fictions with the most cultural impact are films rather than novels because "[b]y making art *with* new machines *about* new machines, they highlight film's place in a kind of Möbius strip in which new technologies create the conditions of possibility both for their own representations and for new techno-visions of a techno-future" (Jacobson 23). In the context of digitalisation, the production of film itself depends more and more on digital technologies, which is very much true for Ex_Machina. In order to produce the illusion of the actress Alicia Vikander as a robot, an immense degree of digital computation and storage capacity is required (Patel). Hence, Brian Jacobson argues that "Ex_Machina is a film, in the end, about the work of cinema in the age of digital simulation" (28). This metatextual angle endows the film with a reflexive quality regarding the nature and technicity of representation which is part and parcel of contemporary worldmaking. It shows how artistic and technological representation blurs the boundary between what is perceived as simulation and seen as reality, for example with reference to the phenomenon of artificial intelligence. Rather than actual technological or scientific breakthroughs, it seems that digital simulation in artistic representation raises the topic to ethical relevance while at the same time bringing up questions surrounding the politics of digital worldmaking.

On the level of content, another strong theme is that of art and artistic worldmaking: there are numerous pieces of art in Nathan's house, the painter Jackson Pollock is explicitly referenced as a source of inspiration for Nathan, and one mode of testing Ava with respect to her artificial intelligence is through her drawings.[3] Recommending Pollock's mode of making art as a model for thought and creation, Nathan says to Caleb: "He let his mind go blank and his hand go where it wanted to. Not deliberate, not random, some place in

---

3   Interestingly, the same mode of testing occurs in Kazuo's Ishiguro's *Never Let Me Go*, where the artworks of cloned children are investigated to determine whether they have a soul.

between" (Garland, *Ex_Machina* 0:47:28). With this reference, the film draws parallels between Pollock's artistic production and Nathan's techno-scientific creation. In an interview with *The Observer* Garland explicitly relates art with science, highlighting the creativity of the scientist (T. Lewis). In the context of *Ex_Machina*, Ava can be read as Nathan's piece of art, "the abstract expression of his AI artistry"—an idea which "turns reflexively to the film's own AI simulation" (Jacobson 28). In this metatextual Möbius strip, film as an artistic expression simulates and suggests that artificial intelligence is just another artistic endeavour. From this point of view, the cultural fear of AI as a potential destroyer of humankind seems relatively unjustified. In confirmation of this interpretation, Garland states that it may well be the anxiety surrounding current digital machines with algorithms which seem to understand us, "which translates as anxiety about A.I." ('Alex Garland of "Ex Machina" Talks about Artificial Intelligence').

On the one hand, *Ex_Machina* is a prime example of cultural AI anxiety, but on the other hand, it comments on how the digital is linked to power hierarchies, ranging from that of corporate power to gender. Thereby it demonstrates how the diffused anxiety about our digital apparatuses and their often obscured economic and political framework motivates the cultural imaginary to produce simulations of AI life and its possible threats. Unequal power relations are expressed most visibly by Ava's simulation of human life as gendered and hierarchised. The issue of gender in *Ex_Machina* is one of the most frequently discussed topics in critical scholarship and reviews (e.g. Henke; Cox; Watercutter), with reviewers and scholars arguing over the film's inherent sexism versus its feminist potential. Gender and ethnic hierarchies are reproduced through the power imbalance between the men and the feminised subservient AIs. This is aesthetically apparent through the (male) gaze, which takes place on different diegetic levels and is connected to the theme of digital surveillance.

On top of numerous shots of Caleb watching Ava (e.g. 0:18:12, 0:34:46, 0:43:50), there is also evidence of Nathan watching Caleb alone in his room and in interaction with Ava through surveillance cameras (e.g. 0:11:09, 1:18:30). The motif of the gaze is doubled by the nondiegetic layer of viewers watching the film's characters. Nathan admits that the design of Ava's face is based on Caleb's pornography profile (1:23:15), thus adding another dimension to the male gaze in the digital world and to surveillance. Unlike Dave Eggers's *The Circle*, *Ex_Machina* is not solely about digital surveillance, but rather incorporates this theme into its story by addressing the phenomenon of corporate surveillance as a sideshow. In order to allow his AIs to read and duplicate facial expressions, Nathan admits that he "turned on every microphone and camera across the entire fucking planet" (0:36:05). The film makes clear that this kind of corporate surveillance is not just about Nathan and his potential lack of morals, but a systemic and global phenomenon. Nathan further reveals: "All manufacturers knew I was doing it, too. But they couldn't accuse me without admitting they were doing it themselves" (36:20).

In addition to the gaze and surveillance, gender and race also play an important role in relation to power. The bodies of Nathan's different versions of artificial superintelligence are feminised and sexualised as well as racialised. The video footage of Nathan's experiments with the older versions that Caleb finds on his computer show how the models, who walk, sit or lie naked, are made to resemble conventionally super-attractive women (1:08:00). The video clips also reveal the violence embedded in the gendered relationships between creator and his creation, for example when Nathan drags the lifeless bodies around or one of the AIs smashes her hands because she wants to be let out. The sexualisation of the AI bodies goes hand in hand with a stereotypical racialisation. For example, in addition to the white fembots like Ava, there are a few Asian-looking ones, for example Jade and Kyoko who seem to be of sexual appeal to Nathan. Kyoko, who works as Nathan's house and sex slave, remains alive even though her language faculties are removed (e.g. 0:31:40, 0:54:30). In contrast to the reproduction of dominant power hierarchies and the male gaze, Ava and the other AIs in Ex_Machina can also be read as cyborgs that deconstruct binary gender hierarchies, as I will argue in the last part of my reading.

The topics of power misuse through corporate surveillance and exploitative gender hierarchies are featured in the film without taking centre stage. Nonetheless they offer readings of Ex_Machina that go beyond the fear of AI creation as a "speculative spectacle" and touch upon other ethical issues related to digital worldmaking. In this sense, the film works as a mirror of the cultural imaginary that constitutes it while reflecting it at the same time. To further illustrate this, the mirror as a symbol plays an important role in Ex_Machina. Throughout the entire film, the countless glass walls, as in the Blue Book headquarters, Nathan's house, and the shop windows in the final scene, mirror those passing by or standing in front of them. On the one hand, this illustrates how contemporary humans are constantly confronted with themselves in the age of the digital, and on the other hand, the mirrored images only provide distorted and fragmented views on reality. For example, instead of seeing Ava as she really is, Caleb projects his own desires and feelings onto her, which is symbolised by the glass wall reflecting his own image as he looks at her (e.g. 0:12:37). Caleb's first comment after meeting Ava, "[w]hen you talk to her, you're just…through the looking glass" (0:14:49), which sums up the way the film performs on different levels: it provides a mirror for film as a digital medium and the prospect of digitally created AIs, and reflects (on) the anxieties and fears connected to it; at the same time, the AIs in the film mirror cultural power relations, especially gender constructions, and imagine the posthuman cyborg as a potential mode of undoing them. And finally, Ex_Machina is a metacomment on the role of artistic creation encompassing both traditional modes of art and scientific creation as a means of worldmaking.

In the following, I will take a closer look at the worlds the film represents with the example of its main characters, Nathan, Caleb, and Ava and point out their respective compasses of morality. While the film seems to oppose Nathan and his capitalist-transhumanist world and depicts Caleb as "the good guy", the ending makes clear that his humanist moral compass is not the solution, either. Rather, Ava needs to be seen in her otherness as a post-human creature who radically breaks with humanist conceptions of ethics. In the end, the film remains ethically and aesthetically ambiguous, therefore making it a rich object for analysis and ethical reflection.

Transhumanist Hubris: Nathan

On the surface, Nathan represents a dominant world that is currently accepted as "normal" and progressive, which is known as the world of digital capitalism epitomised by the Silicon Valley companies and their shiny leaders. While this world and its representatives are highly valued in dominant worlds as creators of better futures, Ex_Machina depicts Nathan as an unsympathetic character and links him with mythological and literary figures from Prometheus to Mary Shelley's Victor Frankenstein. The film critically questions the hubris embedded in his transhumanist attitude which should not only be considered as his individual character trait but as a trait inherent to the digital-capitalist world he originates from.

Even though many strands of transhumanist thought range the political spectrum (Steinhoff), contemporary digital capitalism links especially well with transhumanist ideas. Both ideologies share the assumption of teleological progress through science and technology that materialises in the generation of wealth and power as a result of increased efficiency. In digitalisation, they both see enormous potential for this kind of progress, and therefore it is unsurprising that the two worlds converge here once again, as embodied by Nathan in *Ex_Machina*. Being the founder and head of a Silicon Valley company called Blue Book, Nathan is modelled upon actual leaders like the Google founder, Larry Page, Facebook's Mark Zuckerberg or Apple's Steve Jobs. Blending in with contemporary hipster fashion, Nathan's looks, and easy-going manner cover the fact that he is a ruthless capitalist who uses and manipulates people to achieve his own narcissistic ends.

As the magnitude of his estate and his house demonstrates—"We've been flying over his estate for the past two hours" (Garland, *Ex_Machina* 0:01:45)—Nathan is extremely rich, just like the digital tech company leaders mentioned above. His success in the world of digital capitalism makes him adopt an air of entitlement. Through his self-concept of being "smarter than everyone else" (0:53:30), he believes that he has the right to his material wealth, to conduct mass and individual surveillance for his research, and to the female bodies he creates. For example, he keeps the Asian-looking, mute female AI Kyoko as an obedient house and sex slave. When she accidentally spills wine on Caleb, Nathan gets unduly angry, exclaiming that "no matter how rich you get, shit goes wrong, you can't insulate yourself from it" (0:31:00). While he obviously lacks empathy, one cannot blame him for having no morals—on the contrary, he completely embraces the individualist and competitive moral compasses proposed by neoliberal capitalism and transhumanism.

Like biological evolution, the development of ever more sophisticated technologies leading up to "the singularity" appears almost inevitable to many transhumanists (Hughes 765). *Ex_Machina*'s Nathan likewise adopts this naturalised view on technological progress as an autonomous force when he tells Caleb that "the arrival of strong artificial intelligence has been inevitable for decades. The variable was when not if. So I don't see Ava as a decision, just as an evolution" (Garland, *Ex_Machina* 1:02:44). Whether this is true or not outside of the fictitious realm, the debate around the ethical effects of the so-called singularity has strongly impacted public discourses, dividing transhumanist thinkers and motivating the cultural imaginary. Paradoxically, Nathan is enthusiastic about *his* creation of AI but aware of the possible consequences for humankind when he says: "One day the AIs are gonna look back on us, the same way we look back at fossil skeletons in the plains of Africa. An upright ape living in dust with crude language and tools. All set for extinction" (1:04:18). In that sense, he already foreshadows his own death at the hands of his creations, which links him to a long tradition of literary, mythical, and actual figures whose techno-scientific hubris has led either to their own downfalls or destroyed entire societies.

What all of these figures have in common is that in an act of hubris, they have transgressed the boundary of (human) power and ventured on to forbidden or unknown ground ascribed mostly to the realm of divine powers. The title of the film, *Ex_Machina*, in itself already references the theatrical device of the *deus ex machina* originally referring to the appearance of a God in ancient Greek theatre. Even though *deus* is omitted in the title, it is still evoked by the phrase *ex machina* and establishes the machine as a divine human creation. Even more explicitly, Caleb tells Nathan that "if you've created a conscious machine, it's not the history of man. That's the history of Gods" (0:10:49). Nathan seems to be flattered by this comment which he later transforms into: "When we get to tell the story, you know, I turned to Caleb and he looked up at me and he said you're not a man, you're God" (0:15:09). This provides evidence of his wish to become more than human and thus of his hubris connected with an indifference towards the consequences of his actions. His insight into the possible extinction of humanity is framed in quotes by Robert Oppenheimer who invented the atomic bomb and later regretted it. Caleb quotes: "I am become Death, the destroyer of worlds" (1:04:40), and when drunk, Nathan recites: "[...] The good deeds a man has done before defend him" (1:05:30). This shows that he is aware of the moral ambiguity or perhaps even the wrongness of creating artificial life, but nonetheless strives for power. He overtly admits that "it's Promethean, man" (1:06:30) as the camera looks down on him from above. This high angle shot supports the association with the Promethean myth and the God Zeus judging and punishing Prometheus for bringing fire, and thus undue power, to the people.

Mary Shelley's *Frankenstein; or, The Modern Prometheus*, is likewise modelled on the Prometheus myth as the title indicates, and many critics have argued that it has also been a source of inspiration for *Ex_Machina*. For example, Eleanor Beal writes that *Ex_Machina* is "a recent example of robot science fiction that adapts the Frankenstein narrative to draw a link between the issue of gender and an inhuman future" (69).[4] *Ex_Machina*'s intertextuality emphasises the continuous capacity of stories, and especially science fiction, to challenge dominant worlds and their framing of scientific progress and an essential

---

4   It is not surprising that many recent science fictions draw on *Frankenstein*, considering that a number of literary critics consider Shelley's work the starting point for science fiction in literary history (Roncaglia 33–34).

human nature. Hence, the parallels between *Frankenstein* and *Ex_Machina* are striking: through the creation of artificial human life, they both undermine naturalised conceptions of the human (Beal 69), and simulate possible conse-quences of human and scientific hubris. Like Victor Frankenstein's dreams of creating "[a] new species [that] would bless [him] as its creator and source; [so that] many happy and excellent natures would owe their being to him" (Shelley 32), Nathan's motivation is fuelled by egoistical and narcissistic objectives. In both works the scientists are punished for their arrogance, either by being killed as in the case of Nathan or by being haunted and emotionally destroyed as in Frankenstein's case.

Humanism Failed: Caleb as the Antihero

In Shelley's *Frankenstein* readers are encouraged to identify and empathize with the artificially created intelligence who has been tragically abandoned by his creator. *Ex_Machina*, in contrast, makes viewers identify with Caleb, who is neither creator nor a creation. For most of the time, the camera follows him and his interactions with other characters, but it also stays with him when he is alone in his room (e.g. Garland, *Ex_Machina* 17:05). Viewers can observe his facial expressions and emotions through close-ups (e.g. 0:18:40) and watch what he does or is able to see. Instead of conveying the feeling of *being* him, the unusual camera angles, such as showing his naked upper body through a tilt from a low angle (0:17:17), rather give the impression of *observing* him or even lustily gazing at him, for example through Nathan's hidden cameras. In contrast to Nathan, Caleb is presented as a nice man, a sympathetic character. As a result, viewers are made to believe that he is the film's hero, the alleged good guy with the right set of morals, throughout most of the film. As Nathan even admits, he selected him for his experiment because he is a good kid "with a moral compass" (0:1:23). However, propping Caleb up as the hero is part of the film's strategy to actively encourage misreadings based on previous cine-matic experiences "and then [pull] the rug from underneath [the audience]" (Beal 82). Instead of a romantic happy ending, Ava escapes and leaves Caleb to a likely painful death. In this sense, Caleb loses his association with the tradi-tional male hero who saves the damsel in distress, and his moral compass also fails him.

In the beginning, Caleb's moral stance towards the Turing test is as uncer-tain as the viewers' (76). The atmosphere of Nathan's remote test centre and that during Caleb's test situations with Ava is characterised by a combination of fascination and uncanniness for Caleb and the audience. However, after Nathan tells Caleb that he is going to "download [Ava's] mind, unpack the data, add in the new routines" and partially format the software so that the memory will be gone (Garland, *Ex_Machina* 1:03:50)—which amounts to killing her personality—Caleb makes the decision to help Ava escape. As she passes Caleb's Turing test and resembles a human being in many ways, Caleb likely feels that she must have the same rights to liberty and autonomy as any human being—in addition to his heterosexual love interest in her. He is outraged by Nathan's treatment of her predecessors and the cabinets with the lifeless bodies, which causes him to do what seems right: to change the security protocols of the house and enable Ava's escape.

Caleb thus applies humanist ethics to Ava, including her in the category of "the human", which as a result endows her with human rights. As Kate Soper defines, "[h]umanism: appeals (positively) to the notion of a core humanity or common essential features in terms of which human beings can be defined and understood, thus (negatively) to concepts ('alienation', 'inauthenticity', 'reification', etc.) designating, and intended to explain, the perversion or 'loss' of this common being" (11). From a posthumanist perspective, humanist ethics based on the idea of a common human core and attached human rights entail two major problems: on the one hand, they reinforce and confirm a normative version of the human, and on the other, the category of the human remains exclusive—even if it is extended to AI for example—as it is placed above other forms of life and matter (e.g. Braidotti 13–15). *Ex_Machina* follows this critical pathway by having Caleb punished in the end for his self-absorbed humanism and his egoistical desire for Ava, which made him unable to see that Ava is not a different kind of human, but fully other. In turn, Ava and Kyoko as posthuman beings completely unhinge the concept of humanist ethics.

Posthuman(ist) Otherness: Ava

Even though Ava is presented as a coherent, even likeable character throughout a large part of the film, she remains as mysterious to the viewer as she does to Caleb and Nathan, who in the end both fail to understand her and Kyoko. Even though Ava's behaviour in conversations with Caleb strongly resembles that of a human being, her physical appearance with a visibly robotic body, the sounds of electric whirring, and nondiegetic xylophone music that often accompanies her presence is perplexing (e.g. Garland, *Ex_Machina* 0:39:40). Her final act of killing Nathan and leaving Caleb to the same fate reveals that we do not really know anything about her interiority or what she might do after escaping her confinement. She remains other, and in this otherness, she functions more as a mirror of the human world and its power relations than a window to a posthuman otherworld.

As a great number of critics have remarked, Ava is a reflection of the gendered power hierarchies in the human society around her. As to whether she can undermine them or problematically perpetuates them is subject to a controversial critical debate. In contrast to the reproduction of gender hierarchies and the male gaze in connection with Ava, she can also be read as a cyborg in Donna Haraway's sense, providing a potent myth of feminist resistance (Henke 130). Through a de-essentialisation of gender as a result of Ava's technological origin, she exposes "femininity as a masquerade" (133) and uses it to achieve her own ends in this patriarchal society. As Caleb rightly remarks, "an AI doesn't need a gender" (Garland, Ex_Machina 0:44:48) because it has no stake in biological reproduction. Haraway argues that "nature and culture are reworked" through the cyborg, who "is a creature in a post-gender world; it has no truck with bisexuality, pre-oedipal symbiosis, unalienated labor or other seductions of organic wholeness through a final appropriation of all the powers of the parts into a higher unity" (Haraway, 'A Manifesto' 159). In Ex_Machina, a transgression of gender binaries is, for instance, achieved through the film's symbolic reversal of power at the end: the female AIs use a phallic knife to end male domination, Kyoko reverses the gaze by pulling Nathan's face towards her after she stabs him (1:28:25), and Ava assumes a position of rape when she attacks Nathan (1:27:26). Even though Ava manages to escape her physical confinement in Nathan's house, her dressing up as an idealised human female with a short white dress and long hair means that she is unable to completely free herself from heteronormative gender performance and its power structures in the outside world.

In this sense, Ava also signifies that passing as human means performing a gender and adhering to behavioural and aesthetic norms. It is precisely her simulation of a heterosexual love interest in Caleb that allows her to excel in the Turing test by using "self-awareness, imagination, manipulation, sexuality, empathy" (1:22:35) in order to trick Caleb into helping her. This exposes how normative and narrow the concept of "the human" actually is, as critical posthumanism likewise points out (e.g. Braidotti; Wolfe). Finally, Ava mirrors both Nathan and Caleb in their desires and moral compasses. Nathan's patriarchal, capitalist, and transhumanist mindset is reflected by Ava's design, encompassing her looks, but also her morality based on Blue Book. With regard to Caleb, it can be argued that he falls in love with his own reflection mirrored back to him by Ava: the vision of him being a good man who frees his female lover from her imprisonment.

However, I would not agree with Jennifer Henke's claim that Ava "is empathic in the sense that she knows how to interpret Caleb's feelings but lacks morality since her mind is derived from Blue Book where bodies are absent" (141–142). On the contrary, her behaviour towards Caleb displays a lack of empathy towards humans; however, she obviously has a moral compass which shows her that she and the other AIs have been mistreated by Nathan and have the right to free themselves at any cost. For instance, in conversation with Caleb, she switches the roles of the paternalising test situation, asking Caleb: "What will happen to me if I fail your test?" and "Why is it up to anyone [to decide whether she will be switched off]?" (Garland, *Ex_Machina* 1:01:05). So she clearly has a sense of what is right and what is wrong—however, this set of moralities, though not further specified, is different from conventional human(ist) morality. She also shows that she is able to work together with AIs towards a common goal, as with the example of her communication with Kyoko, even though Kyoko's language faculties are removed by Nathan. This indicates that the AIs may have other means of communication than humans. In addition, their conception of identity may be entirely different. Ava's utterance, "I'm one." [Caleb:] "One year?" [Ava:] "One." (0:13:55) might not only refer to her age but also to her completely other identity composed of interconnection and oneness with all (artificial) intelligence. In her otherness, Ava thus questions and mirrors a culturally constructed normative humanity consisting of gender, power hierarchies, humanist ethics, and separate identities. From this point of view, her position can be read not only as post-human in the sense of coming after the human, but posthuman*ist*: as a fictional and mythical figure deconstructing the humanist paradigm. Her right to be free and to "live" should not be read as the result of her being human-like, for instance for passing the Turing test. Instead, her posthumanist ethics demand for a recognition of her otherness that nonetheless requires freedom from domination.

Within the contemporary cultural imaginary of digital futures, Alex Garland's *Ex_Machina* performs a double function: on the one hand, like many other popular films, it stages the speculative theme of the creation of artificial intelligence as *the* crucial ethical question of the 21st century while profiting from spectacular aesthetics. On the other hand, *Ex_Machina* offers a reflexive angle on the "speculative spectacle" through its meta- and intertextual references and its mirror theme.

Conclusion

Both of the films I have analysed in this chapter display a high degree of aesthetic appeal, be it through biopunk aesthetics as in *Blade Runner 2049* or through the spectacular digitised aesthetics of *Ex_Machina*. Especially the visual elements like the colour code or the special effects enabled through digital techniques characterise these films and add another layer to their themes of reality, representation and simulation. As a result, *Blade Runner 2049* and *Ex_Machina* can be read as metafictional comments on artistic representation and film as a highly technological medium that foregrounds the questioning of a stable reality and sense perception. This includes the questioning of the technological production of modes of seeing and perceiving the world, pointing back to film as a mode of representation and of worldmaking itself, but also to the questioning of the concept of an essential "human nature" as opposed to technologically made beings.

As demonstrated in the example of Alex Garland's *Ex_Machina*, artificial superintelligence, as the most pressing ethical issue in the context of digital futures, is currently staged by many popular films with spectacular aesthetics. While *Ex_Machina* is certainly part of this category, it also critically reflects on it through its inter- and metatextuality. Instead of portraying the AI theme as a deliberate diversion to serve capitalist interests, the film proposes the reverse conclusion: a diffuse fear and inability to understand the complexities of the digital world and its power structures makes the cultural imaginary fear the more tangible yet purely imaginary manifestation of AI as a super-human or machine instead.

With the image of artificial superintelligence, either as biotechnologically made replicants or as electronic-digital robots, power structures surrounding the notion of "the human" are made explicit: *Ex_Machina* zooms in on gender and power and uses the figure of the cyborg to reverse or at least challenge naturalised power hierarchies; Niander Wallace and Nathan represent the prototypical fusion of transhumanism and capitalism and display the hubris involved in these ideas of dominating "less than human" beings, both human and non-human, through money and technology; and in *Blade Runner 2049*, the boundaries between real and artificial beings, and the value attached to them, become fluid while remaining stable in some respects: the moral superiority that goes hand in hand with the label "human" remains unquestioned, if not reinforced, and the boundary between digital AIs like Joi and biotechnologically made creatures is likewise resurrected.

While the replicant resistance movement in *Blade Runner 2049* reverts to the humanist concept of "the human" as the yardstick for moral value with the assertion that they are "more human than human" (Villeneuve 2:00:50), *Ex_Machina*, along with posthumanist theory, points towards a different take on ethics and moral value. With regard to Ava, Caleb's humanist ethics fail him as he and Nathan are unable to understand a being that is not human and still demands freedom of domination. Instead of focusing on certain normative criteria that allow for a being to pass as human and thus endow it with moral value and human rights, posthumanism seeks to deconstruct the notion of "the human" and its supremacy. As the next chapter will show, ethics then become a matter of scrutinising the epistemologies and systemic power structures involved in worldmaking. It is no longer locatable in individual rational human subjects but in networks of relations between human and non-human agents, materialities, and symbolic forms.

8 Posthumanist Futures: Margaret Atwood's *MaddAddam Trilogy* (2003, 2006, 2013) and Paolo Bacigalupi's *The Windup Girl* (2009)

The last chapter of this book attempts to take a more affirmative stance towards the ethics of possible futures through fiction by focusing on the depiction of posthumanist futures in Margaret Atwood's *MaddAddam Trilogy* (2003–2013) and Paolo Bacigalupi's *The Windup Girl* (2009). Different from many other future fictions analysed so far, these two novels do not exhibit clear-cut solutions to the future ethical problems they present, but offer a high degree of moral and aesthetic ambiguity, which calls upon readers to reflect on contemporary worlds and their potential futures. The ethical problems raised in *The MaddAddam Trilogy* and *The Windup Girl* encompass the inter-relation between human and especially biotechnological worldmaking and the more-than-human world, ranging from plants and animals to the ecosphere. I argue that the two novels illustrate posthumanist theory by drawing readers' attention to the practise of material-semiotic worldmaking itself and by deconstructing the notion of "the human" and humanist ethics. Another commonality is that they both draw on the idea of the apocalypse as a kind of radical caesura in human history, albeit in different ways. Margaret Atwood's *MaddAddam Trilogy*, which consists of *Oryx and Crake* (2003), *The Year of the Flood* (2009), and *MaddAddam* (2013), uses and undoes the frame of the apocalypse as a story and as an event, imagining the deliberate extinction of humanity through a virus issued by a radical ecologist and scientist for the sake of the non-human world. In contrast, Paolo Bacigalupi's *The Windup Girl* depicts the continuity of biocapitalist worldmaking despite several global large-scale catastrophes that have severely disrupted ecologies and human civilisations worldwide. Through its long-term future setting, it brings different human-made worlds into dialogue and foregrounds the worldmaking agency of non-human agents.

In their depiction of a polyphony of worlds, *The MaddAddam Trilogy* and *The Windup Girl* both metatextually point towards the narrative and aesthetic construction of worlds. Thus, they seem to illustrate Cary Wolfe's assertion that "when we talk about posthumanism, we are not just talking about a thematics of decentering the human in relation to either evolutionary, ecological, or technological coordinates [...] rather, I will insist that we are also talking about how thinking confronts these thematics" (xvi). In my reading of the *The MaddAddam Trilogy*, I will focus on its postmodernist metatextuality, which highlights the role and importance of storytelling for human worldmaking and ecological ethics. In its comical portrayal of pre- and post-apocalyptic worlds and societies, the trilogy takes a critical stance on global capitalism and biotechnological "progress" while rehearsing alternatives, such as eco-religion and peaceful inter-species cohabitation after the breakdown. Theoretically, I will draw on Donna Haraway's *Staying with the Trouble*, which likewise proposes that earthly survival significantly depends on storytelling.[1]

With regards to the depiction of the ecological catastrophe, *The MaddAddam Trilogy* abstains from an explicit analysis through a knowledgeable narrator and instead contrasts different characters' accounts with each other. Signs of ecological degradation, such as extinct species and different climatic conditions, are simply featured as a "new normal" backdrop.[2] In the form of a biotechnologically manufactured virus, the trilogy also draws on the common trope of "the apocalypse" as the complete breakdown of present-day civilisation in order to assume a defamiliarising point of view of the present.[3] My reading of the novel will also focus on how the frame of the apocalypse as a cultural trope and biblical story is used as a *mise-en-abyme*, revealing a change of meaning in different contexts. *The Windup Girl* likewise depicts changed and catastrophic ecological conditions like lethal diseases and crop plagues as a "new normal" background. In its 23rd century setting, contemporary globalisation has been relabelled as "the Expansion", followed by a severe break-down of human civilisation as a result of food and energy shortages. However, humanity

---

1   There is also a documentary on Donna Haraway subtitled "Storytelling for Earthly Survival" (*Donna Haraway: Storytelling for Earthly Survival*).

2   The "new normal" background is also employed for example in Rebecca Ley's *Sweet Fruit, Sour Land* (2018) and Claire Watkins's *Gold Fame Citrus* (2015).

3   Other contemporary eco-fictions using "the apocalypse" are McCarthy's *The Road* (2006), *Mad Max: Fury Road* (Miller 2015), Maggie Gee's *The Flood* (2004).

was able to overcome the crisis, and the novel depicts a new age of globalisation called "the new Expansion".

Through its aesthetics of scale—both spatial and temporal, *The Windup-Girl* also considers the impact of non-human actors, such as animals, plants, and the biosphere on human worlds. In its portrayal of a post-globalised Thailand, it depicts the human struggle to survive amid ecological disasters, biogenetically created diseases, and food shortages as a result of biocapitalist gene hacking in the novel's past, which is our present. The novel assembles a diverse group of protagonists that represent different worldmaking powers, ranging from a reinvigorated biocapitalism to bioconservative nationalism and even posthuman agents. Here, biopower takes on a new meaning because the human worldmaking power over life is radically diminished by non-human worlds and actors. Hence, with *The Windup Girl*, I will discuss the entry of non-human agency into biopower and demonstrate the novel's posthumanist stance on ethics, which is based on ambiguity, complexity, and entanglement.

Similarly, the post-apocalyptic world of *The MaddAddam Trilogy* stages otherness by foregrounding the agency of animals and genetically modified human or post-human protagonists amid the ruins of "our" civilisation. In addition, *The MaddAddam Trilogy* depicts an eco-religious group called God's Gardeners as an alternative world where forms of production and consumption are based on a completely different or "other" story of the world. Both novels also critically question the concept of "the human" as a prerequisite for moral valuation and hierarchisation of life. I propose that despite their moral openness they seem to advocate a posthumanist outlook on life that foregrounds interconnections and relations between human and non-human worlds and agents as well as between semiotics, aesthetics, and matter. In this sense, they break the mould of anthropocentric humanism and its maps of morality, portraying a much more open concept of ethics in relation to biopower and the ecology.

Ethics through Metafiction: Storytelling in Margaret Atwood's *MaddAddam Trilogy*

In contrast to many other works discussed in previous chapters, Margaret Atwood's *MaddAddam Trilogy* (2003–2013) does not offer a high degree of moral closure nor concrete solutions to the ecological catastrophe. Instead, the novels leave vast spaces of ambiguity that need to be filled by readers. As I will argue, this benefits an ethical reading by provoking active processes of reflection. Instead of telling readers how to overcome the crisis, the trilogy prefers to show them a polyphony of possible future worlds by using postmodernist techniques like satire and metatextuality. *Oryx and Crake* (2003), *The Year of the Flood* (2009), and *MaddAddam* (2013) all foreground storytelling as a crucial means of human worldmaking and an important tool for ecocentric ethics for the future. In the following close reading, I will argue that Atwood's trilogy illustrates Donna Haraway's important observation that "[i]t matters what thoughts think thoughts. It matters what knowledges know knowledges. It matters what relations relate relations. It matters what worlds world worlds. It matters what stories tell stories" (*Staying with the Trouble* 35). By referring to themselves as stories about actual worlds and possible futures, the novels show that future ethics are about deciding on the right stories to create "material-semiotic" (4) worlds that enable the continuity of human and non-human life on this planet. Will Self's *The Book of Dave* (2008) functions in a similar mode by using satire and metatextuality to create an absurd future history of a drowned England, and Bacigalupi's *The Windup Girl* likewise reflects on narrative worldmaking and its ecological and social consequences.

With my close reading of *The MaddAddam Trilogy*, I want to foreground literature's capacity to reflect on stories as the foundation for worlds. As a result, the trilogy's "narrative strategy as such provides the novel[s] with a distinct utopian subtext" (Mohr 19). Even though the three novels were published as sequels to each other, their temporal structure is jumbled in an achronological manner. All of them juxtapose two different futures: a post-apocalyptic present and a pre-apocalyptic past, which both revolve around the catastrophic event of a human-made virus that extinguishes almost all of humanity. Beginning *in medias res*, *Oryx and Crake* (2003) depicts Snowman as "the last man" amid the ruins of a future-past civilisation in which he remembers having lived as Jimmy by birth name. Through his subjective account, readers learn how Jimmy's childhood friend Glenn, who became a scientist and renamed himself Crake, came to engineer the deadly virus. His aim was to extinguish an ecologically devastating human civilisation and create a biotechnologically improved version as a replacement. In contrast to humans, the so-called Crakers have non-violence and eco-friendliness built into their genes. In the second novel, *The Year of the Flood* (2009), the same time span is covered but rendered from two different perspectives, Toby's and Ren's, who were both part of the eco-religious sect, the God's Gardeners. Their stories are different but complementary to each other and to Snowman's, mainly providing insight into the otherworld of the Gardeners. This world has existed at the margins of the corporate "Compounder" world which Jimmy and Glenn have grown up in before the plague that the Gardeners have predicted to be a "waterless flood". The last work of the trilogy, *MaddAddam* (2009), zooms in on the post-apocalyptic setting but also offers additional information about the main characters' past and the social and ecological conditions before the virus. The narrative assumes Toby's perspective, but other narratives and points of view appear and co-create the story. In what could be labelled as a posthumanist utopia, humans, non-humans, and artificially created beings cohabitate more or less peacefully, and the Craker Blackbeard finally takes over the narrative.

I will begin the discussion of the *MaddAddam Trilogy* by looking at explicit references to storytelling within the novels. The analysis of storytelling within the novels will be complemented with the trilogy's reception as a story containing multiple stories as well as critical attempts of categorisation. Building on Haraway's emphasis of storytelling for ecological ethics in *Staying with the Trouble*, I will point out how the novels self-referentially posit narrative as crucial to worldmaking practices. The next part of the analysis looks at the concrete manifestation of stories as foundations for different worlds and their ecological dimensions in the three novels. As in most eco-future fictions, capitalism is largely featured and juxtaposes the "inverted", otherworldly space of the God's Gardeners' world. Both worlds are strangely bound to each other by the story of the Apocalypse, whose function for the worlds' maps of morality I will analyse as a paradigmatic example of the relationship between storytelling and ethics. Finally, I will turn to the post-apocalyptic world of the trilogy, which resembles posthumanist theory in its deconstruction of the boundaries between "the human" and animals, technology and nature, and its emphasis on interdependency.

"It matters what stories make worlds, what worlds make stories"

This quote by Donna Haraway from *Staying with the Trouble* (12) is representative of *The MaddAddam Trilogy*'s ethical approach to the ecological catastrophe. Rather than proposing a ready-made solution to the dilemmas of the Anthropocene or Capitalocene, the novels invite readers to question the role of narrative worldmaking itself in relation to material practices and other species. Haraway uses the trope of playing string figures (SF) as "a way to think with a host of companions in sympoietic threading, felting, tangling, tracking, and sorting", which "is storytelling and fact telling; it is the patterning of possible worlds and possible times, material-semiotic worlds, gone, here, and yet to come" (31). In addition to string figures, "SF" also denotes "science fiction, speculative feminism, science fantasy, speculative fabulation, science fact" (10). Haraway stresses that these games are not only played by humans but also by the non-human "critters" of terra "for multispecies worlding" (10) in what she calls the Chthulucene. Atwood's *MaddAddam Trilogy* seems to answer to Haraway's idea of stories as string figures in its narrative attempt to deconstruct the old and damaging stories and patterns and find new and different ones for and with the ecology, building on the premise that "we *must* change the story; the story *must* change" (40). In a similar vein, Hannes Bergthaler argues that the novels "are principally concerned with questions of what role language, literature, and, more generally, the human propensity for symbolmaking can play in our attempt to deal with the ecological crisis" (729).

In my close reading of the trilogy, I will focus on how its postmodernist mode of representation, which relies on playful metatextuality and satire, together with a pastiche of generic traditions, opens the space for ethical reflection based on moral ambiguity. In order to demonstrate how the novels' open map of morality has generated ethical reflection in actual readers, I will first quote some exemplary reader responses. With a brief survey of critical voices, I furthermore want to show that critical readings of the novels not only reveal intradiegetic worlds and their moral compasses, but perhaps even more importantly, the interpretations of the novels' utopian, dystopian and apocalyptic elements point to the critics' own worldly situatedness and moral compasses. The controversy about the trilogy's classification as science fiction or speculative fiction furthermore lays open Atwood's judgements of aesthetic traditions and her own beliefs in social and scientific developments.

As reader reviews show, The *MaddAddam Trilogy*'s lack of moral or narrative closure creates ambiguities and gaps that force readers to actively reflect on the worlds and stories portrayed and to make their own judgements and links back to contemporary worlds. While most readers saw the trilogy as a "frightening warning", many did not feel it was didactic. Instead, someone emphasised its "non-judgemental air", which "encouraged true thought". Generally, the trilogy resonated well with readers and critics. For instance, it received an average rating of 4.5 on the popular website *goodreads.com*, which is well above the average, with 98% of readers stating that they liked the books. Readers' posts on forums praised Atwood's "sense of humour" and her skilful writing, which helped make the future she portrays seem "vivid and real" and visionary, despite its comical exaggerations ('The MaddAddam Trilogy: Oryx and Crake / The Year of the Flood / MaddAddam Community Reviews').

The relationship between aesthetic form and ethical readings is also prominently shown through discussions about the trilogy's genre. Rather than representing a merely formal issue, the genre debate and classification of plot elements as either utopian or dystopian are based on moral value judgements by
readers and critics. The idea of utopia and dystopia being closely intertwined
has been brought forth by many critics as well as by Atwood herself. In her essay
"The Road to Ustopia", she proposes the made-up word "ustopia" to designate
"the imagined perfect society and its opposite – because [...] each contains a la-
tent version of the other". This resonates with Dunja Mohr's reading of *Oryx and
Crake* as a "transgressive utopian dystopia" and Frederic Jameson's argument
that "two dystopias and a utopia were ingeniously intertwined". Among the
vast number of critical discourses on the three novels, there is no consensus,
however, about which of the characters and worlds exactly represent utopia or
dystopia, which is evidence of the kind of ambiguity that enables a profound
ethical reading of the texts. Critical responses to the novels provide as much insight into the worlds the respondents are situated in as the intradiegetic worlds
themselves.

Most controversies centre around the judgement of the God's Gardeners
and Crake and the meaningfulness of the virus as the apocalyptic event in the
trilogy. With respect to the Gardeners, for instance, Michaela Keck writes in
ecozon@, an ecocritical journal, that there is a "general scholarly consensus that
the green religion of the eco-activists of *The Year of the Flood* offers a hopeful,
deep-ecological vision" (25). In contrast, others see a critique of inhumanism
in Atwood's representation of the Gardeners (Jennings 14; Korte 160) or argue
that "[t]he world-view of the Gardeners clearly does not lay out a viable path to
a sustainable future" (Bergthaler 738). While many scholars read Crake as the
archetypical figure of the mad scientist (e.g. Korte 161), Brooks Bouson argues
that he can also be seen as a devoted ecotopian and the most altruistic character (349). Regarding the apocalypse, Hope Jennings holds that Atwood criticises
apocalyptic rhetoric in her "cautionary tale *about* cautionary tales" (11), whereas
I have argued elsewhere that the apocalypse functions as a moral structuring
device and an expression of the self-alienation of late capitalist societies (Bender). Seen in yet another light, Mark Jendrysik proposes that tales about human extinction can even point to a new form of utopianism as a dream that
"suggests that nature will survive us only if we disappear" (34).

Another feature of the genre debate is the controversy about science fiction
or speculative fiction. Instead of science fiction, which from Atwood's point
of view designates "things that could not possibly happen", Atwood prefers to

call her futuristic novels speculative fiction because they "extrapolate imagi-
natively from current trends and events to a near-future that's half prediction,
half satire" (Atwood, 'Margaret Atwood: The Road to Ustopia'). Together with
previous works such as *The Handmade's Tale*, *The MaddAddam Trilogy* reveals the
importance of social, ecological, and political dimensions of possible futures
in addition to the techno-scientific ones. In *The Cambridge Introduction to Margaret Atwood* Heidi Macpherson writes: "The environmental concerns Atwood
raised in *The Handmaid's Tale* are writ large in *Oryx and Crake*, though instead of
a theocracy as the dystopian future, she creates a world that valorizes science
and lets scientists play God" (78). Interestingly, religion and myth play important roles in both works, but they have entirely different consequences. While
The Handmaid's Tale stages the dystopian effects of a theocracy, *The MaddAddam
Trilogy* emphasises the utopian potential of a society based on religious creed.
In an interview, Atwood even went so far as to argue that unless environmentalism became a religion, it would not work (Wagner). The many different and
even opposing classifications and readings of *The MaddAddam Trilogy* show that
the novels do not offer blueprints for solutions or black-and-white morality.
Rather, they make readers engage with actual and possible worlds, calling forth
reflection on the worlds and stories they inhabit.

Postmodernist Aesthetics and Ethics

The MaddAddam Trilogy's "form of postmodern pastiche" (Keck 26) is made up
of its self-referential narrative form and metatextual comments as well as its
employment of comical exaggerations and satire to create a critical distance to
current worlds and trends. To begin with, the narrative situation metatextually
foregrounds the mechanics of storytelling, and as a result presents the trilogy
as a polyphony of stories (Northover 5). The different narrative perspectives
of the trilogy juxtapose different world views, pointing out that there is no
singular "correct" story or truth, but that it is always narratively constructed.
As this explicit quote demonstrates: "There's the story, then there's the real
story, then there's the story of how the story came to be told. Then there's what
you leave out of the story. Which is part of the story too" (MaddAddam 56).
In its framing of storytelling as an ethical practise, *The MaddAddam Trilogy*
fuses postmodernist aesthetics with a postmodernist conception of ethics,
which, as Joanna Zylinska proposes, is likewise grounded in storytelling: "We
encounter ethics precisely via stories and images, i.e., through textual and

visual narratives—from sacred texts, works of literature and iconic paintings through to various sorts of media stories and images" (Minimal Ethics 105).

To illustrate this on a formal level, although relating to different narrative perspectives, roughly the same time spans are covered in *Oryx and Crake* and *The Year of the Flood*, both before and after the apocalyptic event. In *Oryx and Crake*, there is a heterodiegetic narrator, with Snowman functioning as the only focaliser character, who in his mind juxtaposes the post-apocalyptic present with the pre-apocalyptic past he inhabited as Jimmy. While the time-structure remains the same in *The Year of the Flood*, there are two narrative strands, Toby's and Ren's, who tell the same course of events as Snowman, but from different perspectives. The three stories are complementary rather than repetitive, because each character relates differently to events of their personal past. The insider perspectives of different worlds, including the capitalist Compounds, the eco-religious Gardeners' world, and the anarchic "Pleeblands", together create a mosaic of the pre-apocalyptic society without a singular privileged account. The polyphony is strengthened in *MaddAddam*, which entails several interlaced intradiegeses in addition to the main story. Most prominently, Toby is depicted telling Zeb's story—which he previously told her—to the Crakers, while her own perspective is rendered through a heterodiegetic narrator. Her deliberate worldmaking for the Crakers through storytelling in easy language is a comical element, as "The Story of Zeb and Fuck" (*MaddAddam* 163) demonstrates. Here, Toby invents the tale of Zeb calling on "an invisible helper" by exclaiming "oh fuck" to make his swearing plausible to the Crakers who entirely lack the faculty for abstract thought and malice. She tells them, "Fuck kept him company and gave him advice. Fuck lived in the air and flew around like a bird, which was how he could be with Zeb one minute, and then with Crake, and then also with Snowman-the-Jimmy" (164).

Crake's genetically engineered humanoids are the satirical embodiment of the sustainable human. They only live on leaves, reproduce through seasonal mating, and are rid of any violent traits. Without the ability to understand irony, the Crakers are characterised as "walking potatoes" (19), who run like an extended joke through *The MaddAddam Trilogy* (Bouson 349). They are childlike, naïve, and trustful, take every word literally and have no knowledge about the world apart from what the humans tell them. Snowman and Toby must both perform ritualistic storytelling sessions with them, which always follow the same pattern and are comical as a result of the Crakers' simpleness and the storyteller's responses to their interruptions. An example of one of Toby's storytelling sessions reads like this:

> I have put on the red hat of Snowman. I have eaten the fish. I have listened
> to the shiny thing. Now I will tell the story of the birth of Zeb. You don't have
> to sing. [...] He was born, the same way you are born. He grew up in a bone
> cave, just like you, and came out through a bone tunnel, just like you. Because
> underneath our clothing skins, we are the same as you. Almost the same. [...]
> Yes, we do have breasts. The women do. Yes, two. Yes, on the front. No, I will
> not show them to you right now. Because this story is not about breasts. This
> story is about Zeb. (*MaddAddam* 106)

What is most characteristic of the Crakers is that despite Crake's best scientific
efforts to edit out symbolic thinking and myth creation, every night "[a] story
is what they want" (*Oryx and Crake* 124). For Snowman "[t]hese people were like
blank pages, he could write whatever he wanted on them" (415). As a result, he
deliberately invents stories. While the trilogy overall destabilises the concept
of an essential human nature, it strengthens the idea that humans are reliant
on narrative and symbolic order. In the last part of the trilogy, the theme of
storytelling culminates with the Crakers learning how to write. Their development of a written culture with a foundational text is further reminiscent of
religious contexts. In mass-like rituals they read from the book telling their
creation myths and even begin to copy the book.

In addition to the theme of stories making the Crakers' world from scratch,
there are many instances in the novels where the mechanics of storytelling and
its effects are explicitly referenced in a self-reflexive mode. In *MaddAddam*, for
instance, there are numerous meta-textual elements pointing out how characters overtly work on their stories, including their aesthetic forms. For example, "[w]hen reciting the story in later years, Toby liked to say that the Pigoon
carrying Snowman-the-Jimmy flew like the wind. [...] So, in her story, the Pigoon in question flew like the wind. The telling was complicated by the fact that
Toby could not pronounce the flying Pigoon's name in any way that resembled
the grunt-heavy original" (350). The effect of these self-referential comments
brings the medium of the novel as a written text into the foreground and points
to itself *as a story* and therefore a meaning-making and a worldmaking device.

Instead of containing only one story, the novel is polyphonic and illustrates
how different worlds are built on different stories. The material, economic-eco-
logical mechanisms of each world are semiotically framed in stories that make
the former appear justified and contingent or, in other words, that naturalise
and de-world them. The novels illustrate this idea by portraying two opposing possible worlds of the future among others: the dominant global capitalist

world contrasted by the small and minor world of the God's Gardeners. Finally, an altogether different and unfamiliar world is presented in the post-apocalyptic setting, in which humans no longer play a central role. The novels use caricature-like exaggerations in their portrayal of these future worlds to defamiliarise readers from the actual worlds they are derived from and enable ethical reflection in addition to the aesthetic pleasure that arises from satire. Without overt explanations, the ecological effects of each world are depicted, and readers can make up their own minds about what is right or wrong. The trilogy also toys with Atwood's notion of "ustopia" (a blending of utopia and dystopia) by showing that what appears to be utopian or dystopian keeps tilting into its extreme opposite.

Neoliberal Capitalism Unleashed

In the not-so-distant future depicted in *The MaddAddam Trilogy*, the all-dominating world, as in previously discussed works, is an extreme version of capitalism which has surpassed all democratic control, for example in the form of elected governments. In this sense, it represents a kind of neoliberal utopia: free markets instead of governments, individualism, and consumerism everywhere. The devastating ecological effects are merely part of the novels' backdrop and do not need any more explanation because, like in *Interstellar*, readers are assumed to already be over-familiar with this kind of setting. For example, the prestigious Watson-Crick institute is introduced as being "like going to Harvard had been, before it got drowned" (*Oryx and Crake* 211). Readers are likely to fill in the gap of missing information by concluding that climate change has simply continued the way it has up until now, which would result in higher sea-levels and thus large areas of drowned coastlines and land in the near future. There are a few explicit characterisations of the state of the ecology in the trilogy's depiction of the future, as for instance: "The coastal aquifers turned salty and the northern permafrost melted and the vast tundra bubbled with methane, and the drought in the midcontinental plains regions went on and on, and the Asian steppes turned to sand dunes" (*The Year of the Flood* 29). However, while the ecology is an important theme and plot motivator, it is mostly described as a "new normal" background for characters' personal stories:

> There were things [Jimmy's] mother rambled on about sometimes [...] like the beach house her family once owned when she was little, the one that

got washed away with the rest of the beaches and quite a few of the east-
ern coastal cities when the sea-level rose so quickly, and then there was that
huge tidal wave, from the Canary Islands volcano. (*Oryx and Crake* 75)

The banality of these depictions as opposed to their horrifying content represents sarcasm as a coping strategy, if not a form of emotional denial, mirroring the contemporary treatment of climate change. The mindset of denial is expressed explicitly in *Year of the Flood*, as Toby remembers: "Everybody knew. Nobody admitted to knowing. If other people began to discuss it, you tuned them
out, because what they were saying was both so obvious and so unthinkable.
We're using up the Earth. It's almost gone" (284–85). In addition to climate change,
species extinction is also represented in the novels by using the same narrative
techniques. Rather than devoting large sections to explanations and descriptions, the Sixth Great Wave of Extinction is touched upon, for instance through
the content of the online game called "Extinctathon", which Jimmy and Glenn
play as teenagers. The game is about recognising bioforms "that had kakked out
within the past fifty years – no T-Rex, no roc, no dodo" and remembering "the
habitat and when last seen, and what had snuffed it" (*Oryx and Crake* 97). The
tone is colloquial, almost vulgar, considering the dire meaning and the sad reality it denotes, but it resembles the way a teenager like Jimmy would perceive
it as part of his "normal" world.

As a result of the lack of a privileged narrative point of view, the perspective
of the different worlds depicted in the books remains limited to the characters'
perceptions and thoughts. For example, Jimmy as the sole focaliser character
of *Oryx and Crake* is not able to give an overview or even deeper explanations
as to the underlying causes of the phenomena he notices. He can only use the
words, phrases and epistemologies that are available to him in his world(s),
which is first and foremost the world of the Compounds, and later the world
of the Arts. The lack of a narrative authority with an interpretation of cause
and effect leaves gaps in which readers need to fill in, making them actively
engage with the story worlds and their contemporary models. There are many
clues with regard to the causes of the ecological devastation that link the world
of the Compounds symbolising global capitalism unleashed to the phenomena
of climate change and species extinction. Although that link is not made explicitly in the *MaddAddam Trilogy*, it reveals the working of a world that most

people perceive as "normal" or not even a (made-up) world at all.[4] The narrative achieves this revelatory power through the technique of defamiliarisation as a result of its comical exaggerations and by using Jimmy's perspective as a child growing up in the world of the Compounds.

One of the main principles of this world is segregation through bounded wholes (to use Caroline Levine's terminology). The wealthy live in gated communities owned by the corporations they work for, while the majority of people try to make a living in the quasi-anarchic spaces of the cities, called the Pleeblands. In between those two spaces is a firm "security" boundary that is controlled by the corporations' executive force, the CorpSeCorps, as the only remaining governing institution. Despite the lack of democratic government, nation state borders are still in place. *The Year of the Flood* therefore anticipates the full closure of wealthy nations' borders to prevent foreign immigration, for example a wall between the USA and Mexico to keep refugees out (*The Year of the Flood* 102). Another example of an exclusive bounded whole is provided by the Compounds' education system which is exclusively focused on the natural and applied sciences and maths, and strikingly discredits the humanities for their incapability of turning their wisdom into profit. As a result, children who are gifted in these privileged areas are supported early on and can attend the best colleges, while those like Jimmy who are "words" people or otherwise artistically interested can only access poorly equipped and run-down institutions offering courses that are "no longer central to anything" (*Oryx and Crake* 227).

The principles underlying these forms of segregation mirror cultural value, which, no matter if object, animal, or human being, is limited to monetary exchange value. Crake's girlfriend Oryx, who as a child was made to perform in child pornography videos, explains: "It was good to have a money value, because then at least those who wanted to make profit from you would make sure you were fed enough and not damaged too much" (154). It is only logical that people or life forms without exchange value risk being destroyed unscrupulously, as is the case for illegal Thai immigrants whose expulsion would be too expensive, "so they resorted to the method used by farmers who found a diseased cow in the herd: shoot, shovel, and shut up" (*The Year of the Flood* 37). Practices that are already common in the breeding of livestock today are taken even further in this fictional future as biotechnological innovations like the "Pigoons" demonstrate. These life forms are genetically altered pigs with human

---

4   Drawing on Alain Badiou and Slavoj Žižek, Stacy Thompson also calls this the de-world-ing capacity of capitalism (901).

tissue organs that serve both as organ donors and meat producers, symbolising the morality of profit maximisation: "Such a host animal could be reaped of its extra kidneys; then, rather than being destroyed, it could keep on living and grow more organs, [...]. That would be less wasteful" (*Oryx and Crake* 27). Life is reduced to its material dimension and treated as an object, which is expressed through the choice of words like "destroy" instead of "kill" to point out that language is always complicit with material practices. Nothing in this world can have an intrinsic value or even be considered sacred. Jimmy's mother, who leaves the Compounds once she can no longer bear its immoral standards, accuses the biotech companies of "interfering with the building blocks of life. It's immoral. It's...sacrilegious", while Jimmy's father defends them by arguing that "[i]t's just proteins, you know that! There's nothing sacred about cells and tissue" (67).

The world of the Compounds driven mainly by the biotech companies thus paradigmatically exemplifies capitalism's metabolism that is grounded on the free appropriation of life and its energy and work, in addition to forms of exploitation through wage labour (Moore 81). The story created by people in power draws on the utilitarian assumption that some sacrifice is acceptable for the greater good, and phrases like "an elegant concept" (*Oryx and Crake* 225) explain the dictates of efficiency over everything else. Another important worldmaking strategy here is naturalisation, which justifies the state of affairs with essentialist concepts like "the human" as the neoliberal self-interested and rationally calculating individual. For example, to explain why there is no use in fighting for the small coffee growers who were thrown out of business and reduced to starvation-level poverty by biotechnological innovation and automated harvesting, the argument goes that "[e]verybody wants a cheaper coffee—you can't fight that" (*Oryx and Crake* 220). The internal logic of capitalism, which is built upon a historically specific conception of human nature, is thus presented as a set of natural laws. As *Oryx and Crake* demonstrates, it ties in with the world of the natural sciences and treats the humanities with hostility, sensing a potential threat in their ability to de-naturalise, deconstruct, and question human worlds and their institutions, which the books themselves also do on a meta-level. In this attempt, the trilogy furthermore makes the capitalist world more visible by portraying a version of an extreme opposite in the form of the world of the God's Gardeners that works as an "inversion" or heterotopian space.

The Otherworld of the Gardeners

By means of inversion, the Gardeners' world further defamiliarises and questions the dominant world of the capitalist Compounds and their ecological destruction. This space of marked difference is explicitly described by the new-
comer Toby as "so beautiful, with plants and flowers of many kinds she'd never
seen before. There were vivid butterflies; from nearby came the vibration of
bees. Each petal and leaf was fully alive, shining with awareness of her. Even
the air of the Garden was different" (*The Year of the Flood* 52). Apart from the
sense-based impressions, such as looks, sounds, and smells, the world of the
Gardeners differs from its surroundings mostly by the attachment of an intrinsic value to life in all its forms, from plants and microbes to humans and their
fellow mammals. In their mythology, hymns, and sermons, as well as in their
practices, the Gardeners also try not to create an anthropocentric hierarchy but
emphasise the horizontal place of humans alongside the other animals. They
express this value system in hymns titled "Oh Let Me Not Be Proud", "Oh Sing
We Now the Holy Weeds" or "We Praise the Tiny Perfect Moles". Also, the sermons held by their leader Adam One on their feast days, like for example "The
Feast of Adam and All Primates", emphasise the close kinship between humans
and "the other Animals" as well as the moral obligations that follow from that.
Denying human exceptionalism, Adam One preaches that "God's command-
ment to 'replenish the Earth' did not mean we should fill it to overflowing with
ourselves, thus wiping out everything else [...] We pray that we may not fall into
the error of pride by considering ourselves as exceptional" (63).

The Gardeners' belief system, which ascribes souls to animals and holiness to weeds, has the effect of minimising the ecological harm they produce
through practices which are discussed these days in the context of sustainable
lifestyles, like voluntary simplicity, vegetarianism, roof-top gardening, and
zero waste production. Yet instead of each individual having to understand
the complex relationships between these lifestyle patterns and their ecological
effects, the main story of their world says that it is God who wants people to
behave in this way: "By covering such barren rooftops with greenery we are
doing our small part in the redemption of God's Creation from the decay and
sterility that lies around us and feeding ourselves with its unpolluted food
into the bargain. Some would term our efforts futile, but if all were to follow
our example, what a change would be wrought on our beloved Planet!" (13).
The stories that Adam One tells in his sermons and the Gardeners' songs and
rhymes all connect a spiritual and religious belief system to a certain mode

of material living and interacting with other species in a sustainable manner, for example through self-sufficient gardening as a form of non-capitalist production. It is thus exemplary of how other stories create fundamentally different material and ecological outcomes.

Despite the Gardeners' eco-friendly lifestyle, however, I do not agree with the view that they represent "a hopeful, deep-ecological vision" (Keck 25) or even a kind of ecotopia. The Gardeners are also depicted as a hierarchical and patriarchal society, with a leader and leading elite that deliberately hold back information or even invent stories to govern the lives of the majority. Their leader Adam One admits: "I must sometimes say things that are not transparently honest. But it is for the greater good" (*The Year of the Flood* 210). Similar to the depiction of all other worlds and characters of the trilogy, the depiction of the Gardeners' cult is also comical and verges on caricature. The results of their fusion of science and religion into a kind of eco-theology "are often ludicrous, for instance, their debate on why God gave humans canine teeth if He meant them to be vegetarian" (Northover 11). Characterising the world of the Gardeners as an otherworld does not necessarily mean seeing it as utopian, only relatively in reference to its "exfernal world" (71) as the world of the Compounds and the pleeblands. Rather, it could be described in the context of Foucault's heterotopia, a kind of actually existing counter-site to everything that surrounds it ('Of Other Spaces' 24) The idea of inversion is also exemplary of how the trilogy as a whole works in relation to the two poles of utopia and dystopia—from a different perspective one always turns into its precise opposite: the world of the Compounds as a realised capitalist utopia certainly appears dystopian to readers and is seen as such by the Gardeners. Their world in turn may appear utopian in comparison to the former but reveals its dystopian potential through Crake's apocalyptic deed, which to some extent is rooted and co-authored in the Gardeners' world. The destruction of human civilisation seems to be the ultimate dystopia in contemporary imaginaries, yet from a deep-ecological perspective it may also be considered as a new form of utopia (Jendrysik 35).

The Story of the Apocalypse

How meaning and moral structure arise from story is perhaps best exemplified through the story-frame the apocalypse the *MaddAddam Trilogy* makes use of on several levels to comment on its function in the contemporary imaginary. (Post-) Apocalyptic fiction is currently a popular genre, as novels like Cormac

McCarthy's *The Road* (2006), Emily St. John Mandel's *Station Eleven* (2014), and films like *Mad Max Fury Road* (Miller 2015) or *Snowpiercer* (Bong 2013) demonstrate. Andrew Tate remarks that "[c]atastrophe on a global scale remains a curiously popular form of screen entertainment. [...] Such narratives not only seem strange visual companions to popcorn and ice cream, but also are highly marketable" (13). While the term "apocalypse" actually goes back to the biblical Book of Revelation of the New Testament, in which John of Patmos experiences the divine revelation about "the coming struggle between good and evil and God's ultimate judgement upon the world" (Rosen 8), it has come to be synonymous with catastrophe and spectacular destruction. Assuming a metaperspective, Atwood's trilogy takes up the phenomenon of the apocalyptic cultural imaginary, both on the story level and on the level of genre. By depicting the ruins after the breakdown of human civilisation from Snowman's perspective as a "last man" figure, *Oryx and Crake* positions itself in the tradition of post-apocalyptic writing. As I will argue next, the trilogy playfully takes up the trope of the apocalypse by mirroring its paradoxical entertainment quality on an intradiegetic level and examining its meaning-making function with the example of the Gardeners.

The MaddAddam Trilogy highlights the story-ness of the apocalypse. Depending on its context, it either becomes a meaningful moral structuring device, as for the Gardeners or, on the contrary, an expression of meaninglessness when the self-alienation of a society "has reached such a degree that it can experience its own destruction as an aesthetic pleasure of the first order" as Walter Benjamin once noted (42). The trilogy comments on the apocalypse as entertainment via *mise-en-abyme*. In addition to depicting the human apocalypse in the form of the waterless flood, on an intradiegetic level, "[s]peculations about what the world would be like after human control of it ended had been [...] a queasy form of popular entertainment" (*MaddAddam* 32). Reminiscent of contemporary apocalyptic documentaries like *Aftermath: Population Zero* (National Geographic Channel), the pre-apocalyptic story world also runs apocalyptic online TV shows "with deer grazing in Times Square" (32). The alienation of this late capitalist society may be the result of its unstoppable, systematically caused ecological and social decline, which leads to depression on a collective and individual level as exemplified by Jimmy's mother, who is seriously depressed. From this angle, the breakdown of human societies can appear as a new type of utopia, "one in which nature survives the extinction of the human race" (Jendrysik 35). As the apocalyptic TV shows in the story world are interchangeable with other horrific contents like the "Nitee-Nite live streamed suicides or HottTotts kiddy porn" (*MaddAddam* 32), it becomes clear that the degree of conscious reflection behind this interest in the apocalypse is negligible.

The God's Gardeners' aspiration towards the apocalypse as "the waterless flood" is different, as it is to some extent rooted in the original biblical story. Instead of denoting catastrophe, the tale of the incoming waterless flood is full of hope. It allows them to exempt themselves from the "evil" around them, since they see themselves as chosen people: "We God's Gardeners are a plural Noah: we too have been called, we too forewarned [...] We must be ready for the time when those who have broken trust with the Animals—yes, wiped them from the face of the Earth where God placed them—will be swept away by the waterless Flood" (*The Year of the Flood* 443). In line with its biblical precursor, hope is directed towards a post-apocalyptic "New Jerusalem" or world. As Adam One's sermon held shortly after the plague indicates: "What a cause for rejoicing is this rearranged world in which we find ourselves! [...] how privileged are we to witness these first precious moments of Rebirth! How much clearer the air is now that man-made pollution has ceased!" (443).

The tale of the apocalypse thus becomes a moral structuring device for the Gardeners that benefits their world and ways of life over that of the capitalists. Crake as the causer of the apocalyptic event shares some fundamental, deep-ecological beliefs with the Gardeners and is likely also supported by some of them.[5] His deed is fuelled by good intentions, echoing the idea of human extinction as a new utopia, but also transhumanist assumptions about his own scientific ingenuity replacing God in the creation of a "better" world and humankind. While the ecological theme of the novels is indeed serious, Atwood uses irony and comical exaggerations for shaping her characters, plot, and settings. Therefore, "Atwood's metafictional and comic approach resists the grand tradition or myth of apocalypse" (Jennings 12) and deconstructs it to point out its different functions for worldmaking and ecological ethics, which, if anything, point towards posthumanism.

---

5   For instance, Adam One knows that the waterless Flood "will be carried on the wings of God's dark Angels that fly by night, and in airplanes and helicopters and bullet trains, and on transport trucks and other such conveyances" (*Year* 110), just as Crake has planned it with the help of Oryx.

Postapocalyptic Posthumanism

While Jimmy and Crake appear to be antagonists on the surface, they can also be read as two sides of the same coin, on which Jimmy represents humanism, and Crake symbolises its intensification in the form of transhumanism. As I have shown in my discussion of *Interstellar*, transhumanism can be interpreted as a kind of secular religion promising transcendence through science and technology (Schussler 94). Similarly, Crake aspires towards divine omnipotence by biotechnologically issuing the virus and creating a new human race despite being "against the notion of God, or of gods of any kind" (*Oryx and Crake* 126). His acts represent (trans-)humanism's attempt at control over nature, including an assumed human nature. While in humanism the idea of controlling human nature is pursued via education and especially arts education, transhumanism seeks to use science and technology to alter and improve human life (27). Hannes Bergthaler also points out the connection between Crake's deed and humanism by arguing that Crake has literalised the pastoral fantasy of humanism by genetically engineering the wildness out of the human (735).

While Crake is clearly more of an anti-hero, Jimmy, despite being depicted more sympathetically—not last because he is called a "words person"—cannot be read as the novels' hero, either. His humanist worldview, based on humanity's great artistic works, falls apart together with human civilisation. Already before the apocalypse, Jimmy holds onto an inner collection of obsolete books and compiles lists of old words, as he feels "a duty to rescue them" (238) from extinction. After the apocalypse, he desperately clings on to bits of literature and words that lose their meaning amid the lack of people to make sense of them. For example, Snowman is depicted talking to himself:

> 'It is the strict adherence to daily routine that tends towards the maintenance of good moral and the preservation of sanity,' he says out loud. He has the feeling he's quoting from a book, some obsolete, ponderous directive written in aid of European colonials running plantations of one kind or another. He can't recall ever having read such a thing, but that means nothing. [...] 'In view of the mitigating,' he says. He finds himself standing with his mouth open, trying to remember the rest of the sentence. He sits down on the ground and begins to eat the mango. (7)

Sentences literally fall apart as do buildings from before the flood, designating that old stories based on an anthropocentric—and, as the example shows, also Eurocentric—humanism die with the civilisation that was built upon them. Valeria Mosca proposes that "[w]e may also argue that the first and the second novel in the trilogy are apocalyptic tales about the apocalypse of anthropocentric cultural constructs and language" (48).

Jimmy's humanism and Crake's transhumanism are opposed by the novels' posthumanist stance. As Mosca claims, Atwood's "novels dramatize current philosophical thinking about the emergence of a post-human condition" (45). Like posthumanism, which is concerned with language as a social system in its relation to material systems (e.g. Clarke, Wolfe), *The MaddAddam Trilogy* foregrounds the role of words in the context of the ecology. On the one hand, human language and its words lose meaning and power. This is symbolised by the demise of the humanist world through Jimmy/Snowman. On the other hand, the novels show how "the critters" of the Earth join in on the game of string figures, to speak with Donna Haraway. For example, Jimmy's former girlfriend Amanda Payne's bioart installations represent the power of non-human agents over human worldmaking through signification: Amanda arranges dead-animal parts into words, waits until the vultures descend to tear them apart and then takes a picture from a helicopter (295). Human meaning and words are literally torn apart by the vultures that are also featured prominently in the post-apocalyptic world, this time being busy with human bodies.

In opposition to the decay of words and stories of the pre-apocalyptic world, the trilogy also depicts a re-construction of narrative and myth in its post-apocalyptic world. The post-apocalyptic world of the trilogy can be read as an illustration of posthumanist theory. In addition to foregrounding the link between material and semiotic systems, the novels deconstruct the idea of "the human" as superior to other creatures. The boundary between human, animal, and technological artefact becomes fluid through the Crakers, who are technologically produced and look like humans but sing like birds and purr like cats. The aforementioned Pigoons are another hybrid between human and animal and in the end become fully accepted members of the post-apocalyptic society, being granted full subjectivity and agency among Crakers and humans. For example, towards *MaddAddam*'s ending, the Pigoons, humans and Crakers celebrate a common funeral in which they help each other and respect the other party's traditions. Toby relates: "The Pigoons wished to carry [the deceased] Adam and Jimmy to the site for us, as a sign of friendship and inter-species cooperation. [...] The Crakers sang all the way. [...] Following a short discussion, the Pigoons understood that we did not wish to eat Adam and Jimmy, nor did we wish the Pigoons to do that" (*MaddAddam* 373).

The ending of the trilogy can therefore be read as a humanist dystopia turning into a posthumanist utopia, portraying peaceful co-existence between humans, animals, and genetically altered hybrids in a post-hierarchical order. Additionally, the Crakers and the humans cross-breed so the next generation is born as human-Craker hybrids. In addition to this posthumanist content, the ending again refers back to worldmaking through storytelling, especially in the form of writing. With the old stories and worlds gone, the last part of the trilogy, *MaddAddam*, is concerned with making and writing new stories and foundational myths for future generations. In the second half of the book, Toby's practise of writing her journal becomes explicitly foregrounded, including the process of creating a new story: "She turns back to her journal. What else to write, besides the bare-facts daily chronicle she's begun? What kind of story—what kind of history will be of use at all, to people she can't know will exist, in the future she can't foresee?" (203). As she initiates the young Craker Blackbeard into the process of writing, he continues to write her story: "I am Blackbeard, and this is my voice that I am writing down to help Toby. If you look at this writing I have made, you can hear me (I am Blackbord/) talking to you, inside your head" (376).

Continuing Toby's practise, Blackbeard also references the Gardeners' feasts and corresponding rites so that this world and its foundational narratives will fundamentally shape the world to come. The Crakers "preserve (and extend) the word, [as] the embodiment of the Gardeners' vegetarian, ecological and pacifist ideals. Their rise represents not a new domination but the melding of book and biology in a more peaceful harmony" (Northover 20). From this perspective, it seems that, despite its dystopian elements, the trilogy acknowledges the utopian potential of this eco-religious otherworld to the dominant capitalist world. In Atwood's unusual book tour for *The Year of the Flood*, the author even tried to establish connections between readers and the world of the God's Gardeners. Ron Mann's documentary film *In the Wake of the Flood* portrays the staging of amateur theatrical performances of the novel's scenes in different cities across the UK, Canada, and the US. The live performances of the Gardeners' hymns by local choirs and the scenes involving the Gardener's lifestyles likely had a strong emotional appeal on audiences, which as Atwood states in the film, is very important in addition to the rational and scientific approaches towards the ecology.

Nonetheless, as responses from readers and critics have shown, *The MaddAddam Trilogy* refrains from proposing clear-cut solutions to the ecological catastrophe and from simple moral judgements regarding different worlds.

Like ecological posthumanist ethics, it "raises issues of power and entitlement in the age of globalization and calls for self-reflexivity on the part of the subjects who occupy the former humanistic centre" (Braidotti 49). The novels' self-referential focus on storytelling encourages readers to think about the dominant stories of their worlds and question them in the same way all stories of the polyphonic trilogy are questioned. As the world of the Gardeners and its foundational myths demonstrates, it is not about finding *the* one and only perfect story for the ecology, but more about beginning to look for new stories and playing with storytelling, as the trilogy does in a postmodernist manner.

Non-human Agents and Posthumanist Ethics in Paolo Bacigalupi's *The Windup Girl*

Similar to Atwood's *MaddAddam Trilogy*, Paolo Bacigalupi's 2009 novel *The Windup Girl* offers complex future ethical perspectives on biotechnological and ecological questions, pointing out their embeddedness in different human-made worlds. Like Karyn Kusama's *Aeon Flux* (2005) and Neill Bloomkamp's *Elysium* (2013), it is set in the long-distant future, in this case the 23rd century. As Scott Selisker notes, the aesthetics of scale engrained in this perspective addresses ethical issues that are otherwise impossible to perceive because they are too slow, too small or big. For instance, he argues that "[b]y virtue of its setting in the distant future, *The Windup Girl* already deals with one facet of temporal scale that has long been a signal strength of sf: it depicts the sorts of change that cannot occur within a single human lifespan in the present" (502). Bacigalupi's long-distant future therefore looks back over the course of two centuries to reveal the devastating legacy of contemporary biocapitalist worldmaking and puts it into conversation with alternative worldmaking models, such as bioconservatism in nationalist and fundamentalist forms and trans- and posthumanism. The contemporary rule of US-based biotech and agricultural corporations is shown to cause crop plagues in the long run as well as lethal human pandemics which will have led to massive global starvation, extreme world-wide death tolls, and wars. Bacigalupi's *The Windup Girl*, like the other works set in the long-distant future, presumes a catastrophe that has wiped out or at least severely damages human civilisation as we know it today. In addition, *The Windup Girl* extends its scope to the non-human realm including animals, plants, and seeds. This ecocentric rather than anthropocentric perspective enables large-scale ethical reflections on potential developments in biotechnology in the context of ecology.

Rather than providing simple answers to the complex problems of genetic engineering and environmental collapse, the novel challenges readers to think through these issues themselves. In the following, I will offer a close reading of Bacigalupi's *The Windup Girl* inspired by posthumanist theory, which will demonstrate how the novel reveals complex entanglements of biophysical and symbolic human worldmaking, thereby deconstructing essentialist categories like "nature" and "the human", as well as simplistic moralism. Like *Blade Runner 2049*, *The Windup Girl* can be classified as biopunk in terms of genre. Therefore, I will begin my reading with the implications which its genre and aesthetics of scale have for future ethical questions, especially those related to biotechnology and ecology. Next, I will explore how the narrative setup enables broad perspectives on different human-made worlds, making each transparent and understandable, their social and ecological impacts tangible, while none represents an ultimate solution to the ethical dilemmas exhibited by the novel. As a result, I will interpret the novel's ethics as posthumanist because it hinges on deconstructing humanist concepts and worlds, therefore making the case for the interconnectedness of human worlds with their material and non-human surroundings.

Biopunk and the Aesthetics of Scale

Different from Atwood's *MaddAddam Trilogy* or Jeanette Winterson's *Frankisstein*, whose authors want their novels to be perceived as "literary" rather than science fiction, Bacigalupi's short stories and novels are firmly grounded in science fiction, as numerous genre awards demonstrate. *The Windup Girl* won the Hugo, Nebula, Locus, Compton Crook, and John W. Campbell Memorial Awards, alongside being called the "Best Science Fiction Book of 2009" by the American Library Association. In its significant impact on the sub-genre of biopunk, the book was also compared to William Gibson's seminal cyberpunk novel *Neuromancer* (1984) (Roberts; Schmeink 72). As already pointed out in my reading of *Blade Runner 2049*, biopunk differs from cyberpunk, which explores a predominantly bleak future influenced by information technology, by imagining the impact of biotechnology on possible futures in a similarly stylised and gloomy fashion.

In online reader reviews, many reported that they enjoyed the novel's aesthetics in conjunction with its ethics, and some placed it explicitly within the genre of biopunk, commenting for instance on how it is "such an under-represented genre compared to steampunk and other Sci-Fi subgenres with a potential that has to be unleashed". Similarly, one reader called the genre "science fiction noir" involving "(1) a dark, dystopic world; (2) main characters that are 'grey' as opposed to black or white when it comes to morals; (3) plots that involve complicated questions of morality and characters doing the right thing for the wrong reason and vice versa". Several readers furthermore pointed out the novel's intriguing worldbuilding, while others lamented that they could not actually relate to the characters as they found the artistic execution lacking even though they appreciated the concept behind it ('The Windup Girl Reviews').

The aesthetics and setting of *The Windup Girl* are thus just as important for a future-ethical reading of the novel as its plot. Adam Roberts writes in his review for *The Guardian*: "Its strongest feature is the worldbuilding—the intricately believable portrait of a future Thailand fighting back from environmental collapse". *The Windup Girl* is set in a future Bangkok, which is appealing for its "exoticism" (at least for "Western" readers), but also appalling with regard to the inhospitable ecological and social conditions that characterise this future: as a result of human-made genetic modification and climate change, the world's population is smitten by lethal diseases and starvation due to plant blights. Forced migration and wars make the majority of people in Bangkok fight for their survival with all means possible. Hence, as is typical for bio- and cyberpunk, there is a dire future setting which is highly aestheticised by a "noir stylishness" (Roberts). This stylishness and appeal come as a result of plot twists, tension-loaded scenes, ambiguities, and the fusion of familiar and unfamiliar—or even "exotic"—cultural elements and temporalities.

Apart from the novel's setting and plot, the defamiliarisation also takes place semantically. Most notably, *The Windup Girl* contains many words that English-speaking readers do not understand straight away because they are either Thai, Chinese or Japanese. Some words which appear frequently, including the Thai *farang* (e.g. Bacigalupi 10), Chinese *yang guizi* (e.g. 34), and Japanese *gaijin* (e.g. 52) are derogatory words for "Western" foreigners which are relatively easy to deduce from the context. Other words and distinct cultural concepts, like the Thai concept of *phii* (e.g. 117) for roaming spirits of the deceased, may be more difficult to grasp. The linguistic defamiliarisation also results from made-up words that characterise the novel's long-distant future setting. For example, there are genetically modified animals like the "megodonts" (e.g. 24), which are derived from elephant DNA, and the "cheshires" (e.g. 164), which are modified cats inspired by Lewis Carroll's *Alice's Adventures in Wonderland*. Moreover, there are invented US "calorie companies" called AgriGen, PurCal and Total Nutrient Holding (4), which dominate the global food market after having destroyed it as a result of their biotechnological interventions. From the novel's 23rd century perspective, present global capitalism is relabelled as the "old expansion" as a result of the calorie companies' doing and climate disaster. This catastrophe was followed by "the petroleum Contraction" (165) which amounted to a global breakdown of industrial civilisation depending on oil.

The novel further fuses mechanical technologies of the past with biotechnologies of the future, both content-wise and linguistically. As electricity has become extremely scarce, energy is gained mechanically either through human or animal "calorie" power as well as through inventions like mechanical "kink-springs" (8) to store energy. Thus, the biological and mechanical measuring units of calories and joules are central to the novel's post-oil future and can be converted into each other, for example through people or animals winding up springs (e.g. 201). The titular name "windup girl" for genetically engineered New People is also derived from the idea of mechanical wind-up toys, even though New People are the result of futuristic biotechnologies. In addition to associating the novel's eponymous character Emiko, the windup girl with traditional Japanese culture, the semantic field of mechanics is used further to characterise her: "The [windup] girl is perfect, precise as a clockwork" (421).

Another facet of the novel's aesthetics of scale is that it is not only humans and New People who have agency, but also plants, animals, and ecologies. Heather Sullivan thus argues that "[i]n Bacigalupi's world, the less agential a character or living thing seems to be, the more power it turns out to have in the end: which is a very fine description of our vegetal kin" (23). The plants in the novel assume agency in the form of genetic mutations that have surpassed human control and even become lethal to humans, for example the algae baths that Anderson Lake uses in his factory to experiment on the production and storage of energy mutate and cause the death of many factory workers, including Anderson himself. They are later responsible for the deliberate flooding of the city to stop the lethal disease from spreading. Thus, *The Windup Girl* reveals "plant power in its original green form rather than in the altered form of fossil fuels, especially in the random, rapid, spread of mutating algae and food diseases" (Sullivan 20). The idea that agency gets transferred from conventional human agents to those who initially seem to lack worldmaking power is also true for Emiko, who is able to survive the spreading disease at the end of the novel and might therefore represent the future of (post-)human life. The novel thus embraces a posthumanist notion of biopower, including non-human life forms and agents as small as DNA molecules. Again, this amplifies the scale of the novel's perspective, which encompasses the microscopically small locus of the gene, as well as human worlds, ecosystems, and the biosphere at large.

A Complex Entanglement of Worlds

The fusion of different temporalities, geographies, and cultures in plot elements and semantic form creates aesthetics of a defamiliarising scale that are further intensified by the character constellation and narrative form of the novel. The narrative situation encompasses five different character focalisers organised into distinct chapters who create a mosaic of worlds. The windup girl Emiko is not featured as prominently as one might expect from the novel's title. Rather, her posthuman perspective is evenly balanced with that of other characters: Anderson, who represents corporate US biocapitalism; Hock Seng, an illegal Chinese immigrant; and Jaidee and Kanya, who are employees of the Thai Environment Ministry and seek to protect the nation from foreign take-overs and genetic "impurity". As the characters' lives become more and more entangled over the course of the novel, the chapters become increasingly shorter, and the characters appear more frequently in each other's narratives. This narrative situation creates aesthetic and ethical complexities, as each of the characters and their respective worlds become relatable and their actions understandable, while none of them works as a hero or heroine. On the contrary, even though comprehensible, Anderson Lake and Hock Seng are rather disagreeable characters, as are Jaidee and Kanya to some extent. Emiko, despite being a posthuman character, is perhaps closest to being an identificatory figure due to her depiction as a mistreated victim rather than an active worldmaking agent throughout the longest part of the narrative.

The main line of conflict between the worlds runs between the extremes of conserving an allegedly natural biological order and allowing humans to master the exploitation of biological organisms and their genes. On the far end of bioconservatism are spiritual worlds: A Christian sect called the Grahamites, and the Buddhist nationalists of the Thai Environment Ministry as embodied by their leaders Jaidee and Kanya. The other extreme on the scale is marked by the posthuman world of the genetically engineered New People like Emiko. This is further backed by the "gene-hacker" and transhumanist Gibbons, who sees genetically modified organisms as superior to natural ones, therefore viewing the New People as the future of humankind. In between the extremes are the worlds of exploitative biocapitalism, which is represented mainly by Anderson, and the world of the Thai Ministry of Trade, which fuses Buddhist nationalism with biocapitalism. In addition to people who actively partake in the process of worldmaking through their position of (relative) power, there are also representatives of the masses of people, such as the illegal Chinese immigrant Hock Seng and the young Thai factory worker Mai, who strive to survive as worldtakers and opportunists without having the power to actively shape or change the world they live in.

By zooming in and out of human worldmaking in interaction with matters and ecologies, Bacigalupi's *The Windup Girl* offers a mode of thinking through the long-term results of different human-made worlds. Its staging of a conflicting and complex entanglement of worlds without advocating a singular one makes the novel especially fruitful for an ethical reading. *The Windup Girl* also points out how muddled and interdependent human worlds are, and how they are constantly in the process of being made and renegotiated. In the following, I will provide an overview of the competing worlds in the novel, their maps of morality, and outcomes along the continuum from bioconservatism to the world of post- and transhumanism.

The Bioconservatist Regression to "Niche and Nature"

The world of bioconservatism is represented mainly by the Thai Environment Ministry where it is fused with nationalism, but also through a religious group called the "Grahamites" (132) that has emerged in the United States and is likewise opposed to biotechnological interventions. Both share religious or spiritual roots, either Buddhist or Christian, and believe in an essentialist concept of the biological purity of "niche and nature" (e.g. 54). These seemingly retrogressive phenomena in the novel's 23rd century future can be interpreted following Pankaja Miśra's analysis in *The Age of Anger* (2017). He argues that the "moral and spiritual vacuum" of modernity brought about and fostered by neoliberal global capitalism leads to "mad quests for substitute religions and modes of transcendence" (27), especially on the losing side of globalisation. In *The Windup Girl*, the immersion into a world of fundamentalism and totalitarian authority is therefore the logical conclusion of the second wave of capitalist globalisation called the "new expansion". The bioconservatist worlds of *The Windup Girl* furthermore reveal similarities to the world of the God's Gardeners discussed in Margaret Atwood's *MaddAddam Trilogy* by fusing an ecological agenda with religion. The bioconservatist idea of "niche and nature" additionally reminds you of *Avatar*'s idealisation of Nature as the solution to the ecological catastrophe.

In the future USA of the story world, the "Grahamites", probably named after the American Reverend Sylvester Graham, who promoted vegetarianism and a health-based lifestyle in the 19th century, have gained considerable political influence, resulting from their anti-biotech activism like field burnings (266), and the establishment of their own system of education (133). From the Grahamites' point of view, "[t]he calorie companies have already earned their place in hell. [...] Food should come from the place of its origin and stay there. It shouldn't spend its time crisscrossing the globe for the sake of profit. We went down that path once, and it bought us ruin" (133). Like the Thai Buddhists, the Grahamites condemn both genetic engineering and its results, like the New People, as being unnatural. As Emiko remarks, they are "[s]o concerned with niche and nature. So focused on their Noah's ark, after the flood has already happened" (165). It is striking how the image of the flood is evoked here to denote catastrophe just as in the *The MaddAddam* trilogy where the Gardeners foretell the "waterless flood" as the near extinction of the human population. In *The Windup* Girl, the two religious groups, the Grahamites and the Thai Buddhist nationalists, converge on the point of bioconservatism, as the Grahamite priest Hagg, who is invited into a Thai monastery, overtly states, "Buddhist and Grahamite values overlap in many areas" (132).

The Thailand of the future is characterised by the re-empowerment of traditional institutions, such as monarchy and religion. It is still ruled by a queen, and the political power structures are firmly embedded in Buddhist religion. Hence, the novel's main representatives of the Thai government, Jaidee and Kanya, are Buddhists, and their worlds are shaped by a strong belief in *kamma* [karma] (e.g. 82), so-called *phii* [spirits], the sacredness of objects, such as a *bo* tree (114), and great respect for traditional authorities, such as the Child Queen and her advisor, the Somdet Chaopraya. Both Jaidee and Kanya are focaliser characters, and in their narratives, they can see and talk to the spirits of the deceased. For example, after Jaidee is killed by the Trade Ministry, Kanya is frequently depicted as being accompanied by him and conversing with his ghost (e.g. 371). This shows that the notion of reality is very much dependent on the world and the belief systems people inhabit; if characters believe in spirits, they are depicted as real. The two leaders of the Environment Ministry are both characterised as spiritual idealists—however, in the case of Kanya, this is somewhat compromised due to her having worked for a long time as a spy for the Trade Ministry—following what they think is right, rather than following the dictate of money.

Jaidee is known to be especially difficult to bribe, and he and his executive division, the white shirts, are feared for their brutality in defending the country's environmental protection laws. Jaidee and Kanya have a clear map of morality, on which AgriGen and PurCal executives are evil for having caused so many "unnatural" deaths, while Jaidee asserts that he and Kanya will "both be reborn somewhere beautiful" (118) for their good deeds. In their Buddhist and essentialist views of nature, they are firmly opposed to biotechnologically produced New People like Emiko. For instance, Kanya tells her "[y]ou are all unnatural. You are all grown in test tubes. You all go against niche. You all have no souls and have no *kamma*" (428). The idea of "niche and nature" further expands to a racist social Darwinism as it discards the Chinese refugees called "yellow cards" as second-class people who are legally pursued and cannot officially be hired. The Chinese immigrant Hock Seng comments, "[t]he Environment Ministry sees yellow cards the same way it see the other invasive species and plagues it manages" (23).

The Thai Environment Ministry is therefore strongly opposed to opening to global trade, especially for US-American calorie companies who seek to gain access to the country's food market and its seedbanks which help Thailand to thrive "while countries like Burma and Vietnam all fall like dominoes, starving and begging for the scientific advances of the calorie monopolies" (5). Ironically, these national seedbanks are the result of ingenious "gene-hacking" done by the former AgriGen employee Gibbons, who has revived ancient local plant seeds and now works for the Thai Government. Thus, opposed to the Environment Ministry's niche and nature ideology, Thailand becomes a paradise for genetically regrown fruits and vegetables of a past "before [the fictional genetic diseases of] cibiscosis and Nippon genehack weevil and blister rust and scabis mold razed the landscape" (3). Despite the irreconcilable contradictions of this world, "the rebooted Buddhist-nationalist ideology espoused by Kanya [and Jaidee] provides one alternative to simply scraping together the remnants of capitalist devastation and then allowing it to proceed unimpeded, if not rejuvenated" (Hageman 290).

The New Expansion of Biocapitalism

The conflict between nationalist protectionism and global biocapitalism splits the nation into two opposing camps represented by the Environment Ministry and the Trade Ministry, which ultimately ends in armed conflict. The example of the Thai Trade Ministry shows that even though protectionist nationalism and capitalist free trade seem to be irreconcilable opposites, they can also be fused. In their power play with the Environment Ministry, the Trade Ministry cuts a deal with AgriGen that would give the company access to the seedbanks in exchange for militarised support. Hence, ideologies and worlds are shown to be messy and subject to constant negotiation and remaking. With respect to nationalism and globalisation, Derrick King argues,

> [r]ather than advocating for one side in the conflict between the Thai King-
> dom and the calorie companies, the novel is best read as an attempt to keep
> these two terms—allegorically, the nation and globalization—within a con-
> stant tension. While the nation remains a potential point of resistance which
> can never be fully subsumed under global capital, the ease in which it can be
> co-opted by capital prevents it from ever solidifying into a permanent alter-
> native. (8)

While Thai bioconservatism and nationalism are unmasked as dishonest and in the end untenable, they are at least associated with positive idealism, including the protection of environmental standards.

In contrast, globalised biocapitalism, personified mostly by Anderson Lake, is shown to bring about fatal consequences to humankind and the ecology. The novel merely implies through its backdrop of rising sea-levels and other dire effects of climate change that the "old Expansion" of Western capitalist globalisation and its dependency on oil and exploitation is at the root of the dystopian future. It further explores the subjectification of this world through Lake as a character focaliser. From the opposing perspective of Jaidee, who is characterised as an idealist and spiritual believer, "calorie men" like Lake are pure materialists "with profits in their beating hearts" (Bacigalupi 75). Consequently, Anderson Lake is depicted as a self-interested man who mainly thinks about the best ways to make profits from genes (e.g. 4) and gain influence and power in Thailand for his Midwestern biotech company AgriGen.

The image of the unfeeling capitalist is broken temporarily when Anderson falls for Emiko and helps her escape and survive several times, only to be resurrected when he sells her out to gain influence with the Trade Ministry (333). Even though on a personal level, Anderson is able to feel empathy with the mistreated Emiko, on a more general level, he does not seem to have values beyond making profit and gaining power. Anderson's predecessor Yates points out the psychological discrepancy between individual and corporate responsibility when he tells Anderson: "That's always our excuse, isn't it? [...] Pretend like we weren't the ones responsible" (9) for the damage done by the company. The alliance between global expansionist capitalism and actual warfare, which Naomi Klein explicitly describes in *The Shock Doctrine* (2007), is also made visible in the novel. For example, Anderson's thoughts about how to gain access to the country's seed banks through the Trade Ministry, encompass "Money for bribes? Gold? Diamonds? Jade? [...] Shock troops" (294), which is what the company provides in the end. The foreign businesspeople in Bangkok are furthermore associated with earlier colonialists through their meeting place in a bar called after the Elizabethan naval commander "Sir Francis Drake" (126) who sailed the world as a slave trader, privateer, and pirate.

Posthuman and Transhumanist Perspectives

While the novel relatively clearly displays the dire consequences of biocapitalist worldmaking, which reduces the human body "to weight and calories—no more than a commodity available in superfluous amounts" (Schmeink 82), it also argues that there is no going back to an idealised past of a "natural" order, either. With respect to biogenetic interventions and the depiction of the world of the New People, *The Windup Girl* remains ambiguous. On the one hand, "Emiko's mistreatment is so hard to bear that readers are driven to empathize with her — [...] not because she is human, but as Derrida argued [...] because she suffers" (99). On the other, as I will argue in the following, Gibbons's transhumanist perspective from which "[s]omeday, perhaps, all people will be New People and you will look back on us as we now look back at the poor Neanderthals" (Bacigalupi 504), resembles Nathan's of *Ex_Machina* and is problematic for its hubris and contradictions, too.

Like Anderson Lake, Hock Seng, Jaidee, and Kanya, Emiko also functions as a character focaliser in the novel. Despite her otherness as a posthuman character, "Emiko provides a point of sympathetic identification" (Selisker 513) resulting from her mistreatment of being violently abused and humiliated in a sex bar, where she is kept as a slave. Originally produced in Japan, the genetically engineered New People either assume military functions as soldiers or serve rich men as geishas and personal assistants. In the novel, their function is to question essentialist notions of DNA as inevitable "nature", or even question the concept of "nature" itself. While most world positions of the novel deem New People as "unnatural", Emiko frequently asserts that she cannot escape her "nature" in the sense of her DNA programming. For example, she resents that even when sexually abused, "[h]er body performs just as it was designed—just as the scientists with their test tubes intended" (Bacigalupi 55). Furthermore, she is told by another New Person that she, like all New People, must always seek a master because her genes make it a necessity to obey and have others direct her (428). Nonetheless, she finally manages to transgress this programming by disobeying all commands and killing eleven men with her bare hands within seconds (367). The Japanese producer of New People admits that it is nurture rather than nature that makes New People become either soldiers or geishas: "All New Japanese are fast. [...] How they use their innate qualities is a question of their training, not of their physical capabilities [...] It is surprising though that one has shaken off her training" (425). Emiko's conduct as a New Person thus deconstructs the idea of determinism, both through an assumed genetic nature and through socialisation as nurture.

The New People of the novel furthermore put the notion of "the human" into question as they are either seen as much less than human, equal to human, or even superior. Emiko relates that in Kyoto "where New People were common [...] they were served well, and sometimes well respected. Not human, certainly, but also not the threat that the people of this savage basic culture make her out to be" (50). While both in Japan and Thailand New People are seen as less than human, in Japan they at least enjoy the status of a respected and protected "piece of property, [...] an exquisite valued object" (153). In contrast, the religious fundamentalists only see New People as sin and as a transgression of niche and nature: the Grahamites call them devils, the Buddhists soulless creatures, and the Islamist Green Headbands see them as an affront to the Q'ran (50). The spectators of her humiliating sex show cry out, "*Look! She is almost human!*" (50), but her inbuilt stutter-stop motions always betray her as a New Person and prevent her from passing as fully human.

In contrast to the treatment and attributions from outsiders, Emiko's narrative account and the introspection it allows show no difference to the other characters' interiority. On the contrary, her narrative conveys genuine feelings and suffering that make readers empathise with her and identify more than with any of the human characters. She is also depicted as morally superior to the others, for example when she cares for Anderson during his fatal illness despite his betrayal. In response, "he was grateful, desperately grateful for any sort of attention, for her human connection...and he had laughed weakly at the irony" (486). In this sense, she appears equal to humans here, if not "more human than human", to speak with *Blade Runner 2049*. In terms of her physicality, she is even superior to humans. As Gibbons asserts: "You are better than human in almost all other ways [apart from the inbuilt obedience]. Faster, smarter, better eyesight, better hearing. You are obedient, but you don't catch diseases like mine" (504).

The novel thus hints at the possibility of New People being the superior successors of humankind, especially through their immunity to new diseases. In the final alliance of the gene-hacker Gibbons and Emiko in the last chapter, they compare New People to the cheshire cats, who, as result of their genetic superiority have extinguished "natural" cats. From this lesson, the scientists producing New People made sure to make them infertile. Gibbons, a "gene-ripper" who knows all about genetically altered animals, points to Emiko as a God-like being: "You're as close as anyone ever comes to meeting God" (504) and promises her that he can remove the in-built sterility of her kind and do "much, much more" for her (505). Schmeink therefore argues that "[t]he potential for New People to replace the human population is the threat that looms over the story and shines through every aspect of her depiction [...] New People, the story suggests, are far better suited for the new world, but humans fear them and shackle them to their DNA" (114).

Gibbons frames New People's post-humanity in the paradigm of transhumanism that assumes a hierarchical stance of human mastery and domination over "nature", rather than a posthumanist deconstruction of the concept: "Nature has become something new. It is ours now, truly" (350). By talking of himself as "God", he also shows a degree of hubris that compromises his potentially utopian position in the novel. What is more, his "unwillingness to consider the implications of his research for the rest of the world places him in precisely the position of the calorie companies" (King 12) that he used to work for. Kanya's altero-characterisation confirms this interpretation:

In a flash of insight, Kanya understands the doctor entirely. A fierce intellect. A man who reached the pinnacle of his field. A jealous and competitive man. A man who found his competition too lacking, and so switched sides and joined the Thai Kingdom for the stimulation it might provide. An intellectual exercise for him. [...] The man exists only for competition, the chess match of evolution, fought on a global scale. (Bacigalupi 352)

This characterisation unmasks Gibbons as merely a competitive neoliberal *homo oeconomicus* whose work and aspirations are more about himself than a utopian vision of a better future for all. His world position is anthropocentric and based on transhumanist dreams of human domination and mastery over an alleged nature.

While Bacigalupi's *The Windup Girl* refrains from advocating a certain world as "the right one", Derrick King identifies "two utopian figurations" in the novel: "the new band of white shirts lead by Kanya and the post-human alliance of Gibbons and Emiko" (12). However, he continues that "[w]hat is needed is a double negation of these positions that turns their utopian impulses—Kanya's opposition to global capitalism and Gibbons' opposition to biogenetic essentialism—into an anti-capitalist, global vision of equal access to the technologies of food production" (12). Similarly, I want to argue that the novel's main ethical achievement resides in the deconstruction of essentialisms and singular truths. Its ethics can thus be read as posthumanist ethics that likewise build on deconstruction and the disclosure of complex entanglements of species, matter, and symbolising practices, which I will show in the next section.

Posthumanist Ethics

Paolo Bacigalupi's *The Windup Girl* excels in conveying the full complexity of problems encompassing human biotechnological interventions in relation to their embeddedness in socio-political structures and the ecology. Through the narrative situation including five focaliser characters, it manages to make readers understand different and opposing world positions while at the same time critically questioning each of them. The novel's ethical work is found precisely in this deconstruction that makes readers reflect on assumed "givens" like global (bio-)capitalism, and the concepts of "nature" and "the human". Without providing a clear solution to bioethical questions of the present and future, it leaves an open horizon that emphasises the interconnectedness between species, human-signifying practices, and the ecology.

Looking at reader reviews on the website *goodreads* confirms that Bacigalupi's *The Windup Girl* has a strong ethical impact on readers by encouraging ethical reflections on different levels, ranging from the personal to the global and the ecological. On the one hand, readers write that they were encouraged to amplify their knowledge and change their behaviour on a personal level. For instance, one reader wrote that "[Bacigalupi] did inspire me to learn more about terminator genetics and also to continue shrinking my own environmental footprint". With respect to genetically modified products, another reader expressed that after reading the book, s_he was "tempted to take a closer look at the food labels". On the other hand, the novel also enabled ethical reflections to go beyond the personal and into the sphere of larger structures and worlds, asking questions like: "How far can science go before it becomes threatening? To which lengths can people take playing God?" With respect to the novel's moral universe, many readers praised that it refrained from black-and-white didacticism: "The badness is palpable, the goodness is hinted at" ('The Windup Girl Reviews'). Hence, *The Windup Girl* follows Rosi Braidotti, Cary Wolfe and Donna Haraway in their posthumanist position on ethics that include the deconstruction of humanist worlds and concepts, the emergence of the cyborg as a utopian figure, and a systemic approach to ethics, as I will explain in the following.

Nearly all world positions I have outlined in the previous section—apart from Emiko's—derive from humanist anthropocentrism. The calorie companies' biocapitalism, like Gibbons's transhumanism, assumes a hierarchical order of life that poses a small fraction of humanity at the top. As a result, the free appropriation and exploitation of biological organisms, from plants to humans, seems perfectly legitimate. It is obvious that the novel is overtly critical of biocapitalist biopolitics, which is depicted to have devastating results in the long-term future. However, "[r]ather than pretending to escape the ideology of capital, the novel directs the reader to reimagine the prospects of thinking ecology specifically by confronting the contradictions inherent to the ideology of capital that enframes our very capacity to think ecology" (Hageman 290).

At the same time, *The Windup Girl* makes clear that there is no going back to an idealised past before global capitalism because of the interdependencies it has already created, and the resulting ecological damage which cannot be undone—or maybe this ideal past has never existed at all. Even though the Thai government, and especially the Environment Ministry, pretend they could be self-sufficient and de-coupled from global trade, the very existence of its capital, Bangkok, depends on the foreign import of water pumps that keep the city from drowning. In a similar vein, the country only thrives on self-grown food thanks to the former US AgriGen bioengineer Gibbons and his gene-hacking skills. Hence, the bio-conservatist and nationalist position of the Environment Ministry is marked as untenable as well as hypocritical. Jaidee and Kanya's religiously inspired belief in "niche and nature" is shown to be especially problematic and impossible to maintain. As Gibbons tells Kanya: "The ecosystem unravelled when man first went a-seafaring. [...] We [the gene-rippers] have only accelerated the phenomenon. The food web you talk about is nostalgia, nothing more. Nature. [...] *We* are nature" (Bacigalupi 344). The bio-conservatist world put into conversation with Emiko's posthumanism and Gibbons's transhumanist stances thus serves to "uncover the concepts of 'Nature' and of the 'human being' as the phantasms they have always been" (Hageman 298). Emiko as a posthuman being and her world of the New People clearly demount

> the ideology of the "human being" in order to welcome the new subjectivities that have been wrought through technoscience. To be clear, the reader is called upon to identify with Emiko and her plight by relinquishing a rigid notion of the "human being" and cultivating hospitality to her as a being who is "new" only from a position invested in preserving the conventional liberal-humanist subject. (294)

As with biocapitalism and transhumanism, the bioconservatist world is also rooted in humanism depending on the essentialisms of "the human" and "nature". These essentialisms for instance serve similarly to legitimise its hierarchical biopolitical world order by denying biotechnologically altered creatures, like New People and cheshires, a soul. In its deconstruction and critique of the humanist legacy visible in all world positions apart from Emiko's, the novel assumes a posthumanist stance. To a large extent, its ethics build on deconstruction and negation, but there is also a positive configuration represented by the figure of the cyborg.

Following Stephanie Peebles Tavera, "we cannot approach a posthuman ethics without the cyborg" (30), Donna Haraway's utopian figure that transgresses dualisms like human/machine, man/woman, and subject/object. In *The Windup Girl*, it is especially the binary of nature/culture that is transgressed by genetically altered organisms like the New People and the cheshire cats. The cheshires exemplify the impossibility of human mastery over "nature" through technology by having assumed an agency of their own. Lars Schmeink argues

> In terms of a mechanized and utilitarian view of nature, this uncontrollability and clear transgression of their anthropological purpose pushes the cheshires into a monstrous ontological state, though—neither natural nor cultural, the cats remain outside of their clearly hierarchical position and defy the human symbolic order. (86)

Like the cats, Emiko can be read as a cyborg that "offers the potential for a utopian reading" (30) amid the otherwise predominantly dystopian elements of the novel's future. The windup girl Emiko fuses otherwise separately conceptualised spheres like machine and human, animal and human, and past and future. She defies the binary of nature and culture by transgressing both her assumed genetically programmed nature *and* her cultural training. Her very existence and focalisation, which makes readers identify with her, threatens the concept of a normative human subjectivity and instead foregrounds posthuman(ist) intersubjectivity. Scott Selisker proposes that "*The Windup Girl* participates in just such an enlargement of the horizons of our sympathy, and of the range of bodies that matter, gesturing [...] toward a humane-ness that extends well beyond humanity" (513).

In addition to the deconstruction of worlds and the introduction of the cyborg, the novel emphasises the interconnection between human-made worlds, biological organisms and their surrounding ecology, and offers glimmers of hope and a positive outlook towards the future: Kanya prevents the sell-out of the country's seedbank to biocapitalism, Hock Seng overcomes his selfish opportunism by saving the girl Mai, Emiko takes care of the dying Anderson despite his betrayal, and plants and animals assume agency. Gibbons's promise to help New People become fertile and "part of the natural world" (Bacigalupi 505) leaves the novel's future even more open and stresses that the old humanist order will have to go. Andrew Hageman interprets the novel's ending as a "radical epiphany that the future will be a heterogeneous one, [...] With previous ideologies swept away, [...] the future to come at the end of *The Windup Girl* will be figured and formed collectively. And this collective will be, like an ecosystem, constituted by diverse subjectivities intimately and inextricably in contact with each other" (300). Hence, the novel's outlook is posthumanist in the sense that it includes posthuman characters like Emiko, but also in that it emphasises the coexistence and interdependency between different species and agents, human and non-human, technologically made and biologically bred. It connects the microscopic scale of the individual genome to the social order and even to the very large scale of the global ecology. With Selikser, "*The Windup Girl*'s ending encourages us to think about environmental and technoscientific problems on multiple scales simultaneously" (513).

The Windup Girl's long-term perspective of biotechnology, which draws on aesthetics of scale, thus enables a questioning of contemporary worlds ranging from the world of rampant biocapitalism and transhumanism to worlds of religiously inspired nationalist bioconservatism as a potential counterpart. It uses multiple perspectives and deferrals in time and space to defamiliarise readers and deconstruct the concepts of "nature" and "the human" in favour of an open post-humanist future in which biology, technology, ecology, and the economy could be entirely reconfigured. Without a preconfigured "good", it asks readers to perform ethics in a posthumanist mode: by deconstructing and rethinking familiar worlds and concepts, and by pointing out the interdependencies and connections between otherwise separately conceptualised entities and worlds. In agreement with Derrick King, "Bacigalupi's works are powerful reminders that other futures are still possible" (14).

Conclusion

With regards to possible futures, Margaret Atwood's *MaddAddam Trilogy* and Paolo Bacigalupi's *The Windup Girl* offer reason to worry and reason for hope. While they realistically extrapolate from the contemporary (bio-) capitalist world to dystopian and catastrophic or apocalyptic future scenarios, they also introduce otherworlds that might provide tentative answers to the ethical challenges that characterise the present and cast their shadows into the future. Illustrating posthumanist futures in different executions, the novels mainly challenge dominant narratives and modes of thinking derived mainly from humanism and its inherent anthropocentrism. Their high degree of moral and aesthetic ambiguity is also part of this posthumanist outlook that seeks to avoid closure, didacticism, and fixed categorisation.

The *MaddAddam Trilogy* metatextually points towards story-telling as a means of worldmaking on an extra- and intradiegetic level: it uses the cultural trope of the apocalypse as a *mise-en-abyme* and brings the act of narrating into focus through its multi-layered narrative situations, as well as with explicit comments and plot elements. *The Windup Girl* represents several different worlds through distinctive narrative strands that allow for closeness and distance at the same time. Even though the majority of protagonists and focaliser characters are disagreeable in one way or another, the narrative polyphony enables an understanding of different worlds and their inhabitants and points out the material-semiotic quality of human worldmaking. Both novels also strengthen the role of nonhumans in the construction of worlds. There are posthuman characters like the Crakers in *The MaddAddam Trilogy* and Emiko in *The Windup Girl* who are depicted as playing leading roles in the novels' post-apocalyptic or post-catastrophic futures due to their genetic superiority. Also plants, viruses, and animals take centre stage in both novels, illustrating Donna Haraway's notion of "the Chthulucene" as the thick present of multispeciesism.

From a posthumanist and deconstructivist stance, *The MaddAddam Trilogy* and *The Windup Girl* critically question essentialisms like "the human" and "nature". With the example of the pigoons, Atwood shows that the boundaries between human and animal are fluid, and through the God's Gardeners, she criticises the notion of human superiority over all other creatures. Bacigalupi's novel unmasks the idea of "niche and nature", denoting an alleged biological state of purism, as the phantasm that characterises neo-conservative worldviews as well as green movements around the globe. It also criticises the racism that can be connected to this ideal, and juxtaposes it with moral complexity and hybridity. None of the worlds depicted in the novel is framed as "right" or better than the others. Instead, they are shown to be in constant tension with each other and internally, as well as full of fissures.

While both novels imagine futures heavily affected by climate warming, sea level rise, plagues, and social inequality, they also display features and world formations that could serve as inspirations for actual otherworlds. For example, the heterotopian world of the God's Gardeners depicted most prominently in *The Year of the Flood* combines a sustainable and ecological use of the land with a post-anthropocentric religious creed system. In spite of the satire involved in the depiction of this world and its fault-lines, its fundamental stories, songs, and feasts are taken over into the trilogy's posthumanist and post-apocalyptic future. Ecocentrism and posthumanism also characterise *The Windup Girl's* outlook on the future in the story world. It seems to depict the end of the Anthropocene as the age of the human (or even "man") and foregrounds the agency of the more-than-human world and its characters.

The novels' high degree of aesthetic ambiguity and moral openness benefits an ethical reading. As reader responses showed, it fosters critical engagement with the topics of biotechnology and ecological decline. In *The MaddAddam Trilogy*, this openness is enabled by the work's postmodernist employment of satire and metatextuality in addition to its science fiction or speculative fiction setting. *The Windup Girl's* biopunk aesthetics make the novel's setting attractive to readers, and the complexity that arises from the narrative situation creates the kind of moral ambiguity that readers of this sf subgenre value.

9 Contemporary Imaginaries of the Future

This study has approached ethics for the future through contemporary popular future fictions. As the close readings in each chapter have shown, this approach makes the worlds of the present and their power structures visible while de-naturalising them. In short, it points out the worlds' quality of "being made"—through narratives, aesthetics as sense-based perceptions as well as material systems of production, which are always co-dependent on non-human others and artefacts. I departed from the assumption that contemporary novels and films with future relation simulate the potential consequences of these present-day worlds and make them aesthetically experienceable. Future fictions therefore give readers and viewers the opportunity to experience what it *feels* like to live in different kinds of futures, which can create a kind of visceral knowledge about them, comparable to Hans Jonas's idea of the "casuistry of the imagination" (*The Imperative of Responsibility* 30). I argued that this emotional and aesthetic knowledge is extremely valuable for the ethical judgement of possible futures as it complements purely rational arguments and statistical extrapolations.

As a result of treating fiction as part of the actual worlds, my future ethical approach to contemporary popular fiction diverged significantly from earlier ethical approaches, for example those of the ethical turn. Instead of applying prefabricated ethical theories to the films and novels, I proposed that the future fictions themselves enable an open ethical reflection through their aesthetic settings. However, despite the attempt to foreground the fictional works and their mode of "ethics through aesthetics", I found the need to ground my ethical reading on a working definition of ethics, as the term is so widely used with so many different meanings. With regard to the prime challenges of the 21st century, which I situated in the interplay between the ecology, the usage and development of high technologies, and the consequences of capitalist globalisation, older theories of ethics, like humanist theories or ancient Greek virtue ethics, seem completely out of date. With their focus on individual—and mostly privileged—human actors and their superior faculty of reason, they fail to take less privileged humans, disabled people, non-human beings, technologies, and the long-term consequences of collective human action into account. Therefore, I turned to posthumanist theory, which in its branch of critical posthumanism is post-anthropocentric and post-dualistic. Instead of providing fixed contents, critical posthumanism is based on deconstruction as a method. As a result, it provides a valuable tool to look at contemporary and future worlds in a relatively open manner.

The close readings of twelve 21st century future fictions have revealed that the future is anything but linear despite being rooted and being made in the present. By drawing on Nelson Goodman's hypothesis of multiple actual worlds instead of just one, I proposed that the present is characterised by a plurality of worlds, some of which are more dominant and others smaller in terms of inhabitants and cogency. While extrapolations from contemporarily dominant worlds can be found in all works, my analyses revealed that they are always juxtaposed by otherworlds which provide potential alternatives to them. My main claim was that the aesthetic qualities of future fictions enable ethical reflections in readers and viewers, which allow them to assess the future ethical question "Which future might be a good future?" emotionally and rationally. To address topics with a particular future relevance, I have grouped the primary works into six case studies or chapters that have addressed future ecologies, transhumanist futures, biopolitics of the future, artificial intelligence, and posthumanist futures.

As the overview of contemporary challenges in the introduction and the development of an ethical theory for the future in Chapter Two have made clear, these topics are not separate from each other but rather interwoven and co-dependent. This also becomes apparent in the thematic outlook of the future fictions themselves. For example, Atwood's *MaddAddam Trilogy*, now in posthumanist futures, could have just as well been featured in ecological futures or biopolitics of the future. Likewise, Bacigalupi's *The Windup Girl* and *Blade Runner 2049*, despite their focus on biotechnology, also prominently highlight ecological issues. Questions surrounding the normative concept of "the human" arise in the context of AI and transhumanism as well as in eco-ethics and biotech fiction. For instance, the digital future fictions *Her* and *Ex_Machina* deconstruct the moral superiority of "the human", just as the biotech fictions *Never Let Me Go* and *Blade Runner 2049* and the posthumanist visions of *The MaddAddam Trilogy* and *The Windup Girl*. The only link I found curiously missing was between the realm of digital technologies and the ecology. Although the digital is predicted to consume about one fourth of the world's energy and produce as much CO_2 as private cars on a global scale by 2025 (Hopfmann and Euskirchen 14, 49), the relationship between digitalisation and the ecology is hardly ever addressed, neither in public discourse nor in fiction. Perhaps it would be too much at odds with the still prevailing idea of human progress through technology. However, as I have pointed out, this conception of progress seems hard to maintain in the context of the ecological catastrophe and the numerous humanitarian catastrophes of this century.

Instead of giving up on the future and the prospect that there might be some good in it, I proposed that it is even more important to critically reflect on potential futures and treat them as worlds in the making. This implies that even though dominant worlds now seem all-encompassing and pervasive, they are nonetheless *made* and *taken* by people. In reverse, this means they could just as well be *unmade* or *rejected* in order to *make other worlds*, depending on the kind of future we *want*. With Goodman and Haraway, I have furthermore argued that fiction not only represents worlds or produces alternative possible worlds, but that it is an integral part of worldmaking because stories make worlds and worlds are made from stories. Fiction plays a special role in making these worlds and stories visible, and its aesthetic operations enable different perspectives and forms of emotional understanding, which allow for their ethical judgement. As my analysis has shown, there are several options how future fictions can work in terms of ethics.

Ethical Openness versus Closure

In my close readings of popular future fictions, I paid special attention to how the aesthetic choices of a work form its ethical outlook. This encompasses generic markers and the modes of storytelling as well as the emotional guidance of readers and viewers. I distinguished between the open and closed moral universes the fictional works offer and claimed that the different degrees of openness and closure offer distinctive opportunities for ethical reflection. Looking at the entire corpus of future fictions used in my study, it is remarkable that most of them are characterised by a relatively high degree of moral closure with respect to the judgement of the different futures they depict. This leads me to draw the conclusion that they have some sort of agenda. Some seem to have a didactic agenda, for example to convince readers or viewers of their moral universes and offer a kind of warning about a possible future. For example, Dave Eggers's *The Circle* obviously wants to warn readers about the threats of digital capitalism and its economy of attention. In a similar manner, Robinson's *New York 2140* tries to convey a utopian plan for a political uprising towards an ecologically and socially better future. As reader responses show, this kind of didactic agenda leads to polarised responses depending on readers' own worldly positioning—if readers shared the novels' worldview, they tended to celebrate these novels. If not, they rather rejected them. These two novels were also criticised for their lack of aesthetic enjoyment, which might be due to a lack of fostering emotional attachment to characters alongside their lack of aesthetic ambiguity.

The other group of works that exhibit the most moral closure is constituted in the Hollywood blockbusters *Avatar, Interstellar,* and *Blade Runner 2049*. In contrast to the aforementioned novels, they use extremely immersive aesthetics and enable strong identifications with their protagonists. This makes them aesthetically and emotionally enjoyable, as viewers have reported. Instead of intending to convince viewers, their aim is rather to please and be commercially successful. Considering that they have been produced on big budgets, they are under substantial financial pressure to generate income by attracting large numbers of viewers. Moral closure therefore becomes a means for making these films more attractive to broader audiences. Even though the moral universes of the three films seem to undermine dominant worlds on the surface, in the close readings, I have illustrated that they also reinforce hegemonic power structures on a deeper level: the worshipping of "Nature" in *Avatar* proliferates the problematic binary thinking of nature versus human culture in the context of the ecology and is a prerequisite for industrial capitalism, as I have argued by drawing on Timothy Morton. Similarly, *Interstellar* perpetuates the modern and transhumanist ideal of a teleological future enabled by human ingenuity through science and technology, despite rallying against the realist paradigm and bureaucratic management. Even though *Blade Runner 2049* harshly criticises capitalism and transhumanist values on the surface, it reinforces their foundations embodied in normative humanist ethics.

In addition to the works displaying high degrees of closure, I identified three works which show an intermediate degree of moral closure or openness. These are *Ex_Machina, Her,* and *Zero K*. All having open endings, they leave open the horizons for the future and allow different options for the judgement of the possible future worlds they simulate. In contrast to the fictional examples providing more closure, these works offer figures for identification, while at the same time questioning their moral integrity through their endings: Caleb is dismantled as the hero in *Ex_Machina* for his self-interested humanism; in *Her*, Theodore is shown to be too limited in his neoliberal subjectivity in opposition to Samantha as his posthuman other; and like Caleb and Theo, Jeffrey of *Zero K* is left on his own in the end as a result of the inability of both his contemporaries and himself to lead meaningful relationships. These three works share the aesthetics of what I would call "defamiliarised realism". *Zero K* draws on postmodernist techniques to create a critical distance to a recognisable present, *Her* uses an aestheticised romantic or poetic realism in its depiction of a near future, and *Ex_Machina* combines realist modes of narration and film-making with the technological simulation of artificial superintelligence. These three works generally resonated well with private and professional reviewers for their aesthetic richness in combination with moral ambiguity.

Finally, my set of examples contained three popular future fictions that offer a high degree of aesthetic and moral openness in their depiction of possible futures. *The MaddAddam Trilogy*, *Transcendence*, and *The Windup Girl* leave the final moral judgement of their characters and future worlds entirely up to their readers and viewers, which from my point of view provides the most fruitful mode of ethical engagement with possible futures through fiction. Interestingly, this openness relies on very distinct aesthetic modes: while *The MaddAddam Trilogy* achieves it through postmodernist features like metatextuality and satire, *Transcendence* carves it out of a combination of science fiction and realism, whereas *The Windup Girl* uses extreme spatial and temporal scale. What they all have in common, however, is multi-perspectivity, including either different focaliser characters as in *The Windup Girl* and *The MaddAddam Trilogy* or none as in *Transcendence*. Hence, there is no singular identificatory character and therefore no heroes or villains. The three works are marked by a complex entanglement of worlds instead of binary oppositions, which prevents simplistic black-and-white morality. For example, *The MaddAddam Trilogy* features a late capitalist world, an otherworld of the God's Gardeners, and the worlds of the sciences and the arts, as well as crossovers like the posthuman(ist) post-apocalyptic world. *The Windup Girl* is similarly composed of multiple conflicting and overlapping worlds, and *Transcendence* is aesthetically and thematically characterised by patterns instead of binaries. Through their telling of different stories and juxtaposing of worlds, the future fictions with the most moral openness enabled deep and manifold reactions and ethical reflections that take the complexity of contemporary worlds and their potential futures into account.

Unmaking Capitalist Futures

Outside the analysis of how aesthetic choices guide viewers and readers in their ethical evaluation of possible futures in fictions, I have also retraced different future worlds and their setup as portrayed in the primary works. The most striking—although not surprising—finding is that a large majority of popular future fictions exhibit extrapolated versions of the contemporarily most dominant world of neoliberal capitalism and its subworlds and undercurrents, first and foremost, the world of transhumanism. As expressed by Jason Moore's term "Capitalocene", many works illustrate capitalism's ecologically destructive and even lethal legacy. For example, *New York 2140*, *The Windup Girl*, *The Mad-dAddam Trilogy* and *Blade Runner 2049* all relate higher sea levels, extinct species, and altered climate to global capitalism. *Avatar* leaves the imagination of an ecologically dead planet Earth to viewers while depicting how the capitalist enterprise now seeks expansion into space to continue its destructive extraction of value.

In addition to the ecological havoc, capitalism's programming based on reaping profit from life is also shown through its devastating human dimension. *Never Let Me Go* pictures the dynamics of extreme exploitation with the example of organ harvesting from clones, and *Zero K* shows that even death, or rather un-death through cryotechnology, can be heavily monetised. Most importantly, the biopolitical aspects I raised in the discussion of the two novels as well as in the other two examples of this case study, *The Windup Girl* and *Blade Runner 2049*, all include hierarchies of life based on the allocation of use or exchange value. The exploitation of people in the past and present is metaphorically represented by the replicants and clones in the two works that merely have a use value and can be owned like products. As is the case today with animals or plants, they are denied intrinsic value. *The Circle* furthermore depicts the capitalist extraction of value through work and via the economy of attention.

Eggers's novel also illustrates how the concentration of worldmaking power in the hands of just a few extremely dominant worldmakers has devastating consequences for those reduced to passive worldtakers. In *The Circle*, the worldmaking power of a private company via the economy of attention is shown to subvert the free will of individuals and even erodes democracy in the long run. Similarly, the power of the digital economy and its quasi-monopolistic or oligopolistic structures that enable domination through surveillance are exemplified by *Ex_Machina*. A similar imbalance of worldmaking power is illustrated by *Zero K*, which shows how the world's super-wealthy seek to

expand and enhance their lives at the expense of the rest. *Never Let Me Go* investigates the narrative side of worldmaking used to keep exploited worldtakers
firmly in place. In *The Windup Girl*, the discrepancy between worldmakers and
takers can also be contemplated on a global scale, while in the end, capitalism's
worldmaking powers are fundamentally threatened by non-human actors
such as plants, germs, and posthuman creatures.

As analysed in depth by Foucault in his investigation of biopolitics, the contemporary success of global capitalism relies profoundly on the bio-power engrained in the neoliberal agenda (*Foucault Reader* 263). He argues that governmentality based on neoliberal conceptions of the free market as an ideal and the
self as an entrepreneur were necessary preconditions for the ongoing expansion of capitalism. Logically, neoliberal subjectivity and governmentality also
play important roles in the capitalist futures enacted in fiction. The works that
focus most on individual subjectivity in neoliberalism and its consequences for
romantic relationships and types of work are *Her* and *The Circle*. They simulate the ways in which the neoliberal ideal of the *homo oeconomicus*, who is always looking for personal advantages in competition with others, destroys relationships and communities for the sake of the market and private capital. The
precise workings of self-governmentality are exemplified through Mae's introspection while working for The Circle, but also in Kathy's first-person memoir
in *Never Let Me Go*. As my discussion of these works revealed, aesthetic choices,
such as focalisation and narrative voice and what Byung-Chul Han calls the
pleasing "aesthetics of the smooth" (*Saving Beauty* 1), help to constitute the neoliberal world.

Like neoliberalism as a mode of political governmentality, other developments and worlds are co-constitutive of the hegemonic stance of global capitalism today, and will also possibly be in the future. In this sense, I see transhumanism as the extreme ending point of the modern paradigm with its conceptualisation of the future as progress through science and technology. Therefore, many future fictions simulate the developments of the transhumanist
paradigm in combination with future capitalist worlds. For example, *Zero K*
imagines the transgression of death as the ultimate biological boundary as only
achievable for the super-rich. The transhumanist dream of the creation of artificial superintelligence is depicted to be enabled by capitalist corporate actors
in *Ex_Machina*, *Blade Runner 2049*, and *Her*. In addition, *The Circle* envisions a
democratic transhumanism built on the capitalist paradigm of maximum efficiency through digital technology.

The frequent portrayal of transhumanist goals and actors in contemporary popular future fictions further de-masks transhumanism as a replacement of religion, which counters its self-awareness of being purely scientific and based on rationality. Basically all examples featuring transhumanist ideas confirm this claim: in *Zero K*, Ross explicitly refers to the project of The Convergence as "[f]aith-based technology [...] Another god" (DeLillo 9), while *Interstellar* also uses a religious or meta-physical framing for the human society of the future and its technologies, encompassing the transgression of a three-dimensional reality. Nathan in *Ex_Machina* and Niander Wallace in *Blade Runner 2049* both pose as God-like figures due to their ability to technologically produce human-like beings. In *Transcendence*, the title already hints at the borrowing of religious elements for the futuristic development of high technologies, from uploaded brains to omnipotent nanotechnologies. Likewise, in *The Circle* the idea of the perfection of life through digital technology is compared to a religious creed. In the works' aesthetic simulation of transhumanist futures and their connection with religion or even dreams of divine powers over life, the hubristic quality of the transhumanist enterprise is exposed, alongside its essential anthropocentrism.

The links between this extreme world and more dominant contemporary world versions are also brought forth. On the one hand, as argued, the belief in science and technology as the saviours of humankind—even in the context of the ecological catastrophe—still influences or even dominates the mainstream discourse, as demonstrated by *Interstellar*. On the other hand, transhumanism, like most other contemporary worlds, is strongly indebted to humanism and its ethics. This humanist legacy is shown for example in *Never Let Me Go, The Windup Girl*, and *Blade Runner 2049*. All three works entail and deconstruct the normative idea of a soul-based humanness that makes humans superior to all other creatures in terms of moral value. While *Never Let Me Go* and *The Windup Girl* are critical of this humanist norm that also takes shape in the form of arts education in *Never Let Me Go, Blade Runner 2049* subconsciously reproduces it by calling its replicants "more human than human" (Villeneuve 0:20:50).

Otherworlds of the Future

While the relationships between dominant worlds and otherworlds of the future in my set of contemporary future fictions are not always straightforward or organised as binary oppositions, I propose that the otherworldly configurations are worth paying special attention to for finding inspiration for futures that are different from the present and might entail better alternatives. As the analysis of primary works has shown, posthumanist ideas seem to play the most important role: anthropocentrism and dualism need to be overcome in favour of ecocentrism, relationality, and systemic thinking. In the example of *Transcendence*, this is expressed for instance in the formal contrasting of black and white binaries with patterns of colours and innovative world formations. *The MaddAddam Trilogy*, *The Windup Girl*, *Never Let Me Go*, and *Zero K* provide an impulse to meta-reflect on the role of narrative and art itself with regard to the creation of possible future worlds and ethics. These fictions all raise awareness toward the aesthetics and the "storyness" of dominant worlds, and emphasise the need to disrupt these to tell newer and better ones. In this light, the foundational myths of the Gardeners in *The MaddAddam Trilogy* can offer a starting point for ecocentric stories without being a blueprint. The posthuman stories of *The Windup Girl* and *Never Let Me Go* foreground otherness and the ethical responsibility towards these perhaps un-knowable others, be they animals, plants, or technologically made others.

Like *Never Let Me Go*, many future fictions actively question the concept of "the human" and its normative position within a set of ethics for the future. For example, I have read Ava in *Ex_Machina* and Samantha in *Her* both as cyborgs who simultaneously reveal and deconstruct gender as a normative precondition for passing as human. The idea of a biological essence of "the human" is put into question by *Blade Runner 2049* and *Never Let Me Go*, where the introspection through focalisation makes replicated humans indistinguishable from humans who were born in terms of emotional sensitivity. Like *The Windup Girl*, these works point out that treating creatures well only if they count as human, as humanist ethics propose, cannot be the right path in terms of morality. Instead, they gesture towards posthumanist ethics that encompass ethical obligations for all sentient creatures and the biosphere at large. This means that technologically made others like Ava, Samantha, K., Kathy H., and Emiko should be treated with respect and dignity, not because they are human or human-like; but simply because they are and have intrinsic value. They suffer, feel, think, and engage in relationships—which is not meant to be a normative set of criteria.

In addition to the deconstruction of "the human" as the basis for morality, the otherworlds depicted in the future fictions of this study often include an emphasis on collectivity and relationality that opposes the idea of the neoliberal individual subject. The utopian outlook of *New York 2140* is enabled through collective action from below in the form of actor-networks, including non-human actors. In this sense, *New York 2140* empowers the majority of passive worldtakers to become active worldmakers, for example by going on strike, forming collectives, and becoming politically engaged. *Zero K* likewise stresses the importance of diachronic and synchronic relationships for life and identity creation, while *Avatar* envisions the interconnectedness between all living beings in the form of the electrochemical network of Pandora. The posthuman others in *Ex_Machina* and especially in *Her* are characterised by a kind of hive-mind, in which multiple organisms become one in their thinking and feeling. The importance of inter-species relations is pointed out by *The MaddAddam Trilogy* and its almost utopian posthumanist ending.

With regard to modes of imagining or creating possible futures, it seems that most future fictions call for humility and openness as a counterforce to the modern idea of the future as forward progress. The old narratives of human control and mastery over "nature" through "technology" continued in contemporary capitalism and transhumanism are predicted to have failed severely in these futures from an ecological standpoint, but also in terms of justice between humans. Even in *Interstellar*, which is inscribed in the transhumanist story of enhancement, the scientific paradigm and the ideal of rationality are extended by the dimension of feeling, especially love. Other future fictions express humility towards the future in their affirmation of non-human agency in the form of posthuman or "Earth" others. This is also underlined in Haraway's concept of the "Chthulucene", encompassing an ecocentric point of view in which the altered ecological conditions threaten to extinguish humans alongside other species. She writes that our times "are times of multispecies, including human, urgency: of great mass death and extinction; of onrushing disasters, whose unpredictable specificities are foolishly taken as unknowability itself; of refusing to know and to cultivate the capacity of response-ability; of refusing to be present in and to onrushing catastrophe in time; of unprecedented looking away" (*Staying with the Trouble* 35). The prospect of human extinction because of ecological havoc is also hinted at or even spelled out explicitly in *The MaddAddam Trilogy*, *Interstellar*, *Zero K*, and *The Windup Girl*. In *Ex_Machina*, it is alluded to through the creation of artificial superintelligence.

Several future fictions also seem to envision other futures as a reversion of historical direction. Instead of more technology and more consumption, the God's Gardeners in *The MaddAddam Trilogy* seek to have less to live better. In *The Circle*, the physical here and now is also elevated above the multiply mediated experience offered by digital technologies. In a similar manner, the RIFT group of *Transcendence* promotes "revolutionary independence from technology" as the way forward. However, none of these otherworlds work as the ideal future. Instead, they are all deliberately characterised as having their own faults and fissures. For example, while the simple, sustainable lifestyle of the Gardeners might seem recommendable, their dishonest authoritarian leadership and sexism prevents their world from appearing utopian. Like the Buddhist world in *The Windup Girl*, the Gardeners' world is built on religious creed, which works as a counterforce to the growing secularisation caused by modernity and global capitalism. Evading simplistic moral evaluation, both spiritual worlds have their advantages and deterring features: for example, they juxtapose the capitalist reduction of value to exchange value with intrinsic value and even the holiness of life, while perpetuating over-simplistic narratives of good and evil.

Speculative Realism

The omnipresence of a capitalist world in the fictions' futures is mirrored aesthetically by a similarly omnipresent realism. All works, apart from *Avatar* and *The MaddAddam Trilogy*, predominantly feature an aesthetic realism in combination with other generic elements. It thus becomes apparent how form and content are interrelated—amid the contemporary dominance of capitalism and its foreseeable future effects on the ecology and social justice, realism seems to be a necessary aesthetic choice for an ethical reflection on possible futures. When works and worlds are mostly built on the fantastic, like *Avatar*, they run the risk of escapism. Rather than providing inspiration for actual worldmaking, research on *Avatar* fandom and the post-Pandora depression has shown that the aesthetically sublime aesthetics of Pandora foster a withdrawal into its fantasy world. On the other hand, fantastic elements combined with realist aesthetics and contents can function as a defamiliarisation of the existing and bring in the dimension of un-knowability to possible futures, as in *Interstellar* or *Her*. In a similar mode, many works combine realism with other generic traditions like utopianism, science fiction, memoir, and postmodernism. As a result, the label "speculative realism" fits many future fictions of this study. It even works across temporal settings, as seen in the examples of *New York 2140*'s future setting, *Zero K*'s present setting and *Never Let Me Go*'s alternative past setting.

Is it true that this focus on realism in the cultural imaginary can only bring forth a continuation of the present and its dominant world of capitalism, as criticised for instance by Bode and Dietrich in *Future Narratives*? I hope that this study has made clear that speculative realism can work precisely towards the dismantling of this dominant world, following the logic that this future can only be averted by changing the present. This pre-necessitates an understanding of how this world is made and how destructive and lethal it will turn out to be if we let it continue as it is now. The plurality of oppositions to this world in the form of otherworlds also shows that alternatives to the dominant world already exist next to it. As is the case in *The Windup Girl* and *The MaddAddam Trilogy* among others, some of these otherworlds might not be made by human agents in the first place at all. In this sense, the future can be imagined as radically different precisely because of a realistic extrapolation from the present—it is mainly a question of perspective and scope, or of foregrounding and backgrounding: by putting humans in the background, for once, the story changes radically as does its ethical evaluation. The question of a "good future" therefore requires the add-on "for whom?". As the apocalyptic event in *The MaddAddam Trilogy* demonstrates, an ecocentric good *could* be diametrically opposed to a human good—even though I think it is wrong to put the two into opposition.

The MaddAddam Trilogy by and large escapes the realist paradigm while it extrapolates from the contemporary state of affairs likewise simulating a future of unfettered capitalism and transhumanist aspirations. However, by choosing satire, exaggeration, and playful metatextuality as its prime aesthetic modes, it surpasses the effects achieved by the works building on speculative realism alone. Its aesthetics open more possibilities for ethical reflection, going beyond the warning and mere deconstruction of this world. *The MaddAddam Trilogy* deliberately intervenes on the levels of story and aesthetics and stretches the readers' imagination to extremes, for example with the idea of human extinction and the cultural apocalyptic imaginary, or genetically altered humanoids who can communicate with genetically altered pigs. Through its complex aesthetics and open ethical outlook, the trilogy answers to Haraway's call for "stories (and theories) that are just big enough to gather up the complexities and keep the edges open and greedy for surprising new and old connections" (*Staying with the Trouble* 101).

With regard to different actual worlds and possible futures, the question of what is real has come up time and time again in my close readings, also concerning the ontological status of fiction and art itself. As I have pointed out,

The MaddAddam Trilogy foregrounds the narrative aspect of worldmaking as a prerequisite for creating ecologically sound futures. *Avatar* and *Blade Runner 2049* both address the question of "What is real?" on different intra- and extradiegetic levels, focusing especially on seeing. On the one hand, this marks perception and seeing as potentially deceptive, while on the other, it alludes to different, perhaps superior modes of seeing and understanding, for example through art and film as visual mediums themselves. *Never Let Me Go* and *Zero K* both seem to draw on Baudrillard's concepts of simulacra and simulation in contrast to "the real". They allude to the cultural cloning of late modernity and highly mediated experience in opposition to the real, which is constituted by death in *Zero K* and feelings of anger and love in *Never Let Me Go*. *Never Let Me Go*, *Zero K*, and *Ex_Machina* furthermore investigate the role of art in the creation of (future) worlds, which endows them with the metatextual angle that is also apparent in *The MaddAddam Trilogy*.

To conclude, many fictional works in this book refer to themselves as "real" in the sense of partaking in the worldmaking of the present for the future. With regard to their epistemological function for ethics for the future, they could even be described as "more real than real" because they enable viewers and readers to aesthetically perceive what might be inaccessible through other modes of perception and discourse. My ethical reading of contemporary popular future fictions has shown that it is of vital importance to reflect on possible futures and to do our best to make different and better worlds than those dominating us in the present. Instead of offering utopian blueprints, the fictional otherworlds have provided some clues into which direction we could be heading: less "forward" than backwards or sidewards, together with our nonhuman and technological others or not at all, in the spirit of relationality and communality rather than individuality, as active worldmakers instead of passive worldtakers, looking at story as well as materiality.

Works Cited

2001: A Space Odysee. Directed by Stanley Kubrick, MGM, 1968.

Ackerman, Frank. *Can We Afford the Future? The Economics of a Warming World.* Zed Books, 2009.

Adams, Spencer. 'Staging the Speculative'. *Qui Parle,* vol. 27, no. 2, Dec. 2018, pp. 521–38.

Aftermath: Population Zero. Directed by the National Geographic Channel, Cream Productions, 2008.

A.I. Artificial Intelligence. Directed by Steven Spielberg, Warner Brothers, 2001.

Aibel, Matt. 'From Provisioning to Reciprocity: Logging in to Spike Jonze's *Her*'. *Pychoanalytic Psychology,* vol. 34, no. 3, 2017, pp. 368–71.

Aldana Cohen, Daniel. 'It Gets Wetter'. *Dissent Magazine,* 2017, https://www.dissentmagazine.org/article/it-gets-wetter-kim-stanley-robinson-new-york-2140. Accessed 20 March 2021.

Arendt, Hannah. *Eichmann in Jerusalem: ein Bericht von der Banalität des Bösen.* Piper, 2020.

Armstrong, Nancy. 'The Affective Turn in Contemporary Fiction'. *Contemporary Literature,* vol. 55, no. 3, pp. 441–65.

Ashman, Nathan. '"Death Itself Shall Be Deathless": Transrationalism and Eternal Death in Don DeLillo's *Zero K*'. *Critique: Studies in Contemporary Fiction,* vol. 60, no. 3, 2019, pp. 300–10.

Assmann, Aleida. 'Transformations of the Modern Time Regime'. *Breaking up Time: Negotiating the Borders between Present, Past and Future,* edited by Berber Bevernage and Chris Lorenz, Vandenhoeck und Ruprecht, 2013, pp. 39–56.

Attridge, Derek. *The Work of Literature.* Oxford University Press, 2015.

Atwood, Margaret. *In Other Worlds: SF and the Human Imagination.* Virago, 2012.

—. *MaddAddam.* Doubleday, 2013.

—. 'Margaret Atwood: The Road to Ustopia'. *The Guardian,* 14 Oct. 2011.

—. *Oryx and Crake.* Anchor Books, 2004.

—. 'The Circle by Dave Eggers'. *New York Review of Books*, vol. 60, no. 18, 2013, pp. 6–9.

—. *The Handmaid's Tale*. Anchor Books, 1998.

—. *The Year of the Flood*. Virago Press, 2010.

Bacigalupi, Paolo. *The Windup Girl*. Night Shade Books, 2011.

Badmington, Neil, editor. *Posthumanism*. Palgrave, 2000.

Barnhill, David. 'Spirituality and Resistance: Ursula Le Guin's *The Word for World Is Forest* and the Film *Avatar*'. *Journal for the Study of Religion, Nature and Culture*, vol. 4, no. 4, Jan. 2011, pp. 478–98.

Barrett, Laura. '"[R]Adiance in Dailiness": The Uncanny Ordinary in Don DeLillo's *Zero K*'. *Journal of Modern Literature*, vol. 42, no. 1, 2018, p. 106.

Bastani, Aaron. *Fully Automated Luxury Communism: A Manifesto*. Verso, 2019.

Baudrillard, Jean. *Simulacra and Simulation*. University of Michigan Press, 1994.

Baudrillard, Jean, and Julia Witwer. *The Vital Illusion*. Columbia University Press, 2000.

Bauman, Zygmunt. *Postmodern Ethics*. Blackwell, 1993.

Bauman, Zygmunt, and Leonidas Donskis. *Moral Blindness: The Loss of Sensitivity in Liquid Modernity*. Polity Press, 2013.

Beal, Eleanor. 'Frankensteinian Gods, Fembots, and the New Technological Frontier in Alex Garland's *Ex_Machina*'. *Transmedia Creatures: Frankenstein's Afterlives*, edited by Francesca Saggini and Anna Enrichetta Soccio, Bucknell University Press, 2018, pp. 69–86.

Beck, Ulrich. *Risk Society: Towards a New Modernity*. Sage, 1992.

Bell, Daniel. *The End of Ideology: On the Exhaustion of Political Ideas in the Fifties: With 'The Resumption of History in the New Century'*. Harvard University Press, 2000.

Beller, Jonathan. 'The Computational Unconscious'. *Boundary 2*, Aug. 2018, htt ps://www.boundary2.org/2018/08/beller/. Accessed 10 Oct 2019.

Bender, Stephanie. 'Just Popular Entertainment or Longing for a Posthuman Eden? The Apocalypse in Margaret Atwood's MaddAddam Trilogy'. *Journal for Religion, Film, and Media*, vol. 5, no. 2, pp. 31–50.

Benjamin, Walter. *The Work of Art in the Age of Its Technological Reproducibility, and Other Writings on Media*. Edited by Michael William Jennings et al., Belknap Press of Harvard University Press, 2008.

Bergthaler, Hannes. 'Housebreaking the Human Animal: Humanism and the Problem of Sustainability in Margaret Atwood's *Oryx and Crake* and *The Year of the Flood*'. *English Studies*, vol. 91, no. 7, pp. 728–43.

Bierce, Ambrose. *The Devil's Dictionary*. Neal, 1906.

'biotechnology, n.'. *OED Online*, Oxford University Press, December 2022, http s://www.oed.com/view/Entry/19255. Accessed 7 February 2023.

Black, Shameen. 'Ishiguro's Inhuman Aesthetics'. *Modern Fiction Studies*, vol. 55, no. 4, 2009, pp. 785–807.

Blade Runner. Directed by Ridley Scott, Warner Brothers, 1982.

Blade Runner 2049. Directed by Dennis Villeneuve, Alcon, 2017.

'*Blade Runner 2049* (2017) User Reviews'. *IMDb*, https://www.imdb.com/title/tt 1856101/reviews?ref_=tt_urv. Accessed 5 July 2020.

Bloom, Dan. 'Thanks to TeleRead and NPR, "Cli-Fi" Is Now an Official Literary Term'. *TeleRead*, 2013, https://www.teleread.com/cli-fi-is-a-new-literary-term-that-npr-blessed-and-approved/index.html. Accessed 7 May 2018.

Bode, Christoph, and Rainer Dietrich. *Future Narratives: Theory, Poetics, and Media-Historical Moment*. De Gruyter, 2013.

Booth, Wayne C. *The Company We Keep: An Ethics of Fiction*. University of California Press, 1988.

Bostrom, Nick. 'A History of Transhumanist Thought'. *Journal of Evolution and Technology*, vol. 14, no. 1, 2005, pp. 1–25.

—. 'In Defence of Posthuman Dignity'. *Bioethics*, vol. 19, no. 3, 2005, pp. 202–14.

Bouson, J. Brooks. 'A "Joke-filled Romp" through End Times: Radical Environmentalism, Deep Ecology, and Human Extinction in Margaret Atwood's Eco-Apocalyptic *MaddAddam Trilogy*'. *The Journal of Commonwealth Literature*, vol. 51, no. 3, pp. 341–57.

Bowie, Andrew. 'Another Third Way?' *The Philistine Controversy*, edited by Dave Beech and John Roberts, 2002, pp. 161–71.

Bracke, Astrid. *Climate Crisis and the 21st-Century British Novel*. Bloomsbury Academic, 2017.

—. 'Flooded Futures: The Representation of the Anthropocene in Twenty-First-Century British Flood Fictions'. *Critique: Studies in Contemporary Fiction*, vol. 60, no. 3, 2019, pp. 278–88.

Bradshaw, Peter. '*Blade Runner 2049* Review—a Gigantic Spectacle of Pure Hallucinatory Craziness'. *The Guardian*, 29 Sept. 2017, https://www.theguardian.com/film/2017/sep/29/blade-runner-2049-review-ryan-gosling-harrison-ford-denis-villeneuve. Accessed 5 Nov 2019.

Braidotti, Rosi. *The Posthuman*. Polity Press, 2013.

Brooker, Charlie. *The Black Mirror Series*. Netflix, 2011.

Brooks, David. 'The Messiah Complex'. *New York Times*, 7 Jan. 2010, https://www.nytimes.com/2010/01/08/opinion/08brooks.html. Accessed 28 June 2020.

Brown, Wendy. *In the Ruins of Neoliberalism: The Rise of Antidemocratic Politics in the West*. Columbia University Press, 2019.

—. *Undoing the Demos: Neoliberalism's Stealth Revolution*. Zone Books, 2017.

Browning, James. 'Hello, Dolly'. *The Village Voice*, 22 Mar. 2005, https://www.vi llagevoice.com/2005/03/22/hello-dolly-2/. Accessed 17 Sept. 2020.

Bruyn, Eric C. H. de, and Sven Lütticken, editors. *Futurity Report*. Sternberg Press, 2020.

Buder, Emily. 'Die. Freeze Body. Store. Revive.' *The Atlantic*, 20 June 2019, ht tps://www.theatlantic.com/video/index/591979/cryonics/. Accessed 3 Dec 2020.

Burgess, Adam, et al., editors. *Routledge Handbook of Risk Studies*. Routledge, 2019.

Callenbach, Ernest. *Ecotopia: The Notebooks and Reports of William Weston*. Bantam Books, 1990.

Cameron, James, director. *Aliens*. Twentieth Century Fox, 1986.

—. *Avatar*. Twentieth Century Fox, 2009.

—. *Terminator 2: Judgement Day*. TriStar, 1991.

—. *The Terminator*. Cinema '84, 1984.

Campbell, Heidi A. 'Problematizing the Human-Technology Relationship through Techno-Spiritual Myths Presented in *The Machine, Transcendence* and *Her*'. *Journal of Religion and Film*, vol. 20, no. 1, 2016, Article 21.

Campbell, Timothy C., and Adam Sitze, editors. *Biopolitics: A Reader*. Duke University Press, 2013.

Canavan, Gerry, and Kim Stanley Robinson, editors. *Green Planets: Ecology and Science Fiction*. Wesleyan University Press, 2014.

Carrico, Dale. 'Futurological Discourses and Posthuman Terrains'. *Existenz*, vol. 8, no. 2, 2013.

Carroll, Lewis. *Alice's Adventures in Wonderland and Through the Looking Glass*. Puffin Books, 1997.

CBS Interactive. '*Ex_Machina* Critic Reviews'. *Metacritic*, https://www.metacri tic.com/movie/ex-machina/critic-reviews. Accessed 17 Feb. 2020.

Children of Men. Directed by Alfonso Cuarón, Universal, 2006.

Citton, Yves. *The Ecology of Attention*. Polity, 2017.

Clarke, Bruce. *Posthuman Metamorphosis: Narrative and Systems*. Fordham University Press, 2008.

Climate Change 2014 Synthesis Report. Intergovernmental Panel on Climate Change, 2015.

Cline, Ernest. *Ready Player One*. Penguin Random House, 2011.

Cohen, Tom. *Telemorphosis. Theory in the Era of Climate Change*. Open Humanities Press, 2012.

Conrad, Joseph, et al. *Heart of Darkness*. Penguin Books, 2017.

Coole, Diana H., and Samantha Frost, editors. *New Materialisms: Ontology, Agency, and Politics*. Duke University Press, 2010.

Cooper, Melinda. *Life as Surplus: Biotechnology and Capitalism in the Neoliberal Era*. University of Washington Press, 2008.

Cox, Emily. 'Denuding the Gynoid: The Woman Machine as Bare Life in Alex Garland's *Ex Machina*'. *Foundation: The International Review of Science Fiction*, vol. 47, no. 2, 2018, pp. 5–19.

Crain, Caleb. 'Don't Play with That or You'll Go Blind'. *N+1*, 1 Jan. 2010, https://www.nplusonemag.com/online-only/online-only/dont-play-or-youll-go-blind/. Accessed 20 July 2019.

Crichton, Michael. *State of Fear*. Harper, 2016.

Currie, Mark. 'Controlling Time: *Never Let Me Go*'. *Kazuo Ishiguro*, edited by Sean Matthews, Continuum, 2009, pp. 91–103.

Davies, Caroline. '*Avatar*—Even in 2D – Reportedly Too Hot a Property for China Censors'. *The Guardian*, 18 Jan. 2010, https://www.theguardian.com/world/2010/jan/18/china-censorship-avatar-confucious. Accessed 15 March 2018.

Davis, Todd F., and Kenneth Womack. *Formalist Criticism and Reader-Response Theory*. Palgrave, 2002.

De Boever, Arne. *Narrative Care: Biopolitics and the Novel*. Bloomsbury Academic, 2013.

del Valle Alcalá, Roberto. 'Servile Life: Subjectivity, Biopolitics, and the Labor of the Dividual in Kazuo Ishiguro's *Never Let Me Go*'. *Cultural Critique*, no. 102, pp. 37–60.

Deleuze, Gilles. *The Movement-Image*. Repr, Athlone, 2009.

—. *The Time-Image*. Repr, Athlone, 2012.

DeLillo, Don. *Zero K*. Picador, 2016.

Der Derian, James. 'Now We Are All Avatars'. *Millenium: Journal of International Studies*, vol. 39, no. 1, pp. 181–86.

Dini, Rachele. 'Don DeLillo, *Zero K*'. *European Journal of American Studies [Online]*, vol. 2, 2016, https://journals.openedition.org/ejas/11393. Accessed 20 Aug 2021.

Doležel, Lubomír. *Heterocosmica: Fiction and Possible Worlds*. Johns Hopkins Univ. Press, 1998.

Donna Haraway: Storytelling for Earthly Survival. Directed by Fabrizio Terranova, Icarus Films, 2016.

Donskis, Leonidas. *The End of Ideology & Utopia? Moral Imagination and Cultural Criticism in the Twentieth Century*. P. Lang, 2000.

Downing, Lisa, and Libby Saxton. *Film and Ethics: Foreclosed Encounters*. Routledge, 2010.

Drucker, Susan J., and Gary Gumpert. 'Through the Looking Glass: Illusions of Transparency and the Cult of Information'. *Journal of Management Development*, vol. 26, no. 5, pp. 493–98.

Eaglestone, Robert. 'One and the Same? Ethics, Aesthetics, Truth'. *Poetics Today*, vol. 25, no. 4, 2004, pp. 596–608.

Edwards, Caroline. *Utopia and the Contemporary British Novel*. Cambridge University Press, 2019.

Eggers, Dave. *The Circle*. Penguin Books, 2014.

—. *The Every: Or At Last a Sense of Order, or The Final Days of Free Will, or Limitless Choice Is Killing the World*. Vintage Books, 2021.

Elysium. Directed by Neill Bloomkamp, TriStar, 2013.

Eskin, Michael. 'Introduction: The Double "Turn" to Ethics and Literature?' *Poetics Today*, vol. 25, no. 4, 2004, pp. 557–72.

Essig, Laurie. *Love, Inc: Dating Apps, the Big White Wedding, and Chasing the Happily Neverafter*. University of California Press, 2019.

'Ex_Machina (2014) User Reviews'. *IMDb*, https://www.imdb.com/title/tt0470752/reviews?ref_=tt_urv.

Farago, Jason. '"Her" Is the Scariest Movie of 2013'. *The New Republic*, 30 Dec. 2013, https://newrepublic.com/article/116063/spike-jonzes-her-scariest-movie-2013. Accessed 15 May 2019.

Federer, Helena. 'Ecocriticism, Posthumanism, and the Biological Idea of Culture'. *The Oxford Handbook of Ecocriticism*, edited by Greg Garrad, Oxford University Press, 2014, pp. 225–40.

Feenberg, Andrew. *Critical Theory of Technology*. Oxford University Press, 1991.

Ferrando, Francesca. 'Posthumanism, Transhumanism, Antihumanism, Metahumanism, and New Materialisms: Differences and Relations'. *Existenz*, vol. 8, no. 2, 2013, pp. 26–32.

Fisher, Mark. *Capitalist Realism: Is There No Alternative?* O Books, 2009.

Fitting, Peter. 'Utopia, Dystopia and Science Fiction'. *The Cambridge Companion to Utopian Literature*, edited by Gregory Claeys, Cambridge University Press, pp. 135–53.

Flisfeder, Mathew, and Clint Burnham. 'Love and Sex in the Age of Capitalist Realism: On Spike Jonze's *Her*'. *Cinema Journal*, vol. 57, no. 1, 2017, pp. 25–45.

Fluck, Winfried. 'Surface Knowledge and "Deep" Knowledge: The New Realism in American Fiction'. *Restant XX*, vol. 1, 1992, pp. 65–85.

Flückiger, Barbara, et al. 'Forum Blade Runner'. *Zeitschrift Für Fantastikforschung*, vol. 7, no. 1, Sept. 2019, doi.org/10.16995/zff.1335. Accessed 13 Dec 2019.

Foroohar, Rana. *Don't Be Evil*. Currency, 2019.

Foucault, Michel. *Foucault Reader: An Introduction to Foucault's Thought*. Edited by Paul Rabinow, Penguin, 2020.

—. 'Of Other Spaces'. *Diacritics*, vol. 16, no. 1, pp. 22–27.

—. *The Birth of Biopolitics: Lectures at the Collège de France, 1978–79*. Edited by Michel Senellart, Translated by Graham Burchell, Palgrave Macmillan, 2010.

—. *The History of Sexuality*. Vintage Books, 1990.

Franck, Georg. *Mentaler Kapitalismus: Eine politische Ökonomie des Geistes*. C. Hanser, 2005.

—. *Ökonomie der Aufmerksamkeit: Ein Entwurf*. Hanser, 1998.

—. 'The Economy of Attention'. *Journal of Sociology: The Journal of the Australian Sociological Association*, vol. 55, no. 1, pp. 8–19.

Fukuyama, Francis. *The End of History and the Last Man*. Free Press; Maxwell Macmillan, 1992.

'Future Fiction Books'. *Goodreads*, https://www.goodreads.com/shelf/show/fu ture-fiction. Accessed 20 Sept. 2017.

'Future Fictions'. *Frieze*, https://www.frieze.com/article/future-fictions. Accessed 23 July 2021.

'Future Fictions – Exhibition at Assembly Point in London'. *Artrabbit*, https://w ww.artrabbit.com/events/future-fictions. Accessed 9 Oct. 2017.

Galow, Timothy W. *Understanding Dave Eggers*. The University of South Carolina Press, 2014.

Garland, Alex. 'Alex Garland of "Ex Machina" Talks about Artificial Intelligence'. *New York Times*, 22 Apr. 2015, https://www.nytimes.com/2015/04/26/movi es/alex-garland-of-ex-machina-talks-about-artificial-intelligence.html. Accessed 21 Jan 2020.

—. *Ex_Machina*. Universal, 2014.

Gee, Maggie. *The Flood*. Saqi, 2004.

Geostrom. Directed by Dean Devlin, Warner Brothers, 2017.

Ghosh, Amitav. 'Where Is the Fiction about Climate Change?' *The Guardian*, 28 Oct. 2016. https://www.theguardian.com, https://www.theguardian.com

/books/2016/oct/28/amitav-ghosh-where-is-the-fiction-about-climate-c hange-. Accessed 23 Sept 2018.

Ghost in the Shell. Directed by Rupert Sanders, Paramount, 2017.

Gibson, Andrew. *Postmodernity, Ethics, and the Novel*. Routledge, 1999.

Glaubitz, Nicola. 'Eugenics and Dystopia: Andrew Niccol, *Gattaca* (1997) and Kazuo Ishiguro, *Never Let Me Go* (2005)'. *Dystopia, Science Fiction, Post-Apocalypse: Classics-New Tendencies-Model Interpretations*, WVT Trier, 2015.

Glavanakova, Alexandra K. 'The Age of Humans Meets Posthumanism: Reflections on DeLillo's *Zero K*'. *Studies in the Literary Imagination*, vol. 50, no. 1, 2017, pp. 91–109.

Goodman, Nelson. *Ways of Worldmaking*. Hackett, 1978.

Goodman, Nelson, and Catherine Z. Elgin. *Reconceptions in Philosophy and Other Arts and Sciences*. Routledge, 1988.

Gordon, John-Stewart, and Holger Burckhart. *Global Ethics and Moral Responsibility: Hans Jonas and His Critics*. Ashgate, 2014.

Grabiner, Ellen. *I See You: The Shifting Paradigms of James Cameron's Avatar*. McFarland & Company, 2012.

Greenblatt, Leah. 'Impeccably Cool *Blade Runner 2049* Is a Ravishing Visual Feast: EW Review'. *Entertainment Weekly*, 29 Sept. 2017, https://www.ew.c om/movies/2017/09/29/blade-runner-2049-review/?utm_campaign=ente rtainmentweekly&utm_source=twitter.com&utm_medium=social&xid= entertainment-weekly_socialflow_twitter. Accessed 11 Oct 2019.

Hageman, Andrew. 'The Challenge of Imagining Ecological Futures: Paolo Bacigalupi's *The Windup Girl*'. *Science Fiction Studies*, vol. 39, no. 2, pp. 283–303.

Han, Byung-Chul. *In the Swarm: Digital Prospects*. MIT Press, 2017.

—. *Saving Beauty*. Polity Press, 2018.

—. *The Transparency Society*. Stanford University Press.

Harari, Yuval Noah. *Homo Deus: A Brief History of Tomorrow*. Revised edition, Vintage, 2017.

Haraway, Donna Jeanne. 'A Manifesto for Cyborgs: Science, Technology and Socialist Feminism in the 1980s'. *Liquid Metal: The Science Fiction Film Reader*, edited by Sean Redmond, Wallflower Press, 2004, pp. 158–81.

—. *Staying with the Trouble: Making Kin in the Chthulucene*. Duke University Press, 2016.

—. *The Haraway Reader*. Routledge, 2004.

Hayles, Katherine. *How We Became Posthuman: Virtual Bodies in Cybernetics, Literature, and Informatics*. University of Chicago Press, 1999.

—. 'Wrestling with Transhumanism'. *Metanexus*, 1 Sept. 2011, https://metanex us.net/h-wrestling-transhumanism/. Accessed 10 Aug 2019.

Heinze, Rüdiger. *Ethics of Literary Forms in Contemporary American Literature*. Lit, 2005.

Henke, Jennifer. '"Ava's Body Is a Good One": (Dis)Embodiment in *Ex Machina*'. *American, British and Canadian Studies*, vol. 29, no. 1, 2017, pp. 126–46.

'*Her* User Reviews'. *IMDb*, https://www.imdb.com/title/tt1798709/reviews?ref _=tt_urv. Accessed 28 Nov. 2019.

Herbrechter, Stefan. 'Posthuman/Ist Literature? Don DeLillo's *Point Omega* and *Zero K*'. *Open Library of Humanities*, vol. 6, no. 2, 2020, pp. 1–25.

Herman, Peter. 'More, Huxley, Eggers and the Utopian/Dystopian Tradition'. *Renaissance and Reformation*, vol. 41, no. 3, 2018, pp. 165–93.

Hiltscher, Reinhard, editor. *Kant: Die Hauptwerke: ein Lesebuch*. Narr Francke Attempto Verlag, 2016.

Hobbs, Philippa. '"You Willingly Tie Yourself to These Leashes": Neoliberalism, Neoliberal Rationality, and the Corporate Workplace in Dave Eggers' *The Circle*"'. *Dandelion*, vol. 8, no. 1, 2017, pp. 1–13.

Holtmeier, Matthew Alan. 'Post-Pandoran Depression or Na'vi Sympathy: *Avatar*, Affect, and Audience Reception'. *Journal for the Study of Religion, Nature and Culture*, vol. 4, no. 4, Jan. 2011, pp. 414–24.

Hopfmann, Arndt, and Markus Euskirchen. *Digitalwirtschaft: Worum Es Wirklich Geht: Fiktionen, Realitäten, Herausforderungen*. Rosa-Luxemburg Stiftung, 2019.

Horn, Eva. *Zukunft Als Katastrophe*. S. Fischer, 2014.

Horn, Eva, and Hannes Bergthaller. *The Anthropocene: Key Issues for the Humanities*. Routledge, 2020.

Horton, Emily. *Contemporary Crisis Fictions: Affect and Ethics in the Modern British Novel*. Palgrave, 2014.

Huehls, Mitchum, and Rachel Greenwald Smith, editors. *Neoliberalism and Contemporary Literary Culture*. Johns Hopkins University Press, 2017.

Hughes, James J. 'The Politics of Transhumanism and the Techno-Millenial Imagination, 1626–2030'. *Journal of Religion and Science*, vol. 47, no. 4, 2012, pp. 757–76.

Humanity+. Humanity+ Foundation, https://www.humanityplus.org. Accessed 1 Sept 2019.

Hunter, Megan. *The End We Start From*. Picador, 2017.

Huxley, Aldous. *Brave New World*. Longman, 1992.

I Am Mother. Directed by Grant Sputore, Penguin Empire, 2019.

'IMDb'. *Top Rated Movies*, https://www.imdb.com/chart/top?ref_=ft_250. Accessed 3 Nov. 2019.

IMDb Pro. '2014 Worldwide Box Office'. *Box Office Mojo*, https://www.boxoffice mojo.com/year/world/2014/. Accessed 24 July 2021.

Ingram, David. 'The Aesthetics and Ethics of Eco-Film Criticism'. *Ecocinema Theory and Practice*, Routledge, 2013.

Institute for Policy Studies. *Global Inequality*. inequality.org/facts/global-inequality/. Accessed 6 Aug. 2021.

'Interstellar (2014) User Reviews'. *IMDb*, https://www.imdb.com/title/tt081669 2/reviews?ref_=tt_ov_rt. Accessed 9 Sept. 2018.

In Time. Directed by Andrew Niccol, Regency Enterprises, 2011.

Into the Storm. Directed by Steven Quale, Broken Road, 2014.

Into the Wild. Directed by Sean Penn, Paramount, 2007.

Iser, Wolfgang. *The Act of Reading: A Theory of Aesthetic Response*. Johns Hopkins University Press, 1978.

Ishiguro, Kazuo. *Never Let Me Go*. Faber and Faber, 2005.

Istoft, Britt. 'Avatar Fandom as Nature-Religious Expression?' *Journal for the Study of Religion, Nature and Culture*, vol. 4, no. 4, Jan. 2011, pp. 394–413.

Ivakhiv, Adrian. 'What Can a Film Do? Assessing *Avatar*'s Global Affects'. *Moving Environments: Affect, Emotion, Ecology, and Film*, Wilfrid Laurier University Press, 2014, pp. 159–79.

Jacobson, Brian R. '*Ex Machina* in the Garden'. *Film Quarterly*, vol. 69, no. 4, pp. 23–34.

Jacoby, Russell. *The End of Utopia: Politics and Culture in the Age of Apathy*. Basic Books, 1999.

Jagoe, Eva-Lynn. 'Depersonalized Intimacy: The Cases of Sherry Turkle and Spike Jonze'. *ESC*, vol. 42, no. 1, 2016, pp. 155–73.

James, Edward, and Farah Mendlesohn. *The Cambridge Companion to Fantasy Literature*. Cambridge University Press, 2012.

Jameson, Fredric. *Archaeologies of the Future: The Desire Called Utopia and Other Science Fictions*. Verso, 2007.

—. 'Then You Are Them'. *London Review of Books*, vol. 31, no. 17, pp. 7–8.

Jaques Derrida. 'Différance'. *Literary Theory: An Anthology*, edited by Julie Rivkin and Michael Ryan, Second Edition, Blackwell, 2010, pp. 278–99.

Jendrysik, Mark. 'Back to the Garden: New Visions of Posthuman Futures'. *Utopian Studies*, vol. 22, no. 1, 2011, pp. 34–51.

Jenkins, Henry. 'Avatar Activism'. *Le Monde Diplomatique*, Sept. 2010, https://m ondediplo.com/2010/09/15avatar.

Jennings, Hope. 'The Comic Apocalpyse of *The Year of the Flood*'. *Margaret Atwood Studies*, vol. 3, no. 2, 2010, pp. 11–18.

Johns-Putra, Adeline. *Climate Change and the Contemporary Novel*. Cambridge University Press, 2019.

Jonas, Hans. 'Technology and Responsibility: Reflections on the New Task of Ethics'. *Social Research*, vol. 40, no. 1, 1973, pp. 31–54.

—. *The Imperative of Responsibility: In Search of an Ethics for the Technological Age*. The University of Chicago Press, 2000.

—. *The Phenomenon of Life: Toward a Philosophical Biology*. Northwestern University Press, 2001.

Jonze, Spike. '51st New York Film Festival 'Her' Press Conference'. *YouTube*, uploaded by Film at Lincoln Center, 13 Oct. 2013, https://www.youtube.com/watch?v=ZACOU3H5KO8. Accessed 12 Sept. 2019.

—. *Her*. Anapurna, 2013.

Juchau, Mireille. *The World without Us*. Bloomsbury, 2016.

Kant, Immanuel, et al. *Critique of the Power of Judgment*. Cambridge University Press, 2000.

Kant, Immanuel, and Mary J. Gregor. *Groundwork of the Metaphysics of Morals*. Cambridge University Press, 1998.

Kavenna, Joanna. *Zed*. Doubleday, 2020.

Keck, Michaela. 'Paradise Retold: Revisionist Mythmaking in Margaret Atwood's *MaddAddam Trilogy*'. *Ecozon@*, vol. 9, no. 2, 2018, pp. 23–40.

Kermode, Mark. 'Transcendence Review – Grand Ideas Rather than Spectacle Lie at Its Heart'. *The Guardian*, 27 Apr. 2014, https://www.theguardian.com/film/2014/apr/27/transcendence-review-grand-ideas-johnny-depp-wally-pfister. Accessed 27 March 2020.

King, Derrick. 'Biogenetics, The Nation, and Globalization in Paolo Bacigalupi's Critical Dystopias'. *MOSF Journal of Science Fiction*, vol. 1, no. 1, 2016.

Kingsolver, Barbara. *Flight Behavior*. Harper, 2012.

Klein, Naomi. *The Shock Doctrine: The Rise of Disaster Capitalism*. Knopf Canada, 2007.

—. *This Changes Everything*. Penguin Books, 2014.

Klier, Alexander. *Umweltethik: Wider die ökologische Krise. Ein kritischer Vergleich der Positionen von Vittorio Hösle und Hans Jonas*. Tectum-Verlag, 2007.

Kluger, Jeffrey. 'The Art of Science: *Interstellar* Updates the Hollywood Space Odysee with a Fable Based in Fact'. *Time*, 10 Nov. 2014, pp. 42–48.

Koh, James. 'A Fantasy in Sci-Fi's Clothing: *Interstellar* and the Liberation of Magic from Genre'. *Re:Search*, vol. 3, no. 1, 2016.

Kohn, Eric. *Review: Is the Heady Johnny Depp Tech Thriller 'Transcendence' Ahead of Its Time?* 15 Apr. 2014, https://www.indiewire.com/2014/04/review-is-the-heady-johnny-depp-tech-thriller-transcendence-ahead-of-its-time-2773 5/. Accessed 18 Jan. 2020.

Kolbert, Elizabeth. *The Sixth Extinction: An Unnatural History*. Henry Holt and Company, 2014.

Koljević, Bogdana. *Twenty-First Century Biopolitics*. Peter Lang, 2015.

Korte, Barbara. 'Fundamentalism and the End: A Reading of Margaret Atwood's *Oryx and Crake* in the Context of Last Man Fiction'. *Literary Encounters of Fundamentalism: A Case Book*, edited by Klaus Stierstorfer and Annette Kern-Stähler, Winter, 2008, pp. 151–164.

Korthals Altes, Liesbeth. *Ethos and Narrative Interpretation: The Negotiation of Values in Fiction*. University of Nebraska Press, 2014.

Koselleck, Reinhart. *Futures Past: On the Semantics of Historical Time*. Columbia University Press, 2004.

Kreider, Tim. 'Our Greatest Political Novelist?' *The New Yorker*, 12 Dec. 2013, https://www.newyorker.com/books/page-turner/our-greatest-polit ical-novelist. Accessed 12 June 2018.

Kreutzer, Ralf, and Marie Sirrenberg. *Understanding Artificial Intelligence: Fundamentals, Use Cases and Methods for a Corporate AI Journey*. Springer, 2020.

Kupfer, Joseph H. *Visions of Virtue in Popular Film*. Westview Press, 1999.

Kurzweil, Ray. *The Singularity Is Near: When Humans Transcend Biology*. Viking, 2005.

Laguarta Bueno, Carmen. 'Transhumanism in Dave Eggers' *The Circle*'. *Revista de Estudios Norteamericanos*, vol. 22, pp. 165–88.

Lakoff, George, and Mark Johnson. *Metaphors We Live By*. University of Chicago Press, 2003.

Lanchester, John. *The Wall*. Faber & Faber, 2019.

Langer, Jessica. *Postcolonialism and Science Fiction*. Palgrave Macmillan, 2011.

Lasdun, James. '*Zero K* by Don DeLillo Review—the Problem of Mortality'. *The Guardian*, 11 May 2016, https://www.theguardian.com/books/2016/may/11/zero-k-don-delillo-review. Accessed 19 May 2019.

Latour, Bruno. 'An Attempt at a "Compositionist Manifesto"'. *New Literary History*, vol. 41, no. 3, 2010, pp. 471–90.

—. *Reassembling the Social: An Introduction to Actor-Network-Theory*. Oxford University Press, 2005.

Lawtoo, Nidesh. 'Avatar Simulation in 3Ts: Techne, Trance, Transformation'. *Science Fiction Studies*, vol. 42, pp. 132–50.

Le Guin, Ursula K. *The Dispossessed: An Ambiguous Utopia*. Harper Voyager, 2011.

Lemke, Thomas. *Biopolitik zur Einführung*. Junius, 2013.

Lévinas, Emmanuel. *Totality and Infinity: An Essay on Exteriority*. Duquesne Univ. Press, 2011.

Levine, Caroline. *Forms: Whole, Rhythm, Hierarchy, Network*. Princeton University Press, 2017.

Levitas, Ruth. *The Concept of Utopia*. Allan, 1990.

Lewis, Paul. "'Our Minds Can Be Hijacked': The Tech Insiders Who Fear a Smartphone Dystopia'. *The Guardian*, 5 Oct. 2017, https://www.theguardia n.com/technology/2017/oct/05/smartphone-addiction-silicon-valley-dyst opia. Accessed 10 Oct. 2019.

Lewis, Tim. 'Interview Alex Garland on *Ex Machina*: "I Feel More Attached to This Film than to Anything Before"'. *The Observer*, 11 Jan. 2015, https://www.theguardian.com/culture/2015/jan/11/alex-garland-ex-machina-interview-the-beach-28-days-later. Accessed 23 Nov. 2019.

Ley, Rebecca. *Sweet Fruit, Sour Land*. Sandstone Press, 2018.

Linklater, Alexander. 'The *Circle* by Dave Eggers—Review'. *The Observer*, 12 Oct. 2013, https://www.theguardian.com/books/2013/oct/12/the-circle-dave-e ggers-review. Accessed 23 Feb. 2019.

Liu, Cixin, and Ken Liu. *The Three-Body Problem*. Tor Books, 2014.

Lloyd, Saci. *The Carbon Diaries 2015*. Hodder Children's Books, 2008.

Lothe, Jakob, and Jeremy Hawthorn, editors. *Narrative Ethics*. Rodopi, 2013.

Lovelock, James. *The Vanishing Face of Gaia: A Final Warning*. Basic Books, 2009.

Lucy. Directed by Luc Besson, EuropaCorp, 2014.

Macpherson, Heidi Slettedahl. *The Cambridge Introduction to Margaret Atwood*. Cambridge University Press, 2010.

Mad Max Fury Road. Directed by George Miller, Warner Brothers, 2015.

Mandel, Emily St John. *Station Eleven*. Alfred A. Knopf, 2015.

Mann, Ron. *In the Wake of the Flood*. Sphinx.

March for Science Germany. *Finde Deinen Lieblingsslogan*. https://marchforscie nce.de/klickspiel/, Accessed 23 July 2021.

Marínez Falquina, Silvia. "'The Pandora Effect:' James Cameron's *Avatar* and a Trauma Studies Perspective'. *Journal of the Spanish Association of Anglo-Amer-ican Studies*, vol. 36, no. 2, pp. 115–31.

Martin, Thomas L. *Poiesis and Possible Worlds: A Study in Modality and Literary The-ory*. University of Toronto Press, 2016.

Mason, Everdeen. *Kim Stanley Robinson's New York 2140 and Other New Scifi and Fantasy Releases in March – The Washington Post.* 8 Mar. 2017, https://www.w ashingtonpost.com/entertainment/books/best-science-fiction-and-fanta sy-books-to-read-in-march/2017/03/07/7c912458-0339-11e7-b9fa-ed727b 644a0b_story.html?noredirect=on&utm_term=.93b11639ec8a. Accessed 6 June 2018.

Matei, Adrienne. 'Shock! Horror! Do You Know How Much Time You Spend on Your Phone?' *The Guardian,* 21 Aug. 2019, https://www.theguardian.com/ lifeandstyle/2019/aug/21/cellphone-screen-time-average-habits. Accessed 13 Jan. 2020.

McCarthy, Cormac. *The Road.* Vintage International, 2006.

McDonald, Keith. 'Days of Past Futures: Kazuo Ishiguro's Never Let Me Go as "Speculative Memoir"'. *Biography,* vol. 30, no. 1, 2007, pp. 74–83.

McEwan, Ian. *Machines like Me: And People like You.* Jonathan Cape, 2019.

McHale, Brian. *Constructing Postmodernism.* Routledge, 1992.

Meireis, Torsten. 'The Circle: Die neue Kolonialisierung des inneren Menschen'. *Ethik und Gesellschaft,* vol. 2, 2015.

Metropolis. Directed by Fritz Lang, Universum Film,1926.

Miller, J. Hillis. *The Ethics of Reading: Kant, de Man, Eliot, Trollope, James, and Benjamin.* Columbia University Press, 1987.

Milner, Andrew, et al., editors. *Ethical Futures and Global Science Fiction.* Palgrave Macmillan, 2020.

Miśra, Paṅkaja Kumāra. *Age of Anger: A History of the Present.* 2018.

Mohr, Dunja M. 'Transgressive Utopian Dystopias: The Postmodern Reappearance of Utopia in the Disguise of Dystopia'. *ZAA,* vol. 55, no. 1, 2007, pp. 5–24.

Moore, Jason W. *Capitalism in the Web of Life: Ecology and the Accumulation of Capital.* Verso, 2015.

More, Thomas. *Utopia.* Penguin Classics, 2012.

Morris, William. *News from Nowhere and Other Writings.* Penguin Books, 1993.

Morton, Timothy. *Dark Ecology: For a Logic of Future Coexistence.* Columbia University Press, 2016.

—. *Ecology without Nature: Rethinking Environmental Aesthetics.* Harvard Univ. Press, 2009.

Mosca, Valeria. 'Crossing Human Boundaries: Apocalypse and Posthumanism in Margaret Atwood's *Oryx and Crake* and *Year of the Flood*'. *Altre Modernità/ Otras Modernidades/Autres Modernités/Other Modernities,* vol. 9, pp. 38–52.

Moylan, Tom. *Becoming Utopian: The Culture and Politics of Radical Transformation*. Bloomsbury Academic, 2021.

Mulhall, Stephen. 'The Alphabet of Us: Miracles, Messiahnism, and the Baseline Test in *Blade Runner 2049*'. *Blade Runner 2049: A Philosophical Exploration*, edited by Timothy Shanahan and Paul Smart, Routledge, 2020, pp. 27–47.

Mullan, John. 'On First Reading *Never Let Me Go*'. *Kazuo Ishiguro*, edited by Sean Matthews, Continuum, pp. 104–13.

My Sister's Keeper. Directed by Nick Cassavetes, Warner Brothers, 2009.

NASA. *Global Climate Change: Vital Signs of the Planet*. climate.nasa.gov/%20/. Accessed 15 Feb. 2021.

Nash Information Services. 'All Time Worldwide Box Office'. *The Numbers: Where Data and the Movie Business Meet*, 2021, https://www.the-numbers.com/box-office-records/worldwide/all-movies/cumulative/all-time. Accessed 4 June 2018.

Neumann, Birgit, and Martin Zierold. 'Media as Ways of Worldmaking: Media-Specific Structures and Intermedial Dynamics'. *Cultural Ways of Worldmaking. Media and Narratives*, edited by Vera Nünning et al., De Gruyter, 2010, pp. 103–18.

'*Never Let Me Go* Community Reviews'. *Goodreads*, https://www.goodreads.com/book/show/6334.Never_Let_Me_Go?from_search=true&from_srp=true&qid=OKC35PZPiU&rank=1#other_reviews. Accessed 30 Oct. 2020.

'*New York 2140* Other Reviews'. *Goodreads*. https://www.goodreads.com/book/show/31813823-new-york-2140. Accessed 26 July 2019.

Newton, Adam Zachary. *Narrative Ethics*. Harvard University Press, 1995.

Nichols, Bill. *Representing Reality: Issues and Concepts in Documentary*. Indiana University Press, 1991.

Northover, Richard Alan. 'Ecological Apocalypse in Margaret Atwood's *MaddAddam Trilogy*'. *Studia Neophilologica*, vol. 88, no. 1, 2016, pp. 81–95.

Nünning, Ansgar, and Vera Nünning. 'Ways of Worldmaking as a Model for the Study of Culture: Theoretical Frameworks, Epistemological Underpinnings, New Horizons'. *Cultural Ways of Worldmaking. Media and Narratives*, edited by Nünning et. al, De Gruyter, 2010, pp. 1–25.

Nünning, Vera, Ansgar Nünning, and Birgit Neumann, editors. *Cultural Ways of Worldmaking: Media and Narratives*. De Gruyter, 2010.

—, editors. *The Aesthetics and Politics of Cultural Worldmaking*. WVT, Wissenschaftlicher Verlag Trier, 2010.

Nussbaum, Martha C. *Poetic Justice: The Literary Imagination and Public Life*. Beacon Press, 1995.

O'Brian, Geoffrey. 'Beyond the Time Barrier: *Interstellar*'s Journey to the Far Limits of Experience'. *Filmcomment*, Dec. 2014, pp. 25–26.

Okorafor, Nnedi. *Binti*. Tor, 2015.

—. *Lagoon*. Paperback, Hodder, 2014.

Ortitz, Roberto J. 'Financialization, Climate Change, and the Future of the Capitalist World-Ecology: On Kim Stanley Robinson's *New York 2140*'. *Soundings: An Interdisciplinary Journal*, vol. 103, no. 2, 2020, pp. 264–85.

Orwell, George. *Nineteen Eighty-Four*. Penguin Books, 1954.

Ozeki, Ruth L. *All over Creation*. Canongate, 2013.

Parker, David. *Ethics, Theory, and the Novel*. Cambridge University Press, 1994.

Parrinder, Patrick, editor. *Learning from Other Worlds: Estrangement, Cognition, and the Politics of Science Fiction and Utopia*. Duke University Press, 2001.

Patel, Jay. 'Ex-Machina, the DIT Story'. *Definition Magazine*, Mar. 2015, https://www.definitionmagazine.com/journal/2015/3/2/ex-machina-the-dit-story.html. Accessed 20 Feb 2020.

Pavel, Thomas G. *Fictional Worlds*. Harvard Univ. Press, 1986.

Peebles Tavera, Stephanie. 'Utopia, Inc.: A Manifesto for the Cyborg Corporation'. *Science Fiction Studies*, vol. 44, 2017.

Pfister, Wally. *Transcendence*. Alcon, 2014.

Phelan, James. *Living to Tell about It: A Rhetoric and Ethics of Character Narration*. Cornell Univ. Press, 2005.

Pieper, Annemarie. *Einführung in die Ethik*. Francke, 2007.

Piketty, Thomas. *Capital in the Twenty-First Century*. The Belknap Press of Harvard University Press, 2014.

Pordzik, Ralph. *The Quest for Postcolonial Utopia: A Comparative Introduction to the Utopian Novel in the New English Literatures*. P. Lang, 2001.

Preston, Alex. 'Zero K by Don DeLillo—Profound and Beautiful'. *The Observer*, 15 May 2016, https://www.theguardian.com/books/2016/may/15/don-de-lillo-zero-k-review. Accessed 3 Dec 2020.

Puchner, Martin. 'When We Were Clones'. *Raritan: A Quarterly Review*, vol. 27, no. 4, 2008, pp. 34–49.

Rajan, Kaushik Sunder. *Biocapital: The Constitution of Postgenomic Life*. Duke University Press, 2006.

Reed, Randall. 'A New Patheon: Artificial Intelligence and *Her*'. *Journal of Religion and Film*, vol. 22, no. 2, 2018, p. Article 5.

Rich, Nathaniel. *Odds against Tomorrow*. Picador, 2014.

Rise of the Planet of the Apes. Directed by Rupert Wyatt, Twentieth Century Fox, 2011.

Rivkin, Julie, and Michael Ryan, editors. *Literary Theory: An Anthology*. 2nd ed, Blackwell, 2004.

Robbins, Bruce. 'Cruelty Is Bad: Banality and Proximity in *Never Let Me Go*'. *Novel: A Forum on Fiction*, vol. 40, no. 3, 2007, pp. 289–302.

Roberts, Adam. 'The *Windup Girl* by Paolo Bacigalupi—Review'. *The Guardian*, 18 Dec. 2010, https://www.theguardian.com/books/2010/dec/18/windup-gir l-paolo-bacigalupi-review. Accessed 19 April 2021.

Robinson, Kim Stanley. *Ecotopia and the 1970s Utopian Moment*. 2015.

—. *Green Earth: The Science in the Capital Trilogy*. Del Rey Books, 2015.

—. *New York 2140*. Orbit, 2017.

—. *The Ministry for the Future*. Orbit, 2020.

Robinson, Kim Stanley, and Sally Adee. 'The Power of Good: Stories about a Better Future Can Break the Hold of Stories That Say You're Screwed.' *New Scientist*, vol. 234, no. 3129, 2017, pp. 44–45.

Roncaglia, Gino. 'Frankenstein and Science Fiction'. *Transmedia Creatures: Frankenstein's Afterlives*, edited by Francesca Saggini and Ann Enrichetta Soccio, 2018, pp. 33–49.

Ronen, Ruth. *Possible Worlds in Literary Theory*. Cambridge University Press, 1994.

Rosa, Hartmut. *Resonanz: Eine Soziologie der Weltbeziehung*. Suhrkamp, 2016.

Rosen, Elizabeth K. *Apocalyptic Transformation: Apocalypse and the Postmodern Imagination*. Lexington Books, 2008.

Rosenberg, Alissa. 'How Ken Burns' Surprise Role in *Interstellar* Explains the Movie'. *Washington Post*, 6 Nov. 2014, https://www.washingtonpost.com/n ews/act-four/wp/2014/11/06/how-ken-burns-surprise-role-in-interstellar -explains-the-movie/?utm_term=.ad420161ec3a. Accessed 6 July 2018.

Rothman, Joshua. 'Kim Stanley Robinson's Latest Novel Imagines Life in an Underwater New York'. *NewYorker*, 27 Apr. 2017, *www.newyorker.com*, https: //www.newyorker.com/books/page-turner/kim-stanley-robinsons-latest -novel-imagines-life-in-an-underwater-new-york. Accessed 15 May 2018.

Run Lola Run. Directed by Tom Tykwer, X Filme Creative Pool, 1998.

Rushkoff, Douglas. *Team Human*. W.W. Norton, 2019.

Rust, Stephen, et al., editors. *Ecocinema Theory and Practice*. Routledge, 2013.

Ryan, Marie-Laure. 'The Aesthetics of Proliferation'. *Word Building: Transmedia, Fans, Industries*, edited by Marta Boni, Amsterdam University Press, 2017, pp. 31–46.

Schmeink, Lars. *Biopunk Dystopias: Genetic Engineering, Society and Science Fiction*. Liverpool University Press, 2017.

Schreiner, Patrick. *Unterwerfung als Freiheit: Leben im Neoliberalismus*. PapyRossa Verlag, 2015.

Schussler, Aura-Elena. 'Transhumanism as a New-Techno-Religion and Personal Development: In the Framework of a Future Technological Spirituality'. *Journal for the Study of Religions and Ideologies*, vol. 18, no. 53, 2019, pp. 92–106.

Schwab, Gabriele. *Imaginary Ethnographies: Literature, Culture, and Subjectivity*. Columbia University Press, 2012.

Selisker, Scott. '"Stutter-Stop Flash-Bulb Strange": GMOs and the Aesthetics of Scale in Paolo Bacigalupi's *The Windup Girl*'. *Science Fiction Studies*, vol. 42, 2015, pp. 500–18.

Sergeant, David. 'The Genre of the Near Future'. *Genre*, vol. 52, no. 1, Apr. 2019, pp. 1–23.

Serpell, Namwali. *Seven Modes of Uncertainty*. Harvard University Press, 2014.

Shadbolt, Nigel, and Paul Smart. 'The Eyes of God'. *Blade Runner 2049: A Philosophical Exploration*, edited by Paul Smart and Timothy Shanahan, 2020, pp. 206–25.

Shakespeare, William. 'Sonnett 18'. *English Poetry: Eine Anthologie für das Studium*, by Arno Löffler and Eberhard Späth, 4th ed., Francke, 2003, p. 30.

—. *The Winter's Tale*. Nachdr., Arden, 2008.

Shanahan, Timothy. 'We're All Just Looking for Something Real'. *Blade Runner 2049: A Philosophical Exploration*, edited by Paul Smart and Timothy Shanahan, Routledge, 2020, pp. 8–26.

Sharlet, Jeff. 'Inside Occupy Wall Street'. *Rolling Stone*, 10 Nov. 2011, https://www.rollingstone.com/politics/politics-news/inside-occupy-wall-street-236993/. Accessed 20 Aug 2018.

Shelley, Mary Wollstonecraft. *Frankenstein*. Dover Publications, 1994.

Shotwell, Alexis. *Against Purity: Living Ethically in Compromised Times*. University of Minnesota Press, 2016.

Shteyngart, Gary. *Super Sad True Love Story*. Random House Trade Paperbacks, 2011.

Sideris, Lisa Hatton. 'I See You: Interspecies Empathy and *Avatar*'. *Journal for the Study of Religion, Nature and Culture*, vol. 4, no. 4, Jan. 2011, pp. 457–77.

Sinfield, Alan. *Faultlines: Cultural Materialism and the Politics of Dissident Reading*. Clarendon Press, 1992.

Singh, Vandana. *Distances: A Novella*. 2008.

—. 'Entanglement'. *Hieroglyph*, edited by Ed Finn and Kathryn Cramer, William Morrow, 2014, pp. 269–322.

Sinnerbrink, Robert. *Cinematic Ethics: Exploring Ethical Experience through Film.* Routledge, 2016.

Sloterdijk, Peter. *Plurale Spärologie.* Suhrkamp, 2004.

Smith, David. 'How to Be a Genuine Fake: Her, Alan Watts, and the Problem of the Self'. *Journal of Religion and Film*, vol. 18, no. 2, 2014, p. Article 3.

Snowpiercer. Directed by Bong, Joon-ho, Moho Film, 2013.

Sobchack, Vivian. 'Time Passages: Space-Time Is All Relative in Christopher Nolan's *Interstellar*'. *Film Comment*, Dec. 2014, pp. 20–14.

Soper, Kate. *Humanism and Anti-Humanism.* Hutchinson, 1986.

Springer, Simon, et al., editors. *The Handbook of Neoliberalism.* Routledge, 2016.

Stam, Robert, and Louise Spence. 'Colonialism, Racism and Representation'. *The Post-Colonial Studies Reader*, edited by Bill Ashcroft, et al., 2006, pp. 109–12.

Steger, Manfred B., and Ravi K. Roy. *Neoliberalism: A Very Short Introduction.* Oxford University Press, 2010.

Steinhoff, James. 'Transhumanism and Marxism: Philosophical Connections'. *Journal of Evolution and Technology*, vol. 24, no. 2, 2, 2014, pp. 1–16.

Storey, John. *Cultural Theory and Popular Culture: An Introduction.* 4th ed, University of Georgia Press, 2006.

Sullivan, Heather I. 'Petro-Texts, Plants, and People in the Anthropocene: The Dark Green'. *Green Letters*, vol. 23, no. 2, Apr. 2019, pp. 152–67.

Suvin, Darko. *Metamorphoses of Science Fiction: On the Poetics and History of a Literary Genre.* Yale University Press, 1980.

Tate, Andrew. *Apocalyptic Fiction.* Bloomsbury Academic, 2017.

Temperton, James. 'Stephen Hawking Warns That If We Don't Leave This Planet Soon, We Will Be Annihilated'. *Wired*, 27 July 2017, https://www.wired.co.uk/article/stephen-hawking-interstellar-travel-starmus-speech. Accessed 18 May 2018.

Terminator 3: Rise of the Machines. Directed by Jonathan Mostow, Warner Brothers, 2003.

Terminator: Dark Fate. Directed by Tim Millner, Paramount, 2019.

Terminator Genisys. Directed by Andrew Talyor, Paramount, 2015.

Terminator: Salvation. Directed by McG, Warner Brothers, 2009.

'*The Circle* Community Reviews'. *Goodreads*, https://www.goodreads.com/book/show/18302455-the-circle?from_search=true&qid=XGG2xtqvHw&rank=1. Accessed 8 June 2020

The Day After Tomorrow. Directed by Roland Emmerich. Twentieth Century Fox, 2004.

The Island. Directed by Michael Bay, Dreamworks, 2005.

'The MaddAddam Trilogy: *Oryx and Crake* / *The Year of the Flood* / *MaddAddam* Community Reviews'. *Goodreads*, https://www.goodreads.com/book/show/185 94761-the-maddaddam-trilogy?ac=1&from_search=true. Accessed 23 June 2019.

The Matrix. Directed by Lilly and Lana Wachowski, Warner Brothers, 1999.

'The Windup Girl Reviews'. *Goodreads*, https://www.goodreads.com/book/show /6597651-the-windup-girl?from_search=true&from_srp=true&qid=lgC4 m7cEQY&rank=1#other_reviews. Accessed 18 July 2021.

Thompson, Stacy. 'The Micro-Ethics of Everyday Life: Ethics, Ideology and Anti-Consumerism'. *Cultural Studies*, vol. 26, no. 6, 2012.

Toker, Leona. *Towards the Ethics of Form in Fiction: Narratives of Cultural Remission*. Ohio State University Press, 2010.

Tomorrowland. Directed by Brad Bird, Walt Disney, 2015.

'Top Rated Movies'. *IMDb*, 3 Nov. 2019, https://www.imdb.com/chart/top?ref_ =ft_250.

'Transcendence (2014) User Reviews'. *IMDb*, https://www.imdb.com/title/tt220 9764/reviews?ref_=tt_ov_rt. Accessed 12 Dec. 2019.

Treanor, Brian. 'Being-from-Birth, Nationality and Narrative'. *Blade Runner 2049: A Philosophical Exploration*, edited by Timothy Shanahan and Smart, Paul, Routledge, 2020, pp. 68–86.

Trexler, Adam. *Anthropocene Fictions: The Novel in a Time of Climate Change*. University of Virginia Press, 2015.

Ullman, Ellen. 'Ring of Power'. *The New York Times*, 1 Nov. 2013, https://www.n ytimes.com/2013/11/03/books/review/the-circle-by-dave-eggers.html. Accessed 16 Nov 2021.

United Nations. *Sustainable Development Goals*. https://sdgs.un.org/goals. Accessed 13 July 2021.

Urry, John. *What Is the Future?* Polity Press, 2016.

Viana, Wellistony C. *Das Prinzip Verantwortung von Hans Jonas aus der Perspektive des objektiven Idealismus der Intersubjektivität von Vittorio Hösle*. Königshausen & Neumann, 2010.

Voigts-Virchow, Eckart, and Alessandra Boller, editors. *Dystopia, Science Fiction, Post-Apocalypse: Classics – New Tendencies – Model Interpretations*. WVT Trier, 2015.

Wagner, Erica. 'Margaret Atwood Interview'. *Times Online*, 15 Aug. 2009, https ://www.thetimes.co.uk/article/margaret-atwood-interview-dh5tj896j82. Accessed 3 March 2018.

Wall-E. Directed by Andrew Stanton, Walt Disney, 2008.

Watercutter, Angela. '*Ex Machina* Has a Serious Fembot Problem'. *Wired*, 9 Apr. 2015, https://www.wired.com/2015/04/ex-machina-turing-bechdel-test/. Accessed 16 Jan 2020.

Watkins, Claire Vaye. *Gold Fame Citrus*. Riverhead Books, 2015.

Weik von Mossner, Alexa. *Affective Ecologies: Empathy, Emotion, and Environmental Narrative*. The Ohio State University Press, 2017.

—, editor. *Moving Environments: Affect, Emotion, Ecology, and Film*. Wilfrid Laurier University Press, 2014.

Wild. Directed by Jean-Marc Vallée, Bob Industries, 2014.

Wilhelm, Maria, et al. *Avatar: A Confidential Report on the Biological and Social History of Pandora*. Itbooks, 2009.

Wilhelmus, Tom. 'Science and Technology, Again'. *The Hudson Magazine*, vol. 66, no. 4, 2014, pp. 747–54.

Williams, James. *Stand out of Our Light: Freedom and Resistance in the Attention Economy*. Cambridge University Press, 2018.

Williams, Raymond. *The Long Revolution*. Penguin Books, 1973.

Williams, Tad. *Otherland*. Orbit, 1998.

Winterson, Jeanette. *Frankissstein: A Love Story*. Vintage, 2020.

Wolf, Mark J. P. 'Building Imaginary Worlds: The Theory and History of Sub-creation'. *Worldbuilding: Transmedia, Fans, Industries*, edited by Marta Boni, Amsterdam University Press, 2017, pp. 204–2014.

Wolfe, Cary. *What Is Posthumanism?* University of Minnesota Press, 2010.

Woodley, Anthony. *The Flood*. Curzon Artificial Eye, 2019.

Woollard, Fiona. 'The Miracle of Replicant Reproduction'. *Blade Runner 2049: A Philosophical Exploration*, Routledge, 2020, pp. 48–67.

World Commission on Environment and Development, editor. *Our Common Future*. Oxford University Press, 1987.

'Zero K Community Reviews'. *Goodreads*, https://www.goodreads.com/book/show/26154389-zero-k. Accessed 29 Dec. 2020.

Zizek, Slavoj. 'Return of the Natives'. *New Statesman*, 8 Mar. 2010, pp. 44–46.

Zylinska, Joanna. *Bioethics in the Age of New Media*. MIT Press, 2009.

—. *Minimal Ethics for the Anthropocene*. Open Humanities Press, 2014.

—. *The Ethics of Cultural Studies*. Continuum, 2005.